Deception and Democracy ir

This is the first full-length study of th
lies in classical Athens. Dr Hesk trace
drama, democratic oratory and elite prose writing construct and
theorise a relationship between dishonesty and civic identity. He
focuses on the ideology of military trickery, notions of the 'noble lie'
and the developing associations of rhetorical language with deceptive
communication. *Deception and Democracy in Classical Athens* combines
close analysis of Athenian texts with lively critiques of modern theorists and classical scholars. Athenian democratic culture was crucially
informed by a nuanced, anxious and dynamic discourse on the problems and opportunities which deception presented for its citizenry.
Mobilising comparisons with twentieth-century democracies, the
author argues that Athenian literature made deception a fundamental
concern for democratic citizenship. This ancient discourse on lying
highlights the dangers of modern resignation and postmodern com-
placency concerning the politics and morality of deception.

JON HESK is Lecturer in Greek at the University of St Andrews.

Deception and Democracy
in Classical Athens

Jon Hesk
University of St Andrews

CAMBRIDGE
UNIVERSITY PRESS

CAMBRIDGE UNIVERSITY PRESS
Cambridge, New York, Melbourne, Madrid, Cape Town, Singapore, São Paulo

Cambridge University Press
The Edinburgh Building, Cambridge CB2 2RU, UK

Published in the United States of America by Cambridge University Press, New York

www.cambridge.org
Information on this title: www.cambridge.org/9780521643221

First published 2000
This digitally printed first paperback version 2006

A catalogue record for this publication is available from the British Library

Library of Congress Cataloguing in Publication data

Hesk, Jon.
  Deception and Democracy in classical Athens / Jon Hesk.
    p.   cm.
  Includes bibliographical references and index.
  ISBN 0 521 64322 8 hardback
    1. Democracy – Greece–Athens. 2. Deception–Greece–Athens. I. Title.
JC75.D36   H47   2000
306.2′0938′5–dc21   00-029255

ISBN-13 978-0-521-64322-1 hardback
ISBN-10 0-521-64322-8 hardback

ISBN-13 978-0-521-02871-4 paperback
ISBN-10 0-521-02871-X paperback

Contents

Preface

This book is substantially revised and expanded from its original incarnation as my Cambridge Ph.D. thesis begun in 1991 and there are many debts of gratitude to record for help and support with the project since then. But there are people who deserve thanks for inspiration and teaching long before I started the thesis, particularly Andrew Wilson (formerly of Bedford Modern School) and Ewen Bowie (in Oxford).

The thesis was supervised by Simon Goldhill: my warmest thanks to him for intellectual stimulation, patience, humour, good advice and for not putting up with any rubbish. Several scholars read and usefully criticised drafts of chapters which are still in this book, providing encouragement along the way: thanks to Richard Hunter, John Henderson, Malcolm Schofield, Helen Morales and Paul Cartledge. My Ph.D. examiners were Richard Buxton and Paul Millett: their comments, criticisms and advice were most helpful and much-appreciated.

More recently, I have received friendly advice from Stephen Halliwell: thanks to him for reading the first three chapters and for boosting my confidence. I must also thank the three anonymous readers appointed by Cambridge University Press for swift and extremely good advice on structure, tone and content. Audiences in Oxford, Exeter, London, Bristol, Washington, Glasgow and St Andrews have heard and given useful responses to seminar papers containing material which ended up in this book. The participants in the Classics Faculty literary seminars in Cambridge between 1991 and 1998 were particularly stimulating and I gained enhanced perspectives from presenting material to a distinguished international audience at a colloquium on 'Performance Culture and Athenian Democracy' held at King's College, Cambridge in July 1996.

Much of the research conducted for this book was made possible by a British Academy state studentship. When that money ran out, I received financial assistance from King's College's Supplementary Exhibition Fund, the Cambridge Faculty of Classics, the Cambridge University Jebb Fund and my grandmother Evelyn Hesk. I should also thank the Master and Fellows of St. John's College, Cambridge for electing me to a Research Fellowship in 1995 and thereby enabling me to finish the thesis and begin this book. Since my appointment as a lecturer at St Andrews, friends and colleagues in the School of Greek, Latin and Ancient History have been extremely supportive: thanks especially to Stephen Halliwell and Harry Hine for taking a few hours of teaching off my plate when I needed some crucial days of uninter-rupted writing.

Pauline Hire, my editor, has been extremely patient and kind. I offer her many thanks for efficient handling of editing and publication. It is a real privilege to have had the benefit of her guidance, experience and good advice for my first book. My copy-editor, Linda Woodward has also been excellent and has saved me from many errors.

Over the years, so many friends have helped me to keep going. I cannot thank them all individually here but they should know who they are. Jenny Young deserves a special thankyou for putting up with and sustaining me and for proof-reading various drafts.

Finally, I wish to offer love and thanks to my parents, John and Glenis Hesk, for all their support over many years. They have always taken an intense interest in my work and I could not have started or finished this study without their constant and unconditional love. The book is dedicated to them.

I should point out that I have not been able to take full account of relevant scholarly material published since 1997: after that date, my references are selective and confined to those works which have been easily available, have come to my attention and whose relevance to my arguments has been high enough to require consideration.

Prologue

Liman seemed sympathetic to North for having taken an unanticipated fall. But while presumably disarming North with this tactic, he was also drawing from the witness repeated acknowledgements that his behaviour in lying and deceiving was in violation of the Naval Academy's values of honour and trustworthiness that he had sworn to uphold as a midshipman.[1]

Now Nields would try to lecture North: In certain communist countries the government's activities are kept secret from the people. But that's not the way we do things in America, is it?[2]

A man can do you no greater injustice than tell lies. For in a political system based on speeches, how can it be safely administered if the speeches are not true?[3]

Two congressional committee members attempt to make Oliver North realise that he was wrong to have deceived Congress, the American people and the Iranian government. Liman appeals to an oath he took when he became an American serviceman. Nields makes an explicit link between openness, honesty and normative political behaviour in America. He implicitly grounds that link in America's democratic constitution. He contrasts such ideal behaviour with the practices of countries which are not democratic. The contrast reproduces Karl Popper's influential distinction between 'the open society and its enemies' – even more so when we read Senator Lee Hamilton's verdict on North's testimony.[4] After insisting that North lied to the Iranians, the CIA, the Attorney General, friends, allies, Congress and the people, Hamilton goes on 'I cannot agree that the end has justified

---

[1] From an account of the United States congressional committee hearing on the 'Iran-Contra' affair, where Colonel Oliver North was summoned to give evidence. Quotation from an extract in Kerr (1990) 519. Extract taken from B. Bradlee Jnr. (1988), *Guts and Glory: The Rise and Fall of Oliver North*, New York.

[2] Kerr (1990) 513.

[3] Dem. 19.184: οὐδὲν γὰρ ἔσθ' ὅ τι μεῖζον ἂν ὑμᾶς ἀδικήσειέ τις, ἢ ψευδῆ λέγων. οἷς γὰρ ἐστ' ἐν λόγοις ἡ πολιτεία, πῶς, ἂν οὗτοι μὴ ἀληθεῖς ὦσιν, ἀσφαλῶς ἔστι πολιτεύεσθαι;

[4] Popper (1966).

the means ... The means employed were a profound threat to the democratic process ... Methods and means are what this country is all about.'[5]

In the third of my opening quotations, the fourth-century Athenian *rhētōr* (politician, speaker) Demosthenes represents deceit by elite *rhētores* as a profound threat to democratic process. Mobilising similar arguments to those of Oliver North's inquisitors, he goes on to state that official deceit is relatively unproblematic for a tyranny or an oligarchy, because those systems do not require mass debate and decision-making (19.185–6).

Senator Hamilton is disturbed by North's appeal to the notion that it is sometimes necessary and justifiable to lie to the people. He sees such arguments as threatening to democracy and the ideal identity of his country.[6] North's defence of his deceptions bears some resemblance to arguments offered by Plato's Socrates in the *Republic*. Socrates' ideal polis is governed by rulers who are permitted to lie to their subject-citizens for the good of that state (2.369b7–c6, 3.414b8–415d5).[7] Although embarrassed by his proposal, Socrates also argues that the survival of this state is dependent on the dissemination of and universal belief in a 'noble lie' concerning the natural and biological basis of the state's division of labour. This fiction will convince people that they were born either to rule or be ruled. Plato's Socrates takes the view that lying can be justified when it is deployed for 'good' political ends. Like Congressman Nields and Senator Hamilton, Karl Popper saw this justification of lies by political rulers as a hallmark of totalitarian political thought and he indicted Plato as the originator of such beliefs.[8]

Popper's interpretation of Plato can be, and has been, criticised from a variety of perspectives.[9] But Popper's book, originally published in the wake of the Third Reich and at the onset of the Cold War, illustrates the way in which modern liberal and democratic thought has sought to render notions of 'deceiving the people' as alien to a genuine spirit of democratic government and procedure. Popper locates the

---

[5] Kerr (1990) 520.
[6] See Miller and Stiff (1993) 4: 'In democracies such as the United States ... the prevailing ideology holds that political actors must evince a concern for both political ends and the means used in their pursuit. Stated differently, some communicative strategies are suspect even if they achieve the desired ends because the strategies are at odds with the democratic processes. Two obvious examples of such dubious strategies are deception and coercion.' See also Bok (1978) 165–81.
[7] See Page (1991) 16–26 which traces the development of the argument.
[8] Popper (1966) 138f.
[9] The most direct and sustained criticisms are in Levinson (1953), Wild (1963) and Bambrough (1967).

origin of the 'noble lie' in the writings of a thinker whom most critics would still characterise as out of sympathy with, or at least disillusioned with, the ideals, structures and practices of the democratic society of which he was a member.[10] Brian Vickers, who draws heavily on Popper's views, has mapped Plato's attack on rhetorical theory and practice in democratic Athens onto Plato's authoritarian philosophy.[11] Where Plato sees the use of rhetoric in Athens' assembly and lawcourts as a case of the ignorant few manipulating the ignorant masses, Vickers views rhetorical discourse as the life blood of open debate, pluralism and democracy. Plato is again indicted, not only for his totalitarianism, but for initiating the traditional denigration of rhetoric as a medium for deceptive communication and falsehood.

Vickers and Popper construe Plato's attack on sophistry and rhetoric as hypocritical. On the one hand, Plato champions truth and philosophy through a condemnation of the lies of contemporary politicians and rhetorical theorists. On the other, his moral and political vision, along with the persuasive strategies of his Socrates, give pride of place to the notion that it is acceptable and necessary for the right leaders to tell the right lies to the people. Vickers echoes Aristotle and the Platonic Gorgias when he points out that rhetoric can be used for good or evil ends and that it is no different from any other form of knowledge in this respect.[12] His commitment lies with the deployment of rhetoric 'in a state where free speech is still possible'.[13] He insists that while rhetoric can be deployed in any constitutional system, it is more important to 'understand what rhetoric really can do in the right hands at the right time'.[14]

The argument

One of the aims of this study is to demonstrate that the theoretical denigration of rhetoric as a deceptive technology and the conception of the political 'noble lie' cannot be characterised as a solely 'totalitarian'

---

[10] For Plato as an 'intellectual critic' of democracy see Ober (1998) and, from a specifically rhetorical perspective, Yunis (1996). Von Reden and Goldhill (1999) discuss the 'oblique and difficult relations between Platonic dialogue and the *polis*' (284).

[11] Vickers (1988) 83–147.

[12] See Pl. *Grg.* 456c6–457c3; Arist. *Rh.* 1.1355b1–7. Grimaldi (1980) 30–1 notes the parallel between these passages. See also Garver (1994) 221ff.

[13] Vickers (1988) viii. Contrast the polemical essay of Fish (1994) 102–19. Fish argues that appeals to and endorsements of the notion of 'free speech' can never escape the bind of *restricting* certain arguments or forms of speech. Fish's 'neo-pragmatism' is not free of 'ideology' or 'rhetoric' however: see the excellent critique of Norris (1992) 126–58 and my brief comments below.

[14] Vickers (1988) viii.

or purely Platonic strategy. Nor is Plato's desire to subordinate rhetorical practice to the goals of political and ethical 'truths' and 'goods' completely original to him or solely the product of his anti-democratic agenda. Rather, the emergence of these ideas about rhetoric and deceit can be located in political, legal and cultural discourses which defined Athenian democracy itself.

Modern attempts to separate rhetoric from its dubious connotations fail to acknowledge the way in which the idea of 'rhetoric' was strategically reified and theorised as a mode of deceptive communication in the Athenian democracy's very own competitive institutions of speech and performance. If modern commentators champion Athenian theories and practices of 'rhetoric' as notions which can improve modern institutions of democracy and 'free speech', Athenian oratory's persistent demonisation of the sophist, the logographer and the 'clever speaker' as peddlers of self-serving lies should alert them to the dangers of privileging the ideals of pluralism implied by Greek rhetorical theory over and above the example of how rhetoric comes to be represented and viewed in the 'practical' performances of Athenian democratic discourse itself.[15] I will argue in my fourth chapter that legal and political oratory at Athens deploy what can be termed a 'rhetoric of anti-rhetoric' and a more general 'meta-discourse' concerning the powers and perils of deceptive communication on the part of elite speakers.[16] These anti-rhetorical and 'meta-discursive' strategies do not constitute a philosophical project. Nor do they add up to a treatise on rhetoric and deceit. But they do mark out an area of (self-)representation in which mass-elite democratic discourse could

---

[15] The liberal criticism of Popper (1966) and Vickers (1988) and their defence of 'rhetoric' as the lifeblood of pluralism is curiously close to *some* 'postmodern' accounts of rhetoric. From a 'postmodern' perspective (also hinted at by Foucault (1981) and noted by Dreyfus and Rabinow (1982)) Jarratt (1991) 81–117 calls for the reintroduction of 'sophistic' thought and argumentation to modern western pedagogy without addressing the possibility of their co-optation by dominant regimes of truth and power, not to mention the likely emergence of an 'anti-rhetorical' discourse. See Graff (1989) for 'co-optation'; Fish (1994) 141–79 on why law can never really admit its 'rhetoricity'. Swearingen (1991) also ignores the 'anti-rhetorical' topoi of practical oratory in her (Plato-centred) account of how rhetoric and lies come to be associated. Chomsky (1989) and Arendt (1972) dissect deceptive rhetoric, 'disinformation' and 'noble' lies deployed by the United States federal government in recent decades.

[16] I borrow 'the rhetoric of anti-rhetoric' from Valesio (1980), who uses it to analyse renaissance tracts and speeches in Shakespeare. For references and discussion on what I will be calling 'anti-rhetorical' topoi against opponents, see Dover (1974) 25–8; Ostwald (1986) 256–7. On the orators' attacks on opponents as sophists and 'clever speakers' see Ober (1989) 156–91; on logography see Bonner (1927) 320–3; Dover (1968) 148–74; Kennedy (1963) 126–45; Lavency (1964); Carey and Reid (1985) 13–18; Sinclair (1988) 186; Usher (1976); Cartledge (1990a) 49–52.

self-consciously police and theorise its own risky dependence on the performance of speeches (*logoi*) by both defining and renegotiating classifications of, licences for and limits to deceptive communication and rhetorical performance on the part of elite speakers (*rhētores*) and 'ordinary' citizens (*idiōtai*). This argument seeks to build on, and at the same time modify Josiah Ober's excellent study of Athenian oratory as a discourse of mass-elite negotiation which maintained the relative stability of a democratic constitution despite conditions of financial and educational inequality.[17]

The final chapter of this study continues to isolate 'the rhetoric of anti-rhetoric' as an important trope in Athenian democratic culture. By offering readings of Thucydides, Aristophanic comedy and Euripidean tragedy I seek to show how Athenian historical narrative and civic drama stage the difficulties of securely assessing 'speech's ambiguity' and anti-rhetorical rhetoric in the democracy's political and forensic institutions. These readings will suggest that conceptions of rhetoric as deceptive communication are important for the development of anti-democratic political theory and for our understanding of Attic drama's contribution to the political and cultural education of Athens' democratic citizenry.

My third chapter will show that while Athenian oratory and other Athenian texts constantly censure notions of lying to the democratic community, there are occasions when an (almost Popperian) Athenian ideological distinction between the open and closed society is problematised through the invocation and evaluation of several versions or trajectories of 'noble lies' and 'good fictions'. The contribution of Athenian oratory and civic drama to this area of problematisation and anxiety is marked. I also argue that Plato's 'noble lie', despite its pro-Spartan and authoritarian overtones, is represented in terms which draw on Athenian popular morality and civic mythology. It is especially with regard to these public and philosophical confrontations with the 'noble lie' that I hope to fill some gaps in Marcel Detienne's important study of archaic and classical notions of 'truth', 'oblivion', 'seeming', 'lies' and 'deception' (*alētheia, lēthē, doxa, pseudē* and *apatē*).[18] I argue that Detienne's study is usefully supplemented by an account of Platonic and democratic confrontations with what he calls the problem of 'speech's ambiguity'.

My opening chapter leads off from the ground-breaking work of another member of the 'Paris School' of classicists and establishes a

---

[17] Ober (1989).
[18] Detienne (1967), now available in English with a new introduction as Detienne (1996).

strand of inquiry which runs throughout this study. In three essays, Pierre Vidal-Naquet discusses the association between the myths and practices surrounding the 'liminal' Athenian age-class known as the *ephēbeia*.[19] These essays inform my reconstruction of the crucial role played by representations of deception (*apatē*) within Athenian public projections of civic ideology, national identity and military values. The substance of his arguments and the controversies surrounding them will be raised in the first two chapters and by building on Vidal-Naquet's work I will also reveal some of its limitations.

The first chapter concerns itself with the differing ways in which notions of trickery and deceit are put to work within the areas of national, civic and military identity and within the symbolic fields which enforce and represent 'democratic' conduct. Alongside persistent representations of deceit as 'unAthenian', typically Spartan, feminine and cowardly in a range of texts, we will see the opposition between *apatē* and the Athenian male self being articulated and problematised in Euripidean drama. This problematisation will evoke the threat of deceit in democratic politics. I will also show how legal oratory manipulates and renegotiates some of the ideological, political, legal and religious connotations of the citizen who deceives the demos.

My second chapter concentrates on a range of texts which offer conflicting evaluations of the ideological admissibility of using deceit and trickery against a military enemy. Legal speeches, Platonic dialogue, tragedy, historiography, theories of *paideia*, sophistic display and vase painting will attest to the moral and ideological 'negotiability' of military trickery at Athens. But this range of evidence reveals some significant limits to, and colourings of, military trickery's negotiable status. Xenophon's writing adds other dimensions here; a supposedly pro-Spartan writer who commonly speaks of the necessity of military trickery nevertheless allows his historical characters to discourse anxiously on the wide social implications of using certain forms of education to instil the practice and value of military trickery.

Approaches and methods

Twenty years ago, W. Kendrick Pritchett remarked in the context of military trickery that 'there is clearly a need for further investigation of

---

[19] These are Vidal-Naquet (1968), reprinted and revised in Vidal-Naquet (1986a); additional thoughts and assessments in Vidal-Naquet (1986b). See also Vidal-Naquet (1988) which applies these ideas concerning the *ephēbeia* to a reading of Sophocles' *Philoctetes*.

the concept of ἀπάτη (*apatē*: deception) in Greek society'.[20] There is still no full-length study of deceit and trickery in ancient Greek culture and society, but a lot of work has been done in the meantime. I suspect that Pritchett may have had in mind different material to that presented in, say, Detienne and Vernant's investigation of the semantic field and cultural connotations of 'cunning intelligence' (*mētis*) as a category of thought in ancient Greek culture and society.[21] I should make it clear that I do not intend to speculate on who was really lying in a lawcourt speech or reconstruct the complex *Realien* of Athenian military tactics. But it must also be made clear that I do not dispute recent anthropological, sociological and comparative studies which suggest that lying and trickery (not to mention self-deception and 'misrecognition') were crucial strategies in the various performances that constituted Athenian social, commercial, cultural and political relations.[22]

My interest lies in examining *representations* and *evaluations* of deception (*apatē*), lies (*pseudē*) and trickery (*dolos*) in Athenian texts. As anthropological work repeatedly demonstrates, individuals do not necessarily preach what they practise when it comes to lying – and this is also true for the relationship between a culture's stated norms and the behaviour of its members. Recent studies also show that different cultures vary enormously as to whether their dominant representations of deceit are positive or negative. But it is hard to find a culture where norms and evaluations of deceit are consistent and non-negotiable.[23] What constitutes a 'lie' can vary enormously. Friedl describes the way in which the modern Greek word *psemata* is sometimes used of 'lies' which are actually tall stories performed in social contexts where all participants are aware that the stories are not true. She also records that parents in a Greek village will tell lies to their young children as a means of teaching them not to take other people's action and behaviour at 'face value'.[24] Du Boulay argues that although the Greek word *psema* can be translated as 'lie' it does not carry the overtones of moral failure that 'lie' does in English.[25] Lying, and representations of it, are culturally specific phenomena, but it seems that every culture needs

---

[20] Pritchett (1979) 330.

[21] Detienne and Vernant (1978).

[22] On the sociology of lying in twentieth-century Western society: Goffman (1974) 83–123; Barnes (1994) who has a comprehensive bibliography; Bok (1978). On deceit in modern Mediterranean societies: Friedl (1962); Campbell (1964); Herzfeld (1985); du Boulay (1974), (1976); Bourdieu (1977). For applications to ancient Greece and Athens see Walcot (1977); Winkler (1990b) 173f.; Cohen (1991), esp. chs. 2 and 3.

[23] See Barnes (1994) 136–46.

[24] Friedl (1962) 78–81.

[25] Du Boulay (1976).

deceit both as a practice *and* as an idea (which can be *either* praised *or* blamed according to context) in the exercise and control of power and knowledge.[26] The nature of an ethical evaluation of deceit depends on *who* is making the evaluation, who is receiving it, and *what* is perceived to be at stake in that evaluation. It is with the modern social anthropologist's sensitivity to areas of contradiction or conflict in normative systems and her awareness of individual actors' strategic manipulations of norms and values that I attempt to approach the Athenian representation of deceit.[27]

Having said this, I do not intend to make extensive use of 'comparative' material from recent anthropological work on modern Mediterranean societies. This is partly because, as I have already suggested, much of this work is focused on deception as a practice or process, rather than its *representation*. Where representations are discussed, the context of those representations makes them of limited use for my project. But a brief look at some anthropological work on twentieth-century Mediterranean deception will help to locate my own concerns.

Juliet du Boulay offers a fascinating account of the 'defensive' and 'offensive' use of lies on the Greek island of Euboea. Lies are told with great frequency in order to preserve family honour or to increase family wealth or to make mischief on the government. Lying in court on oath is frowned upon as unChristian. But the villager has a 'moral duty to quarrel with, cheat or deceive the outsider in support of the house' and there is a Euboean saying that 'God wants people to cover things up.'[28] Du Boulay argues that Euboeans have less opportunity to use violence for the maintainence of honour and reputation than the Lebanese community studied by Gilsenan.[29] In the Lebanon the use of lies and slander was tempered by the threat of retaliatory violence. In Euboea, individuals could use offensive lies much more freely.

Michael Herzfeld's superb analysis of sheep-stealing ('kleftism') in a Cretan mountain village shows how the 'Glendiots' whom he studies regard kleftism as a mark of *poniria* ('low cunning'). There is a bewildering array of protocols and poetic possibilities through which the Glendiots can extend networks of friendship, exact vengeance and increase revenge through kleftism. Sheep-stealing is also regarded as a

---

[26] Cultural specificity: Simmel (1950) 312–16; Barnes (1994) 144–5. On the ubiquity of lying in systems of power and control, see Gilsenan (1976) 191. As far as I know, the *representation* of lies as a component of modern civic or democratic ideologies has not received much attention.
[27] See Bourdieu (1977); Herzfeld (1985) and the approach of Cohen (1991) 24–34.
[28] Du Boulay (1974) 74, 82.
[29] Du Boulay (1976); Gilsenan (1976).

mark of the Glendiots' distinctive identity as mountain shepherds. The Glendiots regard their *poniria* as an expression of manliness (*andrismos*) and their quintessential 'Greekness' but, as Herzfeld points out, this is a 'far cry' from 'that nationalist rhetoric which treats all forms of "brigandage" as foreign importations' and official attempts to re-describe sheep-stealing as 'cowardly and demeaning'.[30] Furthermore, not all Glendiots are proud of their 'kleftic' reputation. Sheep-stealing and its attendant qualities of cunning and opportunistic deceit are prized by traditional shepherds, but the Glendiots who have taken up different occupations are embarrassed by kleftism and are unimpressed by the shepherds' additional arguments that sheep-stealing is an economic necessity.

These findings demonstrate that lying and its evaluation are closely related to the politics and ideology of reputation. As Cohen, Winkler and Hunter have shown, Athenian forensic oratory reveals a similar emphasis on honour and reputation in classical Athens.[31] It may be that Athenian parents taught their children that 'Zeus wants people to cover things up': we will see that a fragment of Aeschylus says something similar. But Herzfeld's analysis shows how a community's evaluation of deception can be contested by 'official' discourse and social or economic conflict. The 'manliness' or 'Greekness' of deception and cunning in one Cretan village cannot be viewed as synecdochal for a 'Greek' outlook. Thus, regionalism, Christianity, and divergences between 'official' and 'local' ideology all make a comparative anthropological approach to classical Athens' representation of deception highly problematic. However, du Boulay's account of a relationship between deception and the operations of a 'surveillance culture' and Herzfeld's nuanced emphasis on the relationship between 'kleftism' and differing conceptions of national identity and manhood do at least lend general support to the *focus* of this book.

Whilst my starting point has been to trace the usage and significance of the nouns *apatē, pseudos, dolos* and their cognates, this study demonstrates that all three terms are deployed across a range of discourses (dramatic, legal, political, epideictic, paideutic, philosophical, historical . . .). These different discourses often share the same social, political and cultural anxieties or evaluations concerning deceit, but they also exhibit some telling idiosyncracies, silences or internal conflicts. It emerges that *apatē, pseudos* and *dolos* are associated with or opposed to other significant terms (*phobos*: 'fear', *paraskeuē*: 'preparation', *poikilia*:

---

[30] Herzfeld (1985) 41, 45.
[31] Cohen (1991), (1994); Winkler (1990b); Hunter (1994).

'intricacy', *technē*: 'craft', *sophistēs*: 'sophist', *nikē*: 'victory', *hoplitēs*: 'hoplite'). However, these relations of opposition or association will often be revealed as unstable and slippery.

I do not wish to deny that the specific notion of *mētis* (which often involves the performance of deception) was an important category of thought in Athenian culture.[32] To be sure, actions and achievements which come under the rubric of 'cunning intelligence' as identified by Detienne and Vernant were often represented as admirable. But it is clear from their study that not all manifestations of *mētis* involve the deployment of *apatē*, *pseudē* or *dolos*, and I have found that not all representations of deceit necessarily fall within the semantic field of *mētis* with its various demands of 'stochastic' thought, adaptability, craftsmanship and opportunism.

Occasionally, I will indicate that a discussion or representation of deceit seems to be located within the semantic field of *mētis*. But the material I have selected should demonstrate that in Athenian writings, any pre-democratic notion of deception and trickery as an admirable facet of cunning intelligence is placed under severe strain by the new circumstances of democratic culture and ideology. While we will see the positive public representation of the military trickery and self-sacrifice of the Athenian king Codrus as an example of *apatē* and laudable *mētis* going hand in hand, we will also confront images of sophistic deception where it is hard to detect any clear evocation of this wider category of thought. At the same time we will see Thucydides suppressing Themistocles' skill in deception when he finally appraises the general's life. His qualities of adaptability, foresight and quick-wittedness are reiterated and emphasised by the historian and these are qualities which clearly mark him as a man with *mētis*. But it seems that Thucydides cannot reiterate his triumphant trickery on behalf of the polis.

Apatē, intentional *pseudē* and *dolos* are not so much categories of thought as categories of communication and behaviour.[33] Detienne and Vernant have a tendency to mix and match sources spanning several centuries in their quest for *mētis'* special operations. Although I have left many texts and considerations to one side, I hope that my study of the representation of deceit over a period of roughly one hundred and twenty years (440–320 BC) in texts produced in, or for Athens will exemplify the importance of considering a category of

---

[32] See Detienne and Vernant (1978).

[33] Whilst *apatē* denotes an intentional lie or trick, *pseudos* can denote either an intentional or an unintentional falsehood. See Pratt (1993) 56 and Ferrari (1989) 112.

communication with careful attention both to diachronic pressures on the manner in which that category is put to work and a synchronic picture based on a wide variety of texts (legal, dramatic, philosophical, medical . . .). My approach is one which combines general analysis (for example of the Athenian representation of Spartans as deceitful or of 'noble lies') with detailed exploration of particular texts. I focus on these texts because they are exemplary of certain orthodoxies in the representation of deceit *or* because they are significantly heterodox *or* because they exhibit telling negotiations and anxieties over the use and abuse of deceit.

I have not devoted a specific chapter or a section to the exploration of the already well-documented Athenian association of 'femininity' with deceit, and although it will have an extensive bearing in my third chapter, the archaic and classical description and discussion of (what we would term) literary or poetic 'fiction' as *apatē* or a *pseudos* will not be a primary focus.[34] This is partly because of a wealth of bibliography already devoted to these two areas, but also because I believe that some fresh thoughts on them can be gained through a wider consideration of deceit's trajectory over the terrains of Athenian ideology, public rhetoric and religious discourse.

A reader of this study might be surprised to find that a number of texts do not receive major consideration. The Homeric epics and Hesiod's hexameters are constantly engaged in representing and evaluating deceptive communication and trickery.[35] Homeric or Hesiodic representations and evaluations will inform my discussions, because they clearly informed the representations and evaluations of classical Athenian culture. But this study will not focus on these or other texts which derive from the pre-classical period because I am primarily interested in *democratic* Athens. In order to orientate this primary interest, however, it is perhaps worth making a few remarks concerning the

---

[34] On the ancient Greek association between deception and 'the female' see, for example, Katz (1991) 24–9, 128–30 (Penelope); Rabinowitz (1993) 132f. (Medea), 166–9 (Phaedra); Lefkowitz (1986) 61–79 (esp. on Semonides' characterisation of women as deceptive); Zeitlin (1978) (on Clytemnestra and Athena); Walcot (1996) 91–102 (on ancient Greek mysogyny and fear of female deceit); Buxton (1994), 122–7 (on the representation of *dolos*, deceptive mythical women and 'feminine' crafts); Jenkins (1985) (on weaving, women and trickery). For bibliography on, and discussion of 'lies and fiction' see below pp. 176–88.

[35] On the Homeric representation of *apatē*, *dolos*, and *pseudē*: Walcot (1977); Walsh (1984) ch. 1; Murnaghan (1987); Pucci (1987); Goldhill (1991) ch. 1; Katz (1991); Pratt (1993), chs. 1 and 2; on Hesiod see Rösler (1980), Belfiore (1985), Pucci (1977), Ferrari (1988); on the representation of lying and trickery in lyric, elegiac poetry and Pindar see Gentili (1988) 115–54; Walsh (1984) 37–61; Most (1985) 148–82; Nagy (1985); Donlan (1985); Pratt (1993) chs. 2 and 3.

poetic representation of deception before the fifth century. In Homeric epic, deception is given positive and negative evaluations by its characters. In the *Iliad*, we are presented with Achilles' notorious condemnation of Odysseus: 'More than the gates of Hades, I detest the man who says one thing while thinking another in the depths of his heart' (9.312–13). At the same time, the *Iliad* shows how *mētis* ('cunning intelligence') and what we would call 'rhetorical expertise' are important resources in the pursuit of individual excellence and collective agreement. Furthermore, the *Iliad* does not seem to stigmatise the ambush (*lochos*) as a form of military engagement. In the tenth book, however, we see Odysseus and Diomedes on a night raid where they intercept the Trojan spy Dolon engaged on a similar mission in the opposite direction. Odysseus tricks Dolon into believing that he will be spared if he gives information. Dolon is told 'to have no thoughts of death' but Odysseus and Diomedes kill him once the information has been given (10.380ff.).[36] It is difficult to know how to evaluate this episode but we will see that Odysseus' use of deception and clever speaking in Homer make him 'good to think with' in classical Athenian texts which engage with the morality and ideology of trickery and rhetorical skill. Odysseus' skills as a liar and trickster take centre stage in the *Odyssey*. It would be wrong to suggest that this epic unequivocally celebrates cunning, duplicity and the telling of tall stories. But there is a strong sense in which the *Odyssey* posits its hero's *mētis* and aptitude for falsehood as resources which secure his return home and the re-establishment of his identity.[37] Odysseus' lies are also the means and matter of the perpetuation of his *kleos* (reputation, fame in song).

This final point introduces another important strand in the pre-classical poetic discourse on deception. Odysseus knows how to tell 'lies like the truth' and the *Odyssey* forges a strong connection between Odysseus' ability to tell false tales which are both plausible-sounding and transmit deeper 'truths'. For example, when Odysseus has arrived on Ithaca, he meets the swineherd Eumaeus but does not reveal his true identity (14.122f.). Instead, he pretends to be a Cretan and tells tales of his wanderings, including what he has heard about Odysseus' attempt to return home. Many of the features of these lying tales correspond to the epic's narrative of Odysseus' adventures (some of which are actually presented only by Odysseus himself).[38] Thus the *Odyssey*

---

[36] See Gernet (1981) and Rabel (1992). Rabel argues that the *Doloneia* of book 10 is well-integrated into the *Iliad* and has narrative structural congruence with books 9 and 11.

[37] See Murnaghan (1987); Pucci (1987); Goldhill (1991) 1–68; Rose (1992) 92–140.

[38] On Odysseus' Cretan lies, see Haft (1984); Todorov (1977) 59f.; Walcot (1977); Emlyn-Jones (1986); Goldhill (1991) 36–47.

can be seen to foreground the ways in which certain lies can be both
true and false: they may be false in the details but convey an overall or
deeper 'reality'. They may present fictional situations which nevertheless convey normative or ethical 'truths'.

This awareness that poetry, song and narrative may be either wholly
false or 'lies like the truth' is also articulated in Hesiod's *Theogony*.
There, Hesiod describes how he was given the gift of poetic inspiration
by the Muses. In a difficult pair of lines (27–8) which have generated
much controversy, the Muses tell Hesiod that they know how to tell
many lies like true things (*pseudea . . . etumoisin homoia*), but when they
wish, they also know how to speak 'true' things (*alēthea*). The significance of these lines for our understanding of the *Theogony* and archaic
poetics in general is very difficult to establish. But they do seem to set
out a conception of lying as a form of communication which need not
be opposed to 'truth-telling'.

The idea that poetic narrative is akin to 'lying' is given a moral and
political dimension in late archaic and early classical lyric. For Pindar,
involved as he is in the politics and aesthetics of encomium and aetiology, the possibility that mythological tradition is grounded in poetic
lies allows him to position his own representations as truthful. Thus,
he attempts to rehabilitate the *kleos* of Ajax by impugning Homer as
complicit in Odysseus' lies and cunning self-promotions at Ajax's expense.[39] Xenophanes' verses also question the veracity and ethical appropriateness of poetic tradition.[40] Simonides may have been the first
poet to explicitly characterise his own creations as a form of *apatē*.[41]

In line with the didactic tradition of Hesiod's *Works and Days*, the
elegiac poetry that comes down to us under the authorship of Theognis
also provides important features in the pre-classical representation of
deception. Theognis advises his audience not to trust the outward appearances of fellow citizens and friends (73–4). In the face of social
upheaval in Megara, Theognis recommends that the young aristocrat
conceal his true character and intentions, adapting his *persona* to suit
whatever company he keeps (213–14, 1071–2).[42]

These early poetic treatments of deception will be seen to inform
classical treatments though the new democratic context will place them
in a different light. The reader may also notice certain texts or issues
which are missing from my treatment of Athenian culture. I offer no

---

[39] See Pind. *Nem.* 7.9–30 and 8.19–44 with bibliography cited below p. 118 n. 99.
[40] Xenophanes DK 21 B1, B11 and B12. See Babut (1974); Kirk, Raven and Schofield (1983) 168–70; Pratt (1993) 136–40.
[41] See Plut. *De poet. aud.* 15d; Carson (1992) 53.
[42] See Levine (1985), Donlan (1985) and Cobb-Stevens (1985).

interpretation of the infamous 'deception speech' of Sophocles' *Ajax*.[43] Gorgias' *Encomium of Helen* with its characterisation of *logos* as enacting a form of psychagogic *apatē* will often be mobilised in my argument, but I do not give it privileged treatment.[44] The dramatic and philosophical representation of Odysseus will be considered, but only in relation to broader questions.[45] I will be considering Aristophanes' representation of deceptive rhetoric, sophistry and lying demagogues, but where *Knights* and *Acharnians* will receive some detailed consideration, I will offer no thoroughgoing reading of *Wasps*, *Birds*, *Assembly-Women* or *Clouds*.[46] The speeches of the Attic orators have pride of place in this study but I have not attempted an exhaustive consideration of every discussion of deceit, bribery or sycophancy which they deploy.[47] The *Poliorketika* of Aineias Tacticus could almost be read as a treatise on military trickery but it will only receive a passing reference.[48] These and other texts will be sidelined, partly because they have received recent and productive critical attention. But their relative silence in this study is also a symptom of my belief that there are many other texts (some well known and some not) which have as great a contribution to make in the quest to understand the 'hows and whys' of Athenian culture's representation(s) of deceptive communication and trickery.

Ancient and modern

I began this introduction by setting Oliver North's inquisition alongside Plato and Demosthenes. This is a strategy which will recur throughout the book. Although this study is concerned to understand the representation of deception in classical Athens' democratic culture, there are points where I offer explicit or implicit comparisons with discussions of deception in nineteenth- or twentieth-century British and American texts and political discourse. This species of comparative strategy needs some defence and explanation. It could be argued

---

[43] On the 'deception speech', for example: Knox (1961); Cohen (1978); Goldhill (1988a) 189f.; Blundell (1989) 82–8 (with extensive bibliography).

[44] On Gorgias and *apatē*: Rosenmeyer (1955); Segal (1962); Walsh (1984) 80–106; Verdenius (1981); Wardy (1996b). For fuller bibliography on Gorgias, see pp. 147, 161 and pp. 281–2.

[45] See Stanford (1954).

[46] On *Clouds* see O' Regan (1992) and her bibliography. On *Wasps*, see (for example) Heath (1987b); Henderson (1990); Bowie (1987). For *Birds* see (most recently) the essays collected in Dobrov (1997). On *Assembly-Women*, see Rothwell (1990); Ober (1998) 122–55; Zeitlin (1999) 167–97.

[47] On bribery, see Harvey (1985). On sycophancy see Harvey (1990); Osborne (1990).

[48] On Aineias Tacticus see Whitehead (1988), (1990).

that such comparisons are misleading because they imply that modern America or Britain are in some sense 'the same' as classical Athens. I do not wish these comparisons to imply that Athenian democracy 'translates' into modern democracy or that Athenian representations of deceit are fully explicable in terms of modern analogies. To take one example of *difference* by way of illustration: Herodotus tells us that the general Miltiades was indicted and sentenced to exile by the demos for deceiving them with false promises. Miltiades promised to enrich Athenians if they sanctioned a military campaign. When he failed to come up with the goods, they punished him. Now modern democratic politicians fail to fulfil their pledges all the time and they may get voted out of office as a result. But British and American citizens cannot (or at least, do not) sue a government representative for disappointing them or breaking election promises.

But there are still good reasons for bringing modern representations of deception into play. Firstly, the examples I have selected should help to clarify certain issues which are at stake in my selections and analyses. In the first of my opening quotations Oliver North is subjected to a rhetoric of military identity. This quotation thus serves as a signpost for a key concern of my first chapter: military aspects of Athenian civic identity inform Athenian evaluations and representations of deceit and vice versa. But the North quote will be supplemented with other modern material which will serve to highlight the complexity and difficulty of interpreting (often conflicting) public representations of deception. So the modern comparisons are designed both to highlight the problems encountered in telling a story about the representation of deception in Athens *and* to underline the important points of this story.

Speaking of this book as a 'story' brings me to the second reason for including modern comparisons. These examples can remind the reader that my findings are contingent and conditioned. That is to say that my own position in history is likely to have affected my interpretation of deception in democratic Athens and that such an interpretation does not express some timeless truth either about deception in Athens or about deception *per se*. Rather than pretend that my interpretation is made from some standpoint outside history, my use of modern analogies is intended to signal the likelihood that twentieth-century concerns have shaped the focus and argument of this book. In the current critical climate, one response to the challenge of the inevitable and distorting distance between the interpreter and the ancient culture she seeks to 'read' is to characterise the reconstruction of 'original' meaning as a positivistic and 'realist' illusion. Thus my historical and literary reading of 'deception in classical Athens' is just one story that can be told about that subject – and differing or opposing accounts will be both possible and of similar 'fictional' status.[49] According to this anti-foundationalist, 'textualist' response it would be better to identify the accretions and processes of appropriation which have occurred between the classical period and my own time in order to produce a self-conscious study of the ways in which the relevant ancient texts have been variously received, read and deployed throughout history.[50] It would be interesting to chart the then-to-now 'reception' of the classical material which I present in this book. It would also be interesting to marry this 'reception criticism' with a wider history (or 'story') of the representation of deception. One could draw on a wealth of fascinating material: second sophistic rhetoric and physiognomics, St Augustine, Machiavelli, Nietzsche, House of Commons speeches, political memoirs, modern experimental psychology, nuclear game theory and much more besides.

I have not gone down the 'textualist' road but I do acknowledge that this study is neither *the last word* nor *the only word* on its subject. In a few years' time some of the 'modern comparisons' which I use will date the book rather markedly. This datedness will be a virtue rather than a shortcoming because it will help the reader to judge for herself how historically conditioned or contingent my focus and interpretation is. As for 'textualist' approaches, I think it is both possible and desirable to argue that (for example) a segment of Demosthenes' oratory was informed by a wider contemporary discourse of *apatē* as unAthenian without recourse to a 'textualist' hermeneutic along the lines that this argument is only the product of my contingent late twentieth-century concerns and critical rhetorics (structuralist, Marxist, Foucauldian, empiricist ...) or a significant accretion or appropriation of previous 'readings' of Demosthenes or 'classical Athens'. It is possible because there is still a widespread belief that the past is not hopelessly inaccessible, that there are better and worse accounts of ancient texts, representations or events and that these accounts can be argued about. One reason for this is actually found in 'neo-pragmatist' versions of 'textualism': 'No matter how strongly I believe in the constructedness of fact, the facts that are perspicuous for me within constructions not presently under challenge (and there must always be some for perception even to occur) will remain so. The conviction of the textuality of fact is logi-

---

[49] For the affinities between 'history' and 'fiction' or 'story-telling' see White (1978) and Kellner (1989).
[50] See Martindale (1993) for an example of such a project in relation to Latin literature.

cally independent of the firmness with which any particular fact is experienced.'[51]

Another reason for avoiding 'textualism' is forcefully presented by Paul Cartledge, although his argument here is actually directed towards 'anthropologising' approaches which over-emphasise the 'otherness' of the Greeks:

Are not the Victorian English (say) alien or foreign to us in culturally fundamental respects? But we do not treat their culture as a closed book on principle. In short, although it is not the case, as too many Classicists appear to wish to believe, that 'we are all ancient Greeks' (or Athenians), and although Classical Greek culture is both as a whole and in fundamental details deeply alien, it is nevertheless possible for us to gain a sympathetic understanding of it.[52]

We can recognise and comprehend the Greeks at the same time as we concede their strangeness and otherness. Where the similarities end and the differences begin will always be a matter for disagreement and such debates will be informed by the kinds of theoretical and interpretive controversy which I am grappling with here. If we are neither the same as the Greeks nor entirely different from them (however contingent such an observation might be) then it could be worth working out what the Greeks *actually said* about certain issues. If we identify 'issues' at all in (say) Athenian oratory, we have already found a level of correlation between 'us' and 'them' and this notion of correlation brings me to the final reason why I have chosen to use modern examples.

Stanley Fish argues that any attempt to orientate literary or historical study towards political action beyond the academy is both inevitably doomed and likely to result in bad scholarship. He also argues that his antifoundationalist rhetoric is a form of contemporary 'sophism'. Just as the classical sophists 'shook things up' by arguing that there is no foundational 'truth' and only rhetoric, Fish maintains that his antifoundationalism only persuades people that there is no point in trying to transcend the rhetoric of one's own institutional realm.[53] Whether we are a right-wing academic wishing to teach 'eternal truths' through a strictly censored canon of literature and history or a left-winger who wishes to radicalise students and the wider community with a 'feminist' or 'postcolonial' syllabus, we will not affect the political or ideological outlook of the masses because the academy is too marginal within contemporary political society to have such an effect.[54]

[51] Fish (1994) 248.
[52] Cartledge (1993) 17. See also 1–17 and 175–6.
[53] Fish (1994) 243–56, 281–308.
[54] See also the similar position on intellectual involvement in politics adopted by Rorty (1989).

Of course, an interpretation of Athenian culture or a reading of Sophocles is not going to change government policy, alter voting patterns or give new hope to the unemployed. But where Fish appropriates the rhetorically provocative label of 'sophist' from the (still authoratitive) paradigm of the Athenian 'enlightenment' to describe his antifoundationalism, we can see a lot of 'politics' at work. Fish may not see the 'political' implications of his outlook, but many have argued that his (and Richard Rorty's) antifoundationalism are highly conservative in political and cultural terms.[55] By calling himself a 'sophist', Fish arrogates to himself the image of an intellectual whose rhetoricism and conservative relativism is a provocation to 'mainstream' academia or society as a whole. He celebrates a label which was originally levelled at him as a term of abuse (for similar abusive uses of the term in Athenian oratory see my fourth chapter). 'Sophistry' was undoubtedly a term of abuse in classical Athens, but those intellectuals who (under Plato's own prejudiced taxonomy) have come to be regarded as 'sophists' did not all conform to the Fishian model. Indeed, many of them thought that political excellence was teachable and while some might have been 'conservatives' there were others who clearly did not believe that the status quo was unchangeable or that their profession was incompatible with political agency. This does not mean that Fish is *wrong* to call himself a 'sophist' because the term *can* have precisely the sort of resonance which he gives it. But the label's connotations are not exhausted either by its use as a term for attacking Fish or its reappropriation by him as a rhetorical provocation. And the fact that 'sophistry' is a label which is used at all as a means of attacking, provoking or celebrating critical positions shows that Athenian paradigms have rhetorical and political currency in current intellectual debates about democratic culture. If people are using the example of Athenian culture to advance political arguments concerning modern society (especially when they claim that such uses are *not* political), I think it is legitimate to suggest how my story about deception in democratic Athens can be made politically relevant to our own perceptions of deception in modern Western democracy.

In my epilogue, I will briefly and tentatively outline my (avowedly

---

[55] See Eagleton (1991) 202: '[T]hose who today press the sophistical case that all language is rhetorical ... are quite ready to acknowledge that the discourse in which they frame this case is nothing but a case of special pleading too; but if Fish is genially prepared to admit that his own theorizing is a bit of rhetoric, he is notably more reluctant to concede that it is a bit of *ideology*. For to do this would involve reflecting on the political ends which such an argument serves in the context of Western capitalist society.' See also the political critique of Fish and Rorty in Norris (1992) 126–58.

political and partisan) idea of what this relevance could be. This will not be an attempt to 'do' politics in the conventional sense, but it will trace a few ways in which the representation of deception in the Athenian democracy can suggest a politically oriented agenda for intellectual critique and artistic expression in a modern democracy. The modern analogies which occasionally appear throughout the book will help to clarify that agenda and perhaps encourage the reader to think of (and with) their own connections and analogies.

In my opening quotations, Oliver North is told that his lies are un-American and violate his commitments as an American serviceman. Clearly, evaluations of deceit can be tied to notions of military, political and national identity in the public discourses of a late twentieth-century democracy. I will begin by considering the evaluation of deceit in relation to the ideology of the Athenian citizen-serviceman.

1 Deception and the rhetoric of Athenian identity

British statesmen and public men have never at any time used mendacity as an instrument of war, still less have they uttered such praises of lying as Hitler has done in *Mein Kampf* ... In Great Britain we believe in the ultimate power of Truth.[1]

Viscount Maugham, formerly the British Lord Chancellor, wrote these (partly mendacious) words in a pamphlet published in 1941 entitled *Lies as allies: or Hitler at war*. Hitler was happy to declare the usefulness of deception as a means of achieving his ends and despite the availability of *Mein Kampf* in Britain at the time, Neville Chamberlain had believed the dictator's guarantees of peace in 1938. It makes sense to us now that an establishment pamphleteer would want to represent Hitler's 'praises of lying' as anathema to 'Britishness' and propagate the falsehood that, in contrast to Hitler, British statesmen had never used mendacity as an instrument of war. But Maugham's propaganda, whilst unsurprising, underscores some important points which I will be making in this chapter. Firstly, Maugham mobilises the ideology of 'national character' in his argument. Regardless of the realities of British military and political history, he is able to represent Great Britain as a nation committed to 'Truth'. Secondly, Maugham's contrast between Hitler and 'Britishness' draws its persuasive force from a premise that was essentially true from a British point of view: Hitler had praised lying in his writings and he had proved himself a liar on the international stage. We can characterise the statement as 'propagandistic', 'ideological' or even as occupying the realm of the 'imaginary' in its claims concerning Britishness, but it draws upon aspects of Hitler's philosophy and behaviour which could be documented and understood as accurate or true at the time.[2] Thirdly, the contrast be-

---

[1] Maugham (1941) 11–12.
[2] Maugham's statement about British honesty exemplifies a definition of propaganda offered by the Cambridge classicist Francis Cornford in 1922: 'that branch of the art of lying which consists in very nearly deceiving your friends without quite deceiving your enemies' (recalled in Guthrie's preface to Cornford (1953)).

tween Hitler the Liar and Britain the True obviously relies on a basic assumption that deception is morally wrong and truth-telling is morally good. Finally, the contrast is hardly an adequate or complete guide to British representations of military deceit or national character at the time or in subsequent years. Britain did not shirk from deploying tactics of deception and disinformation against the Axis powers during the Second World War, nor was there a British public outcry when such tactics were revealed after the event.[3]

The points concerning 'national character' and 'morality' in relation to deceit serve to introduce my argument that the representation of deceptive behaviour and communication is an important component in the construction and reproduction of an ideal Athenian citizen identity. I take certain texts that exemplify or relate to this discourse of identity as my starting point because modern scholarship has tended to characterise ancient Greek culture as much more accepting of deceptive behaviour than modern western civic societies. For example, Detienne and Vernant have traced the connotations and valorisation of *mētis* ('cunning intelligence') in a wide range of texts spanning ten centuries from Homer down to Oppian.[4] It would be hard to dismiss the many positive associations which this category of thought is given in the classical period and it is equally hard to find analogues for the concept in modern cultures. It is certainly true that classical Athenian texts offer us many positive evaluations of deceit in certain contexts and I will have much to say about these positive treatments in later chapters. Anthropological studies on rural communities in Greece and elsewhere in the Mediterranean since the Second World War have also been applied to archaic Greece and classical Athens in order to claim that the ancients were not so different from their modern ancestors in prizing and practising deception with vigour.[5] Here, lying is seen to be especially crucial to the conduct of what Cohen calls the 'politics of reputation'.[6] I have already discussed the dangers and advantages of this comparative approach in my introduction. But this chapter attempts to show that in the public spaces of Athenian civic and democratic exchange, there was a strong and persistent ideological construction of deceit and trickery as *negative* categories of communication

---

[3] See Barnes (1994) 23–9; Cruickshank (1979); Cave-Brown (1976).
[4] Detienne and Vernant (1978).
[5] See Walcot (1970), (1977); Scheibe (1979) 83.
[6] Cohen (1991) 36. See also 96 where Cohen concedes that '[F]or Athens we do not have the kind of evidence needed' to demonstrate that deception fulfilled the function of reconciling a need for privacy and the sanctions of public codes described in modern rural Greece by du Boulay (1974).

and behaviour which served to define what it meant to be a good Athenian male citizen. Despite comparative approaches which suggest that deception was a crucial strategy in Athens' 'surveillance culture' and the undeniable value which ancient Greek texts place on 'cunning intelligence' as a category of thought, the *democratic* and *civic* culture of Athens in the fifth and fourth centuries develops powerful representations of deceptive communication as inimical to its very existence.

Where Viscount Maugham was able to forge an image of Britain the True through a contrast with documented examples of Hitler the Liar, we will see that Athenian constructions of 'honest national character' are also often drawing their force from contrasts with solid pre-conceptions about the attitudes and practices of an enemy. The assertion of a contrast between the 'deceptive other' to the Athenian 'self' is sustained by reference to demonstrable features of that enemy's political, cultural and military regimen and past Athenian dealings with it. This 'demonstrability' is important: it is through such demonstrations that Athenian texts can posit the enemy's reliance on deceit as symptomatic of a failure to understand what it is to be (and make) a good citizen.

Maugham's projected image of Britain as a nation that would never deceive an enemy was clearly at odds with the realities of British tactics. It will become clear that Athenian projections of an 'honest' self-image were almost certainly divorced from reality. However, I will have little to say about the extent to which the Athenian ideology of deceit and 'real' practice diverged: as my introduction suggested, this extent of divergence is difficult to gauge given the nature of the evidence available.

I have also stressed that Maugham's image of Britain the True cannot be taken as a complete or adequate guide to the British representation of military deceit during or after the Second World War. If Britain needed to be reassured by the 'ultimate power of Truth' and boosted by an image of itself as an embodiment of Truth, there would be other occasions during and after the war where British Cleverness, Cunning and Duplicity towards enemies would be paraded as virtues without any fear that the two images would be felt to contradict each other. In my second chapter, the Athenian image of military deceit will also reveal itself to be negotiable and open to positive representation. It is crucial to understand, however, that military trickery becomes an area of theoretical anxiety for classical Greek writers. That anxiety will be seen to arise, in part, from a perceived tension between Athenian and Spartan notions of what makes a good citizen-soldier. I will begin by examining how and why that tension is formulated in Athenian public discourse.

Honest hoplites and tricky Spartans

For the Athenian citizen male, his role as a soldier or sailor in wartime was an important component of his civic identity and status: 'in the classical period, military organisation merged with civic organisation; it was not as a warrior that the citizen governed the city, but it was as a citizen that the Athenian went to war'.[7] It was the hoplite class of citizens who formed the nucleus of the citizen land army. To be a hoplite, a citizen had to be able to pay for his heavy armour and, because of this degree of financial qualification, he would probably have belonged to one of 'the three highest classes in the Solonian hierarchy'.[8] This meant that members of the hoplite class tended to be farmers; the sort of men who are caricatured and transformed into comic heroes in the texts of Aristophanes.[9]

The question of how many men made up this class of citizens is difficult to answer with any certainty or precision; the figures given by fifth-century historians may often be generalised or exaggerated. Furthermore, an account of numbers of hoplites or thetes present at a battle may not represent the full muster that was possible. Drawing on evidence from Herodotus, Thucydides and the varied estimates of scholars, Stockton traces an increase in numbers of hoplites deployed in the field from 9,000 at the battle of Marathon in 490 to a figure of 13,000 in 431.[10] The latter estimate is put forward by Thucydides (2.13.6–8) and in addition to this field army, he writes of a further 16,000 hoplites in the forts of Attica and guarding the circuit of the Long Walls. This defensive army was made up of men of metic status

---

[7] Vidal-Naquet (1986a) 85. From a different tradition of scholarship, Pritchett (1971) 27 expresses this merging of the civic and military identity in terms of patriotism: 'The Athenian citizen identified his own interest with that of the state. His patriotism was shown no less in devotion on the battlefield than in financial sacrifice.' See also Vernant (1968) *passim*; Davies (1978) 31f.; Goldhill (1988a) 63; Croally (1994) 47–56. For the Athenian funeral ceremonies (*epitaphioi*) and funeral speeches (*epitaphioi logoi*) as instantiations of the idea that to die fighting for the polis is the finest civic act, see Clairmont (1983) and Loraux (1986).

[8] Vidal-Naquet (1986a) 89. Citizens who were or had been hoplites were known as *zeugitai*.

[9] See especially Trygaeus in Aristophanes' *Peace*: the only Aristophanic hero who is an active hoplite. Although many hoplites were farmers, it is dangerous to generalise about military organisation in fifth-century Athens. The exigencies of the Peloponnesian War and Athens' expanding naval power meant that hoplites often fought at sea. There is also evidence that members of the poorer class of thetes were sometimes equipped for hoplite battle through state finance. We also know that both the hoplite army and the fleet sometimes used metics, free barbarians and slaves. For these and other complexities of fifth-century military arrangements, see Ridley (1979); Vidal-Naquet (1986a) 88f.; Loraux (1986) 32–7.

[10] Stockton (1990) 15f. See Gomme (1933); Jones (1957) 161f.; Hansen (1985).

and citizens who were above or below field-service age. Unfortunately, there is no indication of the proportions of citizens and non-citizens in this second group. Stockton estimates a figure of 18,000 thetes for this time. Even if these figures are exaggerations it seems probable that, from the mid-fifth century onwards, more than half of the male citizen population of Attica had the economic status of a hoplite. In the 430s an older man may have been beyond field-service age but nevertheless retained his hoplite identity. For many, hoplite status was perhaps newly acquired; Jones argues that many thetes became hoplites because of increased prosperity in the mid-fifth century and the possibility that property assessments lagged behind inflationary trends.[11]

It is indisputable that the fifth-century Athenian empire derived its growth and security from a powerful navy rather than its hoplite land army. Nevertheless, Athenian political discourse tended to valorise hoplite identity as opposed to that of the poorer rowing class, and it is clear that to be a hoplite was to be part of a burgeoning 'middle class' whose property and strength in numbers made them the dominant social group in the polis.[12] I will begin by discussing the Athenian projection of an ideology of hoplite endeavour and the representation of *apatē* (deception, trickery) within that projection.

For my purposes, there are two important points about Athenian hoplite warfare that must be stressed. The first point is that a hoplite army was only suited to a set-piece battle, fought in the open and on a site agreed upon by both sides.[13] It is clear from accounts of the Persian and Peloponnesian Wars that battles were fought on a seasonal basis, beginning in Spring and ending in Autumn. Ideally, hoplite warfare involved an open, prearranged contest between two similarly equipped

---

[11] Jones (1978) 166f.

[12] The 'hoplite bias' of public Athenian ideological projections is traced in the *epitaphioi logoi* by Loraux (1986) 155–71. But it would be wrong to suggest that the navy's role in empire and democracy is effaced in Athenian public culture: see Ar. *Vesp.* 1093ff. and *Eq.* 1265–71. Rose (1995) and Rosenbloom (1995) demonstrate how Sophocles' *Ajax* and Aeschylean tragedy engage with the relationship between leadership, politics, sea-power and empire. Naval lists have survived from the fourth century which show that many Athenian triremes were named after key ideological concepts, categories of thought and cultural forms (e.g. *'Demokratia'* – given to four ships over fifty-five years, *'Nike'*, *'Eunomia'*, *'Eleutheria'*, *'Dikaiosune'*, *'Sophia'*, *'Mneme'*, *'Techne'*, *'Tragoidia'*, *'Comoidia'*). See Casson (1971) 350–4 for further examples and discussion. See also Strauss (1996) for an excellent discussion of thetes' ideology and naval service as democratic political education.

[13] See the amazement of the Persian Mardonius at Hdt. 7.9.β1: 'Besides, from all I hear, the Greeks usually wage war in an extremely stupid fashion, because they are ignorant and incompetent. When they declare war on one another, they seek out the best, most level piece of land, and that is where they go to fight. The upshot is that the victors leave the battlefield with massive losses, not to mention the losers, who are completely wiped out' (translation by Waterfield (1998)).

and similarly arranged armies. During and after the Peloponnesian
War, archers, lightly armed troops and ambushes were used increasingly and with devastating effect against heavily armed and relatively
immobile hoplite units.[14] Thucydides recounts instances where Athenian generals attempted to adapt the lineaments of hoplite practice in
order to cope with a stealthy enemy that did not announce itself before
engagement.[15] Several texts of the fifth and fourth centuries attest to
reflection and debate over the relative merits of archery and hoplite
fighting.[16] Nevertheless, it seems clear that 'proper' hoplite fighting was
meant to be a face-to-face trial of strength and courage. This kind of
'up front' massed confrontation was the antithesis of other forms of
fifth-century land warfare. For the hoplite there was none of the trickery associated with ambushes, the protection and distance afforded to
the archer or the mobility allowed to lightly armed and mounted units.
In my second chapter I will argue that this ideological opposition was
not *always* maintained with respect to trickery. For the present discussion, however, it is important to recognise that the ideal of hoplite
practice often excluded the possibility of military trickery from either
side of a conflict.

Commentators have also laid emphasis on the *collective* nature of the
hoplite phalanx. Although other non-democratic Greek cities also had
hoplite armies, it is clear that for post-Cleisthenic Athens the citizen
phalanx served as an important paradigm for Athens' developing ideology of democracy, civic participation and collective responsibility.[17]
The phalanx was only effective and secure if all its members acted as

---

[14] See Thuc. 3.96–8, where Demosthenes' hoplites are wiped out in Aitolia because of
the mobility of their lightly armed opponents.

[15] See Thuc. 4.30–2 where Demosthenes is said to have learnt from his experiences in
Aitolia. See also his use of cunning at 3.112 and the ruse of Paches at 3.34 which I
discuss in more detail in the next chapter. For further references to non-hoplitic tactics
in the Peloponnesian War see Saïd and Trédé (1985). Heza (1974) argues that the
prevalence of ruses in Thucydidean accounts of warfare indicate a change in military
mentality during the Peloponnesian War.

[16] See Eur. *HF* 161ff. and Bond (1981) ad loc.; Soph. *Aj.* 1120; Pl. *La.* 190e5–191e1.

[17] For a sense of this collective responsibility embodied in hoplite organisation we should
note the first four elements of the ephebic oath cited by Siewert (1977) 102–3: 1. 'I will
not disgrace these sacred arms' (οὐκ αἰσχυνῶ τὰ ἱερὰ ὅπλα); 2. 'I will not desert the
comrade beside me wherever I shall be stationed in a battle-line' (οὐδὲ λείψω τὸν
παραστάτην ὅπου ἂν στ⟨ο⟩ιχήσω); 3. 'I will defend our sacred and public institutions'
(ἀμυνῶ δὲ καὶ ὑπὲρ ἱερῶν καὶ ὁσίων); 4. 'And I will not pass on (to the descendants) my
fatherland smaller, but greater and better, so far as I am able, by myself or with the
help of all' (καὶ ο⟨ὐ⟩κ ἐλάττω παραδώσω τὴν πατρίδα, πλείω δὲ καὶ ἀρείω κατά τε
ἐμαυτὸν καὶ μετὰ ἁπάντων). The sentiment of the closely-packed phalanx is already
found in the poetry of the archaic polis: see Tyrt. 8.11–13 and 9.15–19 in the edition of
Prato (1968). For discussion of Tyrtaeus' expression of collective ideology, see Jaeger
(1966); Shey (1976); Tarkow (1983); Goldhill (1991) 126–8.

one tightly-packed unit. To leave your position in this unit was to lay it open to destruction: 'the values of a hoplite are necessarily tied to a sense of collective endeavour'.[18]

A major text, often cited for evidence of these ideal notions of collective action, duty to the polis and the value of the citizen army, is Pericles' funeral speech in the second book of Thucydides. In this speech, the Thucydidean Pericles explicitly contrasts Athenian military values with those of the Spartans. I want to cite a section of the speech in order to illustrate three intertwined strands in the Athenian ideological construction of trickery and deceit as occupying the realm of the 'other' in the second half of the fifth century:

And then we are different to our opponents with regard to military preparations in the following ways. Our city is open to the world, and we have no periodical deportations of foreigners in order to prevent people seeing or learning secrets which might be of military advantage to the enemy. This is because we rely, not on preparations and deceits but on our own real courage with respect to deeds (πιστεύοντες οὐ ταῖς παρασκευαῖς τὸ πλέον καὶ ἀπάταις ἢ τῷ ἀφ' ἡμῶν αὐτῶν ἐς τὰ ἔργα εὐψύχῳ). There is a difference too in our systems of education. The Spartans, from boyhood are submitted to the most laborious training in courage (οἱ μὲν ἐπιπόνῳ ἀσκήσει εὐθὺς νέοι ὄντες τὸ ἀνδρεῖον μετέρχονται), whereas we pass our lives without such restrictions but we are no less ready to face the same dangers as they are. (Thucydides 2.39.1)

This passage has been remarked upon for the extreme emphasis it places on the merits of Athenian non-professionalism.[19] Yet, to use the phrase 'non-professionalism' perhaps introduces a distinction which misses the force of Pericles' statements about Athenian military conduct. He is not so much stressing the non-mercenary aspect of Athenian military participation as emphasising its lack of reliance on acquired knowledge through training. Pericles marks a contrast between the enforced military education and the 'learned courage' of the Spartans on the one hand, and a representation of the Athenians as *naturally* endowed with courage on the other.[20]

This idea of a natural disposition towards prowess in the Athenian character is a commonplace of the funeral orations we have: most

[18] Goldhill (1988) 145.
[19] See Loraux (1986) 150: '... the funeral oration is the privileged locus of Athenian "non-professionalism" in military matters, finding its most extended expression in Pericles' *epitaphios* but referred to in all the orations'. See also Vidal-Naquet (1986a) 89f.
[20] As Mills (1997) 74 points out, this emphasis on Athens' lack of strict and extensive military training allows Pericles to trumpet the fact that Athenians have time for higher concerns: 'We love beauty without extravagance and wisdom (*philosophoumen*) without softness' (Thuc. 2.40.2).

graphically Gorgias' funeral speech attributes 'innate Ares' to the Athenians.[21] Despite a lack of formal training, Pericles boasts that the Athenians have seldom been proved incapable of defeating the Peloponnesian forces.[22] But Pericles also defines the Athenians as trusting in their natural courage as opposed to 'prearranged devices and deceits' (πιστεύοντες οὐ ταῖς παρασκευαῖς τὸ πλέον καὶ ἀπάταις ἢ τῷ ἀφ' ἡμῶν αὐτῶν ἐς τὰ ἔργα εὐψύχῳ). This and the preceding description of Athens as an 'open' and unsecretive city clearly imply a contrast with Spartan practice in military matters. Extensive training, preparation, secrecy and deception are being associated with each other and are being given decidedly negative connotations.

Hornblower finds this chapter of Thucydides 'puzzling': 'its message is that Athenian military arrangements are easy-going and unprofessional by comparison with Sparta's – not a very encouraging thing to be told, one would have thought ... Surely neither Thucydides nor Pericles, who is made to say at 1.142 that naval warfare was a matter of long training, can have thought anything so silly as that effortless superiority could be achieved in land fighting'.[23] Hornblower goes on to point out that there may have been more military training at Athens than Thucydides makes Pericles imply and suggests that this passage is explained by the influence of 'the insouciant, oligarchic attitudes of the cavalry class' on its author.

It is certainly true that the existence and nature of an Athenian cadet-training system (ephēbeia) in fifth-century Athens remains an open question.[24] But there is clear evidence that there was some proto-military training for aspiring Athenian hoplites in the form of disciplined 'war dances'.[25] It is also true that, in reality, Athenian naval warfare required careful training and preparation. Hornblower might have added evidence for the use of deceptive tactics and the need for cunning intelligence in fifth-century descriptions of Athenian naval

---

[21] See Gorgias DK 82 B6. As a foreigner Gorgias is unlikely to have delivered this speech in person at an actual ceremony and it may have been a rhetorical exercise. See also Lys. 2.63.

[22] Thuc. 2.39.2. The author commonly known as the Old Oligarch offers a much less flattering view of the Athenian hoplite force ([Xen.] *Ath. Pol.* 2.1).

[23] Hornblower (1991) 303–4.

[24] For arguments in favour of the probability of a fifth-century *ephēbeia*, see Cawkwell (1972) 262 and (1989) 380; Siewert (1977); Vidal-Naquet (1986a) 97f.; Winkler (1990a) 20f. Wilamowitz (1893) 193–4 used Thuc. 2.39.1 to argue against a fifth-century *ephēbeia*.

[25] See Winkler (1990a) 54f. on the *gumnopaidikē* and the *pyrrhikē* as institutional ephebic dances akin to 'martial arts'. For further discussion of controversies surrounding the Athenian ephebate see below in this section and pp. 86–9.

conduct.[26] But it is precisely the suppression of 'realities' that makes this chapter of the funeral speech so interesting. Pericles is represented as constructing ideal oppositions between Spartan training and Athenian 'natural courage' and between Spartan deceit and Athenian openness. If he suppresses the elements of Athenian naval tactics that involve deception and specialised knowledge, and if he downplays any possible realities concerning Athenian military training, it is because, at the level of ideology, Thucydides' Pericles wants to use an occasion where 'homage to the dead and celebration of the "entire nation" went hand in hand'[27] in order to construct an image of the city for the city which defines it as 'naturally' courageous in contrast to its enemies. Loraux regards this construction, common to virtually all the *epitaphioi logoi*, as another example of the 'aristocratic thinking' that lies behind these speeches. While the oration of Pericles is 'careful not to transform too overtly all Athenian combatants into hoplites and prefers to remain vague' it imbues the Athenian land army with a kind of superior nobility. Pericles 'reserves true glory to hereditary heroism and disdains acquired, and therefore necessarily imperfect, virtues'.[28] Here we see the natural courage of the Athenian collective being given a sharper focus and a stronger emphasis through a construction of the enemy as relying upon contrivance and preparation. The deployment of deception is welded to this idea of acquired and therefore inferior military ability. It would be simplistic to say that military trickery is a completely unproblematic component within the notion of natural, inherited and heroic excellence in Homeric poetry and archaic texts. Nevertheless, the *Iliad* represents the ambush (*lochos*) as an engagement which should be reserved for the 'best of the Achaeans'.[29] By contrast, Thucydides' representation of Pericles' speech emphatically divorces military trickery from the grammar of Athenian excellence and courage on the grounds that it connotes characteristics that are uninherited and not inherent. It can also be argued that the Athenian public ideology of military courage excludes *apatē* because of a very un-Homeric association between trickery of an enemy and *fear* of the enemy. I will return to this association and its implications in my next chapter.

---

[26] Detienne and Vernant (1978) 296–9 discuss details and sources concerning the deceptive naval manoeuvres known as the *periplous* and the *diekplous* which the Athenian navy successfully deployed.
[27] Loraux (1986) 20.
[28] Loraux (1986) 150–2.
[29] See Hom. *Il.* 1.227–9 where Achilles chastises Agamemnon for never taking part in an ambush with 'the best of the Achaeans'.

I have already alluded to another motivation behind Pericles' contrast between Athens' openness and the Spartan enemy's reliance on deception and secrecy, namely the negative relation of notions of trickery to the ideology of hoplite endeavour. As Winkler remarks, the contrast between hoplite warfare and the tactics of deception is particularly important: 'enemy armies might camp quite close to each other without fear of surprise attack ... ambuscades and night attacks were a serious violation of honour, at least between Greeks'.[30] Winkler makes these comments to emphasise the transgressive nature of the myth of trickery associated with the Apatouria festival, an occasion which marked the entry of Athenian adolescents into adult life. Winkler follows Vidal-Naquet's famous analysis of this myth of trickery and its association with a 'coming of age ceremony'. I will briefly summarise Vidal-Naquet's findings because many of my arguments concerning *apatē* and its placement on the terrain of Athenian ideology constitute an explicit engagement with his work.

As I noted above, there is disagreement over the possible existence of an Athenian institution of cadet-training (*ephēbeia*), but there is an inscription from Acharnae of an ephebic oath whose language and style suggest an archaic origin.[31] To be an ephebe was to be at a transitional stage between childhood and full citizenship with all its military, civic and familial responsibilities. For many youths, then, the transformation into adulthood meant the adoption of the military and civic status of a hoplite.

The beginning of a young man's ephebic status was celebrated ritually by the sacrifice of his long hair on the third day of the Apatouria. It was also at this festival that youths were sworn into their phratry. But it is the aetiological myth of the festival and Vidal-Naquet's analysis of it which are instructive.[32] The story of the myth occurs at the frontier between Athens and Boeotia where (there are differing versions) some form of border dispute develops. The Boeotian king is Xanthus ('Fair One') and the Athenian king is Thymoeites, a descendant of Theseus. It is agreed to settle the dispute by a duel but Thymoeites appoints a champion, Melanthus ('Black One'), to fight in his place. Melanthus defeats his opponent by means of a deception. He cries out 'Xanthus, you do not play according to the rules – there is someone beside you!'

---

[30] Winkler (1990a) 33. For general condemnations of deception as a military tactic in Greek drama see [Eur.] *Rhes.* 510–11 and Soph. *Trach.* 270–80 where we are told that Zeus exiled Heracles for killing Iphitus by *dolos*.

[31] See Siewert (1977) and the text contained in n. 17 above.

[32] See Vidal-Naquet (1986a) 108f. He gives an extensive list of sources dating from the fifth century BC through to the Byzantine period.

Xanthus looks round in surprise and Melanthus takes the opportunity to kill him. In one account, Melanthus prays to Zeus *Apātenōr* (Zeus 'deceiver').[33] Many of the sources mention an intervention by 'Dionysus of the black goatskin', a god who is associated with the deception, but all of them explain the name of the Apatouria through a 'paronomastic etymology': the festival commemorates Melanthus' original *apatē*.[34]

In reaction to this myth, Vidal-Naquet asks himself why the story's stress on *apatē* should be offered to ephebes whose oath will bind them to a contrary model of behaviour; 'we have single combat (*monomachia*) and trickery contrasted with fair hoplite fighting on even terms'. Drawing on the insights of Jeanmaire, Lloyd, Lévi-Strauss and Van Gennep, Vidal-Naquet points out that the myth of Melanthus' *apatē* is analogous to the Spartan ephebic institution of the *krupteia* in that it is symmetrically opposite to the life of the hoplite. Through its dramatisation of a negative paradigm, it marks the transition from the marginal status of the ephebe to the positive position of the adult citizen hoplite.[35] Vidal-Naquet's study demonstrates that linguistic and tactical deception are built into the very processes by which young Athenians position themselves for the first time as citizens and hoplites. Melanthus' *apatē* is opposed to the hoplite citizen ideal and yet integral to continuing realisations of citizen identity. This negative position for military trickery clearly informs the Periclean antithesis between Athenian and Spartan character.[36]

Loraux's analysis of the way in which the funeral speeches appropriate aristocratic modes of thought to construct an image of 'natural superiority' is excellent. But where does Pericles' condemnation of Spartan deceit fit into all this? Loraux translates ἀπάταις as 'stratagems' (les stratagèmes) but it is clear from historical and dramatic texts written during the Peloponnesian War that accusations and narrations of Spartan deception and duplicity are common. Indeed there is a strong case for arguing, on the basis of Thucydides' funeral speech and other texts, that the Spartan enemy were being constructed as a para-

[33] *Lexica Segueriana* s.v. *apatouria* in Bekker (1814) 416–17.
[34] As Vidal-Naquet points out, the etymology cannot be dismissed as mere play on words since there was another initiation ritual for young girls which took place at the temple of Athena Apaturia where the founding story of *apatē* involved the union of Aethra and Poseidon. See Schmitt-Pantel (1977).
[35] See Winkler (1990a) 33: 'The ephebate therefore contains ... rites and fictions which dramatise the difference between what ephebes were (boys) and what they will become (men).'
[36] Vidal-Naquet himself hints at a link between Thuc. 2.39.1 and his reading of the myth of Melanthus. See Vidal-Naquet (1986b) 141 n. 8. See also Heza (1974) 44.

digm of 'the deceptive other' in order to mark a difference between these two Greek states who had once been allies.

Alfred Bradford has recently charted the construction of 'the duplicitous Spartan' in a number of fifth-century texts.[37] Although he does not cite Pericles' condemnation of the Spartan deception, Bradford concentrates on the extent to which Thucydides attributes duplicity and hidden motives to Spartan policy and the actions of certain Spartan leaders. He identifies an important distinction within the Athenian representation of Spartan national character. Firstly there is a Spartan 'type', defined primarily in terms of duplicity, and assumed by Euripides, Aristophanes, Thucydides and, to a much lesser extent, Herodotus. But there are also individual Spartans who are 'described by Athenian authors sometimes according to type, sometimes not.'[38] The former category of representation is strikingly evident from the fact that fifth-century texts frequently express the idea that Spartans say one thing while thinking another.[39]

The idea that the Spartan speaks with forked tongue was clearly popular in the second half of the fifth century, but it sometimes surfaces in a context where the prejudicial or 'propagandistic' quality of the idea is foregrounded. For example, Thucydides claims that in 420 Alcibiades tricked Spartan envoys into lying to the Athenian assembly that they had not arrived with full powers to negotiate on behalf of their city. They had previously said the opposite to the Boule, but Alcibiades promised to give them Pylos if they lied. Alcibiades' aim was to destabilise the Peace of Nicias and to establish a new alliance with Argos. Thucydides tells us that Alcibiades' plan was 'to drive a wedge between Nicias and the Spartans, and he also intended by attacking them in the assembly for having no sincerity (ὡς οὐδὲν ἀληθὲς ἐν νῷ ἔχουσιν) and for

---

[37] Bradford (1994). See also Powell (1989).

[38] Bradford (1994) 78.

[39] See Hdt. 9.54.1 where the Athenians 'were well aware of the Spartan tendency to say one thing and think something quite different' (ἐπιστάμενοι τὰ Λακεδαιμονίων φρονήματα ὡς ἄλλα φρονεόντων καὶ ἄλλα λεγόντων). See also Eur. *Andr* 451–2 and Ar. *Lys.* 1233–5. In the last example the Athenian commonplace that Spartans 'say one thing and think another' is being explicitly criticised by Lysistrata as wrong-headed. See also Ar. *Pax* 1063 and *Ach.* 308 (where the chorus vilify Dicaeopolis for making peace with oath-breaking Spartans). After Spartan troops were sent to Epidaurus in 419 and Argos was threatened, the Athenians inscribed 'the Spartans have not kept their oaths' on the base of the stele that had been engraved with the peace treaty between Sparta and Athens in 421 (Thuc. 5.56.1–3). Thucydidean accounts of Spartan treachery or betrayal: the massacre of Plataean prisoners (3.68.1); the slaughter of helots where, in a manner similar to Menelaus' trickery in Euripides' *Andromache*, prominent helots are coaxed out of hiding with false promises (4.80); the betrayal of Scione (5.18.7). See Bradford (1994) and Powell (1989) for further examples in Herodotus, Thucydides, Xenophon and Plutarch.

never saying the same thing twice (οὐδὲ λέγουσιν οὐδέποτε ταὐτά) to bring about the alliance with Argos, Elis and Mantinea' (5.45.3). The historian explains that the Athenians were already feeling cheated by the Spartans. Alcibiades exploits this mood and the commonplace of Spartan duplicity to enact his own trick. The Spartans are tricked into living up to the Athenian prejudice and the Athenian assembly are also deceived by Alcibiades' ruse. This is Alcibiades' first political act in Thucydides' account of the Peloponnesian War and it exemplifies the historian's initial description of him as an ambitious and competitive young aristocrat who sees Nicias as a rival and feels slighted that he had not been approached by the Spartans. Consequently Alcibiades wants to renew hostilities with Sparta but ultimately wishes to revive the strong relationship of *proxenia* which used to exist between the Spartans and his family (5.45.3).[40] The Thucydidean Alcibiades is always a law unto himself. But in the light of the Periclean construction of Athenian 'openness' and Spartan 'dishonesty' which he has presented in book 2, it is striking that the historian presents us with an example of the way in which a prominent young Athenian uses dissimulation to further his own ends and does so by both parading and perpetuating the negative image of Spartans as habitually untrustworthy. While I am primarily concerned here to trace the workings and connotations of the 'ideal', it is important to remember that Thucydides sometimes 'deconstructs' that ideal. In his account of Alcibiades' ruse, the historian narrates an unmasking of the way in which national stereotypes are reproduced and given authority. Alcibiades' lies turn the Spartans into liars and the Athenians are duped because their prejudices are thus confirmed.

Bradford demonstrates the pervasiveness of the 'tricky Spartan' in Athenian authors but he does not ask why or how this stereotype is deployed. It is precisely in Pericles' words that we see the *terms* in which Spartan trickery is opposed to Athenian openness. Deception is not *simply* attributed to the Spartan enemy. Rather, deception is construed in terms of its incompatibility with the ideal Athenian's identity as a hoplite-citizen who is born with the attributes of military excellence and manliness. To stereotype Spartans as deceptive is to imply that they lack natural courage and military excellence and to question their commitment to the honourable lineaments of hoplite battle.

The Athenian construction of Spartans as deceitful in general, and Pericles' comments in particular, also draw their force from perceptions and evaluations of Spartan training and education (*paideia*).

[40] On this, see Ostwald (1986) 298–333.

When he refers to the 'laborious *askēsis*' of the Spartan system of education, the Thucydidean Pericles is clearly referring to what scholars commonly refer to as the *agōgē* and the *krupteia*.[41] Taken together, these two aspects of Spartan *paideia* were the means by which the Spartan state perpetuated its unique reputation as a rigorous authoritarian community of disciplined soldier-citizens. Greek writers of the fourth century evince a persistent fascination with these two extraordinary institutions. As part of the *agōgē* the Spartans were said to have trained young boys from the age of seven for adulthood by forcing them to steal food through hunger and by issuing them with only one cloak. If they were caught stealing from the adult *sussitia* ('common mess') the boys were whipped. This was supposed to instil qualities of military courage, hardness and resourcefulness (*panourgia*).[42] The *agōgē* contained one ritual where boys had to compete in two groups to steal the most votive cheeses from the altar of Artemis Orthia and they were whipped in the process. Xenophon actually argues that this education in deception was designed by Lycurgus to make boys 'more resourceful' and 'better at waging war'.[43] When these boys reached adulthood it seems that some or all of them trained in the *krupteia*.[44] Those boys who go into the *krupteia* supposedly endure pain by going without shoes and bedding, even in winter.[45] They go out into the countryside for a year. With the minimum of food and clothing they had to survive off the land without being caught and in solitude. In a related but separate procedure, the best youths hide by day and kill unwanted helots under the cover of night.[46]

---

[41] As Kennell (1995) 113 points out, the word *agōgē* is never used in extant texts to denote Spartan education until the Hellenistic age: 'writers of the fifth and fourth centuries B.C. rightly presented the rituals of initiation and acculturation as wholly integrated into the unique Spartan way of life, but never attached to it any particular name'. In this book I will nevertheless retain the later term to describe Spartan training practices attested in the classical period.

[42] Xen. *Lac. Pol.* 2.6–9, *Anab.* 4.6.14–15; Plut. *Lycurg.* 16–18. See Hooker (1980) 136f. In the *Lac. Pol.* passage, Xenophon claims that it was the Spartan law-giver Lycurgus who instituted the exercise in theft and trickery.

[43] Xen. *Lac. Pol.* 2.7: ταῦτα οὖν δὴ πάντα δῆλον ὅτι μηχανικωτέρους τῶν ἐπιτηδείων βουλόμενος τοὺς παῖδας ποιεῖν καὶ πολεμικωτέρους οὕτως ἐπαίδευσεν. According to Plut. *Ages.* 20.2, Xenophon put his own sons through the Spartan *agōgē*, at Agesilaus' suggestion. See Cartledge (1987) 66.

[44] Cartledge (1987) 30–1 argues that 'soft' and 'hard' versions of this institution are presented in ancient sources. See also Lévy (1988) and Kennell (1995) 131–2, who both argue that the *krupteia* denotes the one-year period of isolation in the countryside for all trainees and *not* (as is often assumed) the elite helot-killing police duties.

[45] Pl. *Leg.* 1.633b–c.

[46] Plut. *Lycurg.* 28.1–7. On the possible initiatory and symbolic significance of these covert 'police actions' see Lévy (1988); Vernant (1992) 238–9.

Given that Spartan *paideia* was seen to be almost exclusively geared towards the achievement of military excellence and that many aspects of that training involved the practice and rehearsal of theft and trickery, it is hard to resist the conclusion that Pericles' Funeral Speech is exploiting these well-known features of Spartan *askēsis* ('training', 'regimen') and *apatē* in order to define Athenians as naturally courageous and unreliant on 'preparations and deceptions'. But there is more to Pericles' contrast than the construction of Spartan *apatē* as a symptom of anti-hoplitic values and a lack of natural courage which requires rigorous *paideia* as a substitute. There are other texts which suggest that Spartan *paideia* and its emphasis on trickery produce a dysfunctional citizenry. Fifth-century Athenian texts hint at these connections between Spartan duplicity and Spartan education. In the fourth century, we find the connections being more explicitly presented and theorised.[47]

A line in Euripides' *Supplices* (or *Suppliant Women*) offers us a tantalising clue as to how and why Spartan training in duplicity can be figured as the antithesis of Athenian civic and military ideals. More than most Attic tragedies, this play has been seen to resonate with contemporary political and religious significance. We have no secure date for *Supplices* but Angus Bowie has recently argued that it offers a complex 'filtering' of historical events.[48] In the play, the Argive Adrastus appeals to Athens for help when the Thebans refuse to relinquish the bodies of the Seven and the ensuing action can be read as a response to the Thebans' initial refusal to return Athenian bodies after the campaign at Delium in 424. Even if we do not accept that the play has a relationship with events at Delium, there is no doubt that Theseus' encomium of democracy in the play intersects with contemporary Athenian democratic ideology and public discourse.[49] Early on in the play Adrastus explains why he has come to Athens rather than Sparta to seek assistance: Σπάρτη μὲν ὠμὴ καὶ πεποίκιλται τρόπους ('Sparta is wild and intricate in its ways').[50] As a passing comment from a tragedy

---

[47] I will be returning to Xenophon's and Plato's confrontation with the educational role and representation of deceit in later chapters. See my discussion of Xenophon's *Cyropaedia* below at pp. 122–42 and Plato's *Laws* and *Republic* at pp. 151–62.

[48] Bowie (1997) 45–56. See also Collard (1975) 10. Regardless of whether or not they see this play as referring to specific historical events, most critics date this play to the 420s.

[49] For Theseus' praise of Athens and the critique of the Theban herald at Eur. *Supp.* 399–597, see Smith (1967); Shaw (1982); Collard (1972); Burian (1985b); Mills (1997) 97ff.

[50] Eur. *Supp.* 187. As the ensuing discussion will illustrate, my translation of this sentence is necessarily inadequate since it fails to capture the multiple connotations of 'ὠμὴ καὶ πεποίκιλται τρόπους'.

written and performed at some point during the Peloponnesian War, Adrastus' complaint offers some key ideas which inform Athenian denigrations of Spartan duplicity. The phrase πεποίκιλται τρόπους perhaps draws some force from the Homeric epithet πολύτροπος ('of many ways', 'of many turns') as applied to Odysseus and Hermes and fifth-century discussions of its meaning.[51] For the sophist Antisthenes, this epithet did not mean that Odysseus was often changing character and was therefore unscrupulous.[52] Rather, it denoted his *sophia* ('wisdom', 'cleverness') and his skill in adopting figures or manners of speech (*tropoi*) to particular listeners at particular times.[53] For Stanford this is a measure of the extent to which moral problems had come to dominate the evaluation and interpretation of the Homeric Odysseus in that period.[54] Antisthenes may actually be formulating an equation between *sophia* and polytropic skills because of his *admiration* for Spartan national character and behaviour.[55] In the case of Adrastus' complaint in *Supplices*, it seems that Spartans are being negatively

[51] Hom. *Od.* 1.1, 10.330; *Hymn to Hermes* 13, 149; Pl. *Hp. Mi.* 365c–d. On Hermes as an embodiment of *mētis* and *apatē*, see Kahn (1978) 77ff. and 131ff.; Osborne (1985b) 53–4. For Odysseus, see Pucci (1987); Murnaghan (1987); Pratt (1993) to name but a few.

[52] Antisthenes is commonly described as a 'sophist' but while we have evidence that he taught rhetoric, his fragments and doxography suggest that he became close to Socrates. For Antisthenes' 'Socratic' interests, see Rankin (1986). Socrates himself was described or represented as a sophist both before and after his death. See Ar. *Nub.* 627–888; Aeschin. 1.173.

[53] Antisthenes fr. 51 (Caizzi) = Porphyr. schol. ad Hom. *Od.* 1.1. The fragment also describes Pythagoras as 'πολύτροπος' because he adapted his style of speech according to whether he was talking to children, women, archons or ephebes. Odysseus and Pythagoras are two among many *sophoi* who 'if they are clever at dialogue, also understand how to express the same thought in accordance with many *tropoi*' (εἰ δὲ σοφοὶ δεινοί εἰσι διαλέγεσθαι, καὶ ἐπίστανται τὸ αὐτὸ νόημα κατὰ πολλοὺς τρόπους λέγειν). Caizzi (1966) 106–7 compares this fragment's description of Odysseus' ability to associate with anyone to Socrates' teasing characterisation of Antisthenes' 'networking' abilities at Xen. *Symp.* 4.64. See also the Antisthenic tone of Xen. *Mem.* 4.6, where Socrates describes Odysseus as a *rhētōr*. See also Rankin (1986) 66; Pucci (1987) 51f. and Goldhill (1991) 3. Rankin sees fr. 51 as influenced by Socratic and Prodican philology. Pucci applies Antisthenes' interpretation to the original polyvalent meaning of the Homeric epithet but Goldhill points out that this sense of the word is not attested before the fifth century.

[54] Stanford (1954) 99. Critics generally express the ambivalence of fifth-century representations of Odysseus by contrasting his portrayal as a 'negative' unheroic sophistic politician in Sophocles' *Philoctetes* with the more 'positive' portrayal as a humble and cunning mediator in Sophocles' *Ajax*. See Knox (1964) 124; Winnington-Ingram (1979) 57–72, 281–2; Segal (1981) chs. 9 and 10; Goldhill (1988a) 158–60; Rose (1992) 266–330. For my view on Odysseus in *Philoctetes* see pp. 188–201.

[55] See Antisthenes fr. 195 (Caizzi) = Theon *Progymn.* 33, where Antisthenes is reported to have described Sparta as the men's living space and Athens as the women's quarters. Rankin (1986) 114–16 argues that certain fragments display 'laconising' tendencies but is far from convincing.

constructed as changeable and slippery in terms of both character and rhetoric.

Adrastus' association between the quality of *poikilia* and notions of deceit, intricacy, fabrication and beguilement also goes back to Homer. *Poikilia* is commonly used to describe the variegated and shining surface of objects that have been elaborately wrought or woven. Often it is used in the context of female cunning and know-how. In the *Iliad* Aphrodite gives Hera a girdle with which to beguile Zeus erotically and distract him from her interference in the war (14.215f.). This garment is described as ποικίλον (*poikilon*) by the narrator, for all enchantments (θελκτήρια) are figured on it. Aphrodite herself stresses that the girdle is ποικίλον in a speech which seems to be outlining its enchanting qualities (220).[56] In the Hippocratic treatise *On the Sacred Disease* the verb ποικίλλω is used to imply the deceptive and fictional character of explanations offered by those who believe that the Sacred Disease is caused by the gods.[57] So the use of πεποίκιλται at *Supp.* 187 connotes ever-changing and intricate fabrication, fiction and deception.

But in Adrastus' one-line condemnation of the Spartans, the combination of wildness and slippery sophistication in itself seems rather strange. The adjective ὠμή (*ōmē*) connotes rawness, savagery and wild, bestial or uncivilised behaviour.[58] Adrastus' use of the word in conjunction with Spartan deceit perhaps draws its force from ideologically informed Athenian perceptions of the way in which the Spartan *agōgē* and *krupteia* moulded the identity of their pupils. Strong associations between trickery, cunning and those animals that acquire food by stalking and hunting prey are to be found in Greek thought. In animals such as foxes and wolves, there is precisely this combination of sophisticated covert method and savage execution.[59] Where Spartan boys

---

[56] See also Hom. *Od.* 15.105f. where the Spartan Helen has made 'most intricate robes' (πέπλοι παμποίκιλοι) and tries to give Telemachus a robe which is 'loveliest in intricate workings' (κάλλιστος ποικίλμασιν). At *Od.* 8.447 the witch Circe has taught Odysseus the 'intricate knot' (ποικίλον δέσμον) with which he seals a chest of gifts. Furthermore, the Homeric Odysseus is given the epithet *poikilomētēs* (*Il.* 11.482; *Od.* 3.163, 13.293). For a fuller, though by no means comprehensive, discussion of the concept of *poikilia*, see Detienne and Vernant (1978) 18ff. Collard (1975) 157 cites examples where this concept is used to express 'disapproval and moral inconsistency' in tragedy.

[57] Hipp. *Morb. Sacr.* 4.18. See below n. 146 for *poikilia* as a quality of Pindar's poetry.

[58] See Goldhill (1988a) 187: 'It is a word associated with the world of beasts or with attitudes at odds with the norms of human behaviour in society.' At Hom. *Il.* 22.347 the frenzied Achilles desires to eat Hector's 'raw' flesh. See also these connotations of the word at Soph. *Ant.* 471–2 and *Aj.* 548.

[59] See Detienne and Vernant (1978) 34ff. for Greek literature's treatment of *mētis* and deception in animals of prey.

were forced to steal from the *sussitia* without being seen or face a beating if they are caught, Vernant sees a comparison with 'wild animals' and 'beasts of prey': 'the whip does not punish their crime of thievery and its lowness; it denounces ... those who are not able to acquire, as is expected of them, the dangerous qualities of a predator'.[60] Of particular importance here are those elements of the *agōgē* where stealing was accompanied with physical punishment. Xenophon stresses that in the cheese-stealing ritual, the boys who are the most cunning and swift receive the fewest blows from the whip.[61] Vernant sums up the name of the game in this ritual test: 'the best policy is to adopt the roles of the sly Fox and the ferocious Wolf, two animals who have thievery in the blood'.[62]

In the *Politics*, Aristotle criticises these practices and regards them as indicative of flawed Spartan ethics.[63] The Spartans mistake one element of virtue, namely courage or 'manliness' (*andreia*), for virtue itself and by being so preoccupied with the instilling of courage into the young they 'render them like wild animals' (θηριώδεις: *thēriōdeis*) (8.1338b12). Aristotle goes on to argue that the Spartan system of training is not to be emulated because 'what is noble (*to kalon*) must take priority over what is beast-like (*to thēriōdes*). For it is neither a wolf nor any other wild animal that will venture to confront a noble danger; it is only the good man, the brave man' (*anēr agathos*) (8.1338b29–32).[64] The Spartan education fails to instil true 'nobility' and courage as required of the Greek male in battle precisely because it makes him like a beast which cannot display these ethical qualities. The institutions of Spartan training are associated with the behaviour of wild animals, despite (or because of) their emphasis on the deployment of cunning, concealment and deception.[65]

The male chorus of Aristophanes' *Lysistrata* make a similar charge: the men of Laconia 'can no more be trusted than can a ravening wolf'

---

[60] Vernant (1992) 236.
[61] Xen. *Lac. Pol.* 2.9.
[62] Vernant (1992) 236.
[63] Arist. *Pol.* 2.1271b2–6, 7.1333b11–21, 8.1338b11–19.
[64] ὥστε τὸ καλὸν ἀλλ' οὐ τὸ θηριῶδες δεῖ πρωταγωνιστεῖν· οὐδὲ γὰρ λύκος οὐδ' ⟨οὐδὲν⟩ τῶν ἄλλων θηρίων ἀγωνίσαιτο ἂν οὐθένα καλὸν κίνδυνον, ἀλλὰ μᾶλλον ἀνὴρ ἀγαθός. See Loraux (1986) for the honourable description of the Athenian war-dead as *agathoi* ('brave', 'good') in surviving funeral orations.
[65] See Vernant (1992) 242 on this passage: 'An excess of *andreia* runs the risk of resulting in *anaideia* and *hubris*, a shamelessness and unrestrained audacity. Without the tempering and softening effects of *sōphrosunē*, moderation, the kind of excellence to which the tests of trickery, violence and brutality in the *agōgē* are directed shows itself to be perverted and deformed, taking on the form of a bestial savagery, a terrifying monstrosity.'

(628–9).[66] Again, Spartan identity is being constructed in terms of duplicity and the savagery of a (cunning) animal, the wolf.[67] Of course, these statements from comedy are put into the mouths of blustering and bellicose caricatures of Athenian citizenry. As this and other choruses reproduce such stereotyping (and stereotypical) sentiments, it is perhaps the prejudicial character of the 'deceptive Spartan' paradigm that is foregrounded.[68]

Thus it is a perceived affinity between the institutional formation of a Spartan's identity and the behaviour of animals of prey which Adrastus' rhetoric exploits. He glosses the 'raw' or 'savage' liminal period of a young Spartan's training and its similarity to the existence of cunning animals of prey as constituting the character of Spartans of all ages. Spartan 'otherness' to Athens is not simply formulated in terms of a deceptive, slippery national character. It is a particular wild and animalistic form of deceptiveness which is being stressed as antithetical to the civilised conduct of Athens. I will have cause to return to this association between Spartan training and uncivilised cunning in the next chapter when discussing Xenophon's anxious treatment of military trickery in the *Cyropaedia*.

In addition to this conjunction of savagery and cunning, Adrastus' use of 'ὠμή' and 'πεποίκιλται' may have a force deriving from medical terminology which further consolidates Spartan identity as negative. A famous section of Thucydides (3.82.1) describes the progress of civil strife (*stasis*) as ὠμή. Hornblower shows that this phrase (οὕτως ὠμὴ ἡ στάσις προυχώρησε) has a medical flavour and other critics have interpreted Thucydides as using the terminology of the Hippocratic writings to describe *stasis* as a kind of illness affecting the 'body politic'.[69] The adjective ὠμός is frequently used in the Hippocratic corpus to describe bodily discharges which have a 'crude' quality. Such raw discharges are symptomatic of worsening fever and disease.[70] Dis-

---

[66] ... καὶ διαλλάττειν πρὸς ἡμᾶς ἀνδράσιν Λακωνικοῖς, οἷσι πιστὸν οὐδέν, εἰ μή περ λύκῳ κεχηνότι.

[67] See Hom. *Il.* 10.334f. where the unfortunate Trojan spy Dolon embarks on his covert night-time operation wearing a wolf pelt. Gernet (1981) links this episode to the possibility of archaic rites of passage involving the wearing of wolf costumes.

[68] See also Ar. *Ach.* 308, *Pax* 1066, 619f.

[69] See Hornblower (1991) 480 for discussion and bibliography.

[70] See Hipp. *Epid.* 1.11.3–7 in the text and translation of Jones (1923) on unfavourable forms of discharge: 'coctions signify nearness of crisis and sure recovery of health, but *crude* and unconcocted evacuations, which change into bad abcessions, denote absence of crisis, pain, prolonged illness, death, or a return of the same symptoms' (πεπασμοὶ ταχυτῆτα κρίσιος καὶ ἀσφάλειαν ὑγιείης σημαίνουσιν, ὠμὰ δὲ καὶ ἄπεπτα καὶ ἐς κακὰς ἀποστάσιας τρεπόμενα ἀκρισίας ἢ πόνους ἢ χρόνους ἢ θανάτους ἢ τῶν αὐτῶν ὑποστροφάς).

charges which are ποικίλος ('variegated') also indicate disease and in the treatise *Humours*, dangerous discharges from the womb are described as ὠμά and ποικίλα.[71] There may be a sense in which Adrastus' assertion of the crudeness and *poikilia* of the Spartans associates their roughness and propensity for the ever changing formations of trickery with a disordered and diseased condition. The possible play between these different usages of ὠμή and πεποίκιλται τρόπους emphasises that these wild and yet slippery Spartans are not functioning as humans should.

The Thucydidean Pericles' funeral speech, then, is informed by three interrelated components which constitute an Athenian rejection of military *apatē*. Firstly, deception is contrasted with notions of natural courage and inherited, inherent excellence. Secondly, deception is incompatible with an ideal image of hoplite endeavour. Thirdly, the speech's association of deceit with the Spartan enemy, whilst it can be explained in terms of the first two components, can also be related to a wider discourse of 'ethnic stereotyping'. This discourse specifically denigrates the Spartan national character as duplicitous by invoking certain aspects of Spartan education and culture which could be described as 'uncivilised' or 'wild'. Of course, the Spartans utilised hoplite warfare as much as any other Greek state. But the Athenian representation of them as duplicitous was integral to a civic discourse of self-definition.

I have argued that the concepts of deceit and dissimulation were important negative elements of Athens' developing democratic ideology. In the next section I will examine the invocation of similar considerations in Demosthenes' earliest legal oration, *Against Leptines*. In this speech dishonesty is constructed as 'unAthenian' and attributed to his Athenian opponent's proposals and performances. The speech will reappear throughout this study. For it contains some unique and extremely telling strategies of argument. These strategies invoke deceit's (im)morality and ideological significance in relation to three of its most problematic possible trajectories and uses: deceit of the demos, deceit of an enemy, and deceit as a socially or politically beneficial fiction. It might be objected that one should be suspicious of a speech which contains representations and evaluations of deceit which are unparalleled in the rest of Attic oratory. I would reply that in my third chapter it is precisely the exceptional nature of one of these representations

---

[71] From the concordance of Maloney and Frohn (1984) it is clear that ποικίλος is especially used of urine. For one example see Hipp. *Epid.* 1.10.20. On discharges from the womb see Hipp. *Hum.* 3.3–4.

which I find to be significant. Furthermore, it is one of the aims of this study to show that the Athenian public representation of deceit can only be understood if we accept that Athenian democratic discourse is constituted *both* by exceptional creative strategies *and* more frequent and central tenets which persistently inform those strategies. We have seen the Spartan stereotyped as deceitful and have found that stereotype to be a crucial element in Athenian definitions of self. We will eventually see the stereotype of the deceitful sophist as fundamental to Athenian democracy's negotiation of rhetoric's powers and perils. But these powerful and persistent representations of deceit have to be set alongside a host of unique representations and strategies.[72] These strategies are unique in the sense that they are not topoi but they are far from idiosyncratic. For some persistent and common areas of conflict, negotiation and problematisation emerge as underpinning these apparently unique interventions. *Against Leptines* will prove to be exemplary precisely because the concentration and substance of its arguments concerning deceit exhibit this interplay between creative strategic emphasis and an adherence to some underlying common coordinates of representation, negotiation and conflict.

Arguments from (national) character: Demosthenes' *Against Leptines*

In his speech *Against Leptines*, Demosthenes is arguing against a proposal to end the exemptions from taxes (*leitourgia*) which had always been granted to the descendants of officially recognised benefactors (*euergetai*). Early on in the oration, as part of a list of general arguments, Demosthenes claims that it would be 'contrary to the national character' to ratify Leptines' new proposal and he backs up this claim with an example from political history (20.11–12). He recalls how the Thirty Tyrants borrowed money from the Spartans for use against the democratic party in the Piraeus. When the Tyrants were defeated and democracy was restored, Sparta sent envoys to Athens to demand payment of the loan. The problem was discussed and some Athenians argued that only the 'city party' who had supported the Tyrants should

---

[72] The aim here could perhaps be summed up as an attempt to marry the approach of Ober (1989) with that of Cohen (1991) and (1995). Where Ober stresses the importance of 'commonplaces' in Athenian oratory for our understanding of the normative ideology of mass-elite relationships in the democracy, Cohen draws on the reflexive sociology of Bourdieu (1966) and (1977) to emphasise the orators' creative negotiation with, and manipulation of, Athenian 'norms'. See below, pp. 209–41.

be responsible for repayment. Others argued that the debt should be paid by the whole demos as a first sign of reconciliation. Demosthenes points out that the people of Athens decided to pay their contribution and bear their share of the expense so that there should be no breach of the agreement. He goes on to spell out the relevance of this story to his case against Leptines' law:

Will it not be strange, men of Athens, if to avoid cheating the terms of the agreement then, you consented to pay money to those who had wronged you (εἰ τότε μὲν τοῖς ἠδικηκόσιν ὑμᾶς ὑπὲρ τοῦ μὴ ψεύσασθαι τὰ χρήματ' εἰσφέρειν ἠθελήσατε), but now, when you might without any expense requite your benefactors by repealing this law, you prefer to cheat them (ψεύδεσθαι μᾶλλον αἱρήσεσθε)? I for one cannot approve of it. (Demosthenes 20.12)

Demosthenes' example is very carefully selected. This act of past collective honesty represents a 'limit case': it was the time when Athens could have cheated its *enemies* with some justification. But the collective impulse of the Athenian polis towards honesty meant that it couldn't even deceive those who had done it great harm.[73] Furthermore, the prudence and generosity of the democratic collective was manifested in its decision not to place the burden of repayment on the oligarchic party who colluded with the Spartans and were directly responsible for taking on the loan. Such generosity towards the internal enemies of the democratic state is portrayed as coextensive with the notion of an unequivocally honest collective character. Demosthenes' example prompts his jury to ask themselves how they, as 'honest Athenian citizens', could possibly vote to break the city's promise of generosity to its internal benefactors when it had been so honest and generous to external and internal enemies.[74] Here, Demosthenes' conception of deception and cheating involves a failure to reciprocate.

---

[73] Alongside Thuc. 2.39, Demosthenes' argument here contradicts the evidence cited by Dover (1974) 170, on the basis of which he implies that the Athenians always regarded the deception of an enemy as morally commendable.

[74] Demosthenes' representation of the issue rests on a highly tendentious interpretation of the existing law of exemption (*ateleia*) from *leitourgia*. He regards the law as analogous to a binding financial contract. Demosthenes' example of Athens' honest identity deals with the question of whether to honour a loan repayment whereas his opponent's proposed amendment questioned the validity of exempting the *descendants* of benefactors when they themselves may have done little to help the state. The issue of individual responsibility for state finance was particularly pressing at the time of Leptines' proposal because Athens had experienced an increase in its military commitments and a resultant drain on its public finances. Athens had been involved in the so-called 'Social War' of 357–355. For the draining financial effects of this on the Athenian treasury, see Isoc. 7.9. and Sandys (1979) i–ii.

The idea that an intentional *pseudos* or *apatē* can connote 'negative' or 'failed' reciprocity can be found in pre-classical texts, especially erotic poetry, and must be regarded as a fundamental connotation for 'deception' in ancient Greek culture.[75]

Leptines would perhaps have argued that a vote for his new law could not represent a betrayal or a broken pledge because the existing law had been badly framed; why should Athens reward the descendants of benefactors (*euergetai*) with exemptions when it was strictly only the *euergetai* themselves who were owed a favour? And when the state needed more money than ever, wasn't it incumbent upon everybody who possessed wealth to contribute, regardless of an exemption law that was passed in different and less trying circumstances? Demosthenes' mischievous analogy between the existing law and a binding contract attempts to mask these arguments and destroy their relevance.[76] To reinforce his point that Athenians don't break pledges, Demosthenes goes on to speak proudly of the Athenian polis and its 'undeceptive' character:

The instance I have quoted, men of Athens, as well as many others will demonstrate our city's character (τῆς πόλεως ἦθος) to be undeceitful and good (ἀψευδὲς καὶ χρηστόν), and where money is concerned, not asking what pays best, but what is the honourable thing to do (ἀλλὰ τί καὶ καλὸν πρᾶξαι). But as to the character of the proposer of this law, I have no further knowledge of him,

---

[75] See Thgn. 237–54 where Theognis rewards Cyrnus' *apatē* with (initially concealed) 'negative' *kleos* (fame in song). These couplets can be read as a poetic form of reciprocal *apatē* where the addressee (Cyrnus) is tricked by the initial promise of memorialisation.

[76] The seemingly perfect relevance of this historical example to the case in question may also conceal a level of historiographical dishonesty on Demosthenes' part. Demosthenes recounts that the Athenians voted to pay back the Spartan loan collectively because of their natural sense of honesty and their desire to promote political unity following the dismantling of the oligarchic government. The only other source for the motivations behind the assembly's decision is Isoc. 7.66–8. This speech can be dated to 355/354 – the year in which *Against Leptines* was delivered. Isocrates praises the decision of the Athenians to share the burden of the loan repayment collectively. He says that the decision was motivated by the people's desire for reconciliation and unity. Both Isocrates and Demosthenes suppress another possible motivation for paying back the Spartan loan. It seems likely that the decision to pay back the loan was motivated by fear of what Sparta might do if Athens refused. See Weil (1883) 21 and Sandys (1979) 15. The suppression of fear as a motivation in Demosthenes' account is also suggested by the ancient scholia to this speech. See scholia 30 and 32 in Dilts (1986). Isocrates' version also differs from Demosthenes' account by referring to the borrowers as 'those who remained in the city' (68) rather than as the Thirty. Perlman (1961) 155 suggests that Demosthenes refers to the Thirty in order to associate Leptines with oligarchic and pro-Spartan opinion. See below p. 49. Other sources for the loan and its repayment: Lys. 30.22, 12.59; Xen. *Hell* 2.4.28.; [Arist.] *Ath. Pol.* 40; Plut. *Lys.* 21.

nor do I say or know anything to his prejudice; but if I may judge from his law, I detect a character very far removed from what I have described (πολὺ τούτου κεχωρισμένον). I say, then, that it would be more honourable for Leptines to be guided by you in repealing the law than for you to be guided by him in ratifying it, and it would be more profitable for you, as well as for him, that the city should persuade Leptines to assume a likeness to herself (ὅμοιον αὐτῇ) than that she should be persuaded by Leptines to be like him (ὁμοίαν τούτῳ); for even if he really is a good man (χρηστός) – and he may be for all I know – he is not better than the city in character (οὐδὲ βελτίων ἐστὶ τῆς πόλεως τὸ ἦθος). (Demosthenes 20.13–14)

Demosthenes now uses this apparently undisputed picture of honest civic identity and past historical instantiations of it as foils to the character and actions of Leptines. The 'character' (ἦθος: *ēthos*) of Leptines is in direct opposition to that of the Athenian polis. This passage uses the first extant application of the term ἦθος to the polis as a whole. However, Plato's *Republic* does indirectly apply the term to the polis: Socrates states that 'we do contain the same kinds of features (*eidē*) and characters (*ēthē*) as the polis' (4.435e–6a). Thus Socrates sees the *ēthos* of individuals as determined by the *ēthos* of their polis. Socrates later uses the term ἦθος in a similar fashion when describing the *politeia* of a timarchy and this usage is also clearly similar to that of Demosthenes. Socrates has just described the behaviour and personality of the 'timocratic' man (Pl. *Resp.* 8.548e4–549a6). His interlocutor, Adeimantus, confirms this description by pointing out that Socrates' portrait of the timocratic individual corresponds to the ἦθος of the timocratic *politeia* (8.549a7: Ἔστι γάρ, ἔφη, τοῦτο τὸ ἦθος ἐκείνης τῆς πολιτείας). Where Plato specifically wants to make a direct equivalence between the 'character' of a system of government or a polis and that of an individual, he elides the difference between the two by attributing the word ἦθος to a *politeia* or polis when it is usually only applied to individual people by Greek authors of the classical period.[77] By applying this word to the polis, Demosthenes similarly anthropomorphises Athens. At the same time, he subordinates its identity as a collective of individuals to that of a single homogenous being. Athens is thereby given the status of an honest and upright individual.

To contrast the character of Leptines with that of the personified state effectively disembodies him from that state (τούτου κεχωρισμένον). There is the polis and then there is the dishonest figure of Leptines. Demosthenes has identified his opponent's proposal as dishonest and has then cast the perpetrator of dishonesty beyond the

---

[77] One suspects, however, that Plato's attribution of *ēthos* to cities and constitutions may have had sophistic and/or Hippocratic precedents or parallels.

boundaries of his city. Leptines becomes a citizen in name only; his willingness to deceive betrays a character which is antithetical to that of the polis and disrupts its homogeneity. He is not 'like' the polis and so cannot be associated with it.

The terms in which Demosthenes formulates a notion of 'the honest ideal citizen' are partly recognisable as inherited elements of an essentially aristocratic vocabulary which underwent change and development from its first instantiations in Homer through to the elegiac and lyric verse which we associate with the emergence of the Greek polis and the elite social class which dominated it in the seventh and sixth centuries.[78] To describe one's polis as 'good' (χρηστός: chrēstos) is to appropriate a densely significant adjective from its originally aristocratic context of usage where it could denote the civic 'usefulness' to wealthy, noble-born, upright and handsome individuals or a small group of them.[79] Demosthenes reapplies the term to the collective entity of his democratically organised society. The civic body as a whole is defined as χρηστός. The orators did not always give this adjective such a wide democratic redefinition. In the speech Nicocles, Isocrates praises monarchy because it allows the individual who is χρηστός to avoid having to mix with the masses (plēthos) as was the tendency in democratic regimes (Isoc. 3.16). But as Ober points out, this self-confessedly elitist oration was not intended for mass consumption.[80] It is clear from the speeches of orators who participated in and upheld the values of the democracy that to be χρηστός was to be a good democratic citizen of Athenian birth.[81] If Demosthenes' description of his city as χρηστός implies any elitism at all, it surely lies in the patriotic subtext of the passage: 'our national character is superior to that of other states because we valorise truthfulness and honesty above profit'. For Demosthenes, Athens' collective character is as honest, or more precisely, 'undeceitful' (ἀψευδές: apseudes:) as it is 'good' (χρηστός) and has its eye on what is honourable (καλόν) rather than what is most

---

[78] For detailed analyses of the ways in which Homeric and archaic poetry articulate and negotiate key ideological concepts in the vocabulary of feudal and aristocratic Greek elites see Lynn-George (1988), Goldhill (1991) 69–108; Rose (1992) on Homer; Nagy (1990), Nisetich (1989), Kurke (1991) on Pindar; the essays in Figueira and Nagy (1985) on Theognis; Tarkow (1983) on Tyrtaeus.

[79] See Donlan (1980) 303, n. 23: 'One of the most interesting of the aristocratic words is chrēstos (useful, worthy), an old word, used during the archaic period with political force but in the context of civic usefulness, opposed, often to aristocratic luxury. But in the fifth century it was appropriated by oligarchs who proclaimed themselves the useful members of the polis.'

[80] Ober (1989) 16.

[81] Ober (1989) 13, 14, 251, 260. See also Dover (1974) 296–7.

profitable in terms of money. As I have already suggested, there is a need to include the notion of being 'undeceitful' within the wider rubric of terms and ideas which connote ideal civic identity in Athens' public discourses. To be *chrēstos* or to be an *anēr agathos* is to shun deceit (*apatē* or *pseudē*). Demosthenes uses this rhetoric of honest collective identity to shape the outlook of his jury. The jury are actually warned that a vote for Leptines will constitute a hypocritical deception of the demos and benefactors of an earlier era. Demosthenes characterises such a vote as a contravention of the very law (against deceiving the people) which the jury would use to punish other men with death (20.134–5).[82] To vote against Demosthenes would constitute a failure to conform to a historically precedented ideal of honest national character. Leptines is cast in the role of a very 'unAthenian' Athenian precisely because his proposal invites the jury to renege on the commitments made by previous generations of citizens towards their benefactors.

This inclusion of a marked undeceitfulness as an important component of Athens' ideal self-image is also demonstrated later in the speech. Having enumerated the exploits of alien benefactors who had received exemptions, Demosthenes argues that the best men and most numerous benefactors of Athens are her own citizens and that it would be an outrage if they were to have their exemptions repealed (20.67). To prove this point he begins with the case of the general Conon and recounts his achievements; how, with no prompting from the people, he had defeated the Spartans at sea, expelled the Spartan governors from islands in the Aegean and had returned to Athens to restore the Long Walls (68–70). Through these exploits and successes, argues Demosthenes, Conon made the hegemony of Greece once more a subject of dispute between Athens and Sparta. Conon's contribution to Athens' regained power and renown made him worthy of the exemptions which he was awarded as a sign of gratitude. The people also set up his statue in bronze. Demosthenes highlights the praiseworthiness of Conon as a benefactor and the disgrace that would attach to any cancellation of Conon's hereditary *ateleia* through a comparison of what he considers to be Conon's noblest deed, namely the restoration of the Long Walls, with Themistocles' restoration of Athens' defensive walls after the Persian Wars. For Demosthenes, Themistocles was 'the most famous man of his age' and a comparison of the way in which he and Conon accomplished a similar feat will reveal the exceptional qualities of the latter (71–3).

---

[82] On the law and this passage see below, pp. 55–63.

Demosthenes then recounts how Themistocles ordered the Athenians to begin building the city walls and detain any Spartan envoys who might arrive to prevent Athens from becoming too strong in terms of defences. Themistocles himself went on an embassy to Sparta and when reports came that the Athenians were building fortifications, he kept denying the possibility of such reports and told the Spartans to send envoys to Athens. When these did not return he urged the Spartans to send more envoys. With these tactics of deceit and delay, Themistocles ensured that the city walls were rebuilt, despite the Spartans' wishes to the contrary. Demosthenes goes on to draw the lesson from his comparison between Conon and Themistocles:

I expect you have all heard the story of how he [Themistocles] deceived (ἐξαπατῆσαι) them. Now I assert (and I earnestly appeal to you, Athenians not to take offence at what is coming, but to consider whether it is true) that in proportion as openness is better than secrecy, and it is more honourable to gain one's end by victory than by trickery (τὸ φανερῶς τοῦ λάθρᾳ κρεῖττον, καὶ τὸ νικῶντας τοῦ παρακρουσαμένους πράττειν ὁτιοῦν ἐντιμότερον), so Conon deserves more credit than Themistocles for building the walls. For the latter did it by evading those who would have prevented it, the former by being victorious against them (ὁ μὲν γὰρ λαθών, ὁ δὲ νικήσας τοὺς κωλύσοντας αὔτ' ἐποίησεν). Therefore, it is not right that so great a man should be wronged by you, or should gain less than those orators who will try to prove that you ought to deduct something from what was bestowed on him. (Demosthenes 20.73–4)

Themistocles was generally deemed worthy of recognition as a patriotic leader of achievement who operated in the interests of the people he represented. For the orators, he is often invoked as a paradigm of Athenian intelligence, virtue and genuinely democratic leadership. Lysias' *Funeral Oration* emphasises Themistocles' singular abilities at Salamis and Isocrates' *Panathenaicus* styles his leadership as responsible for that victory in contrast to the potentially disastrous strategy of the Spartan general Eurybiades.[83] In the speech *Against Ctesiphon*, Aeschines cites Themistocles as an example of the old style leader who rendered great service to the city and demanded nothing in return.[84] Aeschines makes the point that Themistocles is unlike contemporary politicians such as Demosthenes who expect and demand crowns for non-existent services to the city. In fact, when Themistocles is invoked by the orators, it is generally as a component of the rhetorical topos whereby a present political situation is contrasted with a much more

---

[83] Lys. 2.42; Isoc. 12.51–2.
[84] Aeschin. 3.181. See also 3.259.

glorious and honourable past where Athens' leadership was free of corruption and self-interest.[85]

Such is Themistocles' reputation that Demosthenes has to appeal (or at least make an issue of appealing) to the jury not to take offence at his derogatory remarks about the great leader. He stresses that Themistocles' *methods* of achievement involved the tactics of deceit and dissimulation whereas Conon achieved the same particular result without having to resort to trickery. Thus Conon's achievement, though similar to that of Themistocles in terms of end result, is nevertheless more honourable (ἐντιμότερον) because openness is better than secrecy (τὸ φανερῶς τοῦ λάθρᾳ κρεῖττον). This contrast and its ideological significance are brought out by Demosthenes' postulation of a contrast between victory and dissimulation. It is more honourable to gain one's end by victory than by trickery (καὶ τὸ νικῶντας τοῦ παρακρουσαμένους πράττειν ὁτιοῦν ἐντιμότερον) and whereas Themistocles evaded or slipped past his opponents, Conon conquered them (ὁ μὲν γὰρ λαθών, ὁ δὲ νικήσας τοὺς κωλύσοντας αὔτ' ἐποίησεν). Demosthenes sees victory as a means rather than an end in itself; one can do something by conquering one's opponents or one can achieve the same end through evasion and deceit. Hence 'victory' is equated with success in battle and to succeed through deceit is no victory at all.

The fact that Demosthenes feels able to make these criticisms of Themistocles without damaging his case is perhaps testament to the strength of cultural enmity that Athenians could be made to feel towards notions of trickery and deceit, an enmity that is represented by the orator's invocation of an opposition between victory and deceit. On the other hand, Themistocles' usual status as a leader of great achievement and intelligence might suggest that Demosthenes is drawing attention to a contradiction which the Athenians had previously chosen to gloss over. For in the historians, Themistocles is

---

[85] E.g. Lys. 12.63, 30.28; Dem. 23.196–8, 18.204–5; Din. 1.37; Isoc. 15.233. See however Dem. 23.204 where the speaker points out that Themistocles was finally called to account for bribery as part of his argument that nobody should escape the law, however much they have benefited Athens in the past. See also Isoc. 4.154 where the Persians are derided for giving 'the greatest gifts' to Themistocles who 'in the service of Greece defeated them at Salamis'. Aeschin. 2.9 also seems to hint at this point when he names Themistocles in conjunction with Alcibiades. Lys. 12.63 compares Theramenes' destruction of the city walls, the Piraeus defences and the Long Walls under the Thirty with Themistocles' construction of the city walls 'against the wishes of the Spartans'. He says Theramenes destroyed the walls by deceiving (ἐξαπατήσας) the Athenian citizens. Demosthenes works against this contrast. In his new contrast, it is Themistocles who does the deceiving. See Nouhaud (1982) 219. See also Missiou (1992) 78–82, on Andocides' subversive refusal to name Themistocles.

undoubtedly an ambivalent figure.[86] If we wanted to, we could believe Plutarch's claim that Themistocles was nicknamed 'Odysseus' because of his prudence (*phronēsis*).[87] Detienne and Vernant argue that the accounts and appraisals of Herodotus and Thucydides represent him as a figure who displays many of the qualities which constitute *mētis* as a specific Greek category of thought.[88] He leads Athens to safety through his improvisatory intelligence, opportunism, foresight and a willingness to use deception. But he flees Greece in disgrace, having been ostracised and under a new suspicion of taking bribes from the Persians (Thuc. 1.135). The Attic orators generally suppress this ambivalence and choose to omit the methods that lay behind Themistocles' achievements in order to glorify his benefactions during an ideal Athenian golden age.[89]

Demosthenes reverses the 'golden age' topos by valorising Conon over and above Themistocles and by stressing the latter's use of deception. Where Thucydides ends his account of Themistocles by praising him as an exceptional figure of sagacity and quick-wittedness, Demosthenes chooses to stress the one component of his *mētis* which the historian's final appraisal omits, namely *apatē*.[90] He effectively re-evaluates Themistocles as a popular historical figure and the culturally charged notions of secrecy and deceit are clearly the main constituent elements of that re-evaluation. Of all the ways in which Demosthenes could have chosen to emphasise Conon's honourable status, he opts for a comparison which places him in favourable opposition to a figure of trickery.

Once again, *apatē* is used in an argument towards a definition of

---

[86] See Missiou (1992) 178–82 for references and discussion.

[87] Plut. *De Herodoti Malignitate* 869f.

[88] Detienne and Vernant (1978) 313–14. See Hdt. 8.57–64 where the 'wise adviser' Mnesiphilus is an inspiration for Themistocles' cunning before Salamis and Themistocles himself shows independent skill in manipulating the other Greek leaders. Themistocles' classic ruse comes at Hdt. 8.75.1 where he sends a messenger with a false message to Xerxes which ensures the unity of the Greek fleet and the defeat of the Persian fleet. This ruse is described as a 'Greek's trick' (δόλον Ἕλληνος ἀνδρός) at Aesch. *Pers.* 361–2 though Themistocles is never named in the play and we cannot be certain that an audience in 472 would have associated the trick with Themistocles. On the problem and significance of the absence of direct references in *Persians* to prominent Athenians and the play's possible associations with Themistocles, see Hall (1996) 11–13; Goldhill (1988b) 192–3; Pelling (1997a) 9–13; Sommerstein (1996) 410–13; Harrison (2000). See Thuc. 1.138.3 for praise of Themistocles' improvisatory intelligence.

[89] See Nouhaud (1982) 166–9, 170–7, 218–19 for the orators' glorification of Themistocles. For the few references for Themistocles' receipt of Persian bribes, see above n. 85.

[90] Thuc. 1.138.3. This is not to say that Thucydides does not represent Themistocles lying or using trickery. My point is rather that Thucydides' summing up of Themistocles' qualities discreetly puts his skills in deception out of the picture.

laudable civic behaviour. In the rhetorical construction of the ideal citizen, the deployment of deceit and trickery is rendered problematic for all Athenians, regardless of their status, and even in the face of an enemy. However, the fact that Demosthenes' treatment of Themistocles' building of the walls is apologised for and is unparalleled in oratory, and the fact that Thucydides does not condemn this act of trickery must alert us to the presence of some level of instability in Athenian representations of deception – even at the level of civic ideality. In my next chapter, I will return to Demosthenes' comparison between Themistocles and Conon in order to demonstrate that the ideological position and moral status of military trickery in Athenian public discourse cannot be adequately described in terms of a simple opposition between fair, open confrontation as right and proper and deceptive tactics as transgressive and unAthenian. After all, Demosthenes may argue that Conon's open victory is *better* and *more honourable* than Themistocles' trickery, but he does not condemn Themistocles' trickery as completely *out of order*. Demosthenes places military *apatē* at the lower end of a hierarchy, rather than in a strict opposition which excludes it as a legitimate term.

We have seen how Demosthenes attacks the character of Leptines and the nature of his proposal in terms of an incompatibility between dishonest behaviour and normative civic identity. Ostensibly, the question at issue in the speech *Against Leptines* is not whether Leptines is lying to the people. Rather, Demosthenes and Leptines disagree over a matter of collective policy; should public benefactors be rewarded as they have been in the past? Demosthenes turns this disagreement over policy into a question of which course of action is civically and ideologically appropriate to democratic Athens. He does emphasise the fact that the system of rewards currently in place is in itself an expression of the appropriate exchange of responsibilities between individual and collective within the democratic polis. But by making Leptines' proposal into the breaking of a pledge, Demosthenes also draws on the notion that a dishonest disposition normally has no place in the Athenian character, be it individual or collective. At one point, Demosthenes associates Leptines' desire to end certain rewards for public benefaction with the customs and constitutions of Thebes and Sparta, thereby implicitly accusing his opponent of being out of sympathy with Athens' democratic political culture (20.105ff.). Perhaps there is another link between Spartan identity, anti-democratic views and *apatē* being exploited here. Leptines is thus represented as an Athenian whose character and aspirations are threateningly out of tune with those of a 'true' Athenian democrat.

Leptines was effectively proposing a measure which would have made liturgy and *eisphora* payments more equitable by making a larger number of wealthy citizens liable to such taxation. Leptines' attempt to do away with exemptions amounted to an egalitarian reform of the Athenian tax system. Demosthenes admits that taxation of the rich is desirable but argues that Leptines' proposed methods will have bad side effects. In an important respect then, Leptines was proposing a measure which fell in line with an egalitarian strand of Athens' democratic discourse. His proposal was not obviously selfish, manipulative, undemocratic or inimical to Athens' collective ideology.

In response, Demosthenes avoids many of the topoi of invective which we find in other fourth-century speeches with a political background. There are no accusations of non-citizen birth or inappropriate sexual conduct.[91] Demosthenes makes no accusations of bribe-taking, corruption or outright treason. The issue under dispute hardly fits an accusation of sycophancy but Leptines' ability and willingness to move a major political measure would presumably have made him vulnerable to accusations of over-clever speaking and sophistry.[92] The omission of these strategies is striking and it may be that Leptines' public profile and the egalitarian nature of his proposal made such attacks inappropriate or counter-productive. Demosthenes chooses a different line of argument. He undermines Leptines by appealing to the central importance of the exchange between individual benefaction and collective reward to the past and continued survival of democratic Athens. Leptines' antipathy for the existing system is certainly represented as a failure to understand what makes Athens great, but the arguments concerning honesty and deceit are a crucial component in this representation of national identity.

If Demosthenes characterises Athens as 'undeceitful' does Athenian democratic public discourse ever entertain or value the notion of the 'noble lie'? Or is the idea of performing lies for the benefit of the Athenian polis and demos rejected as 'undemocratic' along the same lines as the Thucydidean Pericles' description of Athens as an 'open

---

[91] Accusations of non-citizen birth: Aeschin. 2.78, 3.171–2; Din. 1.5; Dem. 18.130–1, 21.149. Slavish behaviour or being a slave: Dem. 19.210, 24.124; Hyp. 2.10. See Ober (1989) 266–77. On the Athenian prohibition of speakers who were or had been prostitutes and the topoi of slander that ensue, see Aeschin. 1 and Dover (1978) 19–39; Winkler (1990b); Halperin (1989).

[92] On the common accusation of sycophancy see Ober (1989) index s.v. 'sycophancy'; Osborne (1990); Harvey (1990). On accusations of sophistry and clever speaking see below pp. 209–15. See also Dover (1974) 25–8; Ostwald (1986) 256–7; Ober (1989) 156–91.

society' or Karl Popper's indictment of Socrates' 'noble lie' (*gennaion pseudos*) in the 'closed society' of Plato's *Republic*?[93] These are questions to which I will return in a later chapter and the speech *Against Leptines* will feature surprisingly in my account. For the present, I want to explore the relationship between the ideals of Athenian honesty which Pericles and Demosthenes project and Athenian law. Was the citizen ever indicted for the specific crime of deceiving the people and how was that crime represented?

Symbolic sanctions: the law and the curse against deceiving the demos

Herodotus' *Histories* provide possible evidence for the existence of some form of legislation which specifically prohibited 'deception' of the Athenian demos by an individual in the early fifth century. In the sixth book we are told that Miltiades was appointed a member of the board of generals (*stratēgoi*) in 490/489 (6.104). After the Battle of Marathon, he requested that the Athenians give him command of a military expedition but did not tell them which country he would lead it against. He did say that he would make the Athenians rich if they followed him and that he would 'bring them to a country from which they should easily carry away an abundance of gold' (6.132). However, the expedition failed and Herodotus records that Miltiades returned to Athens with a wound to the knee. Immediately after he returned, a certain Xanthippus brought some form of charge against him for 'deceit of the Athenians' (Μιλτιάδεα ἐδίωκε τῆς Ἀθηναίων ἀπάτης εἵνεκεν) and called for him to be put to death (6.136.1).

Hansen classifies this case as an *eisangelia* ('impeachment') before the *ecclēsia*.[94] Rhodes argues against such certain classification, pointing out that the assembly may have heard cases brought via a variety of procedures and that such procedures may have been far from systematised at this early stage in Athenian legal history.[95] Rhodes conjectures that Miltiades' case may have been referred to the people on an appeal from the Archons and that the assembly judged the case in its role as a mass judicial court (*heliaea*). However, there seems to be little to be gained from guessing precisely what procedure is alluded to in Herodotus' account. We have very little evidence concerning legal

---

[93] See Pl. *Resp.* 3.414b8–415d5 and Popper (1966) 138f.
[94] Hansen (1975) 69.
[95] Rhodes (1979) 104–5. See Hansen (1980) for arguments in reply.

procedure in the early fifth century and it is hard to determine the date of inception for the procedures and institutions referred to in later sources.

Whilst they may disagree over the type of procedure used, all the commentators assume that Herodotus must be referring to a specific charge of 'deception of the people'.[96] This need not be the case. When Herodotus tells us that Xanthippus indicted Miltiades 'because of the deceit he practised on the Athenians' he may only be describing his own perception of the prosecutor's reasons for charging Miltiades. The causal statement may not tell us anything about the specific law which was cited against Miltiades. On the other hand, Miltiades' transgression did involve an unfulfilled promise to the demos. We have five certain references to laws specifically forbidding deception of the demos in fourth-century sources and I will discuss these in more detail below.[97] Four of these references share the conditional phrase ἐάν τις ὑποσχόμενός τι τὸν δῆμον ('if someone, making a promise to the people ...').[98] It seems that in the fourth century at least, the specific charge of 'deceiving the people' was associated with making false or unfulfilled promises. If one of these laws was in existence at the time of Miltiades' trial, then his crime would fit perfectly with prosecution under the auspices of such a law; he promised that he would make the Athenians rich if they allowed his expedition and he singularly failed to make that promise good. If the law(s) against false promises were introduced later in the fifth century, Herodotus may have connected Miltiades' trial with a law against 'deceit of the people (ἀπάτη τοῦ δήμου) precisely because his crime fitted so well with the terms of this later piece of legislation.

Our only other example of a case apparently brought for 'deception of the people' is in Xenophon's account of the notorious trial of the Arginousae generals and its aftermath in 406.[99] Xenophon recounts how six of the generals had been condemned and executed at the bidding of Callixenus. Euryptolemus and Socrates had challenged the legality of Callixenus' proposals but the people said that they should be allowed to do what they wanted – and they wanted the generals to be punished. Not long after the executions, Xenophon describes how the people

---

[96] Harrison (1971) 54 and 60; Hansen (1975) 69; MacDowell (1978) 179; Rhodes (1979) 105.
[97] References to laws against deception of the demos: Dem. 20.100, 135, 49.67; Xen. *Hell.* 1.7.35; [Arist.] *Ath. Pol.* 43.5.
[98] Dem. 20.100, 135, 49.67; [Arist.] *Ath. Pol.* 43.5.
[99] For discussion of the legality of the trial, see MacDowell (1978) 186–9.

repented and called for the prosecution of those politicians who had deceived them:

And not long afterwards, the Athenians repented, and they voted that complaints (*probolai*) be brought against anyone who had deceived the people (οἵτινες τὸν δῆμον ἐξηπάτησαν, προβολὰς αὐτῶν εἶναι), that they provide bondsmen until such time as they should be brought to trial, and that Callixenus be included among them. Complaints were brought against four others also, and they were put into confinement by their bondsmen. But when there broke out a factional disturbance (*stasis*), in the course of which Cleophon was put to death, these men escaped, before being brought to trial. (Xenophon *Hellenica* 1.7.35)

This passage seems to tell us that in 406 it was possible to make 'preliminary complaints' (προβολαί) to the *ecclēsia* against individuals for 'deceiving the demos'. This may be corroborated by a passage of the Aristotelian *Constitution of Athens* which states that in the chief assembly meeting of the Sixth Prytany the people take a vote on whether or not to hold an ostracism, and on προβολαί brought against sycophants and against anyone 'who has failed to perform a promise made to the people' (κἄν τις ὑποσχόμενός τι μὴ ποιήσῃ τῷ δήμῳ).[100] The *ecclēsia* voted for or against the individual accused in the προβολή but the vote was merely 'an expression of public opinion without binding force'.[101] If the *ecclēsia* endorsed a complaint, its author might take his charge to the lawcourts at a later date.[102] The Aristotelian passage states that the number of complaints brought against alleged sycophants was restricted to a maximum of six, divided equally between citizens and metics.[103] On the basis of this statement, Matthew Christ has recently argued that the joining together of the three measures and their re-

---

[100] [Arist.] *Ath. Pol.* 43.5: 'in the sixth prytany, in addition to the business specified, they take a vote on the desirability of holding an ostracism and on *probolai* against sycophants, Athenians and metics, up to the number of not more than three cases of either class and charges against anyone who has failed to perform a promise made to the demos' (ἐπὶ δὲ τῆς ἕκτης πρυτανείας πρὸς τοῖς εἰρημένοις καὶ περὶ τῆς ὀστρακοφορίας ἐπιχειροτονίαν διδόασιν εἰ δοκεῖ ποιεῖν ἢ μή, καὶ συκοφαντῶν προβολὰς τῶν Ἀθηναίων καὶ τῶν μετοίκων μέχρι τριῶν ἑκατέρων, κἄν τις ὑποσχόμενός τι μὴ ποιήσῃ τῷ δήμῳ).

[101] Christ (1992) 339.

[102] For the nature of προβολαί see Lipsius (1905) vol. I, 211–19; Bonner and Smith (1938) vol. II, 63–71; Harrison (1971) vol. II, 59–64; MacDowell (1978) 194–7 and (1990) 13–17. On complaints brought for offences at public festivals see Christ (1992).

[103] Osborne (1990) 94–5 argues that, because the *Ath. Pol.* is not written in the 'best literary Greek', the 'συκοφαντῶν', 'Ἀθηναίων', and 'μετοίκων' of section 43.5 'do not all refer to the same persons and hence the limitation might be that three Athenians and three metics could bring charges against three sykophants in this way annually'.

striction to the Sixth Prytany as described in the *Constitution of Athens* can be dated to some time after 404/403 BC.[104] He sees these measures being linked together as a direct response to the rule of the Thirty (404/403) who used the term 'sycophant' as an excuse to purge Athens of their citizen and metic enemies:

> In the aftermath of an oligarchic coup that had rallied support by condemning democratic excess, the demos asserted its control over extreme oligarchs and extreme democrats through a modification of the Assembly's agenda. Once each year, the demos reminded its elite citizens of its power to expel them through ostracism, while at the same time reminding democrats who frequented the courts and addressed the Assembly that their privileges were not to be abused. These counterbalancing measures accord with the spirit of moderation in which the restored democracy set forth to ensure that civil strife would never again divide the city.[105]

By arguing that the Aristotelian passage reflects a real procedure with significant symbolic force, Christ contradicts earlier scholars who have questioned the likelihood of the notion that accusations against sycophants and deceivers of the demos could only be admitted once a year.[106] Xenophon's description of the complaints laid against those who had secured the execution of the Arginousae generals might go some way towards supporting his thesis, for it describes how the demos effectively scapegoated a group of individuals for its own illegal proposal to judge and condemn the generals *en masse*. The Athenians repented and transferred guilt and blame for the executions onto a small number of active politicians. They achieved this through a legal procedure which allowed them to express the collective opinion that they had been hoodwinked into condemning the generals. The one certain surviving example of charges brought for 'deceit of the demos' (ἀπάτη τοῦ δήμου) indicates the way in which an accusation of deceit could be used to maintain an image of the infallibility and sovereignty of the demos and to exonerate it from any responsibility for unwise or unjust decisions. It is likely that the complaints were initiated by elite politicians who themselves had recognised an opportunity to capitalise on a general mood of repentance in order to get rid of some political competitors. Clearly, as Christ suggests, the law against 'deceit of the demos' was itself open to abusive, dishonest application. The restriction of its possible use offered practical safeguards against such abuses and symbolised the need to police the power of those who would seek

---

[104] Christ (1992) 341ff.
[105] Christ (1992) 346.
[106] E.g. Bonner and Smith (1930) vol. II, 67; Rhodes (1981) 526–7.

to hold politicians and officials to account as well as the power of the politicians themselves.

There seems to be an ambivalence about the law against deceivers of the demos, as with the legislation and rhetoric controlling sycophancy: it is both a perceived check on politicians and a weapon used in elite political competition, a weapon which is itself in danger of being abused. As a potential sanction against individuals who might wish to mislead the people for their own ends, the law symbolised the ideal of the sovereign power of the demos. Its underlying logic of application is analogous to the orators' frequent refusal to question the superior wisdom of the demos: the people do not make mistakes, they are deceived by conniving politicians (*rhētores*).[107] However, while it was still *possible* to be indicted for deceiving the people, the restriction of complaints to the Sixth Prytany also set practical constraints on litigation under the law and signalled the need for such constraints if the integrity of the law's use was to be maintained.

The Demosthenic corpus contains three references to an Athenian law forbidding deceptive promises to the demos:

Of course, you have a law making death the penalty if someone making a promise deceives the demos, Boule or lawcourt. (Demosthenes 20.100)[108]

You have an ancient law, one held in great respect, that if someone making a promise deceives the demos, he shall be brought to trial, and if convicted shall be punished with death. (Demosthenes 20.135)[109]

There are laws which state that if someone making a promise deceives the demos he shall be liable to impeachment. (Demosthenes 49.67)[110]

As Hansen suggests, the first two citations from the speech *Against Leptines* might be references to the law of *probolai* as outlined in the *Constitution of Athens*.[111] I have already discussed the law of *probolē* and the problems of interpreting the Aristotelian description. I wish to concentrate here on the third citation in the speech *Against Timotheus*

---

[107] On the assumption in the orators that the demos will make wiser decisions and have more wisdom than any individual, see Ober (1989) 163–5. In forensic speeches it is often assumed that a bad judgement could only come about if a jury receives false information; unjust or unwise verdicts are the fault of a deceitful litigant and his witnesses, not of the jury.

[108] ἔστι δὲ δήπου νόμος ὑμῖν, ἐάν τις ὑποσχόμενός τι τὸν δῆμον ἢ τὴν βουλὴν ἢ δικαστήριον ἐξαπατήσῃ, τὰ ἔσχατα πάσχειν.

[109] ἔστιν ὑμῖν νόμος ἀρχαῖος ... ἄν τις ὑποσχόμενός τι τὸν δῆμον ἐξαπατήσῃ, κρίνειν, κἂν ἁλῷ, θανάτῳ ζημιοῦν.

[110] ... νόμων ὄντων, ἐάν τις τὸν δῆμον ὑποσχόμενος ἐξαπατήσῃ, εἰσαγγελίαν εἶναι περὶ αὐτοῦ ...

[111] Hansen (1975) 14.

which specifically claims that an individual could be subject to impeachment (εἰσαγγελίαν) if 'making a promise, he deceives the demos'.

One of the problems we have in interpreting Demosthenes' reference to the procedure of *eisangelia* as a means of dealing with deceivers is that there is very little evidence concerning the deployment and development of the law on impeachment (*nomos eisangeltikos*) as a whole. Historians have made educated guesses as to when a source can be said to have offered a *verbatim* quotation from the law, and when it has merely provided a general (and perhaps distorted) gloss. Hansen *presumes* that the citation from the speech *Against Timotheus* contains a direct reference to a clause in the law of impeachment because '*eisangelia* is expressly referred to as the proper remedy to be employed', and the words 'if someone, making a promise, deceives the demos' are a verbatim quotation from the third section of the law on impeachment.[112] Hansen and Rhodes concur on this point and they may be right; it could be that the fourth- and/or fifth-century *nomos eisangeltikos* did include a clause against deceiving the demos by making false promises.[113] However, the fact that the reference from *Against Timotheus* associates deception of the demos with the term εἰσαγγελίαν does not necessarily prove that the *nomos eisangeltikos* contained any clause specifically prohibiting such deception, let alone a clause that is identical with the Demosthenic 'quotation'. Ruschenbusch and Rhodes himself have argued that εἰσαγγελία and εἰσαγγέλλειν and other terms which we take as referring to distinct legal procedures are words 'within whose normal range of meaning one or more technical senses developed'.[114] It was possible that, even in a legal context, terms like εἰσαγγελία or γραφή may not have always been used in their technical legal sense (namely, referring to one procedure as distinct from any other). It was also possible that a set of technical legal terms had not yet crystallised such that each term had its own distinct meaning and no other more general meaning.[115] These possibilities are demon-

---

[112] Hansen (1975) 14.

[113] See Rhodes (1979) 107. The major sources for the offences covered by the *nomos eisangeltikos* are Hyp. 4.7–8, 29, 39; Dem. 24.63; [Arist.] *Ath. Pol.* 8.4, 53.6; Harp. *Suid.* (*EI* 222); Philochorus 328 *FGrH* F199; Poll. 8.51–2. These list offences which Rhodes and Hansen summarise under three headings; (1) Attempts to overthrow the democracy. (2) Treason. (3) Taking of bribes. It is generally held that the charge of deceiving the demos can be added either as part of the third heading or else as denominating a separate fourth heading.

[114] Rhodes (1979) 103. Given Rhodes' caveats, it is surprising that he accepts Hansen's treatment of Dem. 49.67 so uncritically. See also Ruschenbusch (1968) 73–4.

[115] For example, see Goldhill (1988a) 33–56 on the multiple meanings of δίκη, only one of which was 'law-suit.' See also Todd and Millett (1990) 13.

strated in a speech of Isaeus where a charge of mistreating an orphan is referred to as both an *eisangelia* and a *graphē*.[116]

Ruschenbusch has argued that εἰσαγγελία and εἰσαγγέλλειν were originally used of any verbal charge and survived as a term for all charges that were made admissible before the passing of the law that denunciations must be submitted in writing.[117] The word εἰσαγγελία, then, may sometimes refer to a distinct procedure but may also be a general term for a whole cluster of types of denunciation. In the case of the charge concerning *apatē* of the demos, it is simply not possible to determine how old the charge is and whether or not it ever came under the auspices of the *nomos eisangeltikos*. All we can say with any certainty is that *probolai* could be and were brought under the charge of deceiving the people with false promises but that after 404/3 the number of *probolai* which could be brought in a year was severely restricted.

If the procedure and applicability of the law against ἀπατὴ τοῦ δήμου remains obscure, and if we cannot be certain as to the frequency of its actual deployment, we can at least examine the contexts for the Demosthenic references for further clues as to the law's significance within the framework of Athens' political and legal discourse. Such an examination shows that Christ is right to emphasise the symbolic value of the law. But the law's symbolism could be manipulated to convey messages that went beyond a simple warning to the elite that the demos could punish them and a reminder to the demos that they must not abuse that position of sovereignty.

The law against 'deceit of the demos' may have served as a reminder of the fragility of sovereignty of the demos. The placement of complaints against dishonest politicians alongside ostracism and complaints against sycophants demonstrated that the democratic process was always open to the subversions of deceptive communication and corruption. We will see that the law against 'deceit of the demos' is invoked in forensic oratory to remind juries that democracy and deception are incompatible and to represent opponents as transgressive in the light of the law's symbolism. But citation of the law can also constitute a strategy of *self*-representation and can even be a means of mobilising a jury to think in terms of their own identity and collective responsibilities.

The most unsurprising rhetorical use of the law against deception is the reference from the Demosthenic speech (against the prominent

---

[116] Isae. 11.6, 15 (*eisangelia*) 28, 31, 32, 35 (*graphē*).
[117] Ruschenbusch (1968) 73–4.

general Timotheus) which I have just discussed.[118] The speaker, Apollodorus, uses the existence of such legislation as part of his explanation as to why he withdrew an oath-challenge (*proklēsis*) directed at his opponent.[119] He was the first to tender a *proklēsis* to Timotheus and the latter responded in kind:

> For after I had put the oath in the evidence-box, he thought that, by taking an oath himself, he could be quit of the affair. And, if I had not known that he had flagrantly perjured himself in many solemn oaths both to poleis and individuals, I should have allowed him to take the oath. (Demosthenes 49.65)

Apollodorus claims that he is in possession of enough testimony and circumstantial evidence as to make a *proklēsis* unnecessary and continues with a detailed exposition of why a challenge to an oath would be inappropriate legal procedure for dealing with a man like Timotheus:

> It seemed to me ... to be a monstrous thing to give an oath to one who would not only take no care to swear honestly (*euorkēsei*), but who, when it was a question of gain, has not spared even temples. The specific instances of the perjuries he has committed without scruple would make a long story. But I will call to your minds the most flagrant instances and those of which you are well aware. You know that he swore in the *ecclēsia*, imprecating destruction upon himself and dedicating his property to sacred uses, if he should fail to indict Iphicrates as a usurper of the rights of citizenship. Yet, although he has sworn and promised this in the *ecclēsia*, no long time afterwards, in order to serve his own interests, he gave his daughter in marriage to the son of Iphicrates. When a man, then, felt no shame in deceiving you to whom he had pledged his word, though there are laws which declare that if someone making a promise deceives the demos, he shall be liable to impeachment – when, after swearing and imprecating destruction upon himself, he had no fear of the gods in whose name he had perjured himself – was it strange that I was unwilling to allow him to take an oath? (Demosthenes 49.65–7)

---

[118] Dem. 49.67. This speech was delivered by Apollodorus and has a probable dating of 362 BC. Plut. *Vit. Dem.* 15, states that Apollodorus won the suit and that Demosthenes wrote the speech. But Demosthenic authorship has been disputed; see Schäfer (1856–8), vol. III, 137ff.; Blass (1887–98), vol. III, 522ff. Trevett (1992) 50–76 comprehensively surveys the arguments for Demosthenic authorship of the 'Apollodoran' speeches and concludes that 46, 49, 50, 52, 53 and 59 are not the work of Demosthenes.

[119] Apollodorus was prosecuting Timotheus for the return of money which he had borrowed from his father Pasion in the late 370s. Despite the fact that Timotheus was a major public figure and a *stratēgos,* Trevett (1992) 127–8, argues that there was no political motivation behind the case on the grounds that Apollodorus 'makes little attempt to vilify his opponent'. We will see that Apollodorus does vilify his opponent by reference to the law against deceivers of the demos and argues that Timotheus has sworn falsely in the *ecclēsia*. These accusations seem to indicate that Timotheus' public profile as a regular speaker *is* at stake in this speech.

Recent work on the theory lying behind the *proklēsis* procedure and the infrequent attestation of its actual deployment might suggest that Apollodorus is constructing a covering argument here. Todd has shown that oath-challenges were probably constructed in such a way as to ensure that they were turned down by an opponent.[120] If your adversary actually took the oath then there was no possible means of refuting him and the trial would not go ahead. If he challenged you too and both parties agreed to take the oath then they cancelled each other out in their effect. Apollodorus' statement that Timotheus 'thought that by taking an oath himself he could be quit of the affair' (ἠξίου οὗτος καὶ αὐτὸς ὀμόσας ἀπηλλάχθαι) may indicate that a mutual acceptance of a *proklēsis* by both parties meant that further legal proceedings could not occur. Apollodorus indicates that he had the power to get his oath in first and then deny Timotheus of swearing *his* challenged oath by withdrawing that initial challenge. Whether or not this is a distortion of what really happened and hence what was actually permissible is difficult to determine. But if Todd's interpretation of the apparently rare deployment of the *proklēsis* is correct, then there is definitely a case for arguing that Apollodorus *had* to prevent Timotheus from accepting the challenge in order for the case to go to trial. Furthermore, he needed to deal with the fact that his opponent was obviously more than willing to swear an oath. Such intent showed an honest disposition according to the conventions of juridical procedure. To swear the challenged oath was to demonstrate to the public that you had nothing to fear or hide.

In order to turn the incident of the withdrawn oath-challenge to his own advantage, Apollodorus claims that there have been many previous occasions where Timotheus has reneged on sworn oaths. Using the classic rhetorical technique of *praeteritio*, he implies that his opponent is an habitual oath-breaker in the cause of private interest ('the specific instances ... would make a long story'). He actually details only two supposed instances of Timotheus' oath-breaking. Both relate to oaths sworn and promises made to the *ecclēsia*, and the first and most detailed account (quoted above) specifically cites the laws which make anyone liable to *eisangelia* if they are believed to have deceived the demos having made them a promise. Apollodorus points out that by giving his daughter in marriage to the son of Iphicrates, Timotheus

---

[120] Todd (1990) 35ff. See Due (1980) chs. 1 and 5. For a list of references to oath-challenges see Bonner (1905) 74–9 and Harrison (1971) vol. 1, 150ff. On the use of oaths as 'non-artificial' proofs see Arist. *Rh.* 1.1355b39f. and Kennedy (1963) 88–103; Gagarin (1989).

has shown himself to be unconcerned by the sanction of Athens' laws on deception and to be completely unperturbed by the threat of *divine* punishment that might be occasioned by his perjury.

Here, an outraged expression of the way in which democratic sanctions against deceit have been (or might be) disregarded goes hand in hand with an evocation of the sheer transgressive impiety and *hubris* that is to be associated with any supposed occasion when individuals mislead their audience. Apollodorus shows that a speaker who swears by the gods to reinforce his guarantees and is then accused of lying or reneging, is liable to be classed as deceiving the people with false promises. The illegality of the act is backed up with reflection on its impiety: 'promising' (ὑποσχόμενος) in the 'text' of the law is read as including the religious practices and taboos associated with 'swearing' (ὀμόσας).

For Apollodorus, his opponent's perjury can also be interpreted as a willingness to flout the civic laws on deception. When taken together, both interpretations of his transgression (the legal and the religious) demonstrate that Timotheus' acceptance of a *proklēsis* is dangerously meaningless. Timotheus is a deeply irreligious man operating outside laws designed to safeguard the sovereignty of the people. Furthermore, this track record of faithlessness has a direct bearing on the specifics of the case in question as well as the details of the pre-trial procedure. Timotheus stood accused of failing to repay loans made to him by Apollodorus' father Pasion. He denied that he was ever lent the money. But if Timotheus had deceived the demos before, why trust his word now? And if he had taken out loans and promised to repay them, then wasn't it consistent with his past behaviour in public if he had reneged on a private agreement with a banker? If he wasn't afraid of a legal action against making false promises to the people, then he wouldn't think twice about cheating a banker and undergoing a trial for the recovery of the money.

Towards the very end of the speech, then, Apollodorus covers for his opponent's acceptance of a *proklēsis* by demonstrating that he would be impervious to the divine and legal sanctions which would make an oath a symbol of honesty or good intent. At the same time, Apollodorus leaves the audience with an impression of his opponent which would have a direct bearing on the question of which of the litigants was most likely to have told lies or to have cheated on the financial agreement under scrutiny. The citation and interpretation of Athens' laws prohibiting false promises to, and deception of the demos is a crucial element in this nexus of rhetorical strategies.

In Demosthenes' speech *Against Leptines*, the law on *apatē* is referred to twice and in both cases the references are part of rhetorical strategies which are distinct from each other and different to that deployed against Timotheus. In the first case, Demosthenes deals with Leptines' argument that if his own amendment to the law is thrown out, then Demosthenes and Phormio will not introduce their own promised amendment and the old law will remain unchanged. Demosthenes counters this line of attack as follows:

> Now, in the first place, there are many ways open to him, if he wishes, of compelling the amender to introduce his own law. In the next place Phormio and myself and anyone else he cares to name are prepared to guarantee that we will introduce it. You know there is a law making death the penalty for anyone who, making a promise, deceives the demos, the Boule or the lawcourt. You have our guarantee, our promise. (Demosthenes 20.100)

In this argument, Demosthenes does not reinforce his guarantee with an oath but regards a reference to the law against making false promises and its most extreme penalty as sufficient for an indication of his sincerity. By neutralising Leptines' slur with a guarantee and by framing it with the possible legal consequences that might attend the breaking of such a promise, Demosthenes positions himself as having a deep regard for civic law. He places himself as the potential object of the demos' anger and reminds them of the sovereign power they can enforce on him via the terms of an appropriate statute. A little later, Demosthenes uses the same law but realigns its application:

> I now come to speak of a matter about which I feel bound, Athenians, to warn you most seriously. For even if one could admit the truth of all that Leptines will say in praise of his law, it would be impossible under any circumstances to wipe out one disgrace which his law, if ratified, will bring upon our polis. To what do I refer? To the reputation of having cheated our benefactors (τὸ δοκεῖν ἐξηπατηκέναι τοὺς ἀγαθόν τι ποιήσαντας). Now I think you would all agree that this is a distinct disgrace; how much worse in you than others, hear me explain. You have an ancient law, one held in great respect, that if anyone making a promise deceives the demos, he shall be brought to trial, and if convicted shall be punished with death. And are you not then ashamed, Athenians, to find yourself doing the very thing for which you punish other men with death? (Demosthenes 20.134–5)

Demosthenes now places his *audience* in a potentially objective relationship to the law. He characterises the old law guaranteeing exemption from liturgies to state benefactors and their descendants as analogous to a promise to the demos. It is difficult to determine quite what Demosthenes is doing here. Is he arguing that a repeal of the law actually *would be* an example of making a false promise to the demos itself? Or is he simply making a case for the potentially shameful hypocrisy of the civic body if it legally enforces an expectation of individuals to keep their promises to it whilst at the same time having no hesitation in reneging on past promises it has made in law to individuals who are classed as benefactors? It is tempting to conclude that Demosthenes wants his jury to consider the implied charges of collective 'self-deception' *and* the hypocritical treatment of individuals by the collective.

Whatever the precise implications of Demosthenes' argument here, the passage graphically demonstrates the extent to which an orator could manipulate and realign the 'norms of behaviour' that might be implied by a specific rule. He effectively redirects the most obvious thrust of the law concerning false promises. By drawing upon the basic Athenian values of equality and *isonomia*, Demosthenes argues that a law which seems to have been primarily directed against individuals seeking to mislead the collective is equally applicable to the collective itself.[121] He exploits the fact that every citizen is (potentially at least) both subject to, and a beneficiary of, this particular law. Furthermore, the text of the law is not used to threaten each and every member of the jury with prosecution for making false promises. Rather, it is used as a *symbolic* text in order to represent a vote for Leptines as an act of ideological and legal hypocrisy.

The law on deceit offers no concrete legal sanction here but Demosthenes regards its terms as placing a jury in an important bind. He constructs this bind by allowing the law's symbolic meaning to ramify beyond the limits of its normal practical application. But it would be dangerous to read his argument as an exceptional rhetorical conceit. This may be just one instance of the way in which legal statute, ideological 'norms' and actual forensic practice interacted. There may have been codes and rules but an orator could manipulate and incorporate them into his argument; he could create a strategy which placed specific laws and general values on his side; he could even bind his audience to this 'regularising' strategy.[122] We may be making a fundamental mistake if we regard Athenian law as solely functioning to proscribe, deter and punish actions deemed as criminal by consensus. In the case of the laws against deception at least, there has to be a consideration of the extent to which a rule is used to shape a jury's opinion and to manipulate or extend collective self-consciousness. In the search for what the laws on deception 'actually meant', for what actions and be-

---

[121] On these core ideological tenets of Athenian democratic ideology see Ober (1989) 217–19, 240–7 (economic and political equality); Woodhead (1967) and Ober (1989), 74–5 (*isēgoria*).

[122] See Bourdieu (1977) 22. Bourdieu's work on rules, social practice, 'symbolic capital' and 'regularising strategies' has informed this section considerably.

haviours they were 'intended' to proscribe, there has to be a recognition that in both the actual cases brought and in the rhetorical citations as exampled above there was a constant *strategic* re-negotiation of the nature of the laws' relevant applications and significances.

The symbolic and strategic deployment of the law against deceiving the demos is paralleled in the orators' occasional references to the curse proclaimed by a herald before every meeting of the Boule and the *ecclēsia*. The exact content of the curse can only be guessed at from oratory's allusions to it and a parodic rendition in Aristophanes' *Thesmophoriazusae*.[123] Demosthenes certainly regards the curse as including a prohibition on deceit of the demos when he has the curse read out to the jury to show that religion and piety forbid them to acquit Aeschines when he has been proved guilty of lying (19.70).[124] Demosthenes goes on to argue that it would be absurd for the jury to acquit a man whom, through the herald's curse, they enjoin and require the gods to punish. Dinarchus has the curse read out in his speech *Against Demosthenes*. He says that Demosthenes has been proved to have taken bribes and has 'deceived the people and the Boule in defiance of the curse, professing views he does not hold' (ἐξηπατηκὼς δὲ καὶ τὸν δῆμον καὶ τὴν βουλὴν παρὰ τὴν ἀράν, [καὶ] ἕτερα μὲν λέγων ἕτερα δὲ φρονῶν: 1.47). When the curse has been read out, Dinarchus represents Demosthenes as demonstrating his lack of concern for the curse with all his lies (1.48).[125] Dinarchus' speech *Against Aristogeiton* alludes to the curse as directed against those who speak in the *ecclēsia* having taken bribes (2.16).

In Aristophanes' parodic representation of a women's *ecclēsia* (to discuss Euripides), proceedings are prefaced with a long series of curses performed by a female herald, and this is immediately followed by a curse from the chorus. The herald curses anyone who plans evil for the demos of women; anyone who communicates with Euripides or the Medes in order to harm the women; anyone who aspires to tyranny (*Thesm.* 335–8). The objects of the curses then become more ridiculous; anyone who tells a woman's husband that the baby is not her

---

[123] See Andoc. 1.31; Aeschin. 1.23; Dem. 19.70–1, 20.107, 23.97; Din. 1.47–8, 2.16; Lyc. 1.31; Ar. *Thesm.* 295–372. For a reconstruction of the curse see Rhodes (1972) 36–7.

[124] 'To show you that this man is already accursed by you, and that religion and piety forbid you to acquit one *who has been guilty of such lies*. Recite the curse. Take it and read it from the statute' (ἵνα τοίνυν εἰδῆθ᾽ ὅτι καὶ κατάρατός ἐστιν ὑφ᾽ ὑμῶν, καὶ οὐδ᾽ ὅσιον ὑμῖν οὐδ᾽ εὐσεβές ἐστι τοιαῦτ᾽ ἐψευσμένον αὐτὸν ἀφεῖναι, λέγε τὴν ἀρὰν καὶ ἀνάγνωθι λαβὼν τὴν ἐκ τοῦ νόμου ταυτηνί).

[125] 'Despite this, gentlemen of the jury, Demosthenes is so ready with his lies and utterly unsound assertions (Δημοσθένης τῷ ψεύδεσθαι καὶ μηδὲν ὑγιὲς λέγειν ἑτοίμως χρῆται), so oblivious of shame, exposure, or curse, that he will dare to say of me, I gather, that I too was previously condemned by the Boule.'

own; the servant who colludes in a wife's adultery and then informs on her to her husband. There is also a curse against the messenger who brings false reports and the adulterer who 'deceives, telling lies and does not give what he has promised' (ἢ μοιχὸς εἴ τις ἐξαπατᾷ ψευδῆ λέγων καὶ μὴ δίδωσιν ἂν ὑπόσχηταί ποτε: 343–4). Given that the law(s) against deceiving the demos seem to have involved the notion of breaking promises, it seems possible that this is a parodic appropriation of an element in the real curse which specifically condemned 'deceit of the demos' and making false promises to the people.

Whatever the precise wording of the curse, it is clear that the orators invoke it symbolically and strategically to foreground 'deceit of the demos' as transgressive in religious as well as civic terms. Dinarchus makes capital out of the curse's content in order to characterise Demosthenes' deceptions as impious.[126] Demosthenes manipulates the logic of the curse by stressing that its content covers Aeschines' lies to the people. The curse was symbolically apotropaic; it called upon the gods to punish all those who spoke with treasonable intent.

In this section I have tried to show how the Athenian democracy deployed laws and public curses against deception of the demos. I have also argued that these laws were symbolically important in democratic oratory and that the symbolism could be manipulated to embody the responsibilities of the demos as well as those of individual speakers. These symbolic sanctions, alongside Demosthenes' construction of Leptines' proposal as unAthenian dishonesty complement the Athenian representation of deception as 'Spartan', 'anti-hoplitic' and 'uncourageous'. In the next section I will examine an example of Attic tragedy's confrontation with these constructions and representations.

Staging Spartans and *stratēgoi*: Euripides' *Andromache*

The construction of the Spartan 'other' and the Athenian 'self' in terms of an opposition between non-hoplitic trickery and hoplitic openness and a further opposition between deceptive tactics and appearances as culturally acquired on the one hand and a natural, genuine excellence on the other, is well illustrated in the action and narrative of Euripides' *Andromache*.

Vidal-Naquet's interpretation of the Athenian 'coming of age' ceremony has been applied to Athenian dramatic texts in order to demonstrate ways in which they might articulate notions of adult citizen identity and responsibility through their representation of motifs

---

[126] See Worthington (1992) ad loc. (211): 'Curses in Greek society had a political as well as a religious value.'

paralleled in initiation.[127] However, there is a danger that the direct mapping of Vidal-Naquet's posited antithesis (honest hoplite/tricky ephebe) onto the structure and progressions of an Attic tragedy will fail to do justice to its interrogative relationship to the values and ideological oppositions which surround and inform it.[128] For the present, I wish to isolate one thematic element of a complex and rarely discussed play which was written and performed during hostilities with Sparta.[129] I hope to show, however, that this play does not simply reinforce the stereotype of the deceptive Spartan or project an ideal image of hoplitic honesty. For at the same time as these ideal oppositions are played out, the placement of the trickster beyond the boundaries of Athens is rendered problematic through a veiled engagement with the mechanisms of leadership in the contemporary democratic process.

Classical scholarship and criticism on Euripides' *Andromache* has often taken issue with the play's apparent lack of unity and more recently has attempted to find elements and themes in the drama which will give coherence to its tripartite structure.[130] For Lucas, 'the *An*-

[127] Bowie (1987) regards Philocleon in *Wasps* as enacting a reversal of the progression from ephebic to citizen status. See also Bowie (1993) for further applications of Vidal-Naquet's insights to the reversals of Aristophanic Comedy. Vidal-Naquet (1988) reads Neoptolemus' rejection of Odyssean *apatē* in *Philoctetes* as part of a paradigmatic initiation into adulthood; see also Goldhill (1984) 166 on Aeschylus' and Sophocles' Orestes as the ephebic 'cunning hunter' and his false narration of his own death as 'initiatory death'.

[128] For the classic account of Athenian tragedy's questioning relation to Athenian norms, values and ideology, see Vernant and Vidal-Naquet (1988). Goldhill (1984) and (1988a) advance, supplement and refine this approach considerably. See Zeitlin (1986) and (1990) for further exemplary contributions. See Goldhill (1984) 193f. on the inadequacy of too general an application of the motif of initiation to the complexities of the *Oresteia*; see also Winnington-Ingram (1979) and Goldhill (1990) for critiques of Vidal-Naquet's application of 'the Black Hunter' to Sophocles' *Philoctetes*.

[129] There is no firm evidence for the date and place of performance of *Andromache* although all critics put it somewhere between 431 and 421. A scholion on Eur. *Andr.* 445 says that the play did not figure in the Athenian *didaskaliai*. It has been argued by some that the play was not performed at the City Dionysia. Page (1938) 206f. suggested that it was written for performance at Argos, but the negative representation of the Argive Orestes makes this unlikely. See Stevens (1971) 15–21, for an inconclusive survey of opinion. Taplin (1999) 45 whispers the possibility of a non-Athenian primary audience and suggests a Thessalian secondary audience because of the play's 'heavy Thessalian localization' (16–20, 43–4, 115, 1176, 1187, 1211, 1263–9). My reading of the play should hopefully suggest that it was primarily aimed at an Athenian audience. See Lloyd (1994) 12: 'there is nothing peculiar about the style of the play to set it apart from Euripides' plays produced in Athens'.

[130] For a brief but comprehensive survey of critics' misgivings and others' suggestions for 'unifying themes' see Storey (1989) 16–17. See also Phillippo (1995) 355, n. 1. Storey himself sees 'domestic disharmony' as one of its consistent themes. Erbse (1966) regards Andromache's character as the play's unifying idea. Heath (1987a) 93–103, argues that the search for 'unity' of theme or action in this play is erroneous, since such a search is based on anachronistic aesthetic assumptions. Heath (1989) develops these arguments in relation to Greek literature as a whole.

dromache falls mysteriously and feebly to pieces, leaving one with the suspicion that there must be missing clues which would show the play less inept than it seems'.[131] Lesky regards the play as structurally flawed and carelessly written. He takes particular issue with the speeches which seem to be directed against fifth-century Sparta: '... when he [Euripides] allows Peleus to fulminate against Spartan girls (595), who romp naked with young men, it is not political poetry in the higher sense, as we find in Aeschylus, but inartistic propaganda'.[132] Yet it is precisely these contemporarily relevant attacks on Spartan morals and mores which lead Kitto to conclude that the *Andromache* is 'held together by a single idea'. For him the play is a 'denunciation of Sparta, not a tragedy of mankind' and he characterises it more specifically as 'a violent attack on the Spartan mind, on *Machtpolitik*; in particular on three Spartan qualities, arrogance, treachery and criminal ruthlessness'.[133]

Stevens points out that Kitto's reading may not work for the last part of the play.[134] Orestes is related to Menelaus but is described as an Argive (1032).[135] Nobody in the play explicitly suggests that he has Spartan characteristics. However, it is important to note that Orestes is presented as perniciously deceptive and manipulative. In several exchanges which I will discuss later, Andromache and Peleus represent Menelaus as a conniver and a cowardly leader. The play characterises Orestes as a self-interested schemer (993–1008), although the messenger's suggestions that Apollo supports the killing of Neoptolemus make ethical evaluation of these two heroes and the god himself necessarily problematic. Nevertheless, de Jong has shown that the messenger's narration (1085–1172) subtly lays emphasis on the malevolence and impiety of Orestes' tricks and implies that he does not himself actually take part in the ambush of Neoptolemus.[136] It is presumably the similarity between the actions and representations of Menelaus and those of Orestes that led Kitto towards his totalised

---

[131] Lucas (1950) 182.
[132] Lesky (1965) 159.
[133] Kitto (1954) 230–6.
[134] Stevens (1971) 12.
[135] But the text at 1032 is problematic and at 1075 the messenger describes Orestes as Mycenaean. Some MSS omit this line.
[136] See de Jong (1991) 29, 52–3, 57–8, 79, 84, 106, 137, 152–3. Stevens (1971) 211–12 argues, on the basis of Orestes' words at 993–1008 and a possible linguistic interpretation of 1115–16, that Orestes is at Delphi and contrives the plot (995f. and 1085–96) but does not actually take part in the killing. De Jong (1991) 53, n. 144 supports this view, pointing out that at 1125–6 of the messenger speech, Neoptolemus' questions imply that he does not see Orestes among his attackers.

reading of *Andromache* as an anti-Spartan tract. Conacher also seems to assimilate Orestes to a Spartan identity: 'the coming together of the evil elements, Hermione and Orestes, is an essential complement to the ultimate fate of the "good" elements ... it becomes clear that the end towards which the action is leading is the separation of the evil Spartan elements from the noble Trojan and Phthian elements'.[137] Recent work has shown that Kitto's reading fails to consider other important themes which are explored throughout the play; indeed, as Phillipo remarks, it is unlikely that the play can be adequately interpreted in the light of any single 'unifying theme'.[138] But if Kitto cannot justifiably interpret Orestes simply as another 'bad Spartan', his brief analysis nevertheless points to a recurring group of issues which are most explicitly raised by the anti-Spartan speeches of Peleus and Andromache. Critics have interpreted these speeches as having extra-dramatic relevance to the Peloponnesian War and have sometimes attacked their apparent propagandistic content (see Lesky above). Even those critics who have recognised that these passages are 'appropriate' to the drama in itself have said little about the possible thematic interactions between the play's variously formulated attacks on and representations of its 'evil elements'. Kovacs, for example, argues that Peleus' last speech against Menelaus (693f.) 'is from the logical point of view unnecessary' and reads its apparent references to fifth-century political practice as 'anything but democratic'.[139] He grudgingly admits that its contribution to the thematic structure of the play is 'not negligible' but does not consider what the nature of that contribution might be, arguing simply that 'the oppositions in this play here take political form for the first time'. Kovacs does see links between this speech and Andromache's previous discussion of *doxa* (δόκησιν, 696: cf. 319) but he does not explore the significance of similarities, developments and differences between them or their relation to the play as a whole.[140]

There is a need, then, to do more than simply mark a speech as having 'anachronistic' or 'extra-dramatic' contemporary relevance. Nor is it enough to section off the explicit attacks on Sparta or con-

---

[137] Conacher (1967) 173.

[138] Phillippo (1995) 355–6. See also the work of Heath cited above at n. 130. Phillippo concentrates on the play's articulations of family ties through 'significant patronymics' but I agree that '[I]f freed from looking for an idea that will be *the* unifying theme of the play, we look instead at the way certain themes are explored in the context of the play's various elements we may find that Euripides has set up links and patterns ... which help bind the play together' (355–6).

[139] Kovacs (1980) 69.

[140] I discuss Andromache's remarks on *doxa* in relation to Euripidean 'anti-rhetoric' at pp. 279–83.

demnations of *stratēgoi* as propagandistic.[141] There surely has to be an account of the ways in which Menelaus and Hermione are being constructed and assimilated as enemies. Such an account shows how the apparently propagandistic elements of the play relate to and are framed by its recurrent preoccupations with deception. Andromache's tirade (445–63) and Peleus' accusations (590–641, 693–726) have a force which is directly informed by contemporary Athenian politics and ideology, but the position of these speeches within the structure of the play is far from anomalous. Their content and import is carefully prepared for in the drama's preceding exchanges and they highlight issues which continue to be addressed in the rest of the play.

The on-stage action of *Andromache* has been precipitated by an accusation of trickery. From the safety of Thetis' shrine Andromache explains that Hermione is accusing her of secretly administering drugs (φαρμάκοις κεκρυμμένοις: 32) to make her infertile and hateful to her husband Neoptolemus. It is important to note that Hermione is first named in combination with the epithet 'Spartan' (Λάκαιναν: 29) and that when Andromache's prologue first names Menelaus, he is described as 'coming from Sparta' (ἀπὸ Σπάρτης μολών: 41). Andromache starts as she means to go on by emphasising these characters' geographical origin as constitutive of their identity and it is this national identity which will be developed to embrace some damningly negative characteristics.[142]

In fear of Hermione and the arrival of Menelaus, Andromache has fled to the shrine and hidden her child in another's house (ὑπεκπέμπω λάθρα ἄλλους ἐς οἴκους: 47–8). In tragedy, the covert dispatch of the child to another's house often connotes more threatening and destructive deceptions. In Euripides' *Hecuba*, the Trojan queen has sent

---

[141] The introduction of Goff (1995), along with Rose (1995), Gellrich (1995), Foley (1995) and Seaford (1995) point to the importance of a renewed and sophisticated assessment of tragedy's more explicit engagements with the concerns of the fifth-century Athenian polis. On the difficulty of assessing contemporary meaning in Greek tragedy due to its quality of 'heroic vagueness', see Easterling (1997b).

[142] The chorus also stress Menelaus' and Hermione's Spartan identity at 127: 'Are you contending with your masters, a Trojan girl with natives of Sparta (*Lakedaimonos engenetaisin*)?' See Stevens (1971) 115: 'Euripides keeps reminding us of the Spartan nationality of Hermione and Menelaus.' For discussion and bibliography on the process of naming and its importance in Greek culture and literature, see Goldhill (1991) 27. That geographical location and climactic conditions could have a profound effect on human disposition is the major premise of the Hippocratic *Airs, Waters, Places*, although with regard to questions of character, what we have of this treatise concentrates on the effect of such determinants on different non-Greek races. It does, however, correlate the different locations of Greek poleis with specific types of physical strength or dysfunction.

her son Polydorus to the household of the Thracian king Polymestor for his own safety. He has a secret store of gold with him. But Polymestor treacherously murders Polydorus to procure the gold. The vocabulary used of Polydorus' dispatch and the secrecy surrounding it directly echoes the vocabulary used in the *Andromache*.[143] Aeschylus' Clytemnestra sends Orestes away, not for his own protection as she claims, but in order to pursue her adultery and devious murder of Agamemnon with impunity and without interference. So while Andromache's concealment of her son might arouse foreboding, its grounding in genuine motives of protection mark it as a positive ruse in contrast with Clytemnestra's act of concealment which itself concealed the true motives behind it.

When she learns from her *therapaina* that the Spartans have discovered her ruse, Andromache asks her to take a message to Neoptolemus' grandfather Peleus. The *therapaina* doubts that she could conceal the purpose of such a journey from Hermione but Andromache assures her that because she is a woman, she can find many contrivances (πολλὰς ἂν εὕροις μηχανάς· γυνὴ γὰρ εἶ: 85). In making this comment Andromache invokes a dramatic topos, which is particularly prevalent in Euripides but also found in depictions of women in Homer and the other dramatists.[144] But in this play, Andromache's invocation of female wiles conforms to the defensive deceptions of Homer's Penelope and the heroines of Euripides' *Helen* and *Iphigeneia among the Taurians*. Orestes repeats the topos in relation to Hermione's attempt to kill her rival: 'did you weave a plot (ἔρραψας) against this woman as women do?' (911).

Thus the play gives an audience a picture of both the positive and negative aspects to female cunning. Andromache uses it to protect herself and her offspring in the face of evil and in the absence of a male who will defend her. Her covert dispatch of the *therapaina* is designed precisely for the introduction of a sympathetic male in authority. By contrast, Hermione's use of deception is ill-conceived and threatening. Andromache has already used the term μηχανάς once to inquire about the intentions of Hermione and her father (66–7): 'What further plots

---

[143] See Eur. *Hec.* 6: ὑπεξέπεμψε and 10: ἐκπέμπει λάθρᾳ.
[144] See Eur. *Med.* 409, where Medea, like Andromache, is a non-Greek and describes women as 'most clever architects of all kinds of evil' (κακῶν δὲ πάντων τέκτονες σοφώταται). At Eur. *Hipp.* 480–1, the Nurse comments on women's superiority to men in the field of cunning contrivance: 'Certainly men would be late in discovering contrivances, if we women are not going to discover them' (ἦ τἄρ' ἂν ὀψέ γ' ἄνδρες ἐξεύροιεν ἄν, εἰ μὴ γυναῖκες μηχανὰς εὑρήσομεν). See also Eur. *Andr.* 911; *IT* 1032; *Ion* 843f.

(μηχανάς) are they weaving (πλέκουσιν) against my wretched life?' She assumes that the Spartans' attack on her will take the form of 'woven machinations'. Again, the deployment of metaphors for weaving, plaiting and spinning to describe instances of contrivance and deception is commonplace in Greek literature. In Aeschylus' *Choephoroi*, Electra suspects that her as yet unrecognised brother is weaving or plaiting a trap around her: 'what trick (δόλον) are you weaving (πλέκεις) around me, stranger?' (220). A fragment of Aeschylus associates Egyptian trickery with weaving: 'the Egyptians are certainly clever at weaving contrivances' (δεινοὶ πλέκειν τοι μηχανὰς Αἰγύπτιοι).[145] In many dramatic expressions of the anxiety that tricks are being woven, the objects of suspicion are somehow 'other' to the speaking subject; strangers, women, supposedly anti-democratic women, barbarians and here, Spartans who are 'other' to Andromache and are being constructed as such for an Athenian audience.[146] The *therapaina* enhances this picture of malevolent cunning by pointing out that 'as a sentry (φύλαξ), Hermione is no small thing' (86).[147] By the end of the first episode, then, Andromache has represented herself as resorting to deception and concealment in order to protect herself and the life of her son. In the absence of Neoptolemus, Hermione and Menelaus are wrongly accusing her of witchcraft. Their identity as Spartans is foregrounded and their hostility is perceived in terms of malevolent trickery and cunning.

Hermione's entrance speech affirms and supplements the representation of her offered by Andromache and the *therapaina*. 'Adornment' is her opening word (κόσμον: 147) and her subsequent self-description gives expression to a theme that will develop throughout the play. She proclaims that she is wearing the wealthy and luxurious clothes that

---

[145] Aesch. fr. 373 N² (= Aesch. fr. 373 R).

[146] The Homeric Penelope virtually makes the figurative usage literal when she introduces the ruse of Laertes' web: 'I will weave tricks' (ἐγὼ δὲ δόλους τολυπεύω: Hom. *Od.* 19.137). For the conjunction of ὑφαίνω (weave) with μῆτις (cunning) and δόλος (trick) see Hom. *Od.* 4.678, 739; 9.422; *Il.* 6.187. The chorus of old men at Ar. *Lys.* 630 suspect the women of weaving (ὕφηναν) a plot to bring about tyranny. Pindar uses πλέκω and ὑφαίνω to describe his own act of poetic creation. See Pi. fr. 179M (= fr. 169 OCT) and *Ol.* 6.86 where he weaves a work which is *poikilos*; see also Pi. *Nem.* 4.94. On the connotations of weaving in Homer and lyric see Bergren (1979); Snyder (1981); Jenkins (1985). See Buxton (1994) 122–7 for the (often ambiguous) moral and social connotations of weaving as represented in textual and pictorial versions of Greek myth.

[147] The same term was applied to Hermione's aunt Clytemnestra at Aesch. *Ag.* 914. In that play, the full ramifications of calling Clytemnestra a φύλαξ (sentry, look-out, or guardian) are not realised by the Argive king.

were given to her as wedding gifts by Menelaus (147–53).[148] In doing so, she stresses that these expensive garments derive, not from the house of Achilles or Peleus (149), but from the land of Sparta (ἐκ Λακαίνης Σπαρτιάτιδος χθονός: 151).[149] Of course an audience might immediately have seen Hermione as taking after her extravagantly dressed mother Helen.[150] Through this demonstration of wealth and the implication that there are many more wedding gifts besides (πολλοῖς σὺν ἕδνοις: 153), Hermione may be regarded as explicitly transgressing Athenian democratic norms and legislation governing female behaviour and public display.[151] For an Athenian audience, Hermione's self-representation perhaps connoted a marked violation of codes defining the appropriate conduct of married women in their own society. Andromache certainly criticises her insensitive display of Spartan royal wealth within the less affluent Phthian household: such displays are the cause of Neoptolemus' rejection and make Hermione a bad wife (209–14).

Boulter connects the Spartans' protestations of power through wealth with what she sees as the dominant theme of the play: '. . . the slave-woman, Andromache and the old man Peleus are representations of the old fashioned aristocratic morality based on *aretē* and *eugeneia* while Hermione and Menelaus represent pride and power derived from wealth'.[152] This opposition is articulated through the characters' rhetorical definitions of *sophia* (wisdom, cleverness) and *sōphrosunē* (self-control, moderation, prudence). It is important, however, to stress that

---

[148] Lee (1975) 11, points out that Hermione's reliance on her father is extreme and that having decided to lean on his ineffectual support she is in the end no less bereft of friends (ἔρημος φίλων: 78) than Andromache (see also 805). The appearance of fatherly love and support that his extravagant gifts offer is undercut by his subsequent desertion of Hermione at 746. Hermione believes Menelaus has left her open to Neoptolemus' inevitable wrath (854f.).

[149] See Storey (1989) 19, who argues that Hermione is implying a contrast between the wealth of her father and the poverty of Peleus and his descendants' households.

[150] See Helen's luxurious clothes and living spaces in the *Iliad* and *Odyssey*. See also Hecuba's attack at Eur. *Troad.* 991f.

[151] See Plut. *Sol.* 21.4. Solon introduced laws restricting the conferral of bridal gifts (φερναί). In addition, the property that a woman could bring with her when she married was limited to 'three pieces of clothing and household items of small value'. Arthur (1973) 35 argues that this early legislation was 'primarily intended to put a check on display and extravagance among wealthy families'. See also Thomas (1989) 95ff. Seaford (1994b) 74–105 discusses wider legislative projects of proto-democratic and democratic Athenian politicians as attempts to restrict the conspicuous display of wealth and kinship-autonomy in burial rituals and other ceremonies. Cf. Arthur (1973) 56 concerning the difficult interpretation of Plutarch's use of the term 'φερναί'.

[152] Boulter (1966) 53.

Hermione's valorisation of wealth is also being seen as specifically inappropriate to her gender because it is directly damaging to the *oikos*. Her wealthy appearances threaten to mask her moral bankruptcy and supplant the old system of values which Boulter identifies with the play's 'positive' characters. But through this attempt to use the superficial attributes of wealth as the sole grounds for status, she casts herself in the role of a bad woman whose values disrupt domestic stability and continuity.

Andromache's criticisms show how ascriptions of worth based on material appearances rather than genuine 'nobility' of character cannot be adequate. Furthermore, such prioritising of the superficial and the cosmetic will only destroy the order of the very realm which the woman ought to be protecting. Hermione regards the trappings of wealth as giving her the right to 'speak freely' (ὥστ' ἐλευθεροστομεῖν: 153). Wealth, elitism, Spartan identity and the power that they afford: these are the themes through which Hermione introduces herself and justifies her verbal assault on Andromache.[153] But by opposing her homeland to the houses of her husband's forebears, by describing her affluence in terms of acquired adornment and by dramatising a display of appearances, Hermione's self-representation offers grounds for subsequent accusations that Andromache and Peleus will make concerning her own conduct as a wife and the legitimacy of her father's wealth, status and political reputation. And by offering a critique of Hermione's conduct, Andromache explicates and reinforces Athenian norms concerning the conspicuous display of wealth among women. A *Spartan* woman might behave in this way, but even a *barbarian* can see through such a deceptive rhetoric of appearances and demonstrate its dangers.[154] In turn, Hermione accuses Andromache of witchcraft and glosses it as a characteristically Asiatic form of deception:

[153] Hall (1989) 209 argues that Hermione's valorisation of conspicuous wealth frames her as a 'barbaric Greek' and interprets the play as a whole (213f.) as constructing the Spartans' possession of particularly reprehensible qualities through a contrast with the unusually 'noble' and Greek barbarian Andromache.

[154] Lee (1975) gives an account of this play's exploration of notions of nature, convention, appearance and reality: 'the contrasts and parallelisms which make up the *Andromache* can be seen as an illustration in dramatic form of the confusions of *nomos* and *phusis*. This confusion is seen in relation to several areas of social and ethical thinking which were under discussion in the latter part of the fifth century: the divisions between free man and slave, barbarian and Greek, base born and noble, and the problem of fixed standards of behaviour. Also touched on in the play is the question of what is real and whether we can come to a knowledge of it'. However, there is much that Lee omits, particularly the relation of the play's treatment of *doxa* to Athenian poetics, politics or ideology and the interesting point that while the play undermines *nomoi* concerning barbarians, nobility and *nothoi*, the turpitude of Spartans remains largely uncontested.

... στυγοῦμαι δ' ἀνδρὶ φαρμάκοισι σοῖς,
νηδὺς δ' ἀκύμων διὰ σέ μοι διόλλυται·
δεινὴ γὰρ ἠπειρῶτις ἐς τὰ τοιάδε
ψυχὴ γυναικῶν·

Your drugs make me hateful to my husband and my womb is dead and barren because of you. The mind of Asiatic women is clever at such things. (Euripides *Andromache* 157–60)

When Hermione expresses her barrenness (νηδὺς δ' ἀκύμων), she articulates her failure to fulfil what Athenians would have perceived as a woman's most important role in society.[155] Hermione (falsely) blames her inability to conceive (and hence, in Greek terms, her failure to be a complete 'woman') on Andromache's barbarian powers of cunning witchcraft. Through the construction of Andromache as a stereotypically barbarian witch ('you barbarian creature': 261), Hermione initiates a process of scapegoating. This representation of Andromache conforms to general Athenian dramatic topoi concerning natural traits of duplicity in women as well as the more specific model of malevolent deception in barbarian women which was most graphically exemplified by literary and dramatic portrayals of Medea. As Edith Hall notes, it is precisely the fact that Andromache's character fails to conform to the Medea model which throws the Spartan characters' own transgressive deployments of deception and power into sharp relief.[156] For Hermione believes she will be a match for Andromache (160) and following a lengthy rhetorical altercation between the two women, she threatens Andromache in the language of trickery and concealment: 'such a bait do I have for you. But no more of that, for I will hide my words and the deed will soon speak for itself' (τοιόνδ' ἔχω σου δέλεαρ. ἀλλὰ γὰρ λόγους κρύψω, τὸ δ' ἔργον αὐτὸ σημανεῖ τάχα: 264–5).

Through the metaphorical use of δέλεαρ ('bait' or 'lure'), Hermione represents herself as a cunning huntress and casts Andromache in the role of a hunted animal. The term δέλεαρ is rarely attested in Greek literature. It is used by Xenophon's Socrates in a description of the way in which those who are not self-disciplined enough to be rulers of a state will be 'lured' away from their proper tasks by the prospect of physical indulgences such as food. They will satisfy their stomachs before fulfilling more important duties (Xen. *Mem.* 2.1.4). Hermione's use of the term similarly implies that Andromache's 'natural' inferiority is ripe for easy exploitation. But Hermione's deployment of the term δέλεαρ must also be understood in the light of the Athenian repre-

---

[155] Arthur (1973) 50.   [156] Hall (1989) 213f.

sentations of Spartan education which I discussed earlier. Hermione uses the language of hunting, which Athenian writers isolate as another prominent element of Spartan training, and applies it to her perceived female enemy.[157] In my next chapter I will argue that even a supposedly pro-Spartan writer like Xenophon articulates anxieties about military training in deception and cunning precisely because citizens may misuse trickery within the structures of their own polis or *oikos*. Hermione's self-representation as a cunning huntress, alongside a developing disjunction between her appearance and her character, mark her out as unhealthily duplicitous and her penchant for trickery and cunning are being linked to her Spartan identity. By revelling in her role as huntress and deceiver, Hermione gives herself the paradigmatically cruel and devious Spartan identity that is condemned by Thucydides' Pericles, Aristotle, Adrastus in *Supplices* and which will be elaborated upon in Andromache's extended attack on Spartan deceit (445–63).

It transpires that the lure which the Spartans set up activates a desire in Andromache which is far from base or selfish. When she falls prey to their trap, she does so in an act of self-sacrifice in order to preserve the life of her son. She has lost one son at Troy (10) and had regarded her new child as her one hope, protection and strength against troubles (26–8). These factors make the Spartan trick seem all the more cruel and Andromache's self-sacrifice all the more admirable. Hermione and Menelaus may treat Andromache and her son as sub-human prey and disposable bait but the subsequent action demonstrates the bankruptcy of their conceptions and methods. Later in the play we hear from Peleus that Helen's immorality and transgressive desire was the product of the Spartan woman's licence to join in the training activities of the Spartan male (595–600). Andromache will taunt Hermione with her similarity to her mother (229–31). It is worth noting that in Homer's *Odyssey*, Helen is presented as attempting to lure out the Greeks from the wooden horse by imitating the voices of their wives (4.266f.). For all her sophistication, Hermione's use of hunting imagery types her as following in her mother's footsteps and it becomes clear that it is she and not Andromache who has employed transgressive and inhuman forms of trickery.

In announcing that she will *conceal* her words concerning this trap (264), Hermione is perhaps taunting Andromache with the fact that the attempt to conceal her child has failed. Hermione too can play the game of concealment; she only has to hide her words for the deed of

[157] See Cartledge (1987) 31.

trickery to signify after it has been successfully executed. However, these boasts and threats are ironically framed by Andromache's earlier dispatch of the *therapaina*. As Hermione proclaims her superiority (160) and revels in her powers of deception, the audience knows that Andromache has already set in play another secret attempt to outwit the Spartans. In his first speech, Menelaus also boasts of his cleverness. He interprets his success in discovering Andromache's son as indicating that her mental capacities are inferior to his (ἀλλ' ἐφηυρέθης ἧσσον φρονοῦσα τοῦδε Μενέλεω, γύναι: 312–13). In the exchange of ruses, Hermione and Menelaus will be trumped, precisely because they make a flawed assessment of Andromache's intelligence and overvalue their own. For these 'noble' Greeks, the Asiatic Andromache's cunning is confined to the concoction of potions. At the level of rational planning and contrivance, they both regard themselves as superior. And it is true that Menelaus successfully lures Andromache away from the statue of Thetis. She believes his false guarantee that her child will live if she allows her own death (316f. and 381f.). There is a suggestion, however, that the ruse of a 'barbarian' and her slave have ensured that Peleus will arrive to prevent the disastrous outcome of Menelaus' trick.[158]

When she realises that she has been lured from sanctuary by a false promise, Andromache launches a scathing tirade against the deceptive and duplicitous qualities of Menelaus in particular, and Spartans in general. As Stevens notes, this speech is 'dramatically relevant' because Menelaus has coaxed her away from sanctuary with a false promise. But the tirade 'goes beyond what the situation requires, and was influenced by patriotic sentiment'.[159] There are several details of the speech which merit comment in relation to the notion of a 'hoplite ideal' being constructed through negative paradigms of deceit.

Andromache describes Spartans as 'weavers of evil devices' (μηχανορράφοι κακῶν: 447) which perhaps connotes a pejoratively female aspect of their trickery.[160] They are also dubbed 'lords of lies' (ψευδῶν ἄνακτες: 447). Tragedy employs this metaphorical sense of 'lord'

---

[158] A causal connection between the dispatch of the *therapaina* and the arrival of Peleus is never made explicit. The *therapaina* indicates that Andromache's previous attempts to summon Peleus may have failed because of the disloyalty of previous messengers (85). So there is an implication that the *therapaina's* loyalty will make a successful mission more likely.

[159] Stevens (1971) 148.

[160] See Kovacs (1980) 64: '... they are weavers of μηχαναί which puts them in the sphere of a certain kind of female striving'. (On the weaving of μηχαναί as a female characteristic, see nn. 144 and 146 above.)

(ἄναξ) to suggest mastery of oars or weapons.[161] By contrast the Spartans here have mastery only of the weaponry of deceit. Thus *apatē* becomes perjoratively opposed to the fair exchange of open combat. Andromache goes on to distort the narrative of the *Iliad* when she says that Hector 'often with his spear' made Menelaus into a sailor (ναύτην ἔθηκεν: 457). The immoral and duplicitous Spartan is represented as impotent when confronted with the genuine warrior values of Andromache's Trojan husband. Hector actually deprives Menelaus of his 'hoplite status' because he makes him into a sailor instead. In the following line (458), Andromache elaborates the theme of Menelaus' status as a soldier: 'now, appearing a fearsome hoplite (γοργὸς ὁπλίτης) you will kill me, a woman'. The comment is sarcastic: 'Menelaus can be a grim warrior when his opponent is a woman'.[162] But for a fifth-century audience who have already interpreted Andromache's words as alluding to and reinforcing a picture of their contemporary Spartan enemy as machinatory and deceitful, the phrase 'fearsome hoplite' would do more than simply question Menelaus' status as a 'true warrior'. It would have acted as a 'zooming device';[163] Menelaus, along with his wife (592f.) is being constructed as the archetypal Spartan of both the heroic past and the fifth-century present. He is not worthy of the classification 'hoplite' in the specifically Athenian sense of the word. To constantly rely on deceit and the feminine weaving of tricks, to be forced by one's opponent to become a sailor and to succeed with guile and violence against a woman are the mark of a man to whom the ideal term 'hoplite' could never be applied with any seriousness.

Andromache's construction of Menelaus as an anti-hoplite is paralleled in the play's subsequent representations of the ambush engineered by Orestes against Neoptolemus. When Peleus learns of Orestes' plans he explicitly raises the question of the way in which he will confront Neoptolemus: 'will you ambush him or fight him face-to-face?' (κρυπτὸς καταστὰς ἢ κατ' ὄμμ' ἐλθὼν μάχῃ;: 1064). The Messenger names Orestes as the offspring of his malevolently contrivant mother Clytemnestra (Κλυταιμήστρας τόκος: 1115) and echoes

---

[161] See Aesch. *Pers.* 378; Eur. *IA* 1260; *Alc.* 498; Eur. fr. 700 N².
[162] Stevens (1971) 150.
[163] I borrow the term 'zooming device' from Sourvinou-Inwood (1989) 134f. She uses this term to denote tragedy's deployment of words and ideas with specifically fifth-century application – for example, the description of Creon as a *stratēgos* in Sophocles' *Antigone* seems to connote the powerful elective office of the Athenian democracy. For a powerful critique of the uses and abuses of this critical notion see now Foley (1995).

Andromache's attribution of feminine wiles to Menelaus and the Spartan race (μηχανορράφος: 1116). Neoptolemus is described as a 'fearsome hoplite' (γοργὸς ὁπλίτης: 1123), an admiring application of exactly the phrase which Andromache used sarcastically of Menelaus.[164] In the final assault on him, Neoptolemus dodges projectiles and wields his shield in a 'terrible pyrrhic dance' (δεινὰς ... πυρρίχας: 1135). At Athens the *pyrrhikē* was a dance that was intimately associated with hoplite training for ephebes and involved the manipulation of the heavy hoplite shield.[165] The Athenian of Plato's *Laws* tells us that the *pyrrhikē* 'represents modes of eluding all kinds of shots and blows by swervings and duckings and side-leaps upward or crouching' (7.815a1–3). Thus a correlation between Neoptolemus' self-defence and the identity of a hoplite is being stressed. His hopeless attempts to survive the attack ironically imitate the dance-training designed for coping with similar, but much less treacherous attacks. Menelaus and Orestes are both being characterised as employing methods of deception and embodying values which are antithetical to those of the hoplite. Neoptolemus can hardly be read as a paradigm for sound Athenian citizen values but as a victim of misrepresentation and trickery, and through his confrontation of his attackers, he foregrounds the contrast between the open values of the hoplite and the distanced and underhand machinations of Menelaus and Orestes.

Thus far I have discussed this drama's negative constructions of Spartan identity in terms of non-hoplitic deception, the deceptive appearances afforded by the cosmetics of wealth and an association between pernicious cunning and Spartan education. Andromache's strictures concerning the disjunction between the trappings of wealth and actual merit could be compared with the funeral speech of the Thucydidean Pericles. Pericles boasts that Athenian democracy is premised on the notion that political distinction and public recognition are possible for all citizens of genuine excellence regardless of their

---

[164] This repetition is noted by Stevens (1971) 229. See also Poole (1994) 22–3, who points out that the contrast between the Thessalian Neoptolemus and the Spartan Menelaus can be mapped onto the fact that Thessalian cities were long-standing allies of Athens. He also shows that other Euripidean plays exhibit a contrast between Thessalians and Spartans to the disadvantage of the latter.

[165] For sources and further bibliography on the *pyrrhikē* at Athens see Borthwick (1970); Parke (1977) 36 and Plate 7; Winkler (1990a) 55–6; Von Reden and Goldhill (1999) 269. On Neoptolemus' Pyrrhic dance and Trojan leap (1139) see Borthwick (1967). Borthwick must be right to see a pun on Neoptolemus' other name Pyrrhus (*Cypria* fr. 16 D).

social or financial status.[166] I have already indicated that the character-isation of Menelaus and Hermione as devious and deceitful falls in line with a wider Athenian discourse of stereotyping and self-definition. Again, the Thucydidean funeral speech was seen to offer an exemplary formulation of this discourse. But it may be a gross distortion to read this drama purely as a propagandistic text of Athenian self-definition. Although Menelaus is set up as a paradigmatically duplicitous Spartan, both Andromache and Peleus comment on his position as a military and political leader in terms which bring his questionable conduct much closer to the internal concerns of the Athenian democratic polis. It is far from original to suggest either that this or many other Attic tragedies engage with the structure and rhetoric of democratic poli-tics.[167] However, in the light of recent tendencies to read tragedies *simply* as performance texts which reinforce Athenian constructions of the 'other', and to advance my own argument concerning Athenian representations of deceit in the political sphere, I wish to highlight Andromache's and Peleus' comments on leadership and political reputation.[168]

---

[166] Thuc. 2.37.1: '... in public life men gain preference because of their deserts, when anybody has a good reputation for anything: what matters is not rotation but ex-cellence. As for poverty, if a man is able to do some good to the polis, he is not pre-vented by the obscurity of his distinction' (... κατὰ δὲ τὴν ἀξίωσιν, ὡς ἕκαστος ἔν τῳ εὐδοκιμεῖ, οὐκ ἀπὸ μέρους τὸ πλέον ἐς τὰ κοινὰ ἢ ἀπ' ἀρετῆς προτιμᾶται, οὐδ' αὖ κατὰ πενίαν, ἔχων γέ τι ἀγαθὸν δρᾶσαι τὴν πόλιν, ἀξιώματος ἀφανείᾳ κεκώλυται). The in-terpretation of this passage is vexed: see Hornblower (1991) 300–1 for discussion and bibliography. I am not convinced, *pace* Hornblower's comments and Roberts (1984) 73, that this passage necessarily or simply implies that those who are poor can *only* benefit their city by holding one of the democracy's routine rotating offices as opposed to gaining an elective generalship. Certainly a distinction is made between rotation offices (ἀπὸ μέρους) and rewards of merit (ἀπ' ἀρετῆς). But where Hornblower trans-lates ἀξιώματος ἀφανείᾳ as 'lack of authority' or 'lack of distinction', I would argue that 'obscurity of distinction' could be an equally valid translation. Finley (1973) 24 similarly translates the phrase as 'whatever the obscurity of his condition'. Pericles' point could be that recognised excellence is rewarded by election to an office of higher prestige than routine posts, but that a poor citizen of low profile can still gain recog-nition and then election to a generalship if he benefits the city. Perhaps we have a deliberately vague formulation of the kind identified elsewhere in the speech by Loraux (1986) 250. In this case, Thucydides' Pericles would be espousing the ideal of equality of opportunity whilst implicitly recognising that in practice some citizens are more equal than others. See Ober (1989) 194.

[167] On *Andromache* in particular, see, for example, the low-key comments of Stevens (1971) 173–9. For tragedy's engagement with Athens' legal and political discourses, see for example Zuntz (1963); Saïd (1978); Goldhill (1988a) 222–43; Ober and Strauss (1990). On specific plays' engagement with questions of leadership in the democracy, see Buxton (1982); Sourvinou-Inwood (1989); Griffith (1995); Rose (1995); Rosenbloom (1995); Foley (1995); Bowie (1997).

[168] For an excellent account of the oscillation between 'self' and 'other' in Euripides see Croally (1994) 103–15.

Menelaus marks his first entrance with a vicious ultimatum to Andromache (309–18). He has found her son and will only spare him if she gives herself up to be killed. It transpires later that this is the trap of which Hermione has spoken. Menelaus intends to kill mother and child. Andromache replies with an outburst on the subject of false appearances and undeserved reputation which I will examine in more detail in my final chapter (319–63). Andromache exclaims that Menelaus' reputation (*doxa*) is undeserved and sarcastically wonders whether someone as low (*phaulos*) as him could have led the chosen men of Greece against Troy (319–25).

At the end of her speech, Andromache points out that because of a quarrel over a woman Menelaus destroyed her native city (361–63). Kovacs links these final lines to her earlier reflections on Menelaus' true nature: 'His worthlessness is proved in this present instant by the disproportion between this petty quarrel between two women and Menelaus' grossly exaggerated reaction. But come to think of it, the Trojan War, far from providing prima facie evidence of Menelaus' worth, is in fact another proof of his distorted values, since he raised an army and destroyed Troy all for the sake of a woman.'[169] In his confrontation with Menelaus, Peleus develops this evaluation of the war as caused by Menelaus' base sense of proportion (590–641). Menelaus defends his right to protect the interests of his daughter and criticises Neoptolemus for introducing a Trojan woman into his household (645–77). When he speaks of his generalship (στρατηγίαν: 678), Menelaus' arguments are less convincing. He argues sophistically that Helen was chosen by the gods to commit adultery and thereby enabled Greece to grow to manhood when it had previously been innocent of arms and battles (680–4).[170]

Peleus responds that throughout Greece custom is badly conceived (καθ' Ἑλλάδ' ὡς κακῶς νομίζεται: 693). He continues with some damning comments about generalship. Peleus bemoans the fact that when an army triumphs over their enemy,[171] it is the general (*strategos*) who gains in reputation (*dokesis*) (ὁ στρατηγὸς τὴν δόκησιν ἄρνυται:

---

[169] Kovacs (1980) 61. The notions that the war and suffering at Troy are disproportionately large and that Helen is to be reviled are commonplaces: see Hom. *Od.* 11.438; Aesch. *Ag.* 1455–7; Eur. *Cyc.* 177f. and 280f., *Troad.* 975ff., *El.* 213, *IT* 525; Gorg. *Hel.* 2 (= DK 82 B11.2).

[170] See Helen's self-defence before Hecuba and Menelaus at Eur. *Troad.* 924–50 for a similar argument.

[171] τροπαῖα πολεμίων στήσῃ literally means 'set up trophies of the enemy' but Stevens (1971) 179, argues that the phrase came to mean 'triumph over'. See Eur. *Andr.* 763 and Soph. *Trach.* 1102. But as Stevens notes, the literal sense may also be appropriate here.

696). Those who did all the hard work are ignored. All the talk is about the general (οὐδὲν πλέον δρῶν ἑνὸς ἔχει πλείω λόγον: 698), even though he brandished a single spear like everyone else (697). Arrogantly, those who have authority in the polis think they are better than the people, though they themselves are nobodies (σεμνοὶ δ' ἐν ἀρχαῖς ἥμενοι κατὰ πτόλιν φρονοῦσι δήμου μεῖζον, ὄντες οὐδένες: 699–700). Peleus claims that the masses are infinitely wiser when they are gifted with boldness and purpose (οἱ δ' εἰσὶν αὐτῶν μυρίῳ σοφώτεροι, εἰ τόλμα προσγένοιτο βούλησίς θ' ἅμα: 701–2).[172] He then accuses Menelaus and Agamemnon of basking lazily in their generalship whilst others suffered and toiled (703–5).

It has been suggested that Peleus' criticisms might be directed at the demagogue Cleon, who assumed command of a military expedition during the siege of Pylos in 425.[173] However, there can be no certainty of this and I would prefer (albeit tentatively) to see the attack on *stratēgoi* as a more sweeping reflection on elite leadership and the institution of the *stratēgia* at Athens. Peleus' attack on the undeserved reputation of generals is prefaced as bad custom *throughout Greece*. An Athenian audience could have taken this to be an attack on the priorities of Greek heroic leadership implied in Homeric epic. And the *Iliad's* representation of Agamemnon as a flawed *basileus* sets off a poetic tradition of criticising military commanders: one thinks of the iambic poet Archilochus despising a 'tall *stratēgos*' or one 'who is proud of his hair' and preferring a short and bowlegged man who is 'firm on his feet and full of heart' (fr. 60).[174] Peleus' use of the term *stratēgos* may not have been a 'zooming device' that would provoke the Athenian audience to reflect on 'generalship' in their own present-day experience. Even if it did cause them to think of contemporary leadership, they might have read 'throughout Greece' as referring to everywhere *except* Athens in the same way that modern Britons do not always think of themselves being addressed when politicians refer to 'Europe' or 'Europeans'. But if an Athenian audience *did* interpret

---

[172] These lines (699–702) are bracketed in Diggle's OCT. My argument is not substantially altered by accepting their deletion.

[173] See Stevens (1971) 178 who relates Peleus' words to Ar. *Eq.* 392: κᾆτ' ἀνὴρ ἔδοξεν εἶναι τἀλλότριον ἀμῶν θέρος. For Cleon's assumption of Nicias' command and his joint leadership with the general Demosthenes in the siege of Pylos see Thuc. 4.27ff. The Aristophanic reference perhaps picks up Cleon's claim that if the generals were men they would take another fleet to Pylos and take the Spartans by force. Nicias and the people then forced Cleon to lead the expedition himself, and the Aristophanic line implies that the success he claimed was due to Demosthenes rather than himself. Such a specific reference would mean the play was performed after 425.

[174] On Agamemnon as a bad leader in the *Iliad*, see Taplin (1990).

Peleus' comments as encompassing their own generals, then such an interpretation is significant for the play's representation of honesty and deception.

The term *stratēgos* which Peleus uses has a specific resonance for fifth-century Athens. It is usually translated as 'general' but being a *stratēgos* at Athens involved much more than military leadership.[175] Athenian *stratēgoi* were elected by the people, and until the late fifth century they tended to come from Athens' archaic aristocratic families.[176] Even after Pericles' death, *stratēgoi* and the demagogues who either challenged their power or aspired to it were wealthy. They spoke in the *ecclēsia*, offered advice on policy and moved important legislation. Thucydides commented that Pericles' power and influence over the demos as a general had made Athens a democracy in name only.[177] Although this may be an exaggeration, it is clear that the ten annually elected generals were the most important representatives of the democratic polis.

Like all holders of office, however, *stratēgoi* were subject to official reviews of their conduct. Furthermore, *stratēgoi* and other public speakers were vulnerable to indictment on the proposal of any citizen who judged that they had moved illegal decrees, unlawful laws or a policy which had not worked.[178] They could even find themselves expelled for ten years via the procedure of ostracism.[179] Even if we

---

[175] However, after the death of Pericles and as the Peloponnesian War brought about new, complex forms of warfare, the *stratēgoi* tended to be military specialists and they were away from Athens for long periods. In the late fifth and throughout the fourth centuries, political advisers to the demos often formed a separate group from its military leaders. See Perlman (1963). However, the split between orators and generals was far from complete and there were exceptions. See Roberts (1982) 171–3; Ober (1989) 91–3. As Ober points out (120), even in the fourth century extant speeches indicate that orators (*rhētores*) and *stratēgoi* were perceived as performing parallel functions and as constituting a politically powerful group in contrast to *idiōtai*. See Dem. 18.171; Hyp. 4.27, 5.24; Din. 3.19 for this grouping together of *rhētores* and *stratēgoi* in terms of elite status and political accountability.

[176] Themistocles represents a partial exception. Henderson (1990) describes him as a member of the lesser aristocracy. Cf. Ar. *Eq.* 810–19, where the 'nouveau' politician Cleon compares himself to Themistocles.

[177] Thuc. 2.65.9: 'It was a democracy in name, but in fact it was rule by the first man' (ἐγίγνετό τε λόγῳ μὲν δημοκρατία, ἔργῳ δὲ ὑπὸ τοῦ πρώτου ἀνδρὸς ἀρχή).

[178] See Cartledge, Millett and Todd (1990) 215–40, s.v. *euthunē; dokimasia; eisangelia; graphē paranomōn; graphē; probolē*.

[179] On ostracism, see Kagan (1961); Rosivach (1987); Roberts (1982) 142–4. Christ (1992) and Ober (1989) 73–5, stress the important symbolic message which the practice of ostracism carried for the citizenry. Hence Ober: '[T]he experience of arbitrarily expelling a prominent citizen, for the simple and sufficient error of standing out too obviously from the group, was an important lesson in the collective power of the masses to impose upon elites a degree of conformity to popular conceptions of proper public behaviour' (75).

discount the bitter critiques of certain post-Periclean *stratēgoi* and politicians who aspired to command which we find in Thucydides and Aristophanic comedy,[180] it is clear that the loyalty, honesty and integrity of individual generals was constantly subjected to debate and scrutiny.

If *Andromache* was performed at the City Dionysia, Peleus' comments on *stratēgoi* gained polemical force from the fact that all ten elected *stratēgoi* would have been present in the audience. Prior to the dramatic contests at the festival, all ten elected generals performed libations.[181] While this pre-play ceremony affirmed their status and power as leading representatives in the democracy, Peleus' comments would perhaps have invited the wider citizen audience to question whether those representatives were truly worthy of that power and status. These comments are veiled, as one would expect from a tragedy. Nevertheless, Peleus' emphasis on the tension between the honour and renown solely attributed to generals and the possibilities of collective wisdom and military commitment would perhaps resonate in a polis which afforded power, privilege and recognition to individual *stratēgoi* over and above the demos and yet valorised democratic decision making, equality before the law (*isonomia*) and collective military action as central ideological tenets. As I suggested above, this interrogation of generals' claims to competence and honour, along with an accusation of elitist attitudes, would also sit uneasily with a pre-play ceremony involving Athens' ten *stratēgoi*.

On this reading, Menelaus is not simply characterised as the typically deceptive Spartan. Andromache's verbal attacks and the self-representations of Hermione and Menelaus develop a series of terms through which their deployment of deceit, cunning and wealthy appearances are marked as resolutely unAthenian. But the terms in which Menelaus' status as a *stratēgos* are discussed have more uneasy ramifications for an Athenian audience. His behaviour prompts reflections on leadership which problematise an ideal representation of unscrupulous dishonesty, unwarranted status and a bogus reputation for wisdom as attributes which could not be applied to an Athenian. Menelaus seems to be typically Spartan but if, as Peleus suggests, he is just like a host of other *stratēgoi* throughout Greece (καθ' Ἑλλάδ'), then this play highlights the uncomfortable possibility that Athens' political and military representatives are no better than the enemy.

---

[180] See Henderson (1990).
[181] See Goldhill (1990) 100–1 for the evidence and a discussion of this opening ceremony, one of four which were 'closely linked to a sense of the authority and dignity of the *polis*' (106).

Menelaus' duplicitous character and actions make any description of him as a hoplite problematic. But deception and Athenian generalship are not necessarily incompatible, as a remark from an early fourth-century speech of Andocides demonstrates. Andocides is justifying his decision, as a delegate invested with power to negotiate peace with Sparta, to refer the terms of settlement to the assembly rather than agreeing to those terms on the spot. He represents his consultation with the assembly as a commitment to openness. He says that he opposes those who argue that 'no one ... has ever saved the Athenian people by open persuasion: measures for its good must be secret or disguised' (3.33). Andocides explains his opposition in the following terms:

I admit, Athenians, that in time of war a general (*stratēgos*) who is friendly to the polis and experienced should employ secrecy or deception (*lanthanonta ... exapatōnta*) in leading the majority of his men into danger. But when a peace to include the whole of Greece is being negotiated, an agreement to which sworn assent will be given and which will be recorded on public monuments, I deny that the negotiators should employ secrecy and deception. (Andocides 3.34)

Andocides argues that a *stratēgos* must practise secrecy and deception, even on his own men, but ambassadors[182] must never be deceptive towards the demos. The remark does demonstrate a need to distinguish between deception as practised in the context of the battlefield and deception as practised on the demos. In a sense, then, Menelaus' use of deceit as a *stratēgos* is compatible with Athenian perceptions of a general's military responsibilities. We shall see in the following chapter that the extent to which military deceit is admissible is a charged and negotiable question in Athenian public discourse.

However (and this is an issue to which I will also return) Andocides' distinction between the military responsibility of generals to deploy *apatē* and the internal political responsibility of ambassadors not to deceive the people, tacitly acknowledges the possibility that all Athens' advisers (*stratēgoi* included) may deceive the people. Indeed, he makes the distinction in order to strengthen his view that it was right for his delegation to be open with the people, when others had counselled deception and secrecy. Given that a *stratēgos* was often involved in internal politics as much as military campaigning, the representation and evaluation of Menelaus in the *Andromache* hints at the problem of the deceptive enemy within Athens' democratic process at the same

---

[182] As Ober (1989) 92, remarks, 'ambassadors' effectively refers to Athens' elite politicians.

time as it projects a much stronger image of duplicity as a uniquely Spartan (and therefore unAthenian) characteristic.

In this chapter, I have introduced and discussed many of the key areas of concern for the study of the representation and evaluation of deceit in classical Athens. I have demonstrated that notions of civic and national identity are mobilised in the public evaluation of deceit. I have started to explore the extent to which 'deceit of the demos' is recognised as a problem for Athens' spaces of political and legal debate and the ways in which that problem is represented and negotiated. I have begun my account of the orators' *strategic* manipulation of this problem. In later chapters I will return to the public representation of 'deceiving the demos'. But in the next chapter I wish to focus on the representation of a different trajectory of deceit and a different area of negotiation and anxiety. We turn now to the ideological and moral consequences and connotations of deceiving an enemy as discussed in Athenian oratory, drama, philosophy and historiography.

2 Deceiving the enemy: negotiation and anxiety

We are bred up to feel it a disgrace ever to succeed by falsehood ... we will keep hammering along with the conviction that honesty is the best policy, and that truth always wins in the long run. These pretty little sentiments do well for a child's copy-book but a man who acts on them had better sheath his sword for ever.[1]

These words were written by Sir Garnet Wolseley, a former Commander-in-Chief of the British army, for *The Soldier's Handbook* of 1869. They were recycled in the form of a plaque which hung in the operations room of the London Controlling Section, a secret bureau set up by Churchill during the Second World War which was specifically tasked to plan stratagems to deceive the Germans about Allied operations. Churchill famously remarked that 'in war-time, truth is so precious, that she should be attended by a bodyguard of lies'.[2]

Sociologists, historians and journalists have categorised warfare as an area of human activity where lies are to be expected.[3] But the morality of using deceit against an enemy has often required exploration and explanation. For Christian theologians, the use of lies and tricks against an enemy has been justified by placing such tactics under the general rubric of 'just war theory'.[4] Wolseley's words betray an anxiety at the same time as they proclaim military deceit as a necessity: warfare entails a setting aside of the moral teaching that 'honesty is the best

---

[1] Kerr (1990) 362. Extract taken from Cave-Brown (1976).

[2] Kerr (1990) 366. Taken from Cave-Brown (1976).

[3] See Barnes (1994) 23–9 for discussion, bibliography and references. In 1928 the Labour politician and pacifist Arthur Ponsonby said that 'when war is declared, the first casualty is truth'.

[4] For example, the seventeenth-century theologian Jeremy Taylor makes a distinction between 'deception' of an enemy during hostilities and 'lying' to an enemy when making a peace-treaty: 'In a just war it is lawful to deceive the unjust enemy, but not to lie; that is, by semblances and strategies ... by simulation or dissimulation, "by force or craft, openly or secretly," any way that you can, unless you promise to the contrary ... [B]ut if there be a treaty or a contract ... then to tell a lie or to falsify does destroy peace and justice.' Quotation from an extract of Taylor's essay 'The Rule of Conscience' in Kerr (1990) 121–2.

policy' which is contained in the 'child's copy-book'. Deception in warfare complicates a straightforward education and upbringing in the virtues of truth-telling. One of the concerns of this chapter will be to explore whether the obvious value of military trickery creates moral and educational worries in extant Athenian writing.

This chapter will also be concerned to confront the extent to which Athenian public oratory, drama and philosophical writing can represent 'deceit of an enemy' as positive and praiseworthy. In the previous chapter, much of my discussion centred on Thucydides' funeral speech and its negative evaluation of military deception. This speech and the section on deceit in particular were deemed useful for British official-dom during the First and Second World Wars:

> In 1915, placards on London buses displayed excerpts from Perikles' funeral speech, intended to remind the heirs of Athenian culture of the values for which they were fighting. In 1940, the future head of Scientific Intelligence in Britain quoted from the same speech in an official report, to illustrate the dangers for a state of war of the Athenian quality of openness: 'Athens lost the war.'[5]

This twentieth-century manipulation of the Periclean funeral speech for the purposes of propaganda and military planning serves to illustrate the way in which civic and military ideals can be either promoted, questioned or ignored, depending on the particular rhetorical *strategy* which is being deployed. The head of Scientific Intelligence goes behind the propagandistic value of equating 'Britain the True' with 'Open Athens' to make a strong case for secrecy and deception of the enemy in wartime. Did Athenian writers discard or manipulate the ideology of 'openness' in a similar fashion and how open were they in doing so with respect to military trickery?

Vidal-Naquet, the *ephēbeia* and military trickery

In the previous chapter, I argued that Athenian civic discourse represents military trickery as unAthenian. One of my starting points for an examination of this strand of civic discourse was Vidal-Naquet's analysis of the Apatouria festival and the myth of Melanthus which he associates with it.[6] This analysis has been subjected to several lines of attack. It has been argued, for example, that Vidal-Naquet overstates

---

[5] Millett (1993) 179. Millett is himself drawing on the findings of Turner (1981) 187 and Jones (1978) 109–10.

[6] See Vidal-Naquet (1986a) 86–106, which is a revised version of Vidal-Naquet (1968). See also Vidal-Naquet (1986b) for further thoughts and responses to critics.

the case for the existence of an Athenian ephebate as long as two centuries before the legislation of Lycurgus and his associates in the late
fourth century.[7] The validity of a substantive link between the Melanthus myth and the pre-Lycurgan Apatouria has also been questioned.[8]
On the other hand, there is enough evidence to suggest that, even in
the early fourth century, young men between the ages of sixteen and
eighteen did some form of non-hoplitic military service, much of it involving security duties on the borders of Attica or Athens itself.[9] And it
seems almost certain that, in the fifth century, these young men had to
swear a 'hoplite oath' when they came of age.[10] Of course, neither of
these points proves the existence of an archaic or fifth-century 'liminal'
ephēbeia as envisaged by Vidal-Naquet. However, his idea of an 'in-
between period' involving institutionalised practices and associated
stories which were anti-hoplitic gains some credence when we think of
the deceptive behaviour of young male characters in Attic tragedy.[11]

Vidal-Naquet's argument also becomes more plausible when we remember that his idea of a liminal initiation is exemplified more fully by
the Spartan *krupteia* and has been identified securely in many other
cultures around the world.[12] But even if the Melanthus story is to be
associated with a pre-Lycurgan Apatouria and/or some kind of official
ephēbeia, does the story necessarily attest the symbolic 'liminality' of
the Athenian 'citizen-in-waiting'? Does the myth of Melanthus demonstrate that the Athenian ephebate was the same or performed the
same (practical or symbolic) function as the Spartan *krupteia*?[13] These
questions are important for the study of *apatē* at Athens because they

---

[7] Even before Vidal-Naquet's original article, there had been much debate about a possible archaic or fifth-century origin of an Athenian ephebate. See Pélékidis (1962) 7–17
for a survey of opinion.
[8] See Maxwell-Stuart (1970) 113–16.
[9] For the evidence see Ober (1985b) 91–6 and Reinmuth (1971) 126.
[10] See Siewert (1977). Reinmuth (1971) 124ff., concludes that the *ephēbeia* was begun in
the early fifth century, although Lycurgus' legislative programme in the 330s must have
affected the status of the institution.
[11] E.g. Orestes in Aeschylus' *Choephoroi* or Neoptolemus in Sophocles' *Philoctetes*. See,
however, the critiques of Goldhill (1984) 163 and 196f., (1990) 120–3.
[12] See Jeanmaire (1913) 121–50; (1939) 382–3. On African rites of passage and the notion
of the adolescent *communitas* prior to integration into adult society see Van Gennep
(1909) and Turner (1967), (1969). But see also Kennell (1995) 143–6 on the dangers
of viewing such rites as 'primitive' or unchanging and (hence) a means of reconstructing archaic Greek rituals.
[13] See Winkler (1990a) 34; 'It is not necessarily the case that the youngest Athenian soldiers in this period were much exercised in mountain foraging and ambuscades as
Vidal-Naquet concludes from the Spartan parallel.' However as Winkler concedes,
Vidal-Naquet (1986b) 142 clarifies his position on this point: 'What was true of the
Athenian ephebe *at the level of myth* is true of the Spartan *kruptos* in practice.'

translate into a more specific problem: is the verbal trickery associated with the myth of Melanthus a certain mark of an ideological construction of *apatē* as a notion which is fundamentally opposed to the civic and military image of the ideal Athenian, or could it have had a positive symbolic force? We also need to ask whether *apatē* really is always a purely negative term which defines a positive ideal of civic identity and adult male moral agency. Are these boundaries between honesty and deceit never contested or questioned?

One of the difficulties with Vidal-Naquet's analysis lies in its lack of chronological reference points. This shortcoming is partly dictated by the fact that the evidence pertaining to the Melanthus myth is very late.[14] Vidal-Naquet admits and bemoans this problem but his approach also evinces the influence of structural anthropology, with all the problems such influence *can* have for historicist interpretation.[15] We have to ask ourselves whether the myths and rituals of liminal initiation as identified by Van Gennep and Turner can be insulated from history. Does the symbolic meaning of such rituals remain the same in the face of societal change? Was the myth of Melanthus as symbolically stable for the Athenians as it is for Vidal-Naquet? Did the story simply have meaning in relation to ephebes? Was it told only in the context of the Apatouria? Vidal-Naquet refers briefly to the fact that military tactics involving deceit and trickery became widespread during the Peloponnesian War.[16] He reflects that the mythic trickery of Melanthus and the non-hoplitic behaviour of the ephebe become a reality in the tactics of adult warriors and their leaders in the second half of the fifth century. But he does not consider the possible consequences of this

---

[14] See Vidal-Naquet (1986a) 123 n. 15 for the sources. One possible exception to the lateness of the sources is Hellanicus 323a *FGrH* F23 (Scholiast T on Pl. *Symp.* 208d). I will discuss this source in the next section.

[15] See Vidal-Naquet (1986b) 126–7: 'Rather the "Black Hunter" was the first endeavour, as far as I know, by a Greek Historian to use specifically, if critically, Lévi-Straussian concepts to understand some features of Ancient Greek society.' On the uneasy relationship between *some* versions of structuralism and considerations of historical change and crisis, see Gordon (1981) 1–15, who points out that different members of the 'Paris School' have different perspectives on 'history'. See also the programmatic comments of Buxton (1994) 1–6. Ma (1994) 72 offers an excellent 'meta-scholarly' meditation on the advantages and drawbacks of Vidal-Naquet's approach: 'Because of its aetiological fascination with the archaeology of origins, such an approach cannot adequately deal with the historical, sublunary dimension of things. The intersection between the structuralist gaze and the empirical question: "I wonder what happened?": is a problematic question.'

[16] Vidal-Naquet (1986a) 120. See also Pritchett (1974) 156ff. who argues that ambuscades are still rare in the Peloponnesian War. For a view of Thucydides' account of the war as exemplifying a new emphasis on *apatē* and *technē* in Greek warfare see Heza (1974), *passim*; Saïd and Trédé (1985) 66–72.

change in military conduct for Athens' ideal self-image. Ideologies and collective moral codes have the epistemological status of what Loraux calls 'the imaginary'. But, as Loraux herself demonstrates, the construction of this 'imaginary' can undergo alteration as it seeks to negotiate changes in social structures and discursive practices.[17]

If, at the level of the Lévi-Straussian 'deep structure', the Melanthus myth can represent and mark inversion of normative categories only prior to integration, we still have to consider how the myth or its signifying force could have been manipulated and interpreted in Athens' developing 'surface structure' discourses. Lack of evidence means that such consideration cannot be direct or conclusive. But I hope to show that the ideological notion of *apatē* as unAthenian is sometimes contested or modified. Vidal-Naquet's analysis is based on a conception of Athenian ideology which does not take account of the extent to which Athens' political, legal and philosophical discourses re-negotiate the boundaries of Athenian self-definition in order to include a possible place for *apatē*. In this chapter, then, I want to explore some voices which qualify and problematise any tidy definition of Athenian values as excluding the possibility of deceit and trickery as legitimate practices to use against an enemy. Following discussion of *apatē* in relation to the enemy, I will engage an Athenian text where discussion of an education in military trickery goes hand in hand with anxious discussion of the morality and (un)desirability of deceit between friends (*philoi*) and fellow citizens (*politai*).

Tricky Codrus: son of the 'Black Hunter'

One of the major sources used in Vidal-Naquet's discussion of the myth of Melanthus is a scholion to Plato's *Symposium*.[18] The scholion glosses Diotima's passing reference to Codrus, an early king of Attica. For Socrates' Diotima, Codrus is to be placed alongside Alcestis and Achilles because they all sacrificed themselves for the sake of others. She explains that they only sacrificed themselves because they knew that the memory of their virtue would be immortal.[19] With respect to Codrus, Diotima speaks as if her fictional audiences are fully aware of

---

[17] See Loraux (1986) chs. 2 and 6.

[18] Hellanicus 323a *FGrH* F23 (Scholiast T on Pl. *Symp.* 208d).

[19] Pl. *Symp.* 208d4–6: 'Do you suppose', she asked, 'that Alcestis would have died for Admetus, or Achilles would have sought death on the corpse of Patroclus, or your own Codrus would have welcomed it to save the kingdom of his children, if they had not expected to win a deathless memory for excellence (ἀθάνατον μνήμην ἀρετῆς) which now we keep?'

his story. All she says is that Codrus died 'so as to preserve the throne for his sons'. She does not mention the manner of Codrus' death. She refers to the king as 'your Codrus', implying that he is particularly associated with Athens and perhaps that his story was generally held to be exemplary for Athenians.

The scholion, claiming the fifth-century historian Hellanicus as its source, details the lineage of Codrus. Codrus' father was Melanthus and the scholion describes his duel with Xanthus. The scholiast perhaps included the duel because he was just copying Hellanicus' entire account of Codrus and his lineage, an account which itself highlighted the extraordinary contest. On the other hand, the scholiast may have stitched the narrative together himself, explaining Melanthus' appropriation of power in order to clarify Codrus' reign. But the story of Melanthus' ruse also offers a thematic link with the scholion's account of Codrus' death. The latter is provided as an explanation of Diotima's passing reference.[20] We are told (and the source is probably still Hellanicus) that during the reign of Codrus, the Dorians invaded Attica. The Delphic oracle had told the Dorians that they would defeat Athens if Codrus' life was spared. Codrus heard about this oracle and when the Dorians had surrounded Athens, he disguised himself as a woodcutter. Taking an axe with him, he left the safety of the city and set out towards the enemy. Two Dorian soldiers encountered him and Codrus killed one of them. The other Dorian was fooled by the disguise and killed Codrus. In accordance with the oracle, Athens could no longer be captured and the Dorians withdrew. The scholion says that Codrus' eldest son Medon became king.

If this story really does come from a history by Hellanicus then it may have been circulating in fifth-century Athens. The fifth-century historian Pherecydes may also have written the same story.[21] Inscriptional evidence shows that there was a sanctuary dedicated to Codrus on the outskirts of Athens from the early fifth century onwards.[22] The testimony of Pausanias indicates that the sanctuary was believed to

---

[20] Hellanicus 323a *FGrH* F23. For an exhaustive list of sources referring to Codrus, see Schlering *RE* XI, 984–94.

[21] Pherecydes *FGrH* 1.98.110 (= Poll. 10.128).

[22] See Wheeler (1887) for the text of the inscription and discussion. The inscription is in the form of a decree and can be dated to 418/17. It is concerned with the leasing and maintenance of a sanctuary of the cult of Codrus, Neleus and Basile. See also Wycherley (1960) 60–6; Shapiro (1986) 134–6. Burn (1989) 65–7 argues that Codrus and Basile gained fresh prominence in Athenian cult and art in late fifth-century Athens. For general discussion of the Athenian hero-cult of Codrus and its representation in public art, see Krön (1976) 271 ff.

have marked the spot where Codrus fell.[23] But we cannot be sure that Diotima is referring to exactly the same story as that outlined in the scholion. A kylix vase painting of c. 430 has been used to argue that there was another very different version of Codrus' exploit.[24] It depicts Codrus in full hoplite armour, apparently (though by no means certainly) bidding farewell to an older man called Ainetus.[25] The scene occupies the inside of the cup. The other two scenes on the outside of the kylix seem to depict farewells and departures by mythological figures who have a connection with Athens. Theseus as an armed ephebe leaves his father Aigeus and is accompanied by Phorbas. The latter is dressed as a hoplite and Medea is handing him his helmet. On the other side of the cup, Ajax and Mnestheus take their leave of Lycaeus (brother of Aigeus and eponymous hero of the Athenian district of the Lycaeus) and Melite (eponymous heroine of a city deme). Mnestheus is beckoned on by Athena.[26] So, these outer scenes are linked by the themes of farewell and departure but it is hard to tell which conflict or adventure Theseus is departing for.[27] The Ajax and Mnestheus scene probably depicts their departure for Troy.[28] Given this thematic link between the two outer scenes, it is attractive to see the Codrus scene as a representation of the king before he goes out to fight the Dorian invaders. This representation of Codrus as a hoplite is a far cry from Hellanicus' depiction of him donning the disguise of a woodcutter to confront the Dorians on his own. As Lissarrague has shown, there are many fifth-century vases which depict identified or unidentified hoplite warriors taking their leave of older men, and/or women, and/or lightly armed assistants.[29] It has been suggested that the picture of Codrus on the Bologna kylix does not refer to any mythological narrative circulating in Athens and is an isolated improvisation by the vase painter.[30] But the other scenes do seem to refer to specific events in myth which

---

[23] Paus. 1.19.6; Wheeler (1887); Harrison and Verrall (1890) 228–9.

[24] *LIMC* 1.2 309, Aenetos 1; *ARV*² 1268, no. 1.; *CVA* Bologna PU 273.

[25] Burn (1989) 66 conjectures that Ainetus is a seer who revealed to Codrus the manner of his death or else an otherwise unknown Attic hero.

[26] On the vase, Mnestheus' stance and position parallel that of Phorbas in the other scene. Interestingly, Mnestheus is dressed similarly to the ephebic Theseus in the other scene. Both have the same hat, cloak and do not have shields. Mnestheus' companion Ajax occupies a parallel position to Theseus, but, like Phorbas, he is dressed as a hoplite.

[27] Theseus may be departing to fight the Amazons; Burn (1989) 66.

[28] Burn (1989) 66. At Hom. *Il.* 2.545–56, Mnestheus is the leader of the Athenian contingent in the Greek expedition to Troy.

[29] Lissarrague (1989).

[30] Harrison and Verrall (1890) cxliii.

would have been recognisable. Thus there may have been a simpler story which did not involve a ruse – perhaps a version in which the Athenians engaged the Dorians in battle and Codrus was killed in the fight.[31] I will return to the significance of an alternative version without a ruse later. For the present, I wish to refer to the version outlined by the scholion and a very important instantiation of it in a legal speech from the fourth century.

Like Diotima, Vidal-Naquet gives a passing reference to Codrus.[32] Unlike Diotima, he acknowledges that Codrus is said to have been involved in a military deception. He sees that this story is thematically linked with the ruse deployed by Codrus' father, Melanthus. Because Vidal-Naquet is primarily interested in the details of Melanthus' duel and its representation as an *aition* for the Apatouria, he leaves the Codrus tale to one side and does not explore its significance as an Athenian myth of deception. But if, as Vidal-Naquet recognises, the scholion/Hellanicus fragment demonstrates a kinship between Codrus and Melanthus which is grounded in military *mētis* as well as biology, then we need to take great care in privileging the cultural significance of the one story over the other. The Melanthus story may well be related to an Athenian *rite de passage*. Codrus' ruse is not valorised as an *aition* for any Athenian institution or ceremony but, as I will show, it *is* used ideologically in Athenian public discourse. Furthermore, Vidal-Naquet starts with a premise that the features of the Melanthus tale correspond to notions which are paradigmatically opposed to the Athenan hoplite ideal. It is impossible to deny that *apatē* is a negative term in several texts which discuss and define Athenian identity and values; my previous chapter attempted to show how this strand of ideological opposition is manipulated in Athens' political and legal discourses. But this ideological opposition represents only *one* identifiable construction of *apatē*. Through the figure of Codrus, this section aims to show, not that Vidal-Naquet's particular conclusions are necessarily wrong, but that his and other scholars' premises are too re-

---

[31] Arist. *Pol.* 5.1310b36 refers to Codrus saving the city in the context of a discussion of men becoming kings through recognition of great benefits they have brought about for their community. This implies that there was a tradition in which Codrus saved Athens and survived *before* he became king. Is Aristotle referring to a version where Codrus somehow drives away the Dorians and is made king as a consequence? Or is this another exploit of Codrus entirely? Newman (1902) 420, suggests that Aristotle is making an error, but it is always possible that Aristotle and the Bologna kylix describe a completely different exploit by Codrus and not an alternative version of his death during the Dorian invasion.

[32] Vidal-Naquet (1986a) 110.

stricted and simplistic to serve as a complete guide to Athens' moral and political assessment of military trickery.

According to the model of Vidal-Naquet and Winkler, Melanthus' story primarily operates as a negative paradigm because it depicts single combat and victory through deception. The story of Codrus similarly depicts a small skirmish and a ruse. Unlike his supposed father, Codrus does not survive his confrontation with the enemy. But it is clear from the scholion on Plato that his ruse and self-sacrifice secures the withdrawal of the Dorians, the survival of Athens and the continuity of his family's hegemony. For Plato's Diotima it was the last consequence which motivated the king and she draws on a typically Greek notion of *kleos* to emphasise the fact that the manner of Codrus' defeat ensured his immortal fame. But given that we do not know whether Diotima is referring to the same story as the scholion lifts from Hellanicus, we need another text to offer clues as to the status and significance of Codrus' ruse. There is just one other text, but its invocation of Codrus' use of *mētis* and *apatē* is revealing.

In Lycurgus' speech *Against Leocrates* Codrus' self-sacrifice is deployed as an historical exemplum and it is primarily represented as an act of patriotism; Codrus acts in the interests of the entire city rather than in the narrow interests of his family. The year is 331/330 and Lycurgus is prosecuting Leocrates under the general charge of treason. More specifically, Leocrates stands accused of desertion. Lycurgus contends that he dodged his military service after the Battle of Chaeronea by sailing to Megara. As one would expect, the orator contrasts Leocrates' alleged cowardice with the courageous action of Athenians in past conflicts. His first example of courage is Codrus. Lycurgus' version is essentially the same as that outlined in the scholion described above but it is longer and more detailed. The invaders of Attica are called Peloponnesians rather than Dorians (1.84). The means by which Codrus hears about the Delphic oracle is explained: 'a Delphian Cleomantis, learning of the oracle, secretly told the Athenians'. Lycurgus even sees the offering of secret information as indicative of Athens' former reputation. Cleomantis' help is taken as evidence of 'the goodwill which our ancestors inspired even among aliens'(85).[33] Before he deals with the conduct of Codrus, Lycurgus briefly points out that the Athenians of that time did not desert their country as

---

[33] Κλεόμαντις δὲ τῶν Δελφῶν τις πυθόμενος τὸ χρηστήριον δι' ἀπορρήτων ἐξήγγειλε τοῖς Ἀθηναίοις. οὕτως οἱ πρόγονοι ἡμῶν ὡς ἔοικε, καὶ τοὺς ἔξωθεν ἀνθρώπους εὔνους ἔχοντες διετέλουν.

Leocrates did. He praises his ancestors' decision to remain in Athens, enduring the hardships of a siege in order to preserve their fatherland (85).[34] Lycurgus introduces Codrus by reflecting on the noble kings of the past who preferred to die for the safety of their subjects rather than purchasing their own lives by adopting another country (1.86). He then goes on to illustrate this selfless nobility by giving an account of his ruse:

They say, at any rate, that Codrus told the Athenians to note the time of his death and, taking a beggar's clothes to deceive the enemy (λαβόντα πτωχικὴν στολὴν ὅπως ἂν ἀπατήσῃ τοὺς πολεμίους), slipped out of the gates and began to collect firewood in front of the city. When two men from the camp approached him and inquired about conditions in the city he killed one of them with a blow of his sickle. The survivor, it is said, enraged with Codrus and thinking him a beggar drew his sword and killed him. Then the Athenians sent a herald and asked to have their king given over for burial, telling the enemy the whole truth; and the Peloponnesians restored the body but retreated, aware that it was no longer possible for them to secure the country. (Lycurgus 1.86–7)

In this account, Codrus' disguise involves dressing down to the appearance of a beggar (λαβόντα πτωχικὴν στολὴν). Even more than the guise of the woodcutter as presented in other accounts of this story, Codrus' transformation into a beggar marks a complete reversal of his social status.[35] Like the Homeric Odysseus back on Ithaca, Codrus uses the superficial trappings of the beggar to make his royal status unrecognisable.[36] The content of the oracle makes a ruse involving this effacement and replacement of Codrus' social identity a necessity if Athens is to be saved. Unlike the Homeric Odysseus, however, Codrus regains his identity in memorialisation alone. Odysseus uses deceit and violence to survive and claim back his wife, household and his territorial rights over Ithaca. In short, Odysseus' deceit of the suitors facilitates his return to full social identity as king of Ithaca. Codrus' ruse, although similarly formulated in terms of disguise and violence, is conceived specifically for the purpose of self-annihilation. Codrus dies a beggar, but is remembered as a king. Several sources indicate that Codrus was the last king of Athens because his sons quarrelled over the

---

[34] οὐ καταλιπόντες τὴν χώραν ὥσπερ Λεωκράτης ... ἀλλ᾽ ὀλίγοι ὄντες κατακλεισθέντες ἐπολιορκοῦντο καὶ διεκαρτέρουν εἰς τὴν πατρίδα.

[35] Burkert (1985) 84 sees Codrus' disguise as a beggar and self-sacrifice as a mythical echo of Athenian *pharmakos* ritual. See also Seaford (1994a) 345.

[36] See Murnaghan (1987) 9: 'Odysseus' disguise testifies to the reality of the suitors' challenge but it also belittles it; it is a sign of their temporary ascendancy, but also a resource that ensures his eventual and inevitable triumph over them.' On the Homeric Odysseus as a deceiver and in beggar's disguise, see also Goldhill (1991) 6–12 and 24–56.

throne. In some of these accounts, Athens' monarchy is replaced by the archonship.[37] In several traditions, then, Codrus' death as a beggar on behalf of the polis marks a transformation in Athens' constitutional history.[38] A key stage in Athens' move towards democracy is marked by a story of self-sacrifice on behalf of the collective. Lycurgus clearly sees the story as a significant example of an Athenian placing collective values and the safety of the polis above any regard for personal safety or survival.

There were, however, many other stories available to him which did not revolve around *apatē*. Furthermore, in drawing a lesson from Codrus' exploit, Lycurgus actually emphasises the role of deceit:

ἆρά γ' ὁμοίως ἐφίλουν τὴν πατρίδα Λεωκράτει οἱ τότε βασιλεύοντες, οἵ γε προῃροῦντο τοὺς πολεμίους ἐξαπατῶντες ἀποθνήσκειν ὑπὲρ αὐτῆς καὶ τὴν ἰδίαν ψυχὴν
ἀντὶ τῆς κοινῆς σωτηρίας ἀντικαταλλάττεσθαι; τοιγαροῦν μονώτατοι ἐπώνυμοι
τῆς χώρας εἰσὶν, ἰσοθέων τιμῶν τετυχηκότες, εἰκότως.

Is there any resemblance between Leocrates' love of his fatherland and the love of those who once had royal power *who preferred to die for their country deceiving the enemy*, giving their own lives in exchange for the people's safety? It is for this reason that they and only they have given the land their name and have received honours like gods, as is fitting. (Lycurgus 1.88)

He goes on to stress that Leocrates' desertion makes him unfit to be buried in the same ground as those heroes whose distinction in excellence (*aretē*) had made them eponymous heroes (ἐπώνυμοι: 89).[39] Thus Codrus is ranked alongside the foremost mythological heroes who gave their names to the ten Cleisthenic tribes. Lycurgus speaks of 'those who once had royal power' (οἱ τότε βασιλεύοντες) in the plural and tells his audience that they are worthy of renown because 'they preferred to die for their country, deceiving (ἐξαπατῶντες) the enemy' and because they exchanged their own lives for the safety of the collective. It is difficult to determine why Lycurgus uses the plural οἱ τότε βασιλεύοντες. Perhaps ἐξαπατῶντες really refers only to the exploit of Codrus, and Lycurgus uses the plural for the purpose of rhetorical exaggeration. Or does Lycurgus expect his audience to recall similar acts of trickery by

---

[37] E.g. Paus. 5.10, 7.10; [Arist.] *Ath. Pol.* 3.3. See Dougherty (1993) 17, who argues that the quarrel between Codrus' elder sons Neleus and Medon reflects a theme of political crisis prior to colonisation in Greek myth. The dispute is settled by an oracle which instructs Neleus to colonise Ionia.

[38] Drews (1983) 93 and Seaford (1994a) 345 suggest that Codrus' self-sacrifice may once have been imagined as ending the kingship.

[39] Codrus was prominent in Athenian hero-cult; see Kearns (1989) 55f.; Seaford (1994a) 125. But he is only once included among the ten tribal *eponymoi* on a frieze at Delphi; see Krön (1976) 271ff.

other kings of Attica? It could be that Lycurgus is also thinking of Codrus' father Melanthus and his ruse on the border of Attica. But if Lycurgus is thinking of Melanthus, why does the plural designate 'those who preferred to die deceiving the enemy'? Melanthus deceives the enemy but he does not die. Lycurgus could have Melanthus in mind if we gloss προῃροῦντο τοὺς πολεμίους ἐξαπατῶντες ἀποθνήσκειν as 'were prepared to die for their country, deceiving the enemy'. On this reading, Lycurgus is singling out those rulers of Attica who chose to risk death as well as those who opted for certain death. More significantly, he would be characterising Melanthus (Vidal-Naquet's 'Black Hunter') and his act of trickery as an exemplum of bravery for the Athenian citizen-soldier.

Whomever else Lycurgus does or does not have in mind, it is clear that he has no difficulty in praising Codrus' deployment of deceit to defeat the enemy. The passage cited above shows *apatē* towards the enemy going hand in hand with exemplary leadership, collective values, *kleos* and self-sacrifice. At the most, we could argue that Lycurgus uses Codrus as a paradigm of Athenian bravery *because* his reputation involves the enactment of cunning intelligence and individual deceit. At the very least, we can see that Lycurgus finds nothing objectionable in military *apatē*. He makes no attempt to suppress the element of deceit. His generalising remarks couple the notions of self-sacrifice and trickery to the exclusion of any other way of engaging with the enemy.

This valorisation of military *apatē* runs counter to Pericles' comments in Thucydides' Funeral Speech and, to a large extent, it contrasts with the denigration of Themistocles' ruse against the Spartans which we found in Demosthenes' speech *Against Leptines*. Only twenty years before Lycurgus' praise of Codrus, Demosthenes feels able to represent Themistocles' deception of the Spartans as an achievement that is considerably less worthy than Conon's straightforward preservation of the walls by open combat. How are we to explain these contrasting representations?

If we were to leave Demosthenes' evaluation of Themistocles' trick to one side, we *could* explain away the tension between Lycurgus' praise of military *apatē* and Pericles' dismissal of it in the Thucydidean Funeral Speech. This would involve the construction of an evolutionary historical model to explain the shift from the negative representation of military *apatē* which we find in the Funeral Speech to Lycurgus' positive representation in terms of changes in the *Realien* of warfare in the late fifth and fourth centuries. Such an evolutionary historical model would constitute the traditional response to tensions or contradictions between normative statements relating to military action. According to the evolutionary model, military trickery becomes more admissible in public normative statements because warfare involving trickery has become more prevalent and necessary. Whitehead has recently dismissed a similar evolutionary model.[40] With reference to the notion of theft in Greek warfare (κλοπὴ πολέμου), he argues that military trickery was 'an inescapably ambivalent concept, within the broader ambivalence of ancient attitudes towards appropriate and inappropriate routes to military success and to admirable and despicable human qualities therein displayed'.[41] I will be taking issue with the explanatory power of Whitehead's identification of military trickery as an 'ambivalent' notion, but he is right to emphasise that an evolutionary account fails to recognise the fact that tension over the admissibility of military *apatē* persists throughout the classical period. We need a more flexible and nuanced model that can account for the different and differing discussions of military deceit which appear in Athenian texts. But before I present such a model I want to outline some of the 'evolutionary' factors which undoubtedly informed the representation of military *apatē* during and after the Peloponnesian War.

We could conjecture, for example, that the acceptability of *apatē* to Lycurgus is due to the ever-increasing use of specialised non-hoplite units and professional troops during the Peloponnesian War and into the fourth century.[42] The ruse and the ambush were never really absent from practical Athenian strategy and tactics, but there was a change in emphasis which was dictated by the vulnerability of hoplite units when faced with certain terrains and an enemy that would not play the hoplite game.[43]

Thucydides implicitly charts this change in tactics in several accounts of Athenian campaigns in the war. He tells of a few occasions when Athenian *stratēgoi* deployed military trickery or told outright lies when negotiating with the enemy in order to secure victory or safety.[44]

---

[40] Whitehead (1988). Whitehead's model proposes an evolution between pre-classical and classical combat. He dismisses this model because 'it distorts and caricatures both phases of the supposed development'.

[41] Whitehead (1988) 51.

[42] See Wheeler (1991) 136ff. on the rise of *technē* in the second half of the fifth century, both in the sense of warfare involving deception and as involving a valorisation of teachable skills as opposed to native courage. See also Heza (1974) and Saïd and Tredé (1985).

[43] See Ober (1991) *passim*.

[44] See Thuc. 3.91–112, where the Athenian general Demosthenes deploys some of his hoplites in an ambush after his men have been ambushed on a previous occasion. For other examples in Thucydides, see Heza (1974).

He recounts and seems to admire Themistocles' deception of the Spartans: the same ruse which Demosthenes denigrates.[45] Ironically, it is Themistocles' improvisatory intelligence which makes the ruse possible, a form of intelligence which the deception-hating Pericles certainly regards as an Athenian virtue in his Funeral Speech.

Thucydides also records an occasion when the Athenian *stratēgos* Paches promised to spare the life of Hippias, commander of the Arcadians and Persians who had been called in by a faction to take over the fortified area in the city of Notion (3.34). Paches summoned Hippias on the condition that if his proposals were unsatisfactory he would restore him 'safe and sound' (σῶν καὶ ὑγιᾶ) to the fortress. But when Hippias came out to meet the Athenian general, he was placed under guard although left unfettered (ἐν φυλακῇ ἀδέσμῳ) and Paches immediately made a surprise attack on the fortress. He captured it and put to death all the Arcadians and barbarians. 'As for Hippias', continues Thucydides, 'he then took him into the fortress just as he had agreed to do, and as soon as he was inside, seized him and shot him down' (3.34.3). Like Odysseus' reassurance to Dolon in the *Iliad* (10.383f.), Paches' promise is deceptively ambiguous. Paches promises to restore Hippias safely to the fortress and, as Thucydides realises, he does not strictly go back on that guarantee. But the guarantee is based on the prospect of negotiations. Paches is represented as using the offer of talks and the promise of safety to lure out the enemy commander. By detaining Hippias, Paches is able to launch a successful surprise attack. As with many of the engagements described in Thucydides' history of the war, this is an example of siege warfare and the self-interested annihilation of undesirable political factions within Greek cities. In these circumstances, the open, mutually agreed hoplite confrontation is not a serious option for either side. Thucydides does not pass any comment

---

[45] See Thuc. 1.90–3. I say 'seems to admire' because Thucydides does not explicitly make any evaluation of Themistocles' ruse. However, see my comments above, pp. 47–8 on Thuc. 1.138.3, where the historian frames his account of Themistocles' death by offering a general assessment of his ability, without mentioning his use of *apatē*. Thucydides clearly admires Themistocles' native wit and his ability to instantly apprehend and carry out expedient courses of action. He sums up his view of Themistocles' leadership like this: 'to sum him up in a few words, it may be said that through natural ability and rapidity of action this man was supreme at doing precisely the right thing at precisely the right moment' (καὶ τὸ ξύμπαν εἰπεῖν φύσεως μὲν δυνάμει, μελέτης δὲ βραχύτητι κράτιστος δὴ οὗτος αὐτοσχεδιάζειν τὰ δέοντα ἐγένετο). On Thucydides' emphasis on Athenian appeals to necessity and expediency, see Ostwald (1988); Johnson (1991); Hornblower (1991) 75, 326, 421, 452 (expediency) and 67, 194 (necessity). On Thucydides' valorisation of 'natural' intelligence, see Edmunds (1975). Detienne and Vernant (1978) frequently stress the association between the successful *stratēgos* and qualities which connote *mētis* in Athenian sources.

on the incident at Notion, but as an account of what the Athenian army and leadership actually got up to, Paches' deadly trick ironically gives the lie to Pericles' claim that it is only the enemy who deploy 'devices and deceits'. Within Thucydides' own writing as a whole then, Pericles' ideal image of military *apatē* as an unAthenian quality is contested by accounts of 'real' Athenian military conduct during the war.

If this contestation is already occurring in Thucydides, then we *could* argue that, by the time of Lycurgus' political ascendancy, the conceptual frameworks and polarities of the hoplite ideal shifted in response to changes in the conduct of warfare. Even at the level of ideality, deceit can no longer be necessarily associated with non-Athenian military behaviour. Too much real and notable Athenian deception in war has occurred for this imaginary construction ('othering') of military trickery to be sustained. This would be a plausible way of explaining the contrasting representations and evaluations of military *apatē* which are to be found in Pericles' speech and that of Lycurgus some ninety years later.

There are a number of other factors which could have allowed for some realignment of values so as to include a space for *apatē* as a praiseworthy resource for the ideal Athenian warrior during and after the Peloponnesian War. These would include the reduced effectiveness of hoplite warfare in the light of the increased deployment of mercenaries and lightly armed units;[46] the new requirement to initiate and resolve sieges and associated developments in technology;[47] the complex political intrigues underlying the Peloponnesian War, the Social War and the conflict with Macedon.[48] All of these changes in conditions for military and diplomatic agency involved a real depletion of the efficacy and utility of traditional hoplite warfare. Perhaps these strains and encroachments on hoplite practice helped ease the accommodation of *apatē* in Athens' public discussions of ideal military agency and heroism.

We could also see a space for *apatē* in Athens' evaluative discourses being promoted by changes in defensive military organisation which occurred in the first quarter of the fourth century. Fourth-century decrees and oratory provide Ober with a wealth of evidence to support his view that Athens developed a new 'defensive mentality' after the res-

---

[46] See Vidal-Naquet (1986a) 89–93; Ober (1985a).

[47] Exemplified by the fourth-century work on surviving a siege, the *Poliorkētika* of Aeneas Tacticus.

[48] See Aen. Tact. *Poliork.* 11–22 with the comments of Whitehead (1990) ad loc. and 25–34.

toration of the democracy in 404.[49] For Ober this new mentality involved the strengthening of defence and security for the entire Attic
territory (*chōra*) rather than continued emphasis on protecting the city
of Athens alone and investment in naval power. Ober's arguments for
this new unPericlean mentality have been subject to effective critique,
most notably by Harding and Munn.[50] There may not have been such
a great change in military organisation in the fourth century as an
immediate and sweeping response to 'mistakes' made in the Peloponnesian War. After all, the Athenians rebuilt their fleet and the Long
Walls as soon as they could.[51] Nor did changes in military organisation
necessarily amount to a 'Maginot-line mentality' in the manner that
Ober suggests. Munn argues that fourth-century fortresses were not
designed to repel invaders and could easily be bypassed.[52] Rather, they
offered security and refuge for the property and people situated in the
countryside in the event of attack. But even Munn's account points to
new or renewed investment in the *in situ* protection of those living and
working in the countryside.

This investment must in part have been a reaction against Pericles'
unmanly policy of evacuating the countryside of Attica and leaving it to
be ravaged by the enemy.[53] Even if there was no movement towards a
'Maginot-line' defence of Attica, the evidence does suggest that those
who lived and worked on the frontiers were given more protection. The
public rhetoric of the fourth century emphasises the security of, and
protection within the entire Attic *chōra*; fortifications *were* eventually
built on the borders of Attica, mountain passes *were* watched and, for
the first time, a generalship was created for the specific purpose of
co-ordinating this policy of permanent vigilance.[54] Many scholars, including Vidal-Naquet, have noted evidence from Aeschines that young
men of 'ephebic' age were deployed to patrol the border regions as
peripoloi during this period.[55] Munn argues that it was the Boiotian War

---

[49] Ober (1985a) 51–66.
[50] Harding (1988); Munn (1993) 15–33.
[51] Harding (1988) 64. See Xen. *Hell.* 4.8.10.
[52] Munn (1993) 25–32. On the dangers of interpreting classical Athens' military
arrangements in the light of apparent twentieth-century parallels see Millett (1993)
177–81.
[53] Ober (1985a) 51–7. For Pericles' city-based strategy, see Sealey (1967) 94–5; Ober
(1985b), (1991) 188f.
[54] See Ober (1985a) 59–64 and 87–8 for the Attic orators' and institutional emphasis on
the defence of the *chōra*. See Ober (1985a) 99–207 on new fortresses and border defence. On the creation of a *stratēgos* of the *chōra* some time in the first half of the fourth
century, see Munn (1993) 190–4. Harding (1988) 62 points out that where dates are
known, fortresses were not built until the middle of the fourth century.
[55] E.g. Aeschin. 2.167. Vidal-Naquet (1986a) 107; Ober (1985a) 91–6; Winkler (1990a).

of 378–375 which prompted this new focus for ephebic duties.[56] We can certainly see the *rhetorical* emphasis on the *chōra* of Attica at work in Lycurgus' construction of Codrus' *apatē* as exemplary. Codrus' achievement is to precipitate the withdrawal of the Peloponnesians from the entire territory of Attica (οὐκέτι δυνατὸν αὐτοῖς τὴν χώραν κατασχεῖν ἀπεχώρησαν). Codrus is praised alongside other heroes who give their names to places throughout the *chōra* (τοιγαροῦν μονώτατοι ἐπώνυμοι τῆς χώρας εἰσὶν ἰσοθέων τιμῶν τετυχηκότες, εἰκότως). And, unlike Leocrates, Codrus shares a love of the *fatherland* with other past rulers (ὁμοίως ἐφίλουν τὴν πατρίδα Λεωκράτει οἱ τότε βασιλεύοντες).

It is plausible that this new emphasis on the integrity of the *chōra* could have entailed a parallel movement in the location of the ephebe on Athens' *ideological* terrain. If the ephebe gains an important role in the maintenance of Attica's security, and if the borderlands of Attica are no longer Vidal-Naquet's liminal 'badlands' but crucial markers of territorial integrity and impending attack, then it is at least conceivable that the discursive relation of the ephebe to the hoplite may have become destabilised. Vidal-Naquet sees this discursive relation as an antithesis, and to a large extent it is the association between the ephebe and notions of deceit which constitutes that antithesis. But changes in the character of warfare during and after the Peloponnesian War and the enactment of a new or renewed emphasis on territorial defence may have allowed for this antithesis to be contested by a different relation of complementarity or even supplementarity. In this relation, the tricky ephebe would act as a necessary counterpart to the hoplite. The ephebe would remain, as Vidal-Naquet characterises him, a pre-hoplite and his duties as a *peripolos* keep him on the margins of civilised life, but the *value* and importance of those duties would increase. In this climate, it seems reasonable to ask whether the story of Melanthus' victory in a border dispute would not have gained a significance which was different from, or competed with, the liminal ritual symbolism outlined by Vidal-Naquet. If the tale is archaic in origin and attests to an archaic *ephēbeia*, it may well have started life as a story with negative paradigmatic force in the manner that Vidal-Naquet describes. And this negative force probably continued to inform fifth- and fourth-century constructions of ideal Athenian civic and military identity; I have suggested that this is perhaps one reason why Pericles stresses that Athens does not rely on 'pre-arranged devices and deceits'. However, (and this is an argument that cannot be proved) the changes in defensive ideology in the early fourth century and the fact that Lycurgus can give

---

[56] Munn (1993) 188–9.

Codrus' trickery a very positive paradigmatic force (in a case about desertion of civic and military duty) must point at least to the *possibility* that Melanthus' *apatē* did not sustain an unequivocally negative ideological colouring throughout the classical period.

But if Lycurgus sees military *apatē* as an unproblematically traditional Athenian quality, why is Demosthenes devaluing it only twenty years before? The truth is that there can be no straightforward resolution of these conflicting representations and evaluations of 'deceiving the enemy', but an explication of the conflict is in itself instructive. The evolutionary model I outlined above, whilst it accounts for the construction of a positive space for military *apatē* in Athenian public discourse, does not do justice to the continued ambivalence about 'deceiving the enemy' which can be derived from a range of Athenian texts from the late fifth century onwards. But it is not enough simply to speak (as Whitehead does) of 'ambivalence' or to conclude that pro- and anti-deception attitudes to war 'competed and co-existed with each other'.[57] We need to look for strategies of negotiation and co-optation; I will suggest below that Lycurgus' Codrus exemplifies an assimilation of *apatē* into the ideology of 'la belle mort' and a negotiation between the identity of the trickster and that of the hoplite.[58] Nor is it sufficient to trace the vocabulary of what has been called an 'Odysseus ethic' throughout Greek culture, without framing this lexical approach in terms of context.[59] We also need to ask where, when and by whom is military trickery being promoted or denigrated; we need to isolate what is perceived to be at stake in these conflicting evaluations. We may well be dealing here with something akin to what Foucault has termed 'a form of problematisation' in classical Athens' public, political and philosophical discourses.[60] I would suggest that this problematisation emerged during the Peloponnesian War and continued throughout the fourth century. In the next three sections, I will offer more evidence for, trace the development of, and explain what I mean by, this moral problematisation of military *apatē* at Athens.

Military trickery as a negotiable term

Pritchett seeks to play down the significance of accounts of Greek military trickery in historiography throughout the fifth and fourth cen-

---

[57] Whitehead (1988) 51.
[58] For the notion of 'co-optation' as a ruse of power, see Graff (1989).
[59] See Wheeler (1988) 1–49.
[60] See Foucault (1987) 14–24.

turies.[61] He points out that there are very few recorded examples of
ambushes or surprise attacks being deployed in conflict between hoplite armies. Pritchett maintains that hoplite battle was bound by codes
of openness and agreement between the two sides and implies that this
remained the central mode of land warfare, despite the increasing use
of lightly armed troops and mercenaries. He emphasises that most examples of surprise attack and ambush come from contexts where a city
is under siege or where non-hoplitic forces are involved. Pritchett does
not even mention the verbal trickery of Themistocles or Paches, perhaps because he is primarily interested in establishing the tactics and
techniques of leadership that were used on the battlefield, rather than
verbal negotiations that occurred between opposed generals prior to, or
during a cessation of physical hostilities. The evaluation of past military conduct in the orators is also apparently beyond the scope of his
work, and he tends to extrapolate Greek military values from the relative frequencies of historical descriptions of kinds of military practice,
rather than through any detailed examination of what conduct and
values Greek writers and orators praise or attack.[62]

Such a 'bracketing off' of these aspects and evaluations of military
conduct in Pritchett's work is both troubling and useful. It is useful
because it helps us to gain some sense of what constituted 'normative'
military conduct in classical Greece. It is troubling because it has encouraged commentators to measure any Athenian representation of
military conduct against a single, dominant practice and its associated
value-system, namely hoplite conflict.[63] Thus, Vidal-Naquet and Winkler read the myth of Melanthus' ruse and the Athenian *ephēbeia* in
terms of the opposed practice and ideology of hoplitism. Because
manhood, citizenship and hoplite identity were constituted as inextri-
cably interwoven at Athens, they may be right to interpret the Apatouria in this manner. The notion that hoplite ideology was a central
structuring principle in Athenian society has been fruitfully argued and
applied in recent years. But did the Athenians measure all military
conduct against hoplite values? Or rather, was there any room to set up

---

[61] See Pritchett (1974) 147–89.
[62] Pritchett does use the Attic orators, but he trawls them for evidence of tactics and
military practices, rather than evaluations of military conduct.
[63] As I pointed out in chapter 1 and as Paul Cartledge has emphasised to me, the navy
was in reality far more 'dominant' than the hoplite army during the Athenian empire's
ascendancy in the fifth century. See Thuc. 2.62. It became dominant again in the first
half of the fourth century. The land-based arrangements described by Ober (1985a)
and Munn (1993) were the defensive counterpart to naval offence.

different standards of judgement for different contexts of conflict? I must be clear about what I mean here. I am not denying that it was possible to condemn or criticise any instance or notion of military *apatē* through a tacit or declared appeal to military values which could be described as 'hoplitic'. Demosthenes' denigration of Themistocles' ruse clearly follows these lines. Themistocles uses *apatē* in a non-hoplitic context; he deceives a potential enemy whilst on a diplomatic mission (20.67–75). Yet his conduct is viewed as an engagement with an enemy and as such it is denigrated in comparison with open military conflict as practised by Conon. The fact that Conon's victory was largely the result of naval engagement does not affect Demosthenes' evaluative frame of reference; like the hoplite, Conon fought and beat the enemy openly and fairly and this is why he is better than Themistocles. But we have to ask whether Themistocles' deceit could also have been explicitly praised or defended by an orator, through reference to a different set of values, or even through a different formulation of the hoplite ideal or even a mixture of the two. The fact that Demosthenes has to apologise to his audience for his attack on Themistocles may indicate that his ruse had not previously been singled out or thought of in negative terms at all. Lysias implies that Themistocles' ruse *is* praiseworthy when, as part of his attack on the actions of the Thirty, he compares Theramenes' destruction of the Long Walls with Themistocles' construction of the city walls and the Piraeus defences 'against the wishes of the Spartans' (12.63). Lysias argues that Theramenes destroyed the walls by deceiving (ἐξαπατήσας) the citizens of Athens. Theramenes' deceit of the people is contrasted with Themistocles' ability to outwit the enemy in order to secure Athens' safety, but Lysias does not explicitly characterise the latter achievement as an act of military or diplomatic deception.

As I noted in my first chapter, Themistocles and other fifth-century leaders are often held up by fourth-century orators as great men in very general terms. Their specific actions are sometimes invoked as positive *exempla*, but there was clearly much room for selective and strategic emphasis in such representations. On the one hand, for example, Aeschines can invoke Solon as an ideal orator in terms of appropriate deportment in order to condemn Timarchus through comparison (1.25–7). On the other hand, Demosthenes can attack Aeschines' invocation, pointing out that he bases his discussion of Solonian gesture on a very recent statue whose sculptor could have had no idea of the way in which Solon delivered speeches (19.249). Demosthenes then goes on to cite Solon's verses on corrupt politicians selectively. This

lends weight to his attack on Aeschines' political conduct (19.252–5).[64]
Thus the paradigmatic force of 'great' historical figures is highly mal-
leable *and* contestable. Orators can be creative in their representation
or interpretation of the words and deeds of past figures. This creativity
and selectivity of representation is undoubtedly strategic. Demosthenes
seeks to contrast Themistocles with Conon and denigrate the former's
achievement because he wants to emphasise the exceptional nature of
Conon's achievements. Conon gained exemption from public burdens
both for himself and his ancestors. Demosthenes seeks to promote the
value of the occasional granting of *ateleia* by presenting Conon's actions
as more laudable than those of a figure who is constantly represented as
a great military leader, at least until he was bribed by the Persians.[65]
The ancestors of Harmodios and Aristogeiton were retrospectively
granted exemptions, but the ancestors of fifth-century leaders were not.
Demosthenes' comparison between Conon and Themistocles demonstrates the exceptional superiority of the former and therefore makes
the case for the continued recognition of such achievement through the
reward of the *ateleia*.

However, this strategic representation of Themistocles is still
grounded in something which Demosthenes puts forward as a universal truth, namely that it is better to defeat the enemy in open battle
than to trick him. By applying a supposedly 'universal' belief about the
morality of military trickery, Demosthenes shows that recent benefactors can be more praiseworthy and deserving of rewards than those
who contributed to the survival and expansion of Athens in the first
half of the fifth century. Thus, Demosthenes relies on the same basic
ideological premise which we find in Pericles' Funeral Speech and in
critical generalisations about Athenian hoplite identity, namely that
trickery is viewed with contempt and is seen as 'other' to the ideal
identity of the Athenian citizen-soldier. I would suggest, however, that
Demosthenes' evaluation of Themistocles is tellingly inscribed with the
negotiable moral status of 'deceiving the enemy'. For Demosthenes,
apatē is certainly not *part* of the ideal notion of how an enemy is to be
defeated. But Themistocles' trick is set against a 'universal' view which
states that armed open conflict is *better* than trickery. Trickery is not
viewed as the moral antithesis of open battle ('deceiving bad, fighting

---

[64] See Lowry (1991) 163f. on this exchange of evaluations and Demosthenes' evocation
of Solon's 'shame-causing' speech and ruse to incite an invasion of Salamis.

[65] It has also been argued that Demosthenes focuses on Conon because he was the father
of Timotheus, a politician who was under attack at the time of this speech. See Sandys
(1979) 61.

good'); rather, Demosthenes' universal premise simply prescribes that the former is less praiseworthy than the latter. The Periclean ideal antithesis certainly haunts the comparison between Conon and Themistocles, but Demosthenes does allow a space for *apatē* in the realm of Athenian military agency. If we compare Demosthenes' denigration of Themistocles' trick, Lysias' evaluation of Theramenes and Themistocles, and Lycurgus' positive representation of Codrus, we can see that Pritchett, Winkler and Vidal-Naquet do not take account of the extent to which *apatē* is a morally negotiable term in the late fifth and fourth centuries.[66] For Lysias, Themistocles' trick was constructive for Athens and is therefore praiseworthy when placed *in a relation* to the treachery of Theramenes. For Demosthenes, Themistocles' trick is *relatively* less praiseworthy than the achievement of Conon. In Lycurgus' speech against an alleged deserter, the trickery performed by Codrus and other leaders of the past is unequivocally and paradigmatically praiseworthy in a context where such trickery is *related*, not to the open fighting of other Athenian leaders, but to the cowardice of Leocrates. Thus the positive or negative evaluation of the notion of 'deceiving the enemy' is dependent upon its location within a rhetorical relation.

Whilst discussions and evaluations of Athenian oratory indicate that military trickery is morally negotiable and subject to strategic manipulation, there are, nevertheless, clear limits to the way in which such deceit can be represented as unequivocally positive in *public* discourse. Codrus tricks the enemy, but that act of trickery is also an act of self-sacrifice which is geared towards the preservation of the Athenian polis. Perhaps it is not possible to praise individual trickery in Athens' collective institutions, unless such trickery is welded to a version of hoplite endeavour which is premised upon the notion of self-annihilation for, and on behalf of, the survival of Athens. It is this possibility of a

---

[66] The strategic factors which motivate these orators' explicit normative statements concerning *apatē*, and the areas of negotiation which are revealed by comparing them, demonstrate the difficulty of assuming that such statements give unmediated access to a monolithic and definable Athenian ideology or that *democratic* ideology is indeed to be understood solely as a monolithic 'text' of prescriptions and proscriptions. See Rose (1995) 62: 'By ideology in the Marxist sense I do not refer to what is an increasingly common use of the term by classicists, i.e., a statically conceived worldview or so homogenized an entity as "civic ideology". I refer rather to an eminently combative arena of persuasion and struggle.' See also Eagleton (1991) 221–4. In this study I attempt to demonstrate that the representation of deceit and trickery is a constituent of an identifiable civic ideology which defines and delimits the subject as citizen. But I also believe that the democratic, agonistic and rhetorical quality of public discourse at Athens means that this civic ideology is constituted by strategic amendment, debate and negotiation. On this issue see further below pp. 116–18.

negotiation between *apatē* and a version of hoplite agency which I will now explore further.

Deceit, fear and hoplite courage

It is likely that a military and more general social ethic which promoted the acceptability of 'deceiving the enemy' had always been present at Athens. As I mentioned earlier, the story of Codrus' *mētis* was probably current in fifth-century Athens. Some scholars assume the story to be archaic in origin, but Busolt has suggested that it was invented to provide Athens with a figure who rivalled the Spartan hero-king Leonidas.[67] The story of Leonidas' self-sacrifice is very similar to that of Codrus. Whatever its origins, Codrus' trick may well have been positively paradigmatic in the fifth century.

More certain and obvious evidence of a positive evaluation of military trickery is to be found in Aeschylus' *Persians*. The chorus of Persian elders fear that Xerxes' campaign may be thwarted by the 'cunning deceit of a god' (δολόμητιν δ' ἀπάταν θεοῦ: 92) and the Messenger reveals that the Persian defeat was precipitated by a 'Greek's trick' which Xerxes failed to detect (οὐ ξυνεὶς δόλον Ἕλληνος: 360–1).[68] This is a reference to the trick whose conception Herodotus attributes to Themistocles (8.75.1). However much Themistocles' use of deceit is denigrated in the fourth century by Demosthenes, the Aeschylean reference clearly implies that Athenian trickery got the better of the barbarians.[69] Notwithstanding ongoing debate concerning the extent to which *Persians* is purely a celebration of Athenian superiority and democratic values, the play offers an example of the way in which an instance of military trickery could be packaged as an Athenian virtue.[70]

A fourth-century Apulian krater (the so-called 'Darius Vase') provides further evidence that deception was seen as an important component in the defeat of the Persians.[71] The vase represents a female

---

[67] See Busolt (1897) 220–2. See also Kearns (1989) 56.

[68] Aeschylus clearly explored the issue of divine deception in a play that does not survive. See Aesch. fr. 301–2 N² (= Aesch. fr. 301–2 R), cited at *Diss. Log.* 3.12: 'God does not stand aloof from just deception. There are occasions when God respects an opportune moment for lies' (ἀπάτης δικαίας οὐκ ἀποστατεῖ θεός· ψευδῶν δὲ καιρὸν ἔσθ' ὅπου τιμῇ θεός).

[69] See Hall (1996) 136: 'this incident implies the superiority of the Greeks over the barbarians in cunning intelligence'. As Hall points out, the messenger's use of *dolos* ('trick') and the chorus' use of *dolomētin* call to mind Odysseus' epithet *dolomētis* in Homer's *Odyssey* and Odysseus' tricking of the Cyclops, the 'barbarian of the *Odyssey*'.

[70] For bibliography on the difficulties of interpreting *Persians* see p. 48, n. 88.

[71] *LIMC* 1.2 698, Apate 1; *CVA* Naples 3253; Trendall and Webster (1971) 112, no. III.5, 6.

figure labelled Apatē dressed in a leopard skin and hunting boots. She holds two torches.[72] To her right is the labelled female figure Asia who is attended by Aphrodite. To her immediate left stands Athena and then a female personification of Hellas. Hellas is flanked on the left by Artemis, Nikē (Victory), Apollo and Zeus. Beneath this depiction of the divine and daimonic machinery behind the Persian Wars are two scenes depicting the Persian king Darius at court. In one scene he sits on a throne attended by a guard with drawn sword while a man on a plinth marked 'Persai' gestures to him with two fingers. On the lowest band Darius is represented again but this time he is receiving tribute from kneeling Persians while a servant chalks up the amount of wealth received in talants. The figure of Apatē foregrounds the Persians' error of judgement, although the juxtaposition of Athena and Apatē must also imply a divine source for Greek or specifically Athenian cunning in their campaigns against the Persians. Scholars think it likely that the vase treats the battle of Marathon and have noted the possible influence of tragedy on the vase's depictions. It is possible that the vase represents a lost fifth- or fourth-century tragedy.[73] It is certainly the case that the theme of divine and daimonic *apatē* as a force which deludes Xerxes into military action is recurrent and prominent in Aeschylus' *Persians*.[74]

An equally obvious but more problematic witness to the acceptability of 'deceiving the enemy' in the late fifth and early fourth centuries is Plato. In the second book of the *Republic*, Socrates interrogates the poets' representations of the gods. In the course of his critique, Socrates asks if the gods really resort to deceit and disguise as Homer says they do (2.382a1). Before providing the answer to his own question, he first makes a distinction between 'true falsehood' or 'the true lie' (ὡς ἀληθῶς ψεῦδος) and the 'falsehood in words' or the 'lie in words' (τὸ ἐν τοῖς λόγοις ψεῦδος). I will return to this important distinction in the next chapter. For the present, it is only necessary to explain what Soc-

---

[72] Cornford (1907) 194–6 argues that Apatē is 'about to perform the ritual proper to the declaration of war – the act of throwing a burning torch between the combatants'. Cornford cites a scholion on Eur. *Phoen.* 1377 as evidence for this custom. But see Mastronarde (1994) 534–5 for the point that the scholion may be making this custom up in order to explain *Phoen.* 1377.

[73] On the vase's depiction of history and its probable tragic inspiration, see Anti (1952); Trendall and Webster (1971) 112; Hall (1996) 8. Cornford (1907) 194f. uses the vase's depiction of Apatē to argue that 'deception' as a cause of military folly is a mythic or tragic theme which influences Thucydidean narrative.

[74] See Aesch. *Pers.* 91–114; 361f.; 472f.; 744–50; 1005ff. For the important contrast between the words of Darius' ghost and the other characters' and chorus' postulation of divine deceit and delusion sent by the gods as a cause of the Persian defeat, see Winnington-Ingram (1983) 1–15.

rates seems to mean by the distinction. The true falsehood, as Socrates self-consciously coins it, is hated by gods and men alike and it describes occasions when a man is deceived in his soul about 'things that are' (*ta onta*: 2.382b1–5).[75] Thus it amounts to 'ignorance in the soul' (ἡ ἐν τῇ ψυχῇ ἄγνοια) on the part of the deceived (2.382b7–8).[76] By contrast, the 'lie in words' is 'only a kind of imitation of the affection in the soul and a shadowy after-image, not pure unadulterated falsehood' (2.382b9–11).[77] Socrates seems here to be introducing a theoretical foundation which will later justify deceit of the inhabitants of his ideal state by the philosopher-rulers. It also seems to introduce a justification for his infamous 'noble lie.'[78] For Socrates the 'true' lie or falsehood is one that has no relation to his idea of objective moral and ontological truths and will not bring them about if told and/or believed. The lie that is only 'in words' is that which does not correspond to truth or facts, but which, if told, will bring about some genuinely objective true belief, state of affairs or objective moral good.

Socrates goes on to consider on what occasions the 'lie in words' is usefully deployed: 'When and in what relationship may it be useful (χρήσιμον) and not repugnant to us?' (2.382c6–7). Two examples in his answer will be invoked again in his account of the ideal state. The lie in words is useful 'as a sort of medicine (φάρμακον) or preventative' when friends in a fit of madness or illusion are going to do some harm (2.382c7–10). It is also useful in mythological story-telling, says Socrates, 'because we do not know the truth about ancient times, so we make falsehood as much like truth as we can, and turn it to account' (2.382c10–d3). But the first example of a useful lie 'in words' is that which is employed 'in relation to enemies' (πρός τε τοὺς πολεμίους: 2.382c8–9). Socrates introduces this and the other two examples as generally held beliefs, or at least as beliefs which his interlocutor Adeimantus will not find particularly controversial. It is only later that Socrates appropriates and distorts these ideas about contexts for acceptable and useful lies for his own political and moral theory. At present he is drawing on what he represents as generally held beliefs concerning the occasional acceptability and utility of lying – and he

---

[75] ἐγὼ δὲ λέγω ὅτι τῇ ψυχῇ περὶ τὰ ὄντα ψεύδεσθαί τε καὶ ἐψεῦσθαι καὶ ἀμαθῆ εἶναι καὶ ἐνταῦθα ἔχειν τε καὶ κεκτῆσθαι τὸ ψεῦδος πάντες ἥκιστα ἂν δέξαιντο, καὶ μισοῦσι μάλιστα αὐτὸ ἐν τῷ τοιούτῳ.

[76] Ἀλλὰ μὴν ὀρθότατά γ' ἄν, ὃ νυνδὴ ἔλεγον, τοῦτο ὡς ἀληθῶς ψεῦδος καλοῖτο, ἡ ἐν τῇ ψυχῇ ἄγνοια ἡ τοῦ ἐψευσμένου.

[77] ἐπεὶ τό γε ἐν τοῖς λόγοις μίμημά τι τοῦ ἐν τῇ ψυχῇ ἐστιν παθήματος καὶ ὕστερον γεγονὸς εἴδωλον, οὐ πάνυ ἄκρατον ψεῦδος.

[78] Pl. *Resp.* 3.414b8–415d5. On the 'lie in words' as a prelude to the 'noble lie' see below pp. 153–5; Page (1991) 16–26; Reeve (1988) 208–13.

does so in order to make a brief theological point, namely that the gods never deceive because, unlike mortals, they have no use for deception. Why do gods have no use for lies? Socrates answers as follows; no mad or senseless person can be a friend of a god, so no god needs to lie to his friend. Furthermore, no god need have recourse to mythological invention; it would be absurd to suggest that a god could be ignorant of antiquity (2.382d5–e11). When it comes to the question of gods deceiving enemies, Socrates' solution is very revealing. Like the other two solutions, it is itself couched in the form of a question; 'but would he lie to his enemies out of fear?' (Ἀλλὰ δεδιὼς τοὺς ἐχθροὺς ψεύδοιτο;: 2.382d11). To this, Adeimantus simply replies 'certainly not' and the issue is closed. Socrates introduces the idea that people have a specific motivation for deceiving an enemy. He missed this out when he was actually discussing the motives for acceptable deceit between mortals. The motivation is fear (δεδιὼς). From Socrates' question, then, we can deduce that he assumes that mortals deceive their enemies when they are afraid of them. It is therefore absurd for a poet to represent the gods deceiving their *echthroi* because no god could really be afraid of his or her enemies.[79]

What are we to make of this characterisation of using lies against an enemy? Firstly, it provides more evidence that military trickery is of contested value. Plato's Socrates speaks of 'deceiving the enemy' as if it is generally agreed by his community to be morally acceptable. But when we speak of 'community' here, what do we mean? Does Socrates' view of a 'general' moral belief count as evidence for what all citizens of Athens would believe? Or can we only ascribe this belief to the small political, intellectual and sometimes pro-Spartan, often anti-democratic elite which constitutes Plato's depiction of the Socratic 'circle'?[80] For

---

[79] It is difficult to know if there is any reason why Socrates uses the term *polemioi* in the context of mortal deceit and *echthroi* when talking about immortals. But it is clear that *polemios* delineates a military enemy and therefore it seems fair to assume that, in the context of mortal deceit, Socrates has military hostility in mind, at least in part. However, the fact that Socrates does not make any clear distinction between hostility in warfare and day-to-day enmity within a community should not be ignored. When Socrates identifies the acceptability of 'deceiving the enemy', he may be discussing all forms of enmity without making any distinction between the realms of military conflict, politics or private relations.

[80] On this, see Winkler (1990b) 172: 'Athens was a society in which philosophers were often ignored and, when noticed, were easily represented not as authority figures but as cranks or buffoons.' See also Cartledge (1993) 9–10. For the influence of Spartan oligarchic structures on Platonic thought see Powell (1994). For the Platonic representation of Socratic philosophic activity as 'outside' of and 'alien' to traditional and democratic discourses see Nightingale (1995) 13–59. Von Reden and Goldhill (1999) discuss the way in which Platonic dialogues self-consciously position philosophic discussion in relation to and yet at the margins of democratic sites of performance and social and political exchange.

these reasons, we have to accept that Plato's depiction of 'deceive your enemy' as an unproblematic and universally agreeable moral injunction may conceal more than it reveals about Athenian views on *pseudē* and *apatē*. However, we can say that Plato's text shows us that, although the Thucydidean Pericles characterises military deceit as unAthenian, the notion of military trickery *by* citizens is not inconceivable. Furthermore his attitude bears some affinities to the remarks of Andocides, whom we saw sanctioning the use of military trickery by *stratēgoi*.[81] A similar attitude towards military deceit is also demonstrated by Xenophon's Socrates and other Xenophontic treatises.[82]

At the same time as it contradicts Pericles' view of *apatē* in relation to the citizen soldier, the Platonic Socrates' representation of 'the lie in words' offers us a hint of an explanation as to why the contradiction is there. Despite the reservations of the last paragraph it should be noted that Socrates' representation of 'deceiving the enemy' can be read as an inscription within the wider rubric of a fundamental ancient Greek ethic of social relations, namely 'help friends, harm enemies'.[83] Socrates sanctions deceptive communication towards a friend when that friend is in danger of harming himself or others due to some mental aberration. Thus, the Platonic Socrates believes that, in exceptional circumstances, deception can have a positive role in the enforcement of the 'help friends' ethic. His assumption that it is acceptable to deceive an enemy can also be seen as conforming to the pre-Christian Greek notion that it is right and proper to harm your *polemioi* or *echthroi*.[84]

When placed in the context of civic military agency, however, the idea that it is justifiable to harm an enemy by *any* means will certainly become strained, if certain modes of 'doing harm' are associated with *fear* of that enemy. In the privileged public discourse of the Athenian *epitaphios logos*, descriptions of self-sacrifice and bravery in battle explicitly highlight the idea that the exemplary Athenian warrior does not fear the enemy. In the funeral oration of the Thucydidean Pericles, the war-dead are praised as having rejected the 'shameful word of dis-

---

[81] Andoc. 3.33–4. See above pp. 83–4 and below 169–72.

[82] Xen. *Mem.* 4.2.14ff. See below pp. 122–42 and 151–2 for further references and discussion on Xenophon.

[83] For general accounts of this ethic with examples and bibliography, see Blundell (1989) 26–59; Dover (1974) 180–4; Pearson (1962) 14–20 and 87–9.

[84] At Pl. *Resp.* 1.331c–d, Socrates makes it clear to Polemarchus that 'harm enemies, help friends' is not an adequate definition of justice. But this does not mean that Socrates cannot appeal to this ethic in his creation of a just state. As Tatum (1989) 39 points out with reference to 'harm enemies, help friends' in the *Republic*, 'Socrates does not so much reject the idea as examine it with the fluidity that dialectic permits.' See also Page (1991). Socrates *does* attack the 'help friends, harm enemies' ethic in Plato's *Crito*.

honour' when they stood their ground to face the enemy. They died at 'the crowning moment of glory, rather than fear' (τὸ μὲν αἰσχρὸν τοῦ λόγου ἔφυγον, τὸ δ᾽ ἔργον τῷ σώματι ὑπέμειναν καὶ δι᾽ ἐλαχίστου καιροῦ τύχης ἅμα ἀκμῇ τῆς δόξης μᾶλλον ἢ τοῦ δέους ἀπηλλάγησαν: 2.42.4). Similarly, Lysias' funeral speech emphasises the *absence* of fear among the democratic forces who fought Spartans and oligarchic sympathisers in the aftermath of Aegospotami:

> Nevertheless, having felt no fear of the multitude of their opponents (οὐ τὸ πλῆθος τῶν ἐναντίων φοβηθέντες), and having exposed their own bodies to danger, they set up a trophy over their enemies, and now find witnesses to their excellence, close to this monument, in the tombs of the Lacedaemonians. (Lysias 2.63)

In these public representations of military self-sacrifice, it is crucial that the exemplary Athenian soldier is portrayed as completely unafraid of the enemy and death itself.

Socrates' assumption that mortals deceive enemies *because* they are afraid of them clearly runs counter to these descriptions and prescriptions of ideal Athenian military identity. But the notion that deceit of an enemy is motivated by fear is not the singular invention of Plato. Euripides' Electra begins her infamous rejection of the Old Man's claim that Orestes has made a secret entry into Argos by questioning the possibility that her brother would keep himself in hiding:

> οὐκ ἄξι᾽ ἀνδρός, ὦ γέρον, σοφοῦ λέγεις,
> εἰ κρυπτὸν ἐς γῆν τήνδ᾽ ἂν Αἰγίσθου φόβῳ
> δοκεῖς ἀδελφὸν τὸν ἐμὸν εὐθαρσῆ μολεῖν.

What you say, old man, will get you no credit for wisdom if you suppose that my courageous brother would enter this land furtively for fear of Aegisthus. (Euripides *Electra* 524–6)

Electra clearly associates trickery, deceit and concealment with fear of an enemy and hence with decidedly 'unheroic' behaviour. The irony here is that Orestes *has* entered the borderlands of Argos secretly and he intends to stay near the frontier in order to make good his escape should anyone recognise him (94–7). Electra has already spoken with Orestes without realising it (215ff.). Her view of Orestes is grounded in an 'illusory trust in his heroic qualities' and Electra herself 'will have to drive him to commit the matricide as he hesitates to commit the outrage'.[85] To be sure, there are several moments in extant Attic tragedy when deceit and ambush of an enemy is characterised as shameful or

---

[85] Goldhill (1988a) 253 with Eur. *El.* 961ff.

cowardly in comparison to open confrontation.[86] But Electra's words provide the only instance where the 'unheroic' quality of military deceit is explained in terms of its psychological associations. Like Socrates, Electra sees fear of an enemy as the motivation for hiding from him and deceiving him. Unlike Socrates, she associates this fear and any resultant furtive behaviour with cowardice.

It must be said that the formulations of deceit as in some sense 'unheroic' or 'shameful' which we find in Athenian plays are explicitly questioned by other characters and dramatic events.[87] But Electra's comments simply serve to underline the point that public Athenian constructions of ideal military conduct allowed no place for fear of the enemy within them. The inference of Socrates and Electra that military trickery is a mark of such fear goes some way towards explaining why *apatē*, *dolos* and *pseudē* have such a problematic position in Athenian texts which discuss appropriate military conduct. Despite the Homeric valorisation of the ambush as a tactic requiring the best men and a good dose of courage,[88] we have seen examples in the public discourse of democratic Athens where military trickery is denigrated or associated with the non-Athenian 'other'. Pericles and Demosthenes, for example, could be read as appropriating a different Homeric view of deceit. In the *Iliad*, Achilles views the ambush as a noble military practice, but he also tells Odysseus that he hates a man who says one thing and thinks another (9.312–13). Pericles and Demosthenes seem to view all forms of military *apatē* in a manner which appropriates and reapplies Achilles' general reflection on the culpability of telling lies with the result that 'deceiving the enemy' becomes as undesirable and unheroic as deceit between friends or fellow-citizens.

But Socrates and Electra demonstrate that, in the second half of the fifth and also in the fourth century, tactics of trickery and concealment can have the connotation of fear – a connotation which is clearly absent

---

[86] See [Eur.] *Rhes.* 510–11, where the Thracian king comments on Odysseus' military trickery in a way which implies that such ruses are a mark of cowardice: 'no brave man would choose to kill the enemy by stealth rather than confont him face on' (οὐδεὶς ἀνὴρ εὔψυχος ἀξιοῖ λάθρᾳ κτεῖναι τὸν ἐχθρόν, ἀλλ᾽ ἰὼν κατὰ στόμα). See also Soph. *Phil.* 108 where Neoptolemus assumes that it would be shameful (αἰσχρόν) to take Philoctetes' bow by deceit, although in this case it is precisely the fact that Philoctetes is not strictly an 'enemy' which drives Neoptolemus' dilemma. At 90–1, Neoptolemus is initially ready to take the bow by force (πρὸς βίαν), but not through tricks (μὴ δόλοισιν). He believes that it would be base to get the bow by deceit (νικᾶν κακῶς: 95). At Soph. *Trach.* 274–80, Lichas says that Zeus punished Heracles for killing Heracles by deceit. He says that Zeus would have forgiven Heracles if he had fought Iphitus openly.

[87] For such questioning in Sophocles' *Philoctetes*, see below pp. 188–201.

[88] See Adkins (1960) 32; Pritchett (1974) 178 for a list of examples where courage in the Homeric ambush is valorised.

in Homeric poetry. And while this connotation of fear and cowardice may explain the negative attitude towards deceit often expressed in Athens' political, legal and public dramatic texts, it is significant that the Platonic Socrates does not censure deceit of an enemy and views it as useful.[89] This view is also expressed several times in the didactic dialogue and treatises of Xenophon, another Athenian writer who must be regarded as out of sympathy with Athens' dominant ideology.[90] But before I turn to Xenophon's representation of military trickery, I wish to bring Codrus back into the picture. How can Lycurgus represent Codrus' trick so positively if there is a clear association between *apatē* and fear?

Although Lycurgus praises the deployment of *apatē* towards the enemy, it is crucial to realise that the example of Codrus circumvents any link between military trickery and fear. Codrus can only save his city by disguising himself, provoking the enemy and sacrificing his life. In Lycurgus' account, Codrus' *apatē* is a necessary element in his display of courage rather than a sign of fear. The existence of an oracle predicting failure for the Peloponnesians if Codrus is killed makes the achievement of death through deceit unavoidable if Codrus is to defend Athens in the most effective way. The extraordinary revelation of the oracle makes hoplite battle inappropriate and ineffective; it makes death a necessity rather than a risk; and finally, deceit and disguise become the only means of achieving an heroic death and saving the polis. And although Codrus' mode of engagement with the enemy can be described as the antithesis of 'hoplite' engagement, it is significant that he is represented as conforming to the basic lineaments of the Athenian military values which are constantly redescribed (*repre*scribed, *rein*scribed) by extant *epitaphioi logoi*. He is not afraid to die for his country and he is not afraid of the enemy. Codrus' deployment of deceit neither conforms totally to the ideological paradigm of the hoplite nor does it completely oppose it or break from it. In Lycurgus, then, and perhaps even in the late fifth century, the tale of Codrus' trickery can be seen to offer an ideal Athenian image of civic responsibility and military conduct which carefully negotiates and redefines the boundaries between the positive image of open, fair and collective

---

[89] In Plato's *Hippias Minor*, Socrates expresses a preference for Odysseus over Achilles because the former hero lies knowingly whereas the latter utters falsehoods through ignorance. See below pp. 121–2 and Blundell (1992); Pratt (1993) 154, n. 40.

[90] See Vidal-Naquet (1986b) 128, n. 3 who writes that Xenophon's work on war and hunting and 'his modification of the hoplite tradition' have 'a polemical significance that has hardly been noticed'.

hoplite endeavour and negative associations of individual cunning and deceit of the enemy.

In one sense, the 'hoplite' Codrus represented on the late fifth-century Bologna kylix offers a normative representation of the Athenian king which is totally opposed to the depiction of him in the stories of his trickery and low status disguise which we found in the narrative of Hellanicus and Lycurgus. If we had only Hellanicus' brief and neutral account, it would be possible to read Codrus' use of *apatē* in a manner which is similar to Vidal-Naquet's interpretation of Melanthus. Like his father Melanthus, Codrus wins by playing a trick on the enemy. We can also see Codrus' encounter with the enemy as a *monomachia* (single combat). On the evidence of Hellanicus alone, Codrus' ruse could offer Athens a negative paradigm against which 'normative' hoplite identity is to be defined. However, while it is certainly true that Lycurgus' carefully controlled valorisation of Codrus' ruse *and* the image of him as a hoplite on the Bologna kylix offer two *different* mode(1)s of military agency, it is clear that the orator's representation of Codrus as a trickster cannot simply be taken to be the negative antithesis of the representation on the vase. Lycurgus sees Codrus' behaviour as necessary, praiseworthy and militarily appropriate. As Spence notes, Lycurgus deploys Codrus in a speech where his attacks on Leocrates' cowardice are expressed in explicitly hoplite terms.[91] The 'Codrus as hoplite' portrayal on the vase could be interpreted as an erasure of the morally problematic theme of military trickery, but Lycurgus' Codrus is a hoplite warrior as much as he is a 'trickster-figure'. He behaves and dresses as a trickster, but his attitude to his polis, his enemy and himself conforms to the mentality of Athens' ideal hoplite. This leads me to wonder whether the representation of Codrus as a hoplite on the vase necessarily contradicts the version of Codrus' exploit in Lycurgus and Hellanicus at all. If Codrus' *apatē* paradoxically conforms in so many ways to the democratic Athenian ideals of self-sacrifice and bravery in combat, the depiction of him as a hoplite need not represent the promotion of a different version where Codrus goes out to die in the front line of an open battle. If Codrus' death via deceit is nevertheless to be viewed as noble, then it would be culturally logical to represent him as a hoplite rather than as a beggar or a woodcutter. The vase memorialises Codrus in the image of *what he was as good as*

---

[91] E.g. Lyc. 1.43, where the accused is described as 'neither taking up arms on behalf of his fatherland nor *presenting his body to the generals to place in formation*, but fleeing and betraying the safety of the people'. As Spence (1993) 167 points out, the italicised phrase (τὸ σῶμα παρασχόντα τάξαι τοῖς στρατηγοῖς) confirms that Lycurgus is thinking in hoplite terms.

(hoplite) rather than in the image of what he temporarily had to become in order to achieve 'la belle mort'.[92]

On the other hand, the Bologna kylix may simply mark a different version of Codrus' exploit – a version in which Hellanicus' and Lycurgus' theme of deceit is erased. If that *is* the case, the contrast between the two versions (the contested representation of a civic hero) is still instructive. Two versions would attest to the problematisation of military trickery in 'public' representations in the late fifth century. Perhaps in the 430s it was too problematic for Hellanicus' narrative of Codrus' deception to be represented and valorised, either in public art or rhetoric. After all, the vase dates to around the time when it is the Spartan enemy which is being stereotyped as tricky and dishonest. But a hundred years later, the version in which Codrus tricks his enemy is easily co-opted into Lycurgus' hoplitism, and is in no way problematic for public representation. This may well be due to the fact that the trick is presented in terms of self-sacrifice and collective values. In the realm of Athenian military ideology, the trickster does not always remain at the negative end of a polarised opposition in relation to the hoplite. Whether Vidal-Naquet's interpretation of Melanthus and the *ephēbeia* has any significant purchase on Athenian institutions and ideology in the democracy *before* the official ephebate was instituted remains an open question. But the representations of Codrus that I have discussed must offer a challenge to the idea that public Athens always constituted military *apatē* as ideologically negative or resolutely 'anti-hoplitic'. At the same time, the Bologna image of Codrus as a hoplite remains an important emblem of the Athenian imaginary. Codrus' trickery makes sense as a praiseworthy action only if it is termed within the language and narrative which, at the same time as such trickery runs counter to the lineaments of hoplite *practice*, nevertheless evinces the collective values of hoplite bravery and sacrifice. It is this negotiation between trickery and hoplitism which Lycurgus' rhetoric exemplifies.[93]

It could be objected that my argument needlessly attempts to maintain an opposition between deception and hoplite identity or ephebic trickery and hoplite 'honesty'. If Codrus' ruse is praised by Lycurgus, if *apatē* and *dolos* are implied to be Athens' allies in Aeschylus' *Persians*, if Plato, Xenophon, Andocides and a number of other sources all attest the acceptability of military trickery, then why speak of 'negotiation' at all? Surely, the evidence suggests that Vidal-Naquet and others were

---

[92] For this expression and its resonances, see Loraux (1982).
[93] The positive colour of Codrus' deceit might even be suggested by the bare bones of the story in Hellanicus.

wrong to claim such a strong structural opposition between *apatē* and hoplite ideology in the first place? Lycurgus' praise of Codrus does not 'negotiate' with a pre-existing articulation of *apatē* as anti-hoplitic; rather, Codrus' deception stands simply as an effective story which strategically exemplifies the normative values of military self-sacrifice. His cunning is unproblematic because, while texts *can* articulate deception as the ideological antithesis of normative military identity, there is no law of ideological non-contradiction which renders certain positive representations of military trickery automatically anomalous. In other words, Codrus' deception is not an ideological anomaly which requires an explanation in terms of 'ambivalence' or 'negotiation'. A number of evaluative statements which we define as 'ideological' do not have to cohere in terms of their assessment of a single concept or a practice.[94] Codrus saved his city and the fact that he did so through deception is just not a problem for Lycurgus or his Athenian audience. And this need not be because attitudes towards military trickery had changed. It may simply be that military deception could be praised or despised in accordance with the particular rhetorical relation and strategy being performed: to say that such strategies 'negotiate' with an ideological structure of values may be to falsely reify Athenian 'ideology' and to over-emphasise the purchase of the anti-deception discourse outlined in chapter one.

In response to this possible objection I can only argue that my use of the term 'negotiation' is chosen for good reason. It is simply impossible to recover the extent to which (for example) Lycurgus' praise of Codrus would have been viewed as a *marked* realignment of previous civic evaluations of military trickery. In speaking of 'strategy' and 'negotiation' whilst at the same time insisting on the presence of a 'discourse' or 'ideology' where deception is termed unAthenian or anti-hoplitic, I have aimed to present Athenian views and uses of the notion of 'deceiving the enemy' as *both* over-determined by pre-existing structures of thought *and* subject to local (even individual) strategic invention or practice. In this sense, my approach (if not my language) approximates that of Bourdieu, who uses the term 'habitus' to describe the dialectic whereby social practices (weddings, gift-exchanges, trials of honour) reproduce and constitute 'rules' or 'codes' at the same time as they can be seen to deviate from, bend or strategically interpret existing 'rules' or 'codes'.[95] Bourdieu's point is that social practice can never be re-

---

[94] See Ober (1989) 38–42. For an excellent survey of theories and definitions of 'ideology' and the case of classical Athens, see Croally (1994) 259f.

[95] See Bourdieu (1977) 1–52 and 72–158.

duced to a check-list or diagram of 'norms' or 'structures of thought'. But this masterly attack on the 'objectivism' of structural anthropology is not a claim that social practice lacks reference to structures of belief or codes which in some sense guide the potentialities of actual practice and representation. As with Foucault's concern to investigate 'what it was possible to think' at certain points in history,[96] Bourdieu's 'habitus' is the space in which one sees the divergent, creative and yet (after the event) sociologically explicable ways in which social actors consciously or unconsciously *negotiate* and reproduce prohibitions and protocols *in practice* and for often strategic reasons. My characterisation of military trickery in Athens as 'negotiable' is meant precisely to capture this sense of inextricable dialogue between extrapolated structures of value and belief ('la belle mort', hoplite courage) and particular instantiations of discourse (Pericles' Funeral Speech, Lycurgus on Codrus). My further characterisation of military deceit as 'problematic' or 'problematised' in classical Athens is best justified by the material presented in the remainder of this chapter.

If we turn away from the field of *public* representation and rhetoric and return to Athenian works concerned with philosophy, history and *paideia*, we find three authors who add further definition and depth to our picture of the negotiable and problematic status of military deceit in the late fifth and fourth centuries. The first of these authors is Antisthenes, a pupil of Socrates, and widely regarded as the founding father of the Cynic school of philosophy.[97] The second is the author of the *Hippias Minor*, whom most contemporary scholars identify as Plato and whom I will discuss very briefly. The third is Xenophon, whose engagement with the theme of 'deceiving an enemy' is so anxious and far reaching that it requires more detailed treatment in the next section.

Some time in the late fifth or early fourth century, Antisthenes wrote a pair of speeches as if they had been delivered by Ajax and Odysseus during the infamous dispute over which of them should inherit the armour of the dead Achilles.[98] This mythological *hoplōn krisis* and its outcome provoke Pindar to praise the achievements of Ajax and berate Homer for his (deceitful) perpetuation of Odysseus' undeserved and dishonestly gained *kleos*.[99] The dispute was also a popular subject in Attic vase painting in the fifth century and along with Sophocles' dramatisation of the disastrous aftermath of this dispute, we know that

---

[96] See Foucault (1975), (1982).
[97] See Caizzi (1966); Rankin (1986).
[98] Antisthenes fr. 14 (Ajax) and fr. 15 (Odysseus) (Caizzi).
[99] Pind. *Nem.* 7.9–30 and 8.19–44. See Walsh (1984) 37–61; Most (1985) 148–82; Nisetich (1989) 1–23; Pratt (1993) 121–8.

Aeschylus wrote a tragedy which depicted the *krisis* itself.[100] Antisthenes' pair of speeches undoubtedly constitute an exercise in rhetorical composition and *ēthopoiïa*.[101] It is also likely that some of Odysseus' arguments and character prefigure certain values which embodied Antisthenes' philosophical outlook.[102] But the choice of this particular mythological dispute and the arguments which the speeches mobilise can be seen to illustrate the extent to which the (in)admissibility of military deceit had become a problem for Athenian definitions of the good, courageous warrior. I will briefly summarise the relevant arguments put forward in the two speeches.

In his speech, Ajax makes claim to the armour by belittling Odysseus' theft of the Palladion. The theft served no purpose and he calls Odysseus a 'temple-robber'. Predictably, he claims that Odysseus only wants the armour to sell it; he is too cowardly to wear it. Ajax only wants the armour so that he can give it to Achilles' *philoi*. He contrasts his character with that of Odysseus tellingly; no project exists that Odysseus would undertake openly, whereas Ajax could not bear to do anything underhand.[103] Ajax would rather suffer terribly than gain a bad reputation. Odysseus would not care if he was hanged, if he could profit by it. Odysseus allows himself to be beaten and whipped, dresses up in rags and slips out by night to commit sacrilege in the enemy's temples. Ajax finally belittles mere *logoi* and argues that a man who talks is useless. To judge *aretē* and military conduct, you have to look at deeds (*erga*), rather than words (*logoi*).

Unsurprisingly, Odysseus' speech is longer, funnier and cleverer than the somewhat inept effort of Ajax. He claims that he has rendered the army many good services and points out to the judges that they have engaged in no battle in which he has not participated, while they have not shared in the peculiar dangers which he has faced. Odysseus stresses that the object of battle is to win and that the Palladion belonged to the Greeks in the first place. It was known that Troy could not be taken unless the statue was recovered. Odysseus questions the notion that Ajax is superior just because he acted in the company of the whole army. He belittles Ajax's claims to *aretē*, representing him as rushing around like a wild boar who is likely to kill himself by falling over. The truly brave man should not suffer any injury, whether from himself, a comrade or the enemy. Ajax's use of armour is a sign of

---

[100] See Jebb (1962) xx; Garvie (1998)1–6.
[101] See Kennedy (1963) 170–2; Rankin (1986) 153ff.
[102] Rankin (1986) 161–73.
[103] Fr. 14.5 (Caizzi): ὃ μὲν γὰρ οὐκ ἔστιν ὅ τι ἂν δράσειε φανερῶς, ἐγὼ δὲ οὐδὲν ἂν λάθρᾳ τολμήσαιμι πρᾶξαι.

cowardice; there is no difference between wearing Ajax's armour and sitting behind a fortified wall. Odysseus then discourses on his skill and value as a spy who, without armour, kills armed sentries who are awake and then provides intelligence which will keep the Greeks safe. He describes this role as that of a guardian (*phulax*) and a helmsman (*kubernētēs*). He then defends his use of lowly disguises. War is indeed about action rather than appearances. Odysseus has no special arms. He will fight against one or many in any way. Even though he is tired and everyone else is resting he will have himself whipped, and in a slave's disguise he will attack the enemy by night. He goes on to belittle the importance of Ajax's recovery of Achilles' body as opposed to his own recovery of the armour. Ajax is sick with ignorance and envy, mistakenly believing that his strength constitutes *andreia*.

In this summary I have done little justice to the irony generated by these speeches. Odysseus' arguments and language repeatedly allude to his own future status as an epic hero and the tragedy of Ajax's madness and suicide.[104] This playfulness signals the difficulty of interpreting the two speeches as representing concerns with definition and evaluation of 'proper' military conduct which were more widely held in Athens. As rhetorical exercises or as paradoxical and iconoclastic explorations into the nature of *andreia* and *aretē*, Antisthenes' creations bear the hallmarks of the (often idiosyncratic) intellectual investigations which we associate with 'the first Sophistic' at Athens.[105] Antisthenes demonstrates the ease (and through Ajax's words, the unease) with which techniques of *logos* can be used to relativise traditional evaluations and categories of the 'heroic', the 'useful', and the 'courageous' in the sphere of military excellence.

These opposing speeches are the invention of an intellectual figure whom we might consider to be marginal in relation to Athens' public arenas of debate and representation. Nevertheless, they demonstrate that the public representation and evaluation of deceit along a military trajectory in the late fifth and fourth centuries must not only be set against the backdrop of changes in, and utilisations of new *technai* of warfare. The new teachable technologies of speech and refutative argument exemplified in Antisthenes' exercise also provide a possible impetus for the public negotiability of military trickery. Furthermore, his exercise articulates several (of what I have argued to be) issues at stake in the Athenian public representation and evaluation of military trickery. The two speeches explore the extent to which, and some of

---

[104] Rankin (1986) 153ff. outlines some of these ironies.
[105] See Kerferd (1981a) 78–130; Goldhill (1988a) ch. 9.

the terms in which the definition of military *aretē* and *andreia* could be problematised and renegotiated through an opposition between armed, collective and open confrontation and tactics involving stealth, deceit, secrecy and *monomachia*. Furthermore, Odysseus' cunning and stealth take him into self-confessed 'banausic' activity: as helmsman and guardian of the army he is not afraid to see himself as a 'worker' or to undergo the degradations necessary to be a plausible beggar or slave. There is a sense here of an association between military cunning and 'low' social status which I will have cause to return to in the next section. But Odysseus' arguments clearly pose a serious challenge to Ajax's traditional view of military valour: Antisthenes gives weight to the value of 'getting your hands dirty' and dirty tricks. Taken together, Odysseus' and Ajax's speeches offer us a crude mirror of military deceit's moral and ideological significance and its conflicting public representations.

The Platonic *Hippias Minor* must be placed in a similar intellectual context to that of Antisthenes. In this dialogue Socrates' praise of Odysseus' knowing use of lies and his attack on Achilles' ignorant expression of falsehoods is so paradoxical and self-referential in tone that Stanford refused to take it as a serious example of a positive classical representation of the trickster-hero.[106] Through some cunning (and to modern tastes, pedantic) literary analysis Socrates dismantles Hippias' assertion that Achilles is better than Odysseus because Homer represents Achilles as 'simple and true' (ἀληθής τε καὶ ἁπλοῦς) while he makes Odysseus 'polytropic and false' (πολύτροπός τε καὶ ψευδής: 365b3–5). As evidence for this conclusion the sophist cites the Homeric Achilles' famous attack on Odysseus as the man who hides one thing in his heart and says another (365a1–b2, Hom. *Il.* 9.312–13). Socrates departs from Homeric interpretation and sets out to show that one and the same man can be both 'true' and 'false' (365d9ff.). He argues that the wise and just man who lies or does wrong knowingly is always better than the man who does wrong or utters falsehoods without knowing that he is doing so. Those who possess skills and knowledge can pretend to be unskilled or ignorant, but the unskilled and ignorant cannot be skilled and knowledgeable. He argues that the Homeric Odysseus always lies willingly and with knowledge of the truth. Achilles, on the other hand, either deliberately tells lies or utters false-

---

[106] Stanford (1954) 250, n. 38. For the way in which Socrates seems to enact the qualities of Odysseus, whilst representing himself as the ignorant Achilles and Hippias as the knowledgeable Achilles, see the excellent analyses of Blundell (1992); and Napolitano Valditara (1994) 126–42.

hoods and makes false promises unwillingly and in ignorance of the truth. For example, he tells Odysseus that he will sail home but he never does and he implies to Ajax that he will stay (369d1–371e8). Socrates suggests that Achilles is being *polutropos* and telling lies here. When Hippias refuses to accept this, Socrates concludes that Achilles has uttered falsehoods unwillingly and out of ignorance and is therefore inferior to Odysseus. Most of the discussion departs from Homeric interpretation and explores the question of being 'true' and 'false' at the same time as Socrates demonstrates the superiority of the intentional liar with reference to different crafts and branches of knowledge, including all the skills which Hippias claims for himself (368a9f., 373c3f.). The dialogue ends in *aporia* as Socrates confesses that he is as much disturbed by, and unsatisfied with his own conclusion as Hippias is unwilling to accept its truth (376b1–c7).

The *Hippias Minor* demonstrates how a question concerning the relative qualities of two paradigmatic mythical warriors could be turned towards a much larger question concerning the ethics and epistemology of the intentional and unintentional expression of falsehoods. Like Hippias, one finds it hard to work out how far Socrates' praise of intentional falsehood is to be taken seriously: is Socrates deliberately misleading Hippias like an Odysseus or is he being ignorantly false like an Achilles? But his characterisation of 'Odysseus *polutropos*' as wiser and better than Achilles shows us that 'philosophical' and 'sophistic' discourse in Athens could focus on the subject of deceit as a means of exploring, questioning and playing with received assumptions concerning notions of wisdom, knowledge, excellence, truth and falsehood. A focus on deceit also allowed for reinterpretation of the martial heroes who were seen to embody such notions. The wide social, political and ethical implications of valorising deceit in a military context are even more marked in Xenophon's writing and in his anxious treatment of *apatē* which I will now discuss.

Working with children and animals: teaching deceit in Xenophon's *Cyropaedia*

I have discussed military *apatē* in terms of its morally problematic status. I have argued that this problematisation only partly stems from changes in military practice and mentality from the Peloponnesian War onwards and is just as attributable to strategic manipulation of public norms concerning military conduct. I have shown that the problematisation of military *apatē* sometimes allows the rhetorical negotiation of a positive space for it within certain areas of Athens' public discourse. But Lycurgus' Codrus showed that the positive discursive space for military *apatē* is carefully delimited and informed by the notion of 'la belle mort' and collective values. At other times, military *apatē* is an admissible notion, but it can be denigrated in comparison with achievements in open combat; hence Demosthenes' portrayal of Themistocles and Conon.

Despite these examples of negotiation in lawcourt oratory, the genre of the funeral speech seems to exclude *apatē* through complete silence, or else, as in the case of Thucydides' rendition, to condemn it and associate it with the enemy. I have argued that this silence and condemnation was not simply grounded in an opposition between 'hoplite' identity and *apatē* (open and fair collective battle *contra* individual deceit) but also in a more general association between military trickery and *fear* of the enemy.

We saw that Plato's Socrates took a different attitude. He associated deceit of an enemy with fear, and yet he saw such deceit as useful. We will see that Xenophon's Socrates takes a similar (though not identical) view, but in this section I will be concentrating on a Xenophontic dialogue in which Socrates does not explicitly take part.[107] The dialogue is from the first book of Xenophon's *Cyropaedia* and it involves Cyrus, the future king of Persia and his father Cambyses. A segment of this dialogue constitutes the most extensive theoretical justification and recommendation of military trickery to be found in a classical Athenian text. In discussing this segment, its aftermath (literally its 'after-learning') and related texts, I hope to demonstrate another dimension of the late fifth- and fourth-century problematisation of 'deceiving the enemy'. The dialogue carves out a carefully controlled and anxiously mediated educational programme for military *apatē* which attempts to circumvent the dangers that can result from teaching young boys that deception is sometimes just.

The dialogue between Cambyses and Cyrus the Great comes from a section of the text which constitutes 'the most explicit example of Κύρου παιδεία – the education of Cyrus – to be found in Xenophon's lengthy work'.[108] Cyrus has been summoned by his uncle, the Median king Cyaxares, to lead a Persian army against the Assyrians. This is Cyrus' first major military campaign. His father accompanies him to the Persian–Median border, and the dialogue (*Cyr.* 1.6.1–2.1.1) represents their conversation on the journey. Cambyses instructs and cor-

---

[107] Although I will argue that the ideas and methods of 'Socrates' do haunt the exchange.
[108] Gera (1993) 50.

rects his son on matters of military tactics and leadership; he listens to, and answers, Cyrus' questions. Cyrus has had specialist teaching in the art of generalship, but Cambyses shows him that there are many gaps and faults in his learning. He reviews Cyrus' knowledge and instructs him on the subject of supplies, health, the martial arts, rousing the troops and maintaining their obedience (1.6.16–26). Having discussed these matters of essential knowledge, Cyrus asks his father if a general who has dealt with all these matters should go ahead and attack the enemy as soon as he can. Cambyses replies that a commander should only initiate action against the foe if he expects to 'gain an advantage' over the enemy (εἰ μέλλοι γε πλεῖον ἕξειν: 1.6.26). When Cyrus asks his father to tell him the best way (μάλιστα) to gain such an advantage, Cambyses replies as follows:

'By Zeus', he said, 'this is not a trivial or a simple issue that you ask me about, my son. But know this well that the man who intends to do this must be designing and stealthy, tricky and deceitful, a thief and a robber, overreaching the enemy in all things' (ἐπίβουλον εἶναι καὶ κρυψίνουν καὶ δολερὸν καὶ ἀπατεῶνα καὶ κλέπτην καὶ ἅρπαγα καὶ ἐν παντὶ πλεονέκτην τῶν πολεμίων). (Xenophon Cyropaedia 1.6.27)

Cyrus laughs at this answer, swears by Heracles and exclaims 'what a man you say I must become!' (1.6.27). Cambyses then adds that if Cyrus *does* become such a commander, he would also be 'the most just and law-abiding man' (δικαιότατός τε καὶ νομιμώτατος ἀνήρ: 1.6.27). Cyrus is puzzled by this claim (1.6.28): 'Why used you to teach us the opposite of this when we were boys (παῖδας) and ephebes (ἐφήβους)?' Cambyses replies that Cyrus should *still* regard deceit, stealth and thievery as unjust, if they are deployed on friends and fellow citizens (καὶ νῦν πρὸς τοὺς φίλους τε καὶ πολίτας). However, Cambyses maintains that Cyrus and his contemporaries *did* learn many villainies (πολλὰς κακουργίας) so that they could harm their enemies. Cyrus does not recall any such training, so Cambyses reminds him that he was trained to shoot, throw a spear, to ensnare (δολοῦν) wild boars in nets and catch deer in traps. He also stresses that Cyrus never had to confront lions, bears and leopards in a fair, face-to-face contest; he only confronted wild animals when he had some unfair advantage (μετὰ πλεονεξίας τινός). 'Do you not recognise', Cambyses concludes, 'that all these things are villainies (κακουργίαι) and deceptions (ἀπάται) and tricks (δολώσεις) and gaining unfair advantages (πλεονεξίαι)?' Cyrus concedes Cambyses' point but he recalls that he was only allowed to trick wild animals and not men: 'if I ever even seemed to wish to deceive a man, I know that I got a good beating for it' (1.6.29).[109] Cambyses explains that Cyrus and his friends were permitted to shoot and throw a spear at a target but not at people – this was to prevent the youths from harming their friends (*philoi*) at the time. However the target practice ensured that the boys would be able to aim well at men in the event of a war. Along similar lines, Cambyses then explains that Cyrus was taught to deceive and take advantage only of beasts so that he might not harm his friends: nevertheless such training would enable him to use deception against a human enemy in a future war (1.6.29).

Cyrus is still puzzled (1.6.30). He asks Cambyses why he was not taught how to do good and bad to men, given that Cambyses has pointed out that a military commander also needs to understand the latter branch of knowledge. In response, Cambyses reveals that in former generations there *was* a teacher of the boys who taught them justice in the very manner which Cyrus proposes: 'to lie, and not to lie, to cheat and not to cheat, to slander and not to slander, to take and not to take unfair advantage' (1.6.31).[110] He 'drew the line' (διώριζε) between what one must do to one's friends and what one must do to one's enemies. This anonymous teacher (*didaskalos*) also taught the boys that it was right (δίκαιον) to deceive friends, provided it was for a good end (ἐπὶ ἀγαθῷ), and to steal the possessions of a friend if it was for a good purpose (1.6.31). He trained the boys to practise deceit upon each other, 'just as also in wrestling, the Greeks, they say, teach deception and train the boys to be able to practise it upon one another' (1.6.32).[111] Unfortunately, when some of the boys had become experts in *apatē* and perhaps even *philokerdia* (avarice), they started to take unfair advantage (*pleonektein*) of their friends (1.6.32).

As a consequence of this, important legislation was introduced: 'an ordinance (*rhētra*) was passed which obtains even today, simply to teach our boys, just as we teach our slaves in their relations to us, to tell the truth and not to deceive and not to take unfair advantage' (1.6.33).[112] Cambyses adds that the law requires any boys who flout its

---

[109] Ναὶ μὰ Δί', ἔφη, θηρίων γε· ἀνθρώπων δὲ εἰ καὶ δόξαιμι βούλεσθαι ἐξαπατῆσαί τινα, πολλὰς πληγὰς οἶδα λαμβάνων.

[110] Ἀλλὰ λέγεται, ἔφη, ὦ παῖ, ἐπὶ ἡμετέρων προγόνων γενέσθαι ποτὲ ἀνὴρ διδάσκαλος τῶν παίδων, ὃς ἐδίδασκεν ἄρα τοὺς παῖδας τὴν δικαιοσύνην, ὥσπερ σὺ κελεύεις, μὴ ψεύδεσθαι καὶ ψεύδεσθαι, καὶ μὴ ἐξαπατᾶν καὶ ἐξαπατᾶν, καὶ μὴ διαβάλλειν καὶ διαβάλλειν, καὶ μὴ πλεονεκτεῖν καὶ πλεονεκτεῖν.

[111] ... ὥσπερ καὶ ἐν πάλη φασὶ τοὺς Ἕλληνας διδάσκειν ἐξαπατᾶν, καὶ γυμνάζειν δὲ τοὺς παῖδας πρὸς ἀλλήλους τοῦτο δύνασθαι ποιεῖν.

[112] ἐγένετο οὖν ἐκ τούτων ῥήτρα, ᾗ καὶ νῦν χρώμεθα ἔτι, ἁπλῶς διδάσκειν τοὺς παῖδας ὥσπερ τοὺς οἰκέτας πρὸς ἡμᾶς αὐτοὺς διδάσκομεν ἀληθεύειν καὶ μὴ ἐξαπατᾶν καὶ μὴ πλεονεκτεῖν.

prescriptions be punished, so that they may become more refined citizens (πραότεροι πολῖται). When the boys reached the right age (namely Cyrus' present age), it was deemed safe to teach them 'that which is also lawful (νόμιμα) towards enemies' (1.6.34). Cambyses justifies this shift in ethical teaching as follows:

> It does not seem likely that you would break away and become savage citizens (ἄγριοι πολῖται) after you had been brought up together in mutual respect (ἐν τῷ αἰδεῖσθαι ἀλλήλους συντεθραμμένοι). In the same way we do not discuss sexual matters (περὶ ἀφροδισίων) in the presence of very young boys, lest they immoderately (ἀμέτρως) indulge a powerful lust engendered by lax discipline. (Xenophon *Cyropaedia* 1.6.34)

Cyrus accepts Cambyses' argument from historical precedent and asks his father to teach him how to take advantage of the enemy immediately, because he is late in learning (ὀψιμαθῆ: 1.6.35). In the following sections Cambyses offers some practical guidelines on deceiving and taking advantage of the enemy and, in doing so, he draws liberally on Cyrus' experience in hunting and trapping various kinds of animal (1.6.35–40).

I have summarised this section of dialogue in detail because it reveals some of the important issues at stake in the admission or exclusion of a positive ethic of deceit, particularly that of 'deceiving the enemy'. The discussion is held between two 'historical' barbarians, but few scholars would now dispute the fact that the *Cyropaedia* is largely a fiction; '[Xenophon] was much more interested in the political lessons to be derived from his representation of Cyrus' career, than he was in Cyrus' ethnicity, which he minimised to vanishing point.'[113] Hirsch may be right to highlight Xenophon's accuracy in depicting *some* Persian beliefs, customs and institutions.[114] However, these 'facts' did not relate to the empire of Cyrus the Great (c. 559–530); rather they reflected Xenophon's own experience of, and reports he heard about, life in fourth-century Persia.[115] The section of dialogue which I outlined above exemplifies the 'Greekness' of Xenophon's ideal Persians. Cyrus swears by Heracles and Zeus. Cambyses speaks of Persian youths in terms of their future responsibility as *politai* ('citizens') and he refers to the Greek practice of using wrestling as a pedagogic resource

---

[113] Cartledge (1993) 49–50.
[114] See Hirsch (1985) 61ff.
[115] See Cartledge (1993) 49 and 104–6. Cartledge concedes that Xenophon would have got some of his 'facts' about fourth-century Persia right but maintains that the *Cyropaedia* is basically a fictional narrative.

(1.6.34).[116] Amongst other points of contact, it is also clear that 'the Persian teacher of old described here is a very Greek figure',[117] and I will return to his significance below.

Like Plato, Xenophon undoubtedly has an interest in what Cartledge calls 'a new fourth-century willingness to allow virtue and wisdom to a sole ruler, who is somehow elevated above the common herd of his subjects'.[118] Xenophon spent a lot of time working as a mercenary commander for the Spartan king Agesilaus and for the Persian prince Cyrus the Younger. He was condemned in his absence by the Athenian democracy for working with 'the enemy'.[119] His *Hiero* can be read as a handbook on how to be a good Greek tyrant. Likewise, the *Agesilaus* offers a glowing example of the good Greek hereditary king. And although his treatise on how to be a good Athenian cavalry commander (the *Hipparchicus*) may betray his interest in elite leadership, its advice and instruction is predicated upon a need to serve and negotiate with Athens' democratic structure.[120] Cartledge describes the *Cyropaedia* as reflecting 'a new model of political theory, pro-monarchist and not so much anti- as non-civic'.[121] This may be a fair overview of the tenor of the whole work, but Cambyses' discussion of education and military trickery is couched in civic terms, although not specifically Athenian. I have already mentioned Cambyses' references to 'citizens'. Also, as Gera notes, and as I will have further cause to comment upon, he uses a Spartan term (*rhētra*) for the law forbidding Persian youths to lie.[122] Cyrus is being taught the importance of the enforcement of laws that were made for society's benefit in previous generations. The laws set limits on what could and could not be taught by an individual, what was and was not acceptable behaviour in society. These notions of law and responsibility approximate certain components of Greek civic structures and values as much as, or more than, the structures of an ideal 'non-civic' monarchy.[123]

Despite the dramatic date, setting and monarchic hero of the *Cyro-*

---

[116] For the wrestling analogy see below, n. 133.
[117] Gera (1993) 68.
[118] Cartledge (1993) 105.
[119] See Cartledge (1987) 55–73 for sources and discussion of Xenophon's life and career.
[120] See Xen. *Hipparch.* 1.8.
[121] Cartledge (1993) 55.
[122] Gera (1993) 70.
[123] See Too (1998) who argues that Cyrus' education posits the ideal Greek pedagogical state, an ideal which the Persian king fails to live up to: '[P]edagogy is thus the trope which articulates the political and cultural superiority of the Attic democratic state by inviting the replacement of Persia by Athens and of Cyrus by Socrates' (302).

paedia, then, this discussion of deceit is informed by Greek notions of education and polity. Several moments of intertextuality between Cambyses' words and other Athenian writings (including other Xenophontic works) reinforce the crucial point that these barbarians are speaking for the benefit and edification of a Greek polis-dwelling audience, and I shall discuss these resemblances and echoes in the following analysis of Cyrus' and Cambyses' exchange. But before I turn to that analysis I want briefly to outline Xenophon's stated reasons for writing about Cyrus the Great, because they will have a bearing on part of my analysis. The opening sections of the work, so well discussed by Tatum, show that Xenophon 'is not so much concerned with which form government takes, as with the inherent instability of any system'.[124] Alongside the ephemeral nature of oligarchy, monarchy and democracy, Xenophon conjures up an image of men as more difficult to rule than any other living creature. He reflects that 'human beings conspire against none sooner than those whom they see attempting to rule them' (1.1.2).[125] Xenophon focuses on Cyrus because he sees Cyrus as a ruler who circumvented the problems inherent in political structures and in maintaining the consensus of human beings as obedient and willing subjects; 'we know that people obeyed Cyrus willingly ... [H]e was able to awaken in all so lively a desire to please him, that they always wished to be guided by his will' (1.1.4–5). As Tatum puts it, 'here is the ideal leader and the reason why we want to study him'.[126] Xenophon proposes to concentrate on an account of Cyrus' *ēthos*, *genea* (ancestry) and what sort of *paideia* he received (1.1.6).

Tatum characterises Cyrus as the perfect pupil for a 'wise adviser' like Cambyses; '[T]hroughout this long catechism, Cyrus never resists correction or amplification; he grasps instantly every point his father raises. He is an ideal student of the kind few teachers ever encounter in their experience – it is not in the experience of Socrates, for example.'[127] But if the ideal future king is the ideal pupil and interlocutor, it is significant that Cyrus does *not* instantly grasp Cambyses' point about the suitability of his training in hunting. Cambyses asks 'do you not know that you were learning many villainies?' Cyrus replies, 'No father, not I, at any rate.' And when Cambyses argues that his education in hunting promoted the practice of trickery and deceit, Cyrus still questions the relevance of hunting animals to the requirement of an adult commander that he know how to deceive men. However, the past

---

[124] Tatum (1989) 59 and Xen. *Cyr.* 1.1.1.   [125] On this, see Tatum (1989) 61.
[126] Tatum (1989) 63.   [127] Tatum (1989) 87.

pedagogic disaster of the anonymous *didaskalos* (and the subsequent legislation that was introduced) suggest that Cyrus' misrecognition of his boyhood education in *apatē* is (paradoxically) a sign that this education has operated in the appropriate manner and that Cyrus has learnt from it in the appropriate way.

Without realising it, Cyrus the *pais* and ephebe had been training to deceive a future enemy. He believed, and in accordance with the sanction of the law he was taught, that it was *always* important not to lie, cheat or steal. He was not aware that his time spent learning how to hunt was a preparation for deceiving men in war; hence his surprise when Cambyses reveals that a good commander must be 'designing and thievish, wily and deceitful'. If Cyrus had realised that he was being trained to deceive men when he was a boy and that deceit was sometimes justified, he could have misused his learning against friends and fellow-citizens. This is exactly what Cambyses and his ancestors wanted to avoid and Cyrus' surprise and incomprehension demonstrate that it is possible to train youths in military trickery without having to teach them the complexity of justified and unjustified contexts for deceit at a dangerous age. The revelation of those complexities, and the crucial lesson that it is right and necessary to deceive your enemy, must occur after the boy has become a man and has learnt to respect his friends and fellow-citizens. Our section of the dialogue represents this turning point; a revelatory lesson about the morality of deceit and the significance of hunting.[128]

But there is more behind this discussion of trickery than first meets the eye. The dialogue represents military *apatē* as morally, socially and educationally problematic. Gera states that the *rhētra* prescribes that 'children, like servants, should only be taught the truth, with no lessons in deception or taking advantage'.[129] This is true, but the law *does* allow the (ironically) veiled and mediated lessons in deception which take the form of a practical training in hunting and snaring animals. What the law prevents is an *explicit* lesson which entertains the notion that lying is sometimes admissible. Cambyses stresses that Cyrus and his companions only trapped animals and Cyrus knows that deceiving humans got him into trouble. This restriction to hunting (tricking) animals serves a double purpose in Cambyses' programme. It facilitates an education in deception which can remain misrecognised until

---

[128] Hunting is a constantly recurring, polyvalent motif in the *Cyropaedia* as a whole; see Due (1989) *passim*.

[129] Gera (1993) 68.

the young man is sufficiently mature to be told of its true significance; the pupil does not infer from animals to humans as appropriate objects of deception. Rather, he remains convinced that trickery must be practised only on beasts. At the same time, however, this distinction between ensnared animal and human offers a paradigm for a later distinction between enemy (*polemios*) and friend (*philos*). By training the young boy and the ephebe to trick and harm animals whilst encouraging and enforcing a belief that it is wrong to deceive humans, the authorities imbue youngsters with a notion that the legitimate objects of deceit are a different species to illegitimate objects. The boys learnt a code with the prescription, 'trick and harm animals, do not trick or harm humans'. This was good preparation for the later code – 'trick and harm the enemy, do not trick or harm your *philoi* and *politai*'. When Cyrus learns the later code he already knows that legitimate objects of deceit are different *in kind* from the objects to whom one has obligations of honesty and peaceful transaction. Now he realises that the *polemios* is not the same *kind* of human as the friend.

So, whilst the revelation that it is just to deceive a human enemy constitutes an explicit contradiction of what Cyrus was taught as a boy and an ephebe, the logic of this justice is already implicitly built into the (co)operation of a *paideia* in hunting animals and the dictates of the *rhētra*. This process of setting up distinctions between humans and animals, of thinking and working with anthropomorphic and theriomorphic categories in the search for the ideal ruler and the *paideia* which produces him, is a trope which Xenophon sets in play right at the beginning of the *Cyropaedia*. Xenophon makes an analogy between political rulers and cowherds and shepherds; this places cattle and sheep in an analogous position to a citizenry but Xenophon reflects that domestic livestock are so much better 'citizens' than men because livestock obey their keeper more readily than men obey their rulers (1.1.2). Xenophon implies that 'as specimens of political animal, men are inferior to the animals they rule'.[130] Cambyses and the pedagogical scheme he reveals to Cyrus can thus be seen to mirror Xenophon's own didactic tropes at the opening of the work.

Cambyses' discussion of 'deceiving an enemy' reveals and attempts to resolve a strong anxiety which must draw its force from Xenophon's implication that subject-citizens are potentially unruly. The anonymous *didaskalos*, whom Cambyses invokes as a reason for the *rhētra*, offers arguments concerning deception which are identical to those of Socrates when he destroys Euthydemus in Xenophon's *Mem-*

---

[130] Tatum (1989) 61.

orabilia.[131] The argument that it is just to deceive enemies and sometimes friends is also found in the *Dissoi Logoi* and I have previously
mentioned similar ideas which are expressed in Plato's *Republic*.[132] (I
will be returning to these texts in my next chapter.) The *didaskalos'*
methods, which are thus inscribed with Greek sophistic and 'Socratic'
teaching about *apatē* and *pseudē* demonstrate, through their consequences, a difficulty surrounding the ascription of a moral licence to
military trickery. Cambyses equates such methods specifically, and
perhaps somewhat disparagingly, with the fact that the Greeks use
wrestling to teach deception and train boys to practise it upon one
another (1.6.31). Platonic and sophistic texts frequently associate the
art of wrestling with rhetorical training,[133] but the link between the art
of tricking the enemy and the practice of deception in games is also
demonstrated by one of Xenophon's own texts, the *Hipparchicus*, a
treatise on how to be a good Athenian cavalry commander. The treatise is unequivocal about the importance of knowing how to deceive the
enemy:

The means to employ for scaring the enemy are false ambushes, false reliefs
and false messages. The enemy's confidence is greatest when he is told that
the other side is experiencing difficulties and is preoccupied. But given these
instructions, a man must himself invent a deception (μηχανᾶσθαι ἀπατᾶν) to
meet every emergency as it occurs. For there really is nothing more profitable
in war than deception. Even children are successful deceivers when they play
'guess the number'; they will hold up a few counters and make believe that they
have many, and seem to hold up few when they are holding many. Surely men
can invent similar tricks when they are putting their mind to deception? And
on thinking over the successes gained in war you will find that most and the
biggest of these have been won with the aid of deception (καὶ ἐνθυμούμενος δ' ἂν
τὰ ἐν τοῖς πολέμοις πλεονεκτήματα εὕροι ἄν τις τὰ πλεῖστα καὶ μέγιστα σὺν ἀπάτῃ
γεγενημένα). For these reasons either you should not try to command, or you
should pray to heaven that your equipment may include this capability and you
should contrive on your own part to possess it. (Xenophon *Hipparchicus* 5.8–11)

---

[131] Xen. *Mem.* 4.2.14ff. See Gera (1993) 68–72. Von Arnim (1923) 188–9 argues on the
basis of this parallel that Xenophon wants the reader to identify the *didaskalos* with
Socrates specifically. Gigon (1956) 87–8 has further parallels for an argument that
Protagoras may be the source.

[132] See *Diss. Log.* 3.2–5 in the text of Robinson (1979); Pl. *Resp.* 1.331b1–c9 and 2.382a1–
e11. Nestle (1940) 35–42, argues that the words of Cambyses' *didaskalos* and the
passage in the *Dissoi Logoi* are based on a lost work of Gorgias. But as Gera (1993) 69,
n. 144 points out, he ignores the *Memorabilia* parallel.

[133] E.g. Pl. *Grg.* 456b–57b, where Gorgias compares democratic debate to wrestling or
boxing contests and views rhetoric as analogous to the skills used in these contests.
See Yunis (1996) 150–6 for this comparison as a Platonic emblem of sophistry's
'short-term' view of public rhetoric's goals. See Gera (1993) 68, n. 142, for further
examples.

Like Cambyses, Xenophon sees trickery in boys' games as a possible model for the adult commander who wishes to deceive the enemy. However, Cambyses connects Greek boys' wrestling with the disastrous teaching of the *didaskalos* and does not specifically tie such training down to the ends of *military* deception. The *didaskalos* provided practical training analogous to that of Greek wrestling in order to make the Persian boys proficient in deceit *per se*, including occasions where deceit might be used on friends for their own good. The consequence of this, however, was not the simple lesson which Xenophon hopes to draw from the observance of children in the *Hipparchicus*. The *didaskalos*' pupils did not confine their practice of deceit to games, the detriment of their country's enemies or even the benefit of their friends. Rather than using deceit to gain an unfair advantage over enemies, they deployed it to take unfair advantage of their friends. Like the Xenophon of the *Hipparchicus*, the Cambyses of the *Cyropaedia* is in no doubt as to the utility and justice of deceiving an enemy.[134] But Cambyses reveals that a training in military trickery has to be veiled and mediated for the young. There is a danger that the wrong kind of education in 'deceit of the enemy' will result in the failure of a pupil, whether as young boy (*pais*) or ephebe, to realise the distinction between friend (or fellow-citizen) and foe as (im)proper targets for deceit.

And it is not only the 'Socratic' or sophistic *paideia* in deceit which Cambyses interrogates. I noted above that the law prohibiting boys from being taught or from deploying deceptive communication and behaviour towards humans was described by a Spartan term, *rhētra*.[135] The linguistic provenance of the term and the content of the law must encourage a reader to think of the Spartan *agōgē* and possibly the *krupteia*.[136] We saw in the first chapter that these forms of *paideia* encouraged boys and adolescents to engage in various competitive and co-operative activites of theft, cunning and trickery.

Ironically, Cambyses' *rhētra* expressly forbids the stealing and deception by *paides* and ephebes which the Spartan *agōgē* and *krupteia* explicitly promote. Critics have often seen the *Cyropaedia* as inspired by Xenophon's knowledge of, and admiration for, Spartan culture and political structures.[137] It is certainly difficult to regard Xenophon as

---

[134] See Spence (1993) 170–1, who describes the ambush and the ruse as 'the mainstays of cavalry operations in Xenophon's *Hipparchikos*'.

[135] See Tyrt. 2.8; Plut. *Lycurg.* 6 and 13, *Ages.* 8. Plutarch describes the Spartan law-giver Lycurgus' innovations as *rhētrai*.

[136] Gera (1993) 70 notes in passing that *rhētra* may recall the *agōgē*, and notes Cambyses' disapproval.

[137] See Rawson (1969) 50–1; Tigerstedt (1965) 179.

anything other than a pro-Spartan writer, but I suspect that his Cambyses is a figure who articulates something of the equivocal attitude which an exile can express towards a culture which he both embraces and yet views from the distance of the outsider.

Cambyses' disapproval of an explicit, Spartan-style training in deceit for young boys is made apparent by the way in which he equates it with telling boys about sexual matters when they are too young. Furthermore, he expresses concern that such explicit training at too early an age might make young men into 'savage citizens' (ἄγριοι πολῖται). This connection between an inappropriate education (including an emphasis on deceit) and the creation of wild or savage citizens prefigures the attitude of Aristotle to Spartan education. In sections of the *Politics* which I have already discussed, Aristotle criticises Spartan paideutic practices and regards them as indicative of a flawed political ethic.[138] The Spartans mistake one element of virtue, namely courage, for virtue itself. Through a preoccupation with courage they turn youngsters into wild animals (8.1338b12). Aristotle then argues that the Spartan system of training is not to be emulated because of its 'bestialising' effects:

What is noble must take priority over what is beast-like (*to thēriōdes*). For it is neither a wolf nor any other wild animal that will venture to confront a noble danger; it is only the good man, the brave man (*anēr agathos*). But those who let boys pursue these hard exercises too much and make them untrained in necessary things (τῶν ἀναγκαίων ἀπαιδαγωγήτους ποιήσαντες), in reality render them 'banausic', making them useful in statecraft for one task only, and even for this task training them worse than others do, as our argument proves (βαναύσους κατεργάζονται κατά γε τὸ ἀληθές, πρὸς ἕν τε μόνον ἔργον τῆς πολιτικῆς χρησίμους ποιήσαντες, καὶ πρὸς τοῦτο χεῖρον, ὡς φησὶν ὁ λόγος, ἑτέρων). (Aristotle *Politics* 8.1338b29–36)

Spartan education not only fails to make boys truly brave by giving them the inferior courage of beasts; it also makes boys 'banausic' (βαναύσους). This denigration of Spartan training falls in line with a wider Athenian discourse of stereotyping Spartans as deceitful, a discourse which I outlined in my first chapter. But Cambyses' and his ancestors' strictures and worries about the appropriate location of *apatē* in Persia's system of education are similarly premised ('savage citizens') on the possibility that an explicit training in deceit, or an excessive emphasis upon its practice, will make young citizens more like animals than men. However, the Persian system of training in military *apatē* which Cambyses describes as actually in place (a product of those

---

[138] Arist. *Pol.* 8.1338b11–19, 2.1271b2–6, 7.1333b11–21.

anxieties) limits a blurred distinction between 'the human' and 'the bestial', through the category of huntable animal, to the construction of a state enemy as the only licensed target of deceit. The message here is that if boys and ephebes learn that it is right to deceive men and practise trickery on friends and citizens, they turn out like animals and deceive indiscriminately. If they learn that they must be truthful and honest to friends and citizens, whilst training to trick only animals, they will become responsible citizens and restrict the application of their (un)veiled lessons in deceit to the destruction of enemies.

Thus, while Xenophon's texts always maintain a view that military trickery is right and proper, that it is essential for a commander to be skilled in the art of deceit, the voice of Xenophon's Cambyses interrogates and problematises certain Greek models of education in 'deceiving the enemy', particularly those models (the 'Socratic', and the 'Spartan') which other Xenophontic texts endorse. The *Cyropaedia* seems to go underneath Xenophon's other recommendations of military *apatē* in order to show that such recommendations are implicated in broader questions of morality and civic responsibility, that one trajectory of *apatē* (away from the city and towards the enemy) can easily be turned to form, or be confused with, another trajectory (towards the polis as a collection of *philoi* and *politai*). Unlike Plato and the Xenophon(s) of other texts, the Xenophon who writes Cambyses' lines has a problem with 'deceiving the enemy'. But it is not the 'problem' which we often find in Athens' public, democratic texts of drama and oratory. Cambyses is not ambivalent about the moral or practical merit of military trickery itself. Rather, he is convinced that a training in military trickery must be carefully formulated and patrolled by the state in order to prevent behavioural fall-out amongst citizens which would prove catastrophic for the community.

But if the category distinction between humans and animals sets up a boundary against which the morality of *apatē* can be policed and controlled, and if that boundary can be translated into the successful introduction of a fresh distinction between enemies and friends, the Persian patrolling of the licence to deceive is unwilling to cope with a further complexity. The old *didaskalos* taught that it was just to deceive an enemy, but that it was sometimes just to deceive a friend as well. But Cambyses does not allow for deception of a friend. As Gera puts it, he 'ignores one of the problems he himself raises, for he makes no provision for the Persians to learn to deceive friends for their own good'.[139] Gera does not ask why Cambyses should ignore this issue of

---

[139] Gera (1993) 70.

deceiving one's friends. By invoking a very (intertextually) Socratic or sophistic figure, Cambyses not only distances himself from teaching a complex morality of deceit at too early an age. He also seems to distance himself from one of the tenets of such instruction, namely that one should deceive or steal from a friend when such an action will benefit him. Cambyses is not only anxious to prevent selfish deceit between *philoi*; he also wishes to eradicate deceit between fellow *politai*. Although Cyrus is now old enough to learn about licences for deceit, Cambyses offers no space for deceit between friends and citizens. In fact, the category distinction between animals and humans, which signals and prepares for the *polemios/philos* distinction apparently precludes any blurring of the boundaries between the legitimate and illegitimate objects of deceit.

A passage from Xenophon's *Anabasis* offers a clue as to why Cambyses' advanced *paideia* rejects the methods of the *didaskalos* and eschews the licence to deceive friends. The mercenary army, of which Xenophon is a leading member, are preparing to 'steal' an area of a mountain from the enemy. It is Xenophon himself who has come up with the idea to steal the territory by eluding the enemy's observation. Having outlined his plan, Xenophon turns to the Spartan leader Cheirisophos and makes a joke at his expense:

But why should I be the man to make suggestions about stealing? For as I hear, Cheirisophos, at least those among you who belong to the *homoioi* practise stealing, even from childhood, and count it not disgraceful but honourable to steal anything that the law does not prevent you from taking.[140] And in order that you may steal with all possible skill and not get caught at it, it is the law of your land that, if you are caught stealing, you are flogged. Now, therefore, it is just the time for you to display your training, and to take care that we do not get caught stealing any of the mountain, so that we shall not sustain blows. (Xenophon *Anabasis* 4.6.14–15)

Xenophon jokes about the Spartan *agōgē* as an uncannily suitable preparation for the military task in hand. But the Spartan has a rejoinder:

I hear on my side that you Athenians are terribly clever at stealing the public funds, even though it is terribly dangerous for the stealer, and in fact, that your best people do it most, at least if they really are your best who are deemed worthy to rule; hence it is time for you also to be displaying your training. (16–17)

---

[140] The *homoioi* were an elite group of children from the Spartan upper classes. See Cartledge (1987) 24 who argues that Cyrus' membership of the paideutic group of *homotimoi* is reminiscent of this Spartan institution.

Cheirisophos, whose name ('Cleverhand') connotes the 'banausic' qualitiy which Aristotle describes as a Spartan trait, glosses political corruption and deceit of the demos as an Athenian *paideia* for deceiving and stealing from the enemy. The unsettling twist here is that Xenophon has identified a genuine aspect of Spartan *paideia* (the education of a *pais*), whereas the Spartan's example constitutes a critique of adult Athenian political leadership in the democracy. Both versions of 'training' in deceit involve committing mischief against members of one's own polis, but Cheirisophos' joke foregrounds a representation of adult Athens as a state where citizens mischievously deceive each other and, more specifically, where the leading citizens steal from the rest.

It is this scenario of deceit between *philoi* and *politai* which Persia's old *didaskalos* precipitated with his teachings. Cambyses refuses to endorse the *didaskalos*' view that it is sometimes right to deceive friends, precisely because he sees such teaching as dangerous and difficult to control. The Platonic and Xenophontic Socrates both offer specific examples of occasions when it is right to deceive a friend. But the Socrates of the *Republic* uses this notion of justified deceit within the confines of a polis, in order to sanction the use of his 'noble lie' and an asymmetrical precept that the philosopher-rulers can deceive the rest of the people but the people must be punished for deceiving the rulers.[141] The question that arises from such teaching is 'how does one decide what is for a friend's or citizen's own good?' Indeed, the Athenian in Plato's *Laws* reflects on precisely this question. He concludes that while there is a popularly held view that certain circumstances justify deceit, such a relativistic approach has to be rejected because it leaves the circumstances undefined (7.916d–917b).

In the *Dissoi Logoi*, the *Republic* and the *Memorabilia*, the examples of justified deceit are highly particular and obvious.[142] We are told that the old *didaskalos* of Persia drew the line between the right and wrong moment for deceit of a friend but Cambyses indicates that the *paides* either did not heed this distinction or did not apply it correctly. They merely gained the practical skills to deceive friends in order to take advantage of them. Cambyses perhaps realises that what is deemed for

---

[141] On Socrates' explicit characterisation of his *gennaion pseudos* as a 'lie in words', the justification for which he has already explained in terms of the obvious examples of deceiving enemies or mad friends see Pl. *Resp.* 3.414b8–c1.

[142] See *Diss. Log.* 3.2–5; Pl. *Resp.* 1.331c and 2.382b1–e11; Xen. *Mem.* 4.2.14ff. In all three texts, lying is deemed to be acceptable in relation to enemies, friends who need to be prevented from harming themselves and in story-telling. For the Platonic Socrates' distinction between the occasionally acceptable 'lie in words' and the unacceptable 'lie in the soul' see Page (1991).

the benefit of a friend or fellow citizen is highly debatable and contestable and that the admission of any interpretable licence for deceiving friends can precipitate abusive deceit within one's own community.
As we saw, the *Cyropaedia*'s stated aim was to outline the education
and exploits of a leader who does not abuse his power or his citizens,
who rules in such a way as to elicit the voluntary loyalty of his subjects.
Hence it is unsurprising that Cambyses should reject an education in a
complex and context-dependent moral precept which can so easily be
misinterpreted or misapplied by a ruler. Here Xenophon's Cambyses
can be read as reacting against the relativistic teaching about *apatē*
('sometimes good, sometimes bad') which can lead to the kind of
abuses of power and community relations which Cheirisophos jokingly
refers to in the context of political relations at Athens. However, he still
cites the teachings of the *didaskalos* to Cyrus, giving him privileged
access to the notion that friends can or must sometimes be deceived
whilst at the same time making the young prince aware of the dangers
inherent in such a notion.

Another reason for Cambyses' anxiety concerning relativism and
deception must be that he is concerned to teach Cyrus that a leader of
men must have *real* authority and virtue rather than the mere *appearance* of such qualities. Prior to the discussion of military trickery,
Cambyses argues that it is better to secure willing obedience from
one's subjects than to force obedience upon them (1.6.21). This willing
obedience is achieved by the leader who seems to be wise because
'people are only too glad to obey the man who they believe takes wiser
thought (φρονιμώτερον) for their interests than they themselves do'.
Cyrus asks how the leader may quickly achieve this appearence of
superior wisdom. His father replies that 'there is no shorter road than
really to be wise (τὸ γενέσθαι ... φρόνιμον) in those things in which you
wish to appear to be wise' (δοκεῖν φρόνιμος εἶναι: 1.6.22). He goes on
to outline the disadvantages of *pretending* to be wise when you are not
really wise:

If you wish to seem to be a good farmer when you are not, or a good rider,
doctor, flute player or anything else that you are not, just think how many
schemes you must invent to keep up your pretensions (ἐννόει πόσα σε δέοι ἂν
μηχανᾶσθαι τοῦ δοκεῖν ἕνεκα). And even if you should persuade any number of
people to praise you, in order to give yourself a reputation, and if you should
procure a fine outfit (κατασκευὰς καλάς) for each of your professions, you
would soon be found to have practised deception (ἄρτι τε ἐξηπατηκὼς εἴης ἂν)
and not long after, when you were giving an exhibition of your skill, you would
be shown up and convicted, too, as an imposter (ἐξεληλεγμένος ἂν προσέτι καὶ
ἀλαζὼν φαίνοιο). (Xenophon *Cyropaedia* 1.6.22)

Cambyses clearly believes that the absolute ruler must not be tempted to use *apatē* to promote his authority among his own citizens because such ruses will always be unmasked. It has recently been argued that Xenophon's narrative actually dramatises Cyrus' subsequent rejection of Cambyses' teaching concerning the use and abuse of deception.[143] For example, in book 8 Cyrus arranges for his leaders to wear shoes which make them seem taller than they actually are and they wear make-up so that their eyes appear more handsome than they really are (8.1.41). Such theatrical ruses are described in vocabulary which sometimes recalls Cambyses' language of military trickery.[144] We are also told that Cyrus wants his leaders to be able to 'charm' (*katagoē-teuein*) their subjects. This verb 'suggests deception and it identifies Cyrus' rulers with the stereotype of the fifth- and fourth-century sorcerer-rhetorician, the figure who charms, deceives and overpowers his audience through his skill at deploying a cultural language, above all words'.[145] As Too points out, Cyrus' 'theatre of power' not only connotes sophistic deception but also specifically invokes the emphasis on extravagant costume, cosmetics and display which so impressed Cyrus in book 1 when he stayed with his grandfather, Astyages, in Media (1.3.3). Back then, Cyrus' mother specifically warned her son that his grandfather's realm operated as an absolute tyranny in ways which contradicted the Persian system of justice (1.3.18). For Too, Cyrus has ignored his father's teachings and has drawn upon his experiences in Media instead. This is signalled when Cambyses reappears in book 8 to warn Cyrus against using his power to take advantage of his subjects (8.5.24). Ultimately, the rejection of Cambyses' teaching constitutes 'the failure of Cyrus' Persia to live up to the ideal of the pedagogical state'.[146]

This reading of the relationship between Cambyses' pedagogy and Cyrus' subsequent career is attractive and important. It is noteworthy that in book 7 Cyrus deceives his friends as part of a ruse to allow himself to limit his exposure to the masses (7.5.37–58).[147] Alongside the theatrical deceptions which prioritise appearance at the expense of reality in dealings with subject-citizens, it does *seem* that Cyrus the king moves along precisely those trajectories of deception which Cambyses

---

[143] Too (1998) 293–302.
[144] See Xen. *Cyr.* 8.3.1: *tōn technōn ... tōn memēchanēmenōn*; 7.5.37: *hai technai ... hai memēchanēmenai*; Cambyses' words at 1.6.38–9: *tōn pros tous polemious mēchanēmatōn*.
[145] Too (1998) 295. On the sophistic and pejorative connotations of *goēteia*, see below, pp. 209–15.
[146] Too (1998) 301.
[147] See Gera (1993) 286–7.

explicitly marked as politically and socially disastrous. But does that mean that the 'Medizing' son has *really* rejected or ignored his Persian father-teacher? There are two points about Cambyses' lesson on 'deceiving the enemy' which suggest that Too's reading is a little too tidy.

Firstly, as I noted earlier, Cambyses *cites* the relativistic teaching of the sophistic/Socratic *didaskalos* which he ostensibly rejects and against which the Persian state has legislated.[148] Cambyses stresses that this teaching encouraged *pleonexia* and *philokerdia*. Although Cyrus' father wants to maintain that only enemies must be deceived, his son's curiosity (*philomathia*, an important character-trait: 1.4.3) has forced him to reveal that deception of fellow-citizens and friends can be a significant means of gaining advantages over them. Cyrus' later ruses surely indicate that he has learnt from this revelation whilst disregarding the message that such advantage-taking is wrong and deleterious.

Secondly, Cambyses' claim that the ruler who deceives his people with false wisdom will soon be exposed has to be compared with his enthusiastic lecture on the value of military trickery and its analogy with hunting. I have not yet discussed Cambyses' belief that his son must be creative in his deployment of stratagems against the enemy:

'You must not only use what you learn from others, but you must also be an inventor of devices against the enemy (αὐτὸν ποιητὴν εἶναι τῶν πρὸς τοὺς πολεμίους μηχανημάτων), just as musicians render not only those compositions which they have learned but try to compose others also that are new. Now if in music that which is new and fresh wins applause, new devices in warfare also win far greater applause, for they can deceive the enemy even more successfully. And if you, my son', he said, 'should do nothing more than apply to your dealings with men (ἐπ' ἀνθρώπους) the tricks that you used to practise so constantly in dealing with small game, do you not think that you would make a very considerable advance in taking advantage of the enemy (τῆς πρὸς τοὺς πολεμίους πλεονεξίας)?' (Xenophon *Cyropaedia* 1.6.38–9)

Again, Cambyses cannot avoid giving the impression that deception is a valuable tool for the achievement of *pleonexia*. Cyrus is told that one should only direct *apatē* and *pleonexia* towards enemies. But Cambyses is keen to encourage his son to treat military trickery as an inventive and creative field of endeavour. Cyrus should make up new tunes of trickery as well as relying on old ones. This emphasis on creativity and the musical metaphor can be read as another lesson which Cyrus mis-

---

[148] See Xen. *Cyr.* 3.1.38–40, where another sophistic/Socratic figure is invoked briefly. Cyrus learns that the Armenian king executed a man because he was jealous of him with regard to his influence with his son Tigranes. The man is accused of 'corrupting' (*diaphtheirein*) his son and goes to his death echoing the Socrates of Plato's *Apology* and Xenophon's *Memorabilia*. See Gera (1993) 92.

appropriates for his 'theatre of power'. As Too puts it, 'the author's implication is that Cyrus resorts to the very deceptive devices which Cambyses insists should only be used against one's enemies and never against one's own people'.[149] But to characterise this misappropriation as a rejection of, or departure from Cambyses' lesson is to assume that the lesson itself is clear in terms of what behaviour it (dis)encourages. On the surface, Cambyses could not be clearer in dis(en)couraging deception of 'one's own people'. But has he really turned his son away from deceiving friends and citizens through the display of false wisdom? On the one hand, Cambyses teaches that devices which pretend to wisdom will always be found out. On the other, he argues that success in military trickery is only limited by the creative and inventive capabilities of the trickster. If Cyrus applies such powers of creativity to engineer deceit of his own people so successfully that he will not be found out, then why go to the trouble of being 'truly' wise?

Furthermore, there is a pedagogical problem with the 'game animal: human enemy' analogy which Cambyses maintains throughout our segment of dialogue. In the passage above, Cambyses has to make an intermediate move from animals to 'men', before he can qualify 'men' as the sub-category 'enemies'. This opens up the possibility of misapprehension or deliberate misappropriation on the part of Cambyses' student and on the part of the reader. The huntable enemy can be seen as 'other' to Cyrus in the sense of being an enemy rather than a friend or fellow-citizen (Cambyses' intended lesson). But Cambyses' analogy also points to a reading of the huntable animal as 'other' only in the sense that it represents a human individual who is 'other' to oneself (the hunter-trickster), regardless of that individual's status as friend or foe.

When we place our segment of dialogue within the wider context of the entire work, then, we discover that Cambyses' anxiety concerning the right way to teach military trickery is well founded. Cyrus does not refrain from deceiving *philoi* and *politai*. But Cyrus has not simply ignored Cambyses' teaching out of his love of Median custom or because of his tyrannical nature. Cambyses has done his best to reject moral relativism concerning deceit of friends and citizens. He has tried to warn of the dangers of being unmasked as a pretender to false wisdom. But the requirement to explain, endorse and encourage the practice of military deception has muddied the waters. A young man like Cyrus would be quick to understand that if deception is so important and successful for the achievement of *pleonexia* over enemies,

---

[149] Too (1998) 296.

then it will be easy for him to use deception to take advantage of men already under his rule.

In examining this section of dialogue from the *Cyropaedia*, I have attempted to show that Xenophon's work is not *simply* inscribed with the notion that military trickery is admissible.[150] Through Cambyses, Xenophon explores the problems that attend a valorisation of 'deceiving the enemy' within an organised society. Cambyses interrogates two models of Greek *paideia* in *apatē* and finds them potentially destabilising in terms of the morality and behaviour of the individual citizens they produce. In constructing his own programme, Cambyses institutes a system which expressly veils a positive role for *apatē* among boys and ephebes. As an adult, Cyrus is to learn what this veiled and mediated training, a training which carefully prepares for a difference *in kind* beween the *polemios* who is to be deceived and the *philos* and *politēs* who are not. Cambyses himself maintains that difference by distancing himself from the notion that a friend can be deceived. In the *Cyropaedia*, then, military *apatē* is problematised, not in terms of its inherent morality, but in terms of the dangers of its misapplication through a misguided educational programme. Furthermore, Cambyses can be seen to contribute to Cyrus' misapplication of military trickery at the very point where he takes apparently clear steps to prevent it.

In this chapter I showed that military *apatē* is not always negatively termed in Athens' public discourses. I argued that a view of military *apatē* as a negotiable term was much more helpful than a view of it as an ambivalent term. Lycurgus' negotiation and assimilation between the 'hoplite ethic' and *apatē* led me to conjecture that Melanthus may not always have been conceived of as a negative paradigm or a pre-hoplite in Athens' surface-structure discourses. At the same time, however, I conceded that a negative view of trickery as opposed to open combat also persisted in Athenian public discourse and may in part have been due to a surface-structure association between 'deceiving the enemy' and fear of the enemy. In discussing Xenophon, I have made a case for going beyond this author's many valorisations of military trickery. Even in an author whom we would expect to contradict the dominant Athenian ideology, we find an anxiety about promoting military *apatē* and an (ironically self-defeating?) attempt to work out a programme whereby such a promotion can be safely patrolled and

---

[150] *Contra*, for example, the view of Wheeler (1988) 29f. who views Xenophon as a champion of military *apatē* without any consideration of Cambyses' caveats and anxieties.

mediated in order to head off disastrous effects within the social and political fabric of the polis.

Through the anxieties and conflicts inscribed within the writing of Antisthenes, Plato and (particularly) Xenophon, we have seen how an Athenian discussion about military deceit has to invoke a much wider set of issues concerning the definition of male excellence, the (un)-desirability of deceit between *politai*, and the (un)desirability of licensing civic forms of *paideia* which promote certain contexts or trajectories of deceit as justified. In the following chapters I want to explore the Athenian representation of deceit between citizens further, and with the following questions in mind. How does 'practical' and public Athenian democratic discourse confront the suspicions, opportunities and threats which the spectre of deceit conjures up? And how does the democracy deal with the emergence of forms of *paideia* which harness relativistic thought concerning deception and which promote *technai* of speech and argument? I will start to tackle these questions by exploring a concept which still troubles individuals and societies today. It is time to meet 'the noble lie' head on.

3 Athens and the 'noble lie'

I am only taking up one of the fundamental problems of western philosophy when it poses these questions: why, in fact, are we attached to the truth? Why the truth rather than lies? Why the truth rather than myth? Why the truth rather than illusion? And I think that, instead of trying to find out what truth, as opposed to error, is, it might be interesting to take up the problem posed by Nietzsche: how is it that, in our societies, 'the truth' has been given this value, thus placing us absolutely under its thrall?[1]

God does not stand aloof from just deception. There are occasions when God respects an opportune moment for lies.[2]

In his essay 'The Order of the Discourse', Michel Foucault offers an outline of the character and focus of his future research.[3] He proposes to identify the processes by which in our society discourse is 'at once controlled, selected, organised, and redistributed by a certain number of procedures whose role it is to ward off its powers, to gain mastery over its chance events, to evade its ponderous, formidable materiality'.[4] To this end, Foucault isolates three 'principles of exclusion'. They are prohibition, the division between reason and madness and the rejection of the latter, and thirdly, the opposition between true and false.

According to Foucault, the third principle of exclusion finds its origin in the classical rejection of the sophist and the Platonic foundation of a 'will to truth' or 'will to knowledge'.[5] Ever since Plato, argues Foucault, this will to truth has operated to produce a construction of the discourse of truth as independent of the realms of desire and power. Foucault's claim is that this separation masks desire and

---

[1] Michel Foucault's response to the question 'Doesn't science produce truths to which we submit?' in Kritzman (1988) 107.
[2] Aesch. fr. 301–2 N² (= Aesch. fr. 301–2 R) cited at *Diss. Log.* 3.12: ἀπάτης δικαίας οὐκ ἀποστατεῖ θεός· ψευδῶν δὲ καιρὸν ἔσθ᾽ ὅπου τιμῇ θεός.
[3] Foucault (1981) 50. For critical surveys of this essay see Cohen (1994) 80–1; Barrett (1991) 138–45; Dreyfus and Rabinow (1982) 44–78, 184–204.
[4] Foucault (1981) 51.
[5] Foucault (1981) 60–2.

power's total implication in the will to truth.[6] Post-Platonic Western philosophy asserts the central notion of 'an ideal truth as the law of discourse' and an 'ethic of knowledge which promises to give the truth only to the desire for truth itself and only to the power of thinking it'.[7] These philosophical notions reinforce and perpetuate the three principles of exclusion by denying the reality and force of discourse itself. By contrast, sophistic thought and the pragmatic and poetic discourses of pre-Socratic Greece in general insisted on and celebrated discourse's independent materiality whose powers 'could be mastered to act upon the souls of individuals and communities'.[8] Philosophy worked towards the banishment of this view of discourse so as to ensure 'that discourse should occupy the smallest possible space between thought and speech'.[9] As Michelle Barrett notes, Foucault also locates the *emergence* of the 'will to truth' in pre-Platonic Greek thought, identifying it as 'a shift from seeing truth as a given property of the discourse of those in power to seeing truth as a property of the referent of discourse'.[10] As part of his plan for future research, Foucault proposes to 'consider first the epoch of the sophists at its beginning with Socrates, or at least with Platonic philosophy, to see how efficacious discourse, ritual discourse, discourse loaded with powers and perils, gradually came to conform to a division between true and false discourse'.[11]

It could be argued that Foucault did carry out this project in the sense that his work on medicine, madness and (especially) sexuality all point to the 'the emergence of theoretical knowing among the Greeks as the great turning point in our history'.[12] And in the last lectures he ever gave, Foucault was formulating fascinating readings of the Platonic Socrates' self-representation as a philosopher of truth in dialogues such as the *Laches, Phaedo and Crito*.[13] However, I think it would be fair to say that Foucault never treated the 'fifth-century enlightenment' and the confrontation between rhetoric and philosophy in their own right. Foucault's preliminary reflections stress that the Platonic division between truth and falsehood constituted a rejection of a view of discourse

---

[6] See Cohen (1994) 80: 'For Foucault ... this separation is merely an insidious mask which hides that what is really at stake in this "will to truth" is precisely desire and power – hence his variation on the Nietzschean formulation.'

[7] Foucault (1981) 62.

[8] Cohen (1994) 81.

[9] Foucault (1981) 62.

[10] Barrett (1991) 142.

[11] Foucault (1981) 70.

[12] Dreyfus and Rabinow (1982) 201. See Foucault (1975) 56: 'When Hippocrates had reduced medicine to a system, observation was abandoned and philosophy was introduced into medicine.'; (1980) 79: 'The West has managed ... to annex sex to a field of rationality ... we are accustomed to such conquests since the Greeks.'

[13] See Flynn (1994); Nehamas (1998) 157–88.

as having a material independence and a power to mould and shape belief. Foucault wants to know how this insistence on truth as a property of discourse's referent *emerged*, implying that he sees Plato's position as informed and produced by pre-existing concerns.

In this and subsequent chapters, I want to show how texts written before and around those of Plato were addressing the problem of discourse's 'powers and perils'. As with Plato, these texts focus their attention on political and legal debate as a discourse transformed by a new technology of rhetoric into an 'efficacious discourse' of persuasion – a discourse which always threatened to persuade through deceptive communication rather than truth. But rhetoric is not the only concept which has a bearing on the 'will to truth' and concomitant representations of deception. In this chapter I want to focus on the 'noble lie' because it is conceptualised at the same time as rhetoric becomes the object of philosophical and democratic scrutiny. How far is this concept to be read (in Popperian terms) as the Platonic mainstay of totalitarian thought (or thought-control) as opposed to democratic ideology? And in what way does the 'noble lie' relate (in Foucauldian terms) to the Platonic 'will to truth'?

To some extent, Foucault's call for an examination of the way in which the Platonic 'will to truth' emerged, had already been taken up by Marcel Detienne in his book *Les Maîtres de vérité dans la Grèce archaïque*.[14] Detienne himself has recently related this book to Foucault's essay in his new preface to Janet Lloyd's English translation.[15] I will summarise and assess his findings in the next section, because they will inform subsequent discussion in this chapter. Detienne's book is an outstanding exploration of the changing connotations and discursive location of the concept of 'truth' (*alētheia*) and its opposites in archaic and early classical Greek texts. But his account barely touches upon the representation of *apatē* and *pseudē* in Athenian drama, oratory or historiography and that lacuna in his analysis provides further justification for the focus of my last two chapters.

Detienne and the 'masters of truth'

Detienne anticipated Foucault's suggestive comments, by arguing that Greek notions of truth (*alētheia*) underwent a shift which corresponded to a historical shift from mythical to 'rational' thought. He also saw this change in ideas about the truth as an effect of the movement from the feudal authority of kings to the rise of the polis in the sixth and fifth centuries. The democratisation of speech and power entailed by the

[14] Detienne (1967).   [15] See Detienne (1996) 19.

ascendancy of the citizen phalanx in the new social world of the polis constitutes what Detienne terms the 'laicization of truth'.[16] An examination of Homer, Hesiod and archaic poetry leads Detienne to the conclusion that *alētheia* is conferred through the authority of the just king and the divinely inspired poet. But *alētheia* in the archaic period is defined in terms of what can and should be *remembered*. This close association between *alētheia* and remembering (*mnēmosunē*) means that the archaic conception of 'truth' is primarily opposed, not to notions of falsehood or deception, but to notions of obscurity, silence and forgetting (*lēthē*).

For Detienne, archaic *alētheia* is bound up with a set of semantic relationships which emphasise what he calls 'the ambiguity of speech'.[17] *Alētheia* is involved in an ambiguous relationship with *lēthē* because the poet's conferral of truth through memory also confers truth's opposite, namely the forgetting of pain and sorrow among his audience. At the same time Detienne recognises that archaic poetic *alētheia* is involved in an ambiguous relationship with *apatē* and *pseudē*: 'le "Maître de vérité" est aussi le maître de tromperie'.[18] Thus, in the notoriously difficult couplet of the proem to Hesiod's *Theogony*, the Muses tell Hesiod that they know how to tell many lies like true things (ψεύδεα . . . ἐτύμοισιν ὁμοῖα), but that when they wish, they also know how to speak true things (ἀληθέα).[19] Detienne hints that this equation between poetry and 'lies like the truth', and the use of the same formula in Homer and Theognis might approximate a positive notion of *apatē* as 'fiction' which was later theorised by the author of the sophistic *Dissoi Logoi*.[20]

---

[16] Detienne (1967) 99ff.

[17] Detienne (1967) 51–80.

[18] Detienne (1967) 77.

[19] Hes. *Theog.* 27–8. See Detienne (1967) 75ff. For an excellent discussion of these lines with much of the relevant bibliography see Ferrari (1988).

[20] See Detienne (1967) 76–7 where he cites Hom. *Od.* 19.203 and Thgn. 713, comparing them with *Diss. Log.* 3.10. In the Homeric line the formula 'lies like true things' (ψεύδεα . . . ἐτύμοισιν ὁμοῖα) is used to describe Odysseus' lying tale to Penelope at *Od.* 19.165–200 which, though false, could be said to encapsulate an 'ethical truth' by implying that as *xeinos* he deserves good treatment from her. On this, see Pratt (1993) 91. The tale is 'like the truth' in terms of plausibility, and in the guise of the Cretan his account of his wanderings approximate his 'real' adventures as Odysseus. See also Goldhill (1991) 45. The Theognidean use of the formula describes Nestor's eloquence as a positive *aretē*. At *Diss. Log.* 3.10 it is argued that the better painter or tragedian is the one who knows how to deceive (ἐξαπατᾶν) by making things like the truth (ὁμοῖα . . . τοῖς ἀληθινοῖς ποιέων). The question of (a) whether the archaic self-reflection on poetry constitutes an awareness of a category which we would call 'fictional'; and (b) whether some classical reflections on poetry, *apatē* and *pseudē* constitute an emerging awareness of this category is a vexed issue which I discuss below at pp. 176–9. On these issues, see most recently Finkelberg (1998).

Gorgias' fragmentary description of tragedy as a positive form of *apatē* can also be read in this light.[21] Perhaps even Plato's theory of *mimēsis* (representation, imitation) shares the assumptions of Hesiod's formula.[22] But Detienne also seems to suggest that this and other archaic reflections on speech's ambiguity (truth or lies masquerading as truth?) constitute a developing awareness that language is an unreliable medium for the maintenance of just and fair social exchange.[23]

In the rhetorical and sophistic culture of the fifth-century polis, the 'magico-religious' authority of king and poet to select truth in terms of what should be remembered and memorialised, is challenged. Detienne marks the beginning of this challenge with the fragments of the poet Simonides and the doxography surrounding him. Simonides appeals to the notion of *doxa* (seeming, appearance) as having greater force than *alētheia*.[24] And according to one anecdote he represented his poetry as a form of *apatē*.[25] For Detienne, Simonides anticipates a new climate of secularised dialogue and debate in the fifth century where the unstable realm of *doxa* (seeming and appearance) becomes a reference point which rivals the archaic concept of truth.[26] Detienne rightly locates this valorisation of *doxa* in the concerns of sophistic inquiry and the areas of rhetoric and argumentation.[27] The new democratic culture of fifth-century Athens creates an interest in techniques of verbal persuasion and a realisation that, because men's moral and

[21] See DK 82 B23 where Gorgias writes that tragedy offers *apatē* through *muthoi* ('stories') and *pathea* ('emotions'), and that the tragedian who uses *apatē* is 'more just' (*dikaioteros*) than the one who doesn't, while the spectator who is deceived is 'wiser' (*sophōteros*) than the one who isn't. See Lada (1993) 99 for this and other evidence of *apatē* as 'illusionism' or 'fiction' in the fifth century. Croally (1994) 24, n. 24 follows Laín Entralgo (1970) 221 and Carson (1992) 53 in translating *apatē* as 'fiction' but points out that this is to lose the possible negative connotations of the term. For further discussion see the bibliography cited at p. 176, n. 107.

[22] Detienne (1967) 77. See also Belfiore (1985).

[23] Detienne (1967) 79. See Ferrari (1988), who develops Detienne's reading of Hes. *Theog.* 27–8 more fully in terms of 'lies like the truth' being the means by which 'good exchange' can be subverted by agents of 'bad exchange'.

[24] Fr. 55 Diehl (= *PMG* fr. 93/598): 'seeming/opinion overpowers the truth.' (τὸ δοκεῖν καὶ τὰν ἀλάθειαν βιᾶται). The attribution of this fragment to Simonides is uncertain. See the discussion and bibliography of Detienne (1967) 109, n. 20. Gentili (1964) argues for Simonides' authorship. Bowra (1963) gives strong arguments for the authorship of Bacchylides.

[25] See Plut. *De poet aud.* 15d. See Carson (1992) 53 who regards this as the first recorded usage of the term *apatē* as 'artistic illusion'.

[26] Detienne's argument that the dispersal of authority across a new 'agonistic' framework of the polis gives rise to a proliferation of competing and competitive intellectual discourses is extended and refined by Lloyd (1979) 248ff.

[27] Detienne (1967) 121–2, (1996) 118: 'Both Sophists and orators were thus very much men of *doxa*.' For the sophist Gorgias' point that persuasion and deceit are successful because of the mortal condition of *doxa* see Gorg. *Hel.* 11–12 (= DK 82 B11.11–12).

epistemological knowledge is incomplete, questions of fact and value are open to debate through opposing arguments.[28] In the areas of rhetorical and sophistic theory, the idea that there are two contradictory arguments on any issue is complemented by the idea that persuasion (*peithō*) or *apatē* are the goals of debate or inquiry. Within this agonistic framework, the sophist as intellectual or teacher of rhetoric emphasises the mortal condition of controvertible and unstable *doxa* and the power of persuasion or deception to take advantage of that condition.

At the same time as sophistic thought is excluding a notion of truth in favour of *doxa*, *peithō* and *apatē*, Detienne argues that Orphic and Pythagorean texts are maintaining the priority of *alētheia*. In this 'philosophico-religious' domain *alētheia* becomes the positive term in what he calls a 'logic of contradiction'.[29] Truth becomes unambiguously opposed to the ambiguous world of deception, falsehood, persuasion and opinion. This valorisation of truth as a difficult privileged knowledge to be attained and maintained is found in its most developed form in the fragments of the Eleatic philosopher Parmenides.[30] Whilst Parmenides' views remain obscure and complex, it is clear that he promotes an ontological framework which constitutes *alētheia* and he opposes this truth to the *doxai* of mortals.[31] Furthermore, he associates mortal *doxa* with deceptive communication.[32] This 'logic of contradiction' replaces the 'logic of ambiguity' which constitutes the archaic '*alētheia–lēthē*' relationship. However, for Detienne, these two stages in the conception of truth are linked by the common use of

---

[28] See DK 80 A1 where Diogenes Laertius remarks that Protagoras was the first to argue that there are two *logoi* concerning everything, these being opposed to each other. The classic text which demonstrates this emphasis on the viability of opposing arguments is the *Dissoi Logoi* of the late fifth or early fourth century. On the sophistic preoccupation with 'opposing *logoi*' and the nature of sophistic 'relativism' see Kerferd (1981a) 78–110.

[29] Detienne (1967) 133–5. See also DuBois (1991) 76.

[30] Detienne (1967) 137–41.

[31] See Parmenides DK 28 B1, the famous prologue to his hexameter poem, where the goddess tells the author that he must learn both truth and mortal *doxa* (28–30): 'It is proper for you to learn everything – both the unshakeable heart of well-rounded truth and the *doxai* of mortals in which there is no true reliance' (χρεὼ δέ σε πάντα πυθέσθαι ἠμὲν Ἀληθείης εὐκυκλέος ἀτρεμὲς ἦτορ ἠδὲ βροτῶν δόξας, ταῖς οὐκ ἔνι πίστις ἀληθής). See also Parmenides DK 28 B2. For discussion of Parmenides' poem and its ontology, see Kirk, Raven and Schofield (1983) 241–54.

[32] See Parmenides DK 28 B8, where he moves from discussing the objects of truth to those of opinion (50–2): 'For you here I cease both my trustworthy discourse and thought concerning truth. Henceforth learn mortal *doxa*, listening to a *deceitful ordering of my words*' (ἐν τῷ σοι παύω πιστὸν λόγον ἠδὲ νόημα ἀμφὶς ἀληθείης· δόξας δ' ἀπὸ τοῦδε βροτείας μάνθανε κόσμον ἐμῶν ἐπέων ἀπατηλὸν ἀκούων).

memory. And he is careful to point out that in Parmenides' 'first philosophy', the boundary between *alētheia* and *apatē* is more permeable than that found in the Orphic and Pythagorean material.[33] He suggests that this is because Parmenides is a philosopher more concerned with the radical opposition between 'Being' and 'Non-Being' rather than that between *alētheia* and *apatē*.

Detienne's idea that there is a shift in the definition of the semantic field into which *alētheia* falls, can be criticised on a number of counts. Firstly, the notion of a radical historical break between a time of myth and a time of reason can be viewed as too simplistic.[34] Secondly, Detienne's concentration on sophistic, rhetorical and philosophic *theory* in the early classical period overlooks the question of how democracy's discourses of oratory and drama approach the problem of what he identifies as 'the ambiguity of speech'. If, as Detienne himself hints, archaic thought recognised deceptive communication to be a problem for 'good exchange' in social and political relations, and given that he is interested in the 'laicization' of discourse, it would seem to be imperative to consider how the privileged 'practical discourses' of democracy approach that problem as well as the 'theoretical' texts which he analyses. Sophistic and rhetorical theory subordinate truth to a celebration of *doxa* and *apatē*. By contrast, philosophic theory seeks to maintain truth's priority, sometimes harnessing deceit to achieve that end. How does public democratic exchange respond to these developments and negotiate its own particular concern with the threats and opportunities offered by deceptive communication?

A third problem with Detienne's analysis brings us back to the specific focus of this chapter. It has been argued that there *are* significant examples of Homeric and archaic oppositions between *alētheia* and *pseudē* (truth and falsehoods) or between *alētheia* and *apatē* (truth and deception).[35] It is also apparent that 'philosophical' writers of the fifth and fourth centuries do not always maintain a tidy opposition between *alētheia* and the concepts of *pseudos*, *apatē* and *peithō*. As Detienne himself acknowledges, Parmenides' route to *alētheia* is also the 'path of Per-

---

[33] See Detienne (1967) 141, (1996) 134: 'The philosopher can find traces of *Alētheia* at the heart of the "deceptive" world.'

[34] See the cautionary comments of Lloyd (1979) 4–5; DuBois (1991) 76–7.

[35] See Adkins (1972) for a critique of Detienne's argument in relation to the Homeric evidence. See Pratt (1993) 17–22 for argument and examples which clearly show that Detienne has undervalued the opposition between truth and deception in Homeric and archaic texts in favour of exclusive concentration on the *alētheia–lēthē* relation. Mourelatos (1970) 63–5 stresses that Homeric *alētheia* can connote accurate and undistorted reporting and that the archaic period develops its meaning as 'genuineness, authenticity, or reality'.

suasion'.[36] Detienne's analysis effectively stops at Parmenides, though he does use Platonic material to shed light on the 'philosophico-religious' sects and the sophistic celebration of *doxa*. He certainly regards the Platonic philosopher's domain as completely opposed to the domain of the sophist and the politician.[37] As I have already shown (and will have further cause to discuss) Plato's Socrates argues that an intentional *pseudos* can be deployed to uphold and disseminate what he regards as the truth. In Plato's *Phaedrus*, Socrates concedes that in the *ecclēsia* and lawcourts, an enlightened rhetoric may require the deployment of *apatē*. Socrates' point is that an orator can only deceive properly if he already knows the truth, and it emerges that this truth is to be gained through dialectical inquiry.[38] In the *Hippias Minor*, Socrates ironically praises the Homeric Odysseus because he deceives knowingly, whereas Achilles tells lies without knowledge of what he is doing (though neither hero emerges as having an adequate understanding of justice).[39] The Platonic evidence confounds any expectation that 'the will to truth' entails a blanket ban on the use of lies.

The 'logic of contradiction' is partially complicated by Parmenides' philosophy and Detienne seems to recognise this problem. But it is also complicated by the relativism of the 'noble lie', a notion which Detienne does not consider. In the previous chapter we saw that this notion has a 'sophistic' as much as a 'Socratic' colouring. Furthermore its role and articulation in the polis was a focus of theoretical anxiety in Xenophon's *Cyropaedia*. In the rest of this chapter I will try to outline some of the ways in which Plato's 'noble lie' can be seen to challenge any tidy conception of Platonic thought as constituting a 'will to truth'. If 'theoretical' texts are formulating the idea of the 'noble lie' and anxiously debating the effects of its deployment in a polis, it will also be this chapter's concern to show that oratory, drama and historiography participate in this anxious debate by addressing the (in)admissibility of 'noble lies' in a specifically *democratic* state. The *democratic* inscription

---

[36] Parmenides DK 28 B2: 'The one, that [it] is and that it is impossible for [it] not to be, is the path of Persuasion (for she attends upon Truth)' (ἡ μὲν ὅπως ἔστιν τε καὶ ὡς οὐκ ἔστι μὴ εἶναι, Πειθοῦς ἐστι κέλευθος ('Αληθείη γὰρ ὀπηδεῖ)). Mourelatos (1970) 160 argues that *Peithō* is one of the faces of divinity who controls 'the Parmenidean what-is'.

[37] Detienne (1967) 121.

[38] Pl. *Phdr.* 261a6–262c4. Socrates claims that orators must assimilate and dissimilate at will and this may have to involve *apatē*. But to deceive effectively the orator must assimilate and dissimilate accurately. He must therefore be free of self-deceit and this entails apprehension of the truth. See Ferrari (1987) 40–5. Murray (1988) 283–4 connects this section of the *Phaedrus* with the logic of the 'noble lie' at Pl. *Resp.* 3.414b8–415e4.

[39] Pl. *Hp. Mi.* 370e–373c. See Blundell (1992) for an excellent analysis of this dialogue's ironic complexity. See also Napolitano Valditara (1994) 126–42.

of the 'noble lie' will reveal the shortcomings in Popper's approach to state-sponsored deception.

Plato's pharmacy: the 'noble lie' in the *Republic*

For Xenophon's Cambyses, a relativistic approach to lying should not be entertained in the education of young boys. We saw that this relativistic approach is put forward in the sophistic *Dissoi Logoi* and Xenophontic and Platonic accounts of Socrates' philosophy. Why do these texts introduce the idea that lying can sometimes be justified?

In Xenophon's *Memorabilia* and Plato's *Republic* lying is used as a notion which undermines a simple definition of justice. In the *Republic*, Socrates (rather unfairly) interprets Cephalus as arguing that justice consists in giving back what one is owed and telling the truth (1.331b1–c5). Socrates quickly points out that this definition cannot hold for all cases of human interaction. To tell the truth and give back what one is owed is 'sometimes to act justly and sometimes unjustly' (1.331c4–5):

Take this case, as an example of what I mean: everyone would surely say that if a man takes weapons from a friend when the latter is sound of mind, and the friend demands them back when he is mad, one must not give back such things (οὔτε χρὴ τοιαῦτα ἀποδιδόναι), and the man who gave them back would not be just, and moreover, one should not be willing to tell someone in this state the whole truth (πάντα τἀληθῆ). (Plato *Republic* 1.331c5–9)

Particularly noteworthy here is Socrates' stress on necessity (χρή). To avoid doing an injustice to the insane friend, one *must* deceive him. Socrates makes a similar move in the *Memorabilia* in order to shake Euthydemus' confidence in finding a definition for justice (4.2.14–19). Alongside the case of lying to a depressed friend who might harm himself, Euthydemus is confronted with more examples of righteous deception. Euthydemus has to concede that it is just to deceive an enemy in war (4.2.15). It is just to trick an ailing son into taking the medicine he needs (δεόμενον φαρμακείας) if he refuses to take it (4.2.17). It is also just for a general to lie to his disheartened troops by telling them that allied forces are approaching if such a lie raises their spirits (4.2.17). The *Dissoi Logoi* also present the examples of administering medicine to relatives or preventing self-harm through deception. Again, this sophistic treatise regards these as cases where 'it is right to lie and deceive' (3.2). But this time, the unknown author has the specific agenda of demonstrating that 'the same thing is both right and wrong': in other words, deceptive communication can be used for just or unjust ends depending on the context of its deployment. Thus 'the same thing' (deception) can be described as just or unjust.

These three relativistic discussions of lying share a common theme, namely that deception can be used where what we might call 'paternalism' is justified. Person x decides that person or group y must be successfully deceived for their own good. The case of lying to one's own troops about approaching allies in order to boost morale may strike the modern reader as particularly controversial. But an ancient reader might recall the manner in which Homer's Odysseus is explicit about lying to his demoralised crew: he admits that he did not tell them about the imminent threat of the monster Scylla for fear that they would panic (*Od.* 12.210–20). Furthermore, a comment made by Andocides in his speech *On Peace with Sparta* suggests that such deception would not be regarded as reprehensible by the demos of classical Athens. As we saw in chapter one, and as we will see further in the next section, Andocides regards it as *necessary* for a general to deceive his men when leading them into danger (ἄνδρα στρατηγὸν . . . λανθάνοντα δεῖν τοὺς πολλοὺς ἀνθρώπων καὶ ἐξαπατῶντα ἄγειν ἐπὶ τοὺς κινδύνους: 3.33). The parallel between Xenophon's *Memorabilia* and Andocides' oratory would suggest that, despite (or because of) the implication of paternalism, these examples of justified deceit are seized upon precisely because they would strike their contemporary readership as uncontroversial. Although these lies are not always explicitly described as 'necessary', it is clear that they are brought forward as cases where deception is the only available tactic for the achievement of a just or good outcome: the mad or depressed friend is saved from harming himself, the army's morale is boosted where it would otherwise remain dejected, the son's health is restored where he would otherwise remain ill.

That Plato believes that certain situations make lying a moral necessity is made clearer from the manner in which the Socrates of the *Republic* introduces his infamous 'noble lie' (*gennaion pseudos*). Aware that his educational programme may not be enough to maintain the tripartite hierarchy of guardians, auxiliaries and producers in his ideal city ('Kallipolis'), Socrates argues that all three groups need to believe that their upbringing and education was in fact a dream (3.414d5). They are to be told that the real reason why they find themselves in one of three distinct groups is that they are all born from the earth. Thus all the citizens are to view each other as brothers (3.414e5). But this myth of autochthony has a twist. Some of Kallipolis' autochthonous citizens have gold mixed into their souls (guardians). Others have silver (auxiliaries) and the farmers and other producers have bronze or iron (3.415a4–7). Socrates prefaces this 'noble lie' by asking what sort of lie is needed to ensure that all the citizens in his ideal state will adhere to the division between the three classes of philosopher-kings, guardians and workers:

'How might we', I said, 'contrive one of those lies that come into being in a case of necessity (τῶν ψευδῶν τῶν ἐν δέοντι γιγνομένων) of which we were just now speaking, some one noble (γενναῖόν) lie to persuade, in the best case, even the rulers, but if not them, the rest of the city?' (Plato *Republic* 3.414b8–c1)

When Socrates speaks of necessary lies here, he must be referring to his earlier elaboration (2.382a4–d3) of the distinction between 'lies in words' and 'lies in the soul' which I mentioned in the previous chapter.[40] In that earlier discussion Socrates asks when and to whom the 'lie in words' is useful (*chrēsimon*) rather than hateful. He puts forward the familiar instances of deceiving enemies and deceiving friends 'who are attempting to do some wrong through madness or ignorance' in order to turn them away from it (2.382c8–9). He says that the lie then becomes 'useful like a drug' (*hōs pharmakon chrēsimon*: 2.382c10). Socrates sees 'good lies' as 'pharmacological' because they are designed to correct unhealthy defects of belief or understanding in an individual or groups of individuals.[41] His final example of a useful 'lie in words' is *muthologiai* or 'story-telling':

And in the case of those stories (*muthologiais*) which we mentioned just now, those told because we don't know the truth (*talēthes*) about these ancient things, making the lie as much like the truth as we can (ἀφομοιοῦντες τῷ ἀληθεῖ τὸ ψεῦδος) don't we also make it useful? (Plato *Republic* 2.382c10–d2)

Again, Socrates refers to an earlier argument. It should be remembered that this discussion of the distinction between 'the lie in the soul' (always bad) and 'the lie in words' (sometimes useful, necessary and good) has come about because Socrates wants to prove that the gods never use deception because they do not need to. This argument about the gods is, in turn, part and parcel of his argument that the children of his ideal state must only be told the right stories as part of their education. This precludes reciting the tales told by the poets who portray gods and heroes in a way which is socially detrimental for the future citizens of Kallipolis. For Socrates, it is not necessarily wrong to tell tales that are not factually correct or verifiable.[42] Indeed, tales which

---

[40] That Socrates is thinking in terms of the 'lie in words' is argued by Reeve (1988) 183; Page (1991); Gill (1993) 32.

[41] See Page (1991) 18–19.

[42] See Guthrie (1975) 457; Ferrari (1989) 113; Gill (1993); Pratt (1993) 121; Janaway (1995) 88–9.

are lies 'like the truth' about the unknowable past can convey 'ethical'
or 'religious' truths.[43] It is only wrong to tell tales which harm the listener because they encourage him to imitate a weeping Achilles or to
believe that the gods are immoral and selfish. Socrates objects when 'a
man in speech makes a bad representation of what gods and heroes are
like' (ὅταν εἰκάζῃ τις κακῶς τῷ λόγῳ, περὶ θεῶν τε καὶ ἡρώων οἷοί εἰσιν:
2.377e1–2). But such a person should not be blamed for lying *per se*: he
should be blamed for 'not lying well' (ἐάν τις μὴ καλῶς ψεύδηται:
2.377d9).

For Socrates then, the 'lie in words' is useful when it is an instance of
'lying well'. And the Myth of Metals is one of those instances – it conforms to the general notion that some lies are not 'real' or 'true' lies
because they bring about morally 'true' outcomes. But it also conforms
to some aspects of 'fiction': stories may be deliberate untruths, but the
right kind of stories can promote the moral health of a community and
they are not to be criticised if the 'untruth' of the story conveys a
deeper moral truth which restores or maintains such communal health.
Socrates' endorsement of myths and stories which 'lie well' can be
paralleled in other archaic and classical texts which offer metatextual
commentary on the functions and effects of poetry and story-telling.[44]
I will return to the significance of such popular assumptions in the
next section. But what interests me here is the way in which Socrates
equates the 'Dream' and the 'Myth of Metals', not only with a *popular*
notion of good story-telling as 'good lying', but also with *uncontroversial* examples of lies which are like drugs because they turn friends
away from harm and towards safety in very exceptional and specific
circumstances.[45]

Before Socrates gets to the 'Dream' and 'the Myth of Metals', his
conception of 'good lies' as 'pharmacological' is put forward to show
that Kallipolis' philosopher-rulers must be allowed to lie to the rest
of its citizens while those citizens must never lie to the rulers. Having
ruled out the poetic representation of the gods grieving or laughing as
unsuitable for the youth of Kallipolis, Socrates stresses that the young
must be taught to take the truth seriously. He concedes that lies can be
'useful as a form of remedy' (χρήσιμον ὡς ἐν φαρμάκου εἴδει: 3.389b4).
But this means that such lies 'must be assigned to doctors while private

---

[43] See Murray (1996) 151–2 on *Resp.* 2.382d2.
[44] See Belfiore (1985); Pratt (1993) 131–56; Gill (1993) 66–87; Murray (1996) 151–3.
[45] Murray (1996) 150–1 on *Resp.* 2.382c6–7 rightly points out that 'Socrates's justification of lying in certain circumstances is not as radical as has sometimes been
supposed.'

men (*idiōtais*) must not put their hands to it' (3.389b5). His interlocutor, Adeimantus, agrees and Socrates then concludes that it is fitting for the rulers (*archontes*) of Kallipolis to lie 'for the benefit of city in cases involving enemies or citizens' (3.389b8–9). For the private citizen to lie to the rulers is 'a fault the same as, or greater than, for a sick man or a man in training not to tell the truth to the doctor or the trainer or for a man not to say to the pilot the things that are concerning the ship and the sailors, lying about how he himself or his fellow sailors are faring' (3.389c1–6).

Thus Socrates' argument moves from 'the lie in words' told to children or friends to the wholesale deception of his ideal citizens through a myth of origins and an asymmetrical licence afforded to rulers to lie to the ruled. Citizens, however, are forbidden to lie to their rulers because such deceptions will hamper the rulers' ability to do their job properly. Indeed, the point at which this licence and prohibition are introduced is also the first appearance of a distinct group of 'rulers' in the *Republic*: 'lying is not some merely incidental topic grafted onto a consideration of the obligations of good government; the need for political rule and the need for the drug of deceit emerge at the same time'.[46] For Popper, this convergence of needs constitutes the core of the *Republic*'s totalitarian vision. But Plato's pharmacological analogy has been used to defend him from Popper's charges of totalitarianism. Critics of Popper have argued that Plato does not conceive of the rulers' lies or (rigorously censored) paideutic lies as a means of limiting individual freedom.[47] They are designed simply to help every individual to realise their best interests and to identify those interests with their correct role within the structure of the ideal state. Children particularly need help with such self-realisations and so may adults if their psychological make-up is found to be imperfect.[48]

The extent to which such defences are credible depends on our own definition of the nature and possibilities of human freedom, not to mention our own conception of human nature itself. Furthermore, these defences seem to be predicated on the assumption that political theory *can* arrive at a defintion of what will make an objectively good

---

[46] Page (1991) 18.
[47] See Page (1991) 20: '... there are some choices, according to Socrates that are more profoundly in error because they directly compromise the most basic responsibilities of human, political life. They are choices that can confound the realization of full human freedom itself. To ignore completely the goods of the city is not eccentric, but pathological, and if lying can help correct the radical subversion of the city's goods (which are still human goods), then it cannot be good to dismiss lying out of hand.'
[48] See Page (1991) 10; Reeve (1988) 212.

and just community. Socrates does not make this claim exactly but he seems to believe that his blueprint for Kallipolis will provide the conditions through which such a community might be achieved. If official 'noble lies' are necessary to maintain such conditions, then we can either agree that such lies are necessary because Kallipolis is desirable and workable or we can disagree on the basis that such lies will maintain a community that is not desirable, and could never become objectively 'good' or 'just'. The idea that an objectively 'just' community is conceivable or achievable is doubtful in so many ways. And it is far from clear how the *Republic* can be seen to promote individual freedom through its discussion of pharmacological lying, if we regard such freedom as crucially dependent on access to certain truths: the real circumstances of our birth and upbringing, the actual structures that regulate our political or social lives, the content of those stories we were *not* told when we were children. However, the so-called 'authoritarianism' implied by the *Republic*'s discussion of lying is not radically different to certain educational assumptions and political practices exhibited in the so-called 'free' societies of the twentieth century. Democratic governments *have* undoubtedly lied to their people for supposedly 'noble' ends and it is questionable whether any civil society could maintain itself without its government withholding or fabricating information in certain circumstances. Plato's 'noble lie' thus provokes difficult, interesting and fundamental questions for political and ethical theory. But these questions are not my concern here. Instead, I want to concentrate on two features of the *Republic*'s treatment of lying which serve to locate the notion of 'the noble lie' within the specific context of *Athenian* culture and thought.

Firstly, Socrates' vision of a state which maintains its structure through the promulgation of a 'noble lie' and licenses strategic deceptions on the part of its rulers is rooted in the claim that 'pharmacological' lying is part and parcel of everyone's lives: *everybody* knows that certain special situations make lying a necessity in order to secure just and beneficial outcomes. In the case of story-telling, people may be mistaken if they think that the poets tell good lies, but Socrates' belief is clearly that story-telling *should* amount to another everyday example of positive pharmacological lying. Socrates does not make it clear whether the requirement that nobody can lie to the rulers precludes other citizens from lying pharmacologically to each other. Socrates may have departed from his initial representation of 'the lie in words' as something which *everybody* can and must occasionally deploy. But there can be little doubt that each time Socrates makes a case for lies which will benefit the polis as a whole, he always takes the interlocutor back to a 'common-sense' viewpoint that it is sometimes necessary to lie well.

What is the significance of this appeal to 'common-sense' examples of justified deception? In the first chapter, I argued that Athenian public discourse mobilised images of Spartan education and national character in order to construct notions of trickery and deception as unAthenian. There is another aspect to the Athenian description of Spartan duplicity which I highlighted only very briefly in chapter two, namely the use of lies as a technique of political control. Anton Powell has recently pointed out that Athenian sources emphasise the prevalence of 'official deceit' in Sparta.[49] This 'official deceit' included misleading helots as to whether they would be killed or rewarded and tricking enemies in wartime.[50] Thucydides and Xenophon record how the Spartan authorities trapped the traitors Pausanias and Cinadon by means of elaborate deceptions.[51] More significantly for my purposes, Xenophon twice represents Spartan officials lying to their own citizens about the outcome of battles involving Spartan forces.[52] For Powell, what distinguishes Sparta in Athenian writing is 'not self-interested mendacity by ambitious individuals, but high-minded, often elaborate, official conspiracy: deceit for a good end, to borrow a phrase from the *Laws* (663d)'.[53] Powell cites from Plato because he is concerned to show that Platonic discussion of the 'noble lie' as a legitimate technique of statecraft to be practised on citizens by their official superiors is one of the elements of the *Laws* which engages with (Athenian representations of) Spartan political practice. The Athenian of the *Laws* is much more reticent and allusive about the legitimacy of official 'noble lies' than the Socrates of the *Republic*.[54] This is particularly evident in the area of the political manipulation of religion and oracles. It is easily forgotten that part of the *gennaion pseudos* of the *Republic* is an invented oracle (3.415c8). Xenophon claims that the Spartan law-giver Lycurgus secured obedience to his new laws by having them sanctioned by the Delphic oracle. The historian argues that this was the finest of Lycurgus' 'contrivances' (μηχανημάτων), because he was able to have it enacted that disobedience to his laws was impious as well as illegal.[55]

---

[49] Powell (1994) 284–7
[50] Deceiving helots: Thuc. 4.80; deceiving the enemy: Xen. *Ages.* 1.17.
[51] Pausanias is lured to a hut where hidden ephors can hear him incriminate himself: Thuc. 1.133. Cinadon is lured away from Sparta on the pretext of an official errand: Xen. *Hell.* 3.3.8–11.
[52] Xen. *Hell.* 1.6.36f. and 4.3.13f.
[53] Powell (1994) 285.
[54] Powell (1994) 286–92.
[55] Xen. *Lac. Pol.* 8.6.

There are many other examples of official use of oracles at Sparta to authorise policy or changes of policy, but it is only Lycurgus' use of divination which is explicitly characterised as a ruse.[56] In the *Laws*, religious beliefs and oracles are frequently invoked as a means of securing the obedience of subjects, but in contrast to the 'noble lie' of the *Republic*, they are never explicitly characterised as pragmatic fictions.[57]

For Powell the more subtle treatment of official deceit in the *Laws* can be explained by its intended audience.[58] A Spartan or pro-Spartan audience didn't need to have the value and drawbacks of official deceit spelled out to them in black and white. And they would be sensitive about how Spartan practices might be portrayed to any non-Spartan readers. The *Republic* drew upon the Spartan notion of the necessity of 'noble lies' more explicitly because it was intended for an audience who were less familiar with the notion in the first place. An Athenian audience would be more shocked by the notion and would therefore require extensive and explicit explanation of its application and validity. Socrates is indeed anxious about the reception which his interlocutors will give to his *gennaion pseudos*: 'you'll think my hestitation quite appropriate when I do speak' (3.414c9). Adeimantus is definitely shocked by it: 'not without reason were you for so long ashamed to tell the lie' (3.414e9). Adeimantus' shock and Socrates' shame must be significant. But it does not seem to me that shock is automatically commensurable with unfamiliarity. Mary Whitehouse (veteran guardian of British public 'decency') is doubtless familiar with human nudity and sexual intercourse; this does not prevent her from being shocked by their depiction in certain public contexts. Nor is it clear that the *Republic*'s passages of justification for official deceit represent a requirement to breed familiarity. Official deceit could have demanded justification to an Athenian readership precisely because of its well-known associations with the tight oligarchy of Sparta. I have already shown that Spartan duplicity was a frequent image in Athenian public texts. It is hard to believe that Thucydides' and Xenophon's stories of Spartan 'noble lies' were not a widely-known component of that image.

The state-sponsored 'noble lie' had Spartan connotations and those

---

[56] Powell neglects to mention that political and official manipulation of oracles by Athenian democratic leaders is also represented and criticised in Athenian texts. See Ar. *Eq.* 125ff. and 927ff. But the Aristophanic representation stresses the selfish motives of the manipulator rather than deceptive manipulation of oracles as a genuine means of benefiting the polis.

[57] Powell (1994) 288. But see Pl. *Leg.* 5.738b–c, where, as Powell points out, 'indifference to the truth of certain religious beliefs is clearly hinted at'.

[58] Powell (1994) 291–2.

connotations were widely known. The manner in which Plato's Socrates characterises the *gennaion pseudos* in the *Republic* can be seen as an attempt to explain official deceit in terms which side-step anti-Spartan prejudices in the dialogue's Athenian audience. Paternalistic lying on the part of Kallipolis' rulers and Socrates himself is represented, not as a systematic 'Spartan-style' policy of state control but as an 'occasional' *pharmakon* which must be administered in specific circumstances where the health and unity of the community would otherwise be in jeopardy. Pharmacological lies are appropriate in education, in the creation of a foundation-myth and in the maintenance of the division of the three classes. In addition, the rulers are at liberty to lie to the ruled whenever such lies will maintain the health of the state. These official lies are all built on the simple moral foundation that it is just and proper to save your friends from harm by lying to them when there is no other way to achieve that end. Thus the *Republic* is able to explain or justify official lies in terms which would either distance them from perceived Spartan practices or at least persuade the reader that they are simply a wider application of a 'common-sense' view that lies can sometimes be useful. This is not to claim that the discussions of everyday pharmacological deception are somehow 'tacked-on': the *Republic* integrates its specific analysis of the nature and role of lying with its moral, political and epistemological vision.[59] But by starting with everyday cases where 'paternalistic' lying makes sense, Plato attempts to 'naturalise' his representation of the 'lie in words' as a form of social interaction which is acceptable in *any* polis, rather than as the hallmark of an undemocratic city such as Sparta.[60]

My point here, which will be developed throughout this chapter, is that the 'noble lie' (in the *Republic* and in Athenian texts in general) cannot be characterised *simply* as a 'totalitarian' ploy. Crucially, Socrates legitimises its use by arguing that good lies are part of the fabric of contemporary social life and that legitimation is reinforced through agreement with interlocutors in dialogue. Where Adeimantus expresses shock and highlights Socrates' shame and hesitancy concerning the 'Myth of Metals', the dialogue carefully enhances this process of legitimation. The transformation of 'common-sense' deceit into state propaganda is acknowledged and marked as problematic at the same time as it is deemed to be necessary.

The second point I wish to make concerning Plato's 'noble lie' is

---

[59] As Page (1991) and Reeve (1988) demonstrate.
[60] On 'naturalisation' as a ruse of ideology see Eagleton (1991) 59–61. The classic account of 'naturalising' strategy is Barthes (1972) 125.

related to the first insofar as it concerns the manner in which the 'positive' use of lies is represented. Alongside the analogy with the pharmacological 'lie in words', the 'Myth of Metals' is presented by Socrates as 'nothing new but a Phoenician thing' (μηδὲν καινόν ... ἀλλὰ Φοινικικόν τι: 3.414c4). Now it has been forcefully argued that the *gennaion pseudos* is 'Phoenician' because the Phoenicians were associated with trade and money-making. The lie prevents the mingling of the different classes and Glaucon later points out that if the bronze and the iron classes do mix, the ideal city will be pulled towards money-making (8.547b) and the result will be a bastardised regime of masters and slaves rather than rulers and ruled. The lie is 'Phoenician' because it limits materialistic and self-interested desires which will ultimately destroy Kallipolis.[61] Of course, the fact that the 'noble lie' involves gold, silver, iron and bronze elements also makes it 'Phoenician' in the sense that it is grounded in a metaphor for coinage and monetary value. But there is an even more obvious reason why Socrates' *gennaion pseudos* is a 'Phoenician thing'. The tale he wants to tell is one of autochthonous brotherhood. Cadmus was a Phoenician who founded Thebes with a race of giants who sprang from the earth after he had sown the dragon's teeth.[62] As Page points out, Cadmus' giants eventually kill each other off – precisely the kind of strife which the 'noble lie' aims to avoid.[63] By calling his lie 'Phoenician', Socrates places it alongside traditional foundation-myths involving autochthony.

Plato is explicit about the value of such myths and their exemplary status as 'noble lies' in the *Laws*. In this dialogue, the Athenian is convinced that the 'unjust life' is more unpleasant than the 'just life' (2.663d1–3). But he surmises that even if this were not the case, a lawgiver could not find a more profitable (*lusitelesteron*) or effective lie (*pseudos*) to persuade all men to act justly of their own free will (2.663d5–10). Clinias replies that truth is a fine and enduring thing but it is not easy to persuade men of it (καλὸν μὲν ἡ ἀλήθεια, ὦ ξένε, καὶ μόνιμον· ἔοικε μὴν οὐ ῥᾴδιον εἶναι πείθειν). The Athenian retorts that it was easy enough to persuade (*peithein*) men of the 'Sidonian story' (*Sidōnion muthologēma*), incredible (*apithanon*) though it was, and there were countless other similar stories (2.663e4–5). At Clinias' request, he then elaborates on the nature and value of these stories:

---

[61] See Page (1991) 21–6.
[62] This explanation for the 'noble lie' being 'Phoenician' is offered by Adam (1963) 195 and Guthrie (1975) 462.
[63] Page (1991) 22, n. 20.

The tale of the teeth that were sown, and how the armed men sprang out of them. Here, indeed, the law-giver has a notable example of how one can, if he tries, persuade the souls of the young (*peithein tas tōn neōn psuchas*) of anything, so that the only question he has to consider in his inventing is what would do most good to the polis, if it were believed; and then he must devise all possible means to ensure that the whole of the community constantly, so long as they live, use exactly the same language, so far as possible, about these matters, alike in their songs, their tales (*muthois*), and their speeches (*logois*). (Plato *Laws* 2.663e9–664a8)

Here, as in the *Republic*, there is an expression of the value of myths of autochthony as lies which are good for a polis. An *Athenian* would know this: Athens had such a myth of its own.[64] Socrates is not sure if the first generation of Kallipolitans can be persuaded of his Phoenician tale but Adeimantus is certain that subsequent generations will be persuaded (*Republic* 3.415d1–2). And the Athenian of the *Laws* is similarly concerned with the process of *persuasion*. Clinias seems to believe that it is actually true that the just life is also the most pleasant but the Athenian's point is that even if it proved to be untrue, some kind of myth should be told to make it seem true. Such a lie will be profitable and the trick is to use the highly persuasive medium of a myth.

Much has been written about Plato's deployment of mythical or pseudo-mythical discourse and such studies reveal that Platonic myths should always be considered in the context of the dialogues which frame and constitute them.[65] However, the equation between myths of origin and 'noble lying' in the *Republic* and the *Laws* indicates that Plato's 'pharmacological' conception of deception is firmly rooted in what Foucault calls 'efficacious discourse' and what Detienne would call 'the ambiguity' of archaic *alethēia*. Scholars have noted that the Platonic conception of 'lies which imitate truth' approximates Hesiod's claim that the Muses know 'lies like the truth'.[66] Plato's 'Myth of Metals' also has a Hesiodic ring to it and, as the Athenian of the *Laws* makes clear, foundation-myths are crucial for stabilising a polis.[67] The notion of the 'lie in words' as a *pharmakon* is a twist on Gorgias' account of persuasive *logos* as a form of *apatē* which is akin to a drug – sometimes poisonous, sometimes palliative.[68] It is important that Socrates and the Athenian are anxious only to use the 'drug of deceit' as a curative and preventative medicine. But it is equally significant that

---

[64] On the ideological importance of Athens' myth of autochthony, see Loraux (1993).
[65] See, for example, Segal (1978); Brisson (1982); Smith (1986); Gill (1979), (1993).
[66] See Hes. *Theog.* 27–8 with Belfiore (1985).
[67] See Hes. *Op.* 106ff. for the myth of the five ages of mankind.
[68] See Gorgias *Hel.* 14 (= DK 82 B11.14) with Murray (1996) 151; Segal (1962) 106; Verdenius (1981); MacDowell (1982) 12–16.

Plato's pharmacology of lying and its manifestation in persuasive civic myths is put forward as the means by which the philosopher secures and maintains his ideal polis. The 'will to truth' still needs the persuasive *pseudē* of archaic and classical mythological paradigms to cure the city. The comparison of these paradigms with *pharmaka* is an adaptation, rather than a depature from the sophistic and Gorgianic celebration of speech's pharmaceutical effects.

When Socrates starts to narrate the Myth of Metals, he says that the Kallipolitans will be told that 'the god in fashioning/moulding those of you who are competent to rule, mixed gold in at their birth' (3.415a4–5). The Greek for 'the god fashioning/moulding' is *ho theos plattōn*. This phrase suggests a pun: the Greek *sounds* like it could also mean 'the god Plato'.[69] Just as Plato 'fashions' a 'noble lie', the god 'fashions' the citizens of Kallipolis from a range of metals. Plato plays god by moulding a myth which will, in turn, mould his ideal hierarchy of citizens. The Myth of Metals may be a 'lie in words' but it is designed to change the Kallipolitans' sense of what they are made of. Plato's 'noble lie' thus signals its own 'materiality' as discourse.

The Platonic philosopher may be the new 'master of truth', but he has to dispense lies from his pharmacy to realise that regime of truth: he is dependent upon mastering the independent materiality of discourse and its effects on the 'souls of individuals and communities'. This materiality – the old persuasive spell of 'lies like the truth' – makes it difficult to characterise Platonic discourse as significantly different to pre-Socratic representations of 'truth' in the manner which Foucault suggests. Detienne is far from clear as to where he would place Plato in his account of the Greek history of *alētheia*. But I hope to have shown that his treatment of elements of sophistic and pre-Socratic thought is usefully extended and nuanced by an examination of the 'noble lie' in Plato. The Platonic 'master of truth' is also the master of lies and in that sense he shares his mode of communicating and establishing authority with the archaic king, poet or prophet, the classical sophist, and all the institutions of the classical city which transmit myths of its own origins and identity.

If Platonic dialogue explicitly acknowledged and theorised a positive role for deceptive communication within a polis, did the public discourses of Athenian democracy allow such notions to be aired? Did the paternalistic, Spartan (oligarchic) and sophistic/Socratic connotations of the 'noble lie' preclude any admission that a 'noble lie' was compatible with democracy? I now turn to these questions.

---

[69] This pun is noticed by Clay (1988) 19 and Rose (1992) 354.

The 'noble lie' in democratic oratory

In the first chapter we saw that the notion of 'deceiving the demos' was specifically prohibited by law. References to that law and its application indicated that it was ideologically symbolic, as was the curse against deceiving the people proclaimed by a herald before every trial or meeting of the *ecclēsia*. In the case of the speech *Against Leptines*, we also saw that a general notion of ideal citizen identity could be invoked to characterise the supposed dishonesty of a proposal or an opponent as 'unAthenian'. The law and curse against 'deceiving the demos' are certainly inscribed with the idea that deceit and democracy are incompatible. And a community which created and applied specific laws against deception of the demos, false witnessing in trials and deception in commerce, as Athens did, certainly regarded the possibility of deceptive communication as a threat to 'good exchange'.[70] In modern Western democracies the idea that executive government or related officials could lie for the benefit of the state is often condemned as incompatible with democratic ideology. But how far did Athenian public discourse regard deceit as a specific problem for a *democratic* political system?

The reasons why a democracy, rather than any other political system, must be vigilant against deceit are explicitly raised by Demosthenes in his speech *On the False Embassy*. His opponent Aeschines stands accused of misconduct in his role as an ambassador to Macedon in 346. Demosthenes, who was a member of the same embassy, claims that Aeschines has taken bribes from Philip and has deliberately lied about the embassy to the Athenian *ecclēsia* with treacherous intent.[71] Unsurprisingly, the speech abounds with accusations of deceit on the part of Aeschines, but at one point Demosthenes predicts that his opponent will complain that he alone of all those who address the people is to be called to account for his *logoi* (19.182).[72] He replies to this objection by

---

[70] On the charge of false witnessing (*dikē pseudomarturiōn*) see Harrison (1971) 192–8; Todd (1993) 261–2. Andoc. 1.74 indicates that three convictions for false witnessing could mean the loss of citizen rights. For legal sanctions against deceit in the *agora* see MacDowell (1978) 157 and [Arist.] *Ath. Pol.* 51.1; Dem. 20.9; Hyp. 3.14.

[71] For the details of the charges and the political background to the case, see Vince and Vince (1926) 232–42; Harris (1995) 63–123. On the complexity of Athenian diplomacy at this time see the essays in Perlman (1973).

[72] Aeschines' formulation in his defence speech is slightly different. At Aeschin. 2.178, he complains that he is being called to account for *erga* when he only had *logoi* under his control and that he is the only one of ten ambassadors to be called to account in this manner.

stating that if Aeschines has deliberately deceived the people for money as an ambassador, then the jury must not listen to the suggestion that he should not stand trial for the things he said. With heavy sarcasm, Demosthenes poses a question: 'for what are we to bring any ambassador to justice if not for his words?' (183). He then points out that ambassadors are given control, not over triremes, military positions, hoplites or citadels, but 'words and opportunities' (ἀλλὰ λόγων καὶ χρόνων). It is wrong for an ambassador to waste opportunities for the state, but the implications of giving false reports to the demos are represented as more profoundly damaging:

τοὺς δὲ λόγους εἰ μὲν ἀληθεῖς ἀπήγγελκεν ἢ συμφέροντας, ἀποφευγέτω, εἰ δὲ καὶ ψευδεῖς καὶ μισθοῦ καὶ ἀσυμφόρους, ἁλισκέσθω. οὐδὲν γὰρ ἔσθ' ὅ τι μεῖζον ἂν ὑμᾶς ἀδικήσειέ τις, ἢ ψευδῆ λέγων. οἷς γάρ ἐστ' ἐν λόγοις ἡ πολιτεία, πῶς, ἂν οὗτοι μὴ ἀληθεῖς ὦσιν, ἀσφαλῶς ἔστι πολιτεύεσθαι;

If the words of his reports are true and profitable words, let him be acquitted. If they are false, venal and damaging, let him be convicted. A man can do you no greater injustice than telling lies; for, where the political constitution is based on speeches/words, how can it be safely administered if the words/speeches are false? (Demosthenes 19.183–5)

I used this passage at the beginning of my introduction as an emblem of Athenian democracy's confrontation with the problem of deceptive communication. In his speech *Against Leptines*, Demosthenes represented the *ēthos* of the Athenian polis as 'honest' (*apseudēs*) and 'noble' (*chrēstos*) (20.13). But here, Demosthenes is not discussing Athenian national character. Rather, he stresses that the democratic constitution of Athens is a system based on 'words' or 'speeches'. Aeschines' lies to the *ecclēsia* are the worst kind of injustice because the democratic 'city of words' is extremely vulnerable to this exploitation of what Detienne calls 'the ambiguity of speech'. In his oration *On the Crown*, Demosthenes argues that deceiving the people by not saying what one thinks is the worst crime a *rhētōr* can commit.[73] This sentiment is echoed by other extant orators, including Dinarchus who, in addition to condemning Demosthenes himself for 'deceiving the people and the council in defiance of the curse', also attacks him for 'saying one thing

---

[73] Dem. 18.282: 'And who is the deceiver of his city? Surely the man who does not say what he thinks. For whom does the herald read the curse justly? For him. For what graver crime can be charged to an orator than that his thoughts and words are not the same?' (καίτοι τίς τὴν πόλιν ἐξαπατῶν; οὐχ ὁ μὴ λέγων ἃ φρονεῖ; τῷ δ' ὁ κῆρυξ καταρᾶται δικαίως; οὐ τῷ τοιούτῳ; τί δὲ μεῖζον ἔχοι τις ἂν εἰπεῖν ἀδίκημα κατ' ἀνδρὸς ῥήτορος ἢ εἰ μὴ ταὐτὰ φρονεῖ καὶ λέγει;)

while thinking another'.[74] Demosthenes' words contribute to a picture of the way in which public oratory is a medium for the negotiation of mass-elite relations in the democracy.[75] As Ober puts it, 'when the Athenians paid a politician with the coin of their trust and their willingness to weaken ideological restraints, they expected to be paid back with the best and most heartfelt advice he could come up with. Anything less was treason'.[76] This view of deceit of the demos is, as Ober and others have stressed, particularly apparent when the orators connect an elite official's dishonesty with the taking of bribes.[77] When Dinarchus accuses the *stratēgos* Philocles of having taken bribes from Harpalus, the treasurer of Alexander the Great, he is described as having 'deceived every Athenian'. Philocles 'betrayed the trust which he did not deserve to receive from you, and so has done all he can to destroy everything in the polis'.[78] The orators also gloss deceit as 'katapolitical' (against the polis) by associating its perpetrators with sophistry or sycophancy.[79] And a number of commentators have shown how these topoi of accusation reflect and reproduce a democratic ideology whereby the representative power, wealth and the privileged education of elite speakers is kept in check and continuously monitored.[80]

---

[74] Din. 1.47 in the text of Conomis (1975): ἐξηπατηκὼς δὲ καὶ τὸν δῆμον καὶ τὴν βουλὴν καὶ παρὰ τὴν ἀρὰν, καὶ ἕτερα μὲν λέγων ἕτερα δὲ φρονῶν ... See Lys. 18.16 where the speaker complains that the people do not realise that orators have a hidden agenda of private gain against the public interest. See also Hyp. 5.17. and Dem. 24.124. Din. 3.6–7 states that there is nothing more troublesome than the unnoticed *ponēria* of a politician. See also the view of Cleon at Thuc. 3.37.4–5, to be discussed further below. See also Arist. *Rh.* 2.1399a30–2 and *Soph. Ref.* 172b36–173a6 for the topic of confronting an opponent with secret wishes which run counter to noble public statements.

[75] Demosthenes' comments at 19.182–6 constitute a topos to the extent that they convey the idea, found in other speeches and orators, that an orator can do nothing worse than lie to the demos. They are nevertheless unique in the extant corpus of oratory to the extent that they contain an explicit link between the injustice of deceit and the fact that a democratic *politeia* is based on *logoi*. See below, pp. 168–9.

[76] Ober (1989) 330–1.

[77] Ober (1989) 236–8 and 331–2. See Harvey (1985), who concludes, '[T]he majority of Hypereides' fellow-Athenians regarded taking bribes against the interests of the state as particularly heinous' (112).

[78] Din 3.4: ὁ δὲ πάντας Ἀθηναίους ἐξηπατηκώς, καὶ προδοὺς τὴν πίστιν ἣν παρ' ὑμῶν οὐκ ἄξιος ὢν ἔλαβε, καὶ τὸ καθ' αὑτὸν μέρος ἅπαντ' ἀνατετροφὼς τὰ ἐν τῇ πόλει.

[79] On the orators' use of 'anti-rhetorical' topoi against opponents, see below pp. 202–41. See also Dover (1974) 25–8; Ostwald (1986) 256–7. On the orators' attacks on opponents as sophists and 'clever speakers' see Ober (1989) 156–91; on logography see Bonner (1927) 320–3; Dover (1968) 148–74; Kennedy (1963) 126–45; Carey and Reid (1985) 13–18; Sinclair (1988) 186; Usher (1976); Cartledge (1990a) 49–52; Too (1995) 115f. On the topoi concerning sycophancy see Osborne (1990) and Harvey (1990).

[80] See Harvey (1985); Ostwald (1986); Ober (1989), (1994); Osborne (1990); Wilson (1991).

These and other topoi in the extant corpus of Athenian oratory represent the key areas of concern in a continuing process of ideological negotiation between the demos and those who had the leisure, wealth and ability to become its advisers. Over time elite speakers 'helped to create a vocabulary of social mediation which defined the nature of mass-élite interaction for the Athenians and legitimated both the power of the masses and the special privileges of the élites'.[81]

So, when Demosthenes says that telling lies to the demos is a singular crime in the passage cited above, he rehearses a topos. But Demosthenes moves beyond this standard topos, by explaining that deceit is *peculiarly* unacceptable in a democratic system because that system is 'logocentric'.[82] He also goes on to make a further point about deception in democracy by claiming that 'the filching of opportunities' for debate in the polis through false reports is a worse crime in a democracy than it would be in an oligarchy or a tyranny (185). In these undemocratic systems everything is done promptly by command, while in the case of democracy the Boule must be informed and a draft resolution must be drawn up. Then the *ecclēsia* must be convened on a statutory date so that a debate can take place and, after further time for dialogue and consideration a decision can be reached (185–6). Here, Demosthenes foregrounds deceptive communication as a threat to a central tenet of Athenian democratic ideology, namely the valorisation of forethought, discussion and debate prior to action. This tenet is neatly expressed in the Thucydidean Funeral Speech of Pericles:

---

[81] Ober (1989) 306.
[82] In Derridean terms, democracy is represented here as 'logocentric'/'phonocentric' (reliant on speech and what Derrida would see as a myth of speech's 'self-presence') *and* as vulnerable to phenomena of speech (deceit is a radical symptom of speech's *lack* of 'self-presence') which 'logocentric'/'phonocentric' prejudices usually suppress and attribute to *writing*. See, especially, Derrida (1981) and Norris (1987) 28–96. However, in line with Derrida (1981) and its famous analysis of Plato's *Phaedrus*, the tendency of democratic oratory to attribute deceit of the demos to the workings of the sophist and the logographer can be seen as a mark of the encroachment of 'logocentric' prejudice in democratic discourse against writing as a phenomenon which contaminates 'self-present' spoken communication. Derrida's view that the *Phaedrus*' distinction between 'good speech' and 'bad writing' is self-undermining is criticised by Ferrari (1987) 214–22 who points out that Socrates attempts to map out a distinction between 'good' and 'bad' writing. See Halperin (1992) for application of Derridean insights to Plato's *Symposium*. Sometimes, orators and characters in civic drama praise writing as an *aide-mémoire* and a guarantee of *isonomia* through the visibility and permanency of inscribed laws. See Thomas (1989) 21, n. 22, and 61–2 with n. 151. Derrida would perhaps point to the ways in which these eulogies assume that such writing is self-present or 'like' speech.

... and we ourselves judge affairs or at least endeavour to arrive at a correct understanding of them[83] in the belief that it is not words that harm actions, but rather not to be instructed by words before the necessary time comes for action (ἀλλὰ μὴ προδιδαχθῆναι μᾶλλον λόγῳ πρότερον ἢ ἐπὶ ἃ δεῖ ἔργῳ ἐλθεῖν). For we have this point of difference over others, to be the most daring in action and yet at the same time we are most given to reflection (ἐκλογίζεσθαι) upon the ventures we mean to undertake. (Thucydides 2.40.2–3)

Pericles is implicitly contrasting the virtues of Athenian democratic deliberation with Sparta's political system.[84] It must be noted that both here and elsewhere, the Thucydidean Pericles is particularly concerned to premise his praise of deliberation and good decision-making with a self-authorising notion of the *rhētōr* giving good prior *instruction* (προδιδαχθῆναι).[85] Yunis has very recently shown how Demosthenes also deploys a similar self-authorising model of instructional rhetoric to that of the Thucydidean Pericles.[86] Demosthenes contributes to this valorisation of '*logoi* before *erga*' by stressing that a deceptive politician can rob the demos of its right to deliberate and the advantages associated with that right. We will see below that Andocides had already articulated a similar opposition between deceit and democratic debate.

In direct contrast to Pericles, the Thucydidean Cleon attacks the Athenian obsession with careful deliberation when he opens his speech in the Mytilenean debate (Thuc. 3.37.3–5). And in partial contrast to Demosthenes' argument he claims that the slow process of debate actually proliferates the possibilities for deceit of the demos. Furthermore, those who want the *ecclēsia* to reconsider its previous decision on the Mytilenean affair must either have been bribed to do so or are confident in their abilities as 'clever speakers' to mislead their audience

---

[83] On the vexed interpretation of αὐτοὶ ἤτοι κρίνομέν γε ἢ ἐνθυμούμεθα ὀρθῶς τὰ πράγματα, see Hornblower (1991) 305–6.

[84] See Hornblower (1991) 305. Pericles' comments are similar to those of Democritus DK 68 B66: 'It is better to deliberate before actions than to consider them afterwards' (προβουλεύεσθαι κρεῖσσον πρὸ τῶν πράξεων ἢ μετανοεῖν). On the affinity between Democritean moral and political thought and representations of political discourse in Thucydides, see Hussey (1985).

[85] As argued by Yunis (1996) 75ff.

[86] Yunis (1996) 256–7, 276–7. In my view, Yunis' assumption of direct Thucydidean influence on Demosthenes and his belief that the speeches of the Thucydidean Pericles were meant to represent an ideal and unique 'model' of rhetoric leads him to underestimate the extent to which Demosthenes' statements about deliberation may be versions of a more widely deployed discursive strategy as much as (or more than) they constitute a unique and heartfelt personal vision. See Hesk (1999b). However, as I suggest below, Demosthenes certainly *represents* himself as having unique political theoretical insight by reflecting on the effects of deceit in different constitutional systems.

(38.2–4). Cleon's opponent Diodotus replies that this is itself a deceptive argument; Cleon is attacking the wisdom of careful deliberation and manufacturing suspicion against those who want to re-open
discussion of Mytilene's fate because further debate may result in a
decision which he opposes (42.2–6). Diodotus claims that the climate
of suspicion which people like Cleon encourage actually forces good
advisers to use *apatē* in order to re-establish their credibility (43.2–4).
Diodotus' statement that orators have to use *apatē* to avert the suspicion created by other speakers is unique, but his argument that good
advice is hindered by an atmosphere of suspicion is closely paralleled
in one of a collection of mostly deliberative preambles which is usually
attributed to Demosthenes.[87] Thucydides seems here to articulate a
peculiar problem which democracy faces in relation to *apatē* and it is a
problem which provides an important frame for Demosthenes' comments about the 'logocentricity' of the Athenian legal and political
system. The *rhētōr* can, as Demosthenes and Diodotus claim, destroy
the demos' control over its own affairs by deceiving them in such a way
as to deny them the opportunity to debate important issues. But by
emphasising democracy's dependence on *logoi*, Demosthenes also follows Cleon's point that conduct of free debate is no guarantee against
the threat of deceptive communication. We will see in my final chapter
that Diodotus adds a further twist by highlighting the possibility that an
opponent's invective against the threat of deceptive communication to
democracy is itself an insincere *strategy* to discredit the character and
motives of his opponent. And we will see that even Diodotus' remarks
invite the reader to reflect on the sincerity and motives of his own
rhetoric.

Thucydides' account of the exchange between Diodotus and Cleon
foregrounds the difficulty of determining a 'bottom line' democratic
ideological attitude towards deception in the lawcourts or assembly.
As the orator pronounces on the dangers of the opponent who will
hoodwink the demos he is always attempting to impugn the sincerity
of his opponent and he does so by marking that insincerity as anti-
democratic or symptomatic of democracy's *malaise*. While Dem-

---

[87] Dem. *Pr.* 37 in the text of Clavaud (1974). On the questionable authenticity of the
Demosthenic collection of preambles see Clavaud (1974) 5–55; Yunis (1996) 287–9.
Even if Clavaud and Yunis' arguments for Demosthenic authorship are wishful thinking, I know of no arguments to suggest that this collection is not a genuine fourth-
century product. Yunis (1996) 288, n. 4 provides late evidence from the *Suda*, Athenaeus and Hermogenes that Antiphon, Thrasymachus and Critias wrote collections of
preambles. Cratinus *PCG* fr. 197 parodies a judicial preamble; Xen. *Mem.* 4.2.3–5
parodies a deliberative preamble. These parodies suggest to Yunis 'a general awareness of diction that was standard to preambles well before Demosthenes' time' (288).

osthenes' attack on deception as a subversion of the democracy's 'logocentricity' seems to preclude any possibility that an orator would be able to sanction the use of 'noble lies' to benefit the demos, it has to be taken as a *strategic* act of self-authorisation. It may embody a fundamental tenet that democracy and deceit do not mix but Demosthenes' little departure into political theory is undoubtedly designed to represent Aeschines as an anti-democratic villain. By contrast, Demosthenes promotes himself as an articulate democratic statesman who understands the fundamental constitutional principles which make Aeschines' lies ideologically heinous. Demosthenes' comments are built around a commonplace but his *particular* reflection on deception as a threat to the democracy's 'logocentric' constitution is a unique embellishment in the extant corpus. This interplay between topos and creative 'spin' is a feature of the orators' 'anti-deception' rhetoric which I will have cause to return to. But my point here is simply that the orators' repeated attacks on the notion of a *rhētōr* deceiving the demos should not lead us to assume that democratic discourse precluded public articulation of the notion that a speaker could lie to the demos for its own benefit. If Thucydides could have Diodotus argue openly that prejudice and suspicion could force a speaker to use deceit to neutralise such suspicion, then it is worth asking how far, and in what circumstances a democratic orator could give deceit a positive colouring.

For the rest of this section, then, I want to test Demosthenes' categorical rejection of deceit as inimical to democratic process and principle. How far do the orators reject deception because it is *strategically* necessary to impugn opponents or is it really the case that public democratic discourse can *only* represent the ambiguity of speech as a threat to the demos? In other words, is there a place for the 'noble lie' in democratic ideology? Do the orators ever claim that it can be right to lie to the demos?

An apparently Popperian antithesis between the principles of the open society and 'lying to the people' is articulated in a passage from Andocides' speech *On the Peace With Sparta*, a passage which I have already discussed in relation to deceit and Athenian *stratēgoi*. Andocides expresses an awareness that a number of his audience in the *ecclēsia* are anxious to conclude a peace treaty with the Spartans as quickly as possible. These citizens are critical of Andocides and his fellow ambassadors for not coming to terms with the Spartans during their meeting with them. They argue that the embassy was sent with full powers in order to avoid further reference of the matter to the *ecclēsia*. Andocides goes on to attribute the following viewpoint to these critics:

Our desire to secure our position by such a reference [to the *ecclēsia*] they call nervousness, since no one, they argue, has ever saved the Athenian people by open persuasion (οὐδεὶς πώποτε τὸν δῆμον τὸν Ἀθηναίων ἐκ τοῦ φανεροῦ πείσας ἔσωσεν). Rather, it is necessary to benefit them through concealment or deception. This is an argument I do not support. (ἀλλὰ δεῖ λαθόντας ἢ ἐξα-πατήσαντας αὐτὸν εὖ ποιῆσαι. Τὸν λόγον οὖν τοῦτον οὐκ ἐπαινῶ.) (Andocides 3.33)

We know that Andocides' attempt to secure the peace between Athens and Sparta failed and that both he and his fellow-delegates were exiled from Attica.[88] His creation of an image of a substantial body of citizens chastising him for not having made peace on the spot may therefore be a desperate exaggeration of the popularity of Sparta's proposals in Athens. But this passage shows us that it is possible for Andocides to present the demos with the idea that they can only be benefited if they are actively deceived or if facts are concealed from them. He speaks of the idea as if it is a well-known strand of thought. And yet, it is an idea which Andocides categorically rejects. As we saw in the first chapter, he goes on to draw a distinction between a *stratēgos* who may deceive his troops in war and ambassadors who, in the process of negotiating peace for all of Greece, must never use secrecy or deceit.[89] He maintains that he and his colleagues deserve praise rather than blame for bringing the Spartans' proposals back to the *ecclēsia* for careful consideration and debate (34).

Anticipating Demosthenes, Andocides creates an opposition between deceit of the demos and a model of open and considered deliberation. His comments are further inscribed with a paradigm of *peithō* as 'good exchange' and this is opposed to the 'bad exchange' of *apatē*. But the evocation and dismissal of the idea that the demos can only be saved by *apatē* rather than open *peithō* represents a category distinction which was far from stable in Athenian public discourse. As Richard Buxton has shown, the relationship between the notions of *dolos* (trickery) and *apatē* on the one hand and *peithō* on the other, is 'much more variable and ambiguous than that between *bia* and *peithō*'.[90] This variability and ambiguity is particularly noticeable in Athenian drama. In drama *peithō* is sometimes characterised by frankness and is opposed to *dolos* or

---

[88] See Missiou (1992) 168–72.
[89] Andoc. 3.34, quoted above p. 83.
[90] Buxton (1982) 64. However, Buxton does acknowledge that while *peithō* and *bia* are usually opposed to one another, *peithō* can be described as violent (Aesch. *Ag.* 385–6) or as equivalent to violence/force (Gorg. *Hel.* 12 = DK 82 B11.12). See Adcock (1948) who describes Greek *peithō* as 'an ambiguous friend' (13). See also Rothwell (1990) 26–43, who stresses the ambiguity of *peithō* with reference to connotations of erotic deception or seduction.

apatē.[91] At other moments *peithō* slips out of this position and becomes virtually synonymous with trickery or deceit.[92] Gorgias' *Encomium of Helen* also seems to blur the distinction between *logos* as *peithō* and as *apatē*, probably because the author is concerned with the power of language to seduce and charm the listener like a drug (*pharmakon*).[93] But Andocides' opposition between *peithō* and *apatē* falls in line with the eulogy found in Lysias' funeral oration, where 'to persuade by argument' (λόγῳ ... πεῖσαι) is valorised as the hallmark of civilisation and democracy (2.18–19).[94]

One can only speculate as to whether the ambiguous representation of *peithō* in drama or sophistic exegesis would have made an audience sceptical of Andocides' claims for *peithō* as a democratic notion which could and should be kept distinct from notions of deceit. But Andocides could have made his point by praising *peithō* and deliberation without any reference to the concept of justifiable deceit. So why does he bother to invoke the concept at all? He clearly believed that ideological mileage could be gained from dismissing the concept of the 'noble lie'. After Popper, it is apparent that the 'noble lie' can easily be associated with 'the closed society', but would it have had the same connotations for the Athenian citizenry?

I have already argued that 'official deception' would have been closely associated with the practices of Spartan oligarchy. When Andocides condemns those who argue that the Athenian demos can only be saved or benefited if it is misled, he does so primarily because he is attempting to persuade an Athenian audience to make peace with Sparta. By dismissing a notion which that audience would associate with the practices of Spartan oligarchy and the beliefs of laconisers, he is attempting to neutralise the suspicion that he is acting as an agent of an undemocratic enemy state in order to secure a peace treaty which serves that state's interests more than those of Athens.[95] Again, the

---

[91] See Soph. *Phil.* 50–120, where Odysseus and Neoptolemus discuss how to win over Philoctetes in terms of a choice between *peithō, bia,* or *apatē/dolos.* See Buxton (1982) 65 and 118–32 and my analysis below pp. 193–9.

[92] See Aesch. *Cho.* 726 where the chorus invoke *Peithō dolia* (treacherous/tricky Persuasion) to help Orestes in the murder of Aegisthus and Clytemnestra. See also Buxton (1982) 65 and 109. See Ar. *Pax* 622 and *Vesp.* 101 where compounds of *peithō* describe the effects of deception and bribery respectively.

[93] Gorg. *Hel.* 8–14 (= DK 82 B11.8–14). See Verdenius (1981); Segal (1962); Rothwell (1990) 27.

[94] For the equation between *peithō* and civilised human society see also Isoc. 15.254 and 4.48. At 15.230–6, Isocrates claims that Solon, Cleisthenes, Themistocles and Pericles all relied on their powers of eloquence and persuasion. See Buxton (1982) 54–5.

[95] Missiou (1992) argues that Andocides' speech follows a pro-Spartan agenda. If this is the case then Andocides' rejection of 'noble lies' is an attempt to mask that agenda.

orator's description of deceit as 'undemocratic' constitutes a strategy of self-representation and self-authorisation.

It would be tidy and simple if I could leave my discussion here to conclude that Athens' public democratic discourses always represent the political theory and practice of 'the noble lie' as an unacceptable trait of closed societies. Unfortunately, neither the evidence of Athenian oratory nor drama permits this simple conclusion. We have seen that Andocides himself has no problem with a *stratēgos* who deceives his own troops in order to lessen their fear and thereby enhance their performance in battle, but other texts demonstrate that this context for deceit was viewed as a legitimate special case.[96] Only once does an extant orator actually support the notion of lying to the demos for their own benefit in a public speech. Ironically, and significantly, this single instance occurs in Demosthenes' *Against Leptines*, a speech which I have already shown to contain detailed and sustained *attacks* on deceit of the demos as contrary to law and Athenian national character. I have also shown that the speech devalues deceit of an enemy in comparison to open confrontation.

Demosthenes advocates a 'noble lie' in the context of an argument concerning the conduct of heroic historical figures of the fifth century. He anticipates that his opponents will argue that even at Athens in previous generations, men who had done great services to the polis received no material rewards from the demos (20.112).[97] This argument, if Leptines and his supporters really intended to use it, would establish a precedent for their proposal that the descendants of officially recognised *euergetai* no longer be granted exemption from *leitourgia*. According to Demosthenes they will argue that Cimon was only rewarded with an inscription in the *agora* (112).[98] Demosthenes does not counter this claim with evidence of a more substantial material reward, either for Cimon or his descendants. He argues instead that Leptines' party are accusing the Athenian polis of ingratitude. Furthermore, their claim is a distortion; in the past, rewards and honours reflected the character of the age, and he is confident that men such as Cimon did get everything that they wished from the state (114). He also cites the example of Aristides' son Lysimachus, whom he claims to have received considerable benefits of land and money in recognition of his father's services to Athens (115). Even if the methods

[96] Cf. Xen. *Mem.* 2.2.17; *SVF* III 513; Onas. *Strat.* 23. See Blundell (1989) 36; Pritchett (1979) chs. 2, 3 and 12.
[97] On the pervasive trope of 'anticipating' an opponent's argument, see Dorjahn (1935).
[98] The inscription is cited at Aeschin. 3.183. Cimon was honoured for capturing Eion in 476.

were different in the past, Athens did honour its *chrēstoi*. Demosthenes concludes his attack on his opponents' argument from historical precedent in the following manner:

> Is it just then, Athenians, to honour your benefactors? It is just. Then, to observe your oaths, act on that principle yourselves; resent the imputation that your ancestors acted otherwise; and as for those who cite such instances, alleging that your ancestors rewarded no man for great benefits received, look upon them as villains (*ponērous*) and uneducated (*apaideutous*). They are villains because they falsely charge your ancestors with ingratitude. But they are unlearned (*amatheis*) because they do not see that even if the charge was completely proven, it would be more appropriate for them to deny it rather than to say it (εἰ τὰ μάλιστα ταῦθ' οὕτως εἶχεν, ἀρνεῖσθαι μᾶλλον ἢ λέγειν αὐτοῖς προσῆκεν). (Demosthenes 20.119)

Leptines and his followers have lied about the jury's ancestors. But even if it were true that the demos of the fifth-century Athens did not reward and honour benefactors, it would have been 'appropriate' (προσῆκεν) to deny this fact rather than proclaim it. Effectively, Demosthenes is arguing that it would be better to lie than tell an unpalatable truth about Athens' past failings in collective reciprocity if such failings proved to be a reality. Indeed, to tell the truth in this case would be to betray ignorance and a lack of education (hence ἀπαιδεύτους and ἀμαθεῖς). He does not actually say 'it would have been more appropriate to lie', but he makes it clear that a 'denial of the facts' would be fitting. The phrasing is reminiscent of the euphemisms and semantic acrobatics recently deployed by British ministers and senior officials when confronted with overwhelming evidence that they have told lies.[99] But Demosthenes is prepared to claim, on this issue, that it would be appropriate to mislead the demos or conceal the truth from them.

The fact that this is the only instance I can find of such an admission in extant oratory is not surprising. It is almost unheard of for a modern

---

[99] E.g. the notorious exchange between lawyer Malcolm Turnbull and the British Cabinet Secretary Sir Robert Armstrong in the 'Spycatcher trial' on 18 November 1986. See Kerr (1990) 495–510 for the relevant extract of trial transcripts taken from M. Turnbull (1988) *The Spycatcher Trial*, London. Under questioning Armstrong claimed that he had never lied for what he perceived to be reasons of national security. When Turnbull presented a letter as strong evidence that he had lied for such reasons, a long semantic tussle ensued. Armstrong said the letter contained a 'misleading impression' but 'not a lie'. When asked what the difference was, Armstrong said a lie was a 'straight untruth' whereas a 'misleading impression' was 'perhaps being economical with the truth' (503). See also *The Guardian* 2 February (1990) 7: 'Mr David Treddinick (C. Bosworth) said that given 300 terrorist murders the army was absolutely justified in using disinformation. Mr Seamus Mallon (SDLP. Newry and Armagh) said disinformation was a euphemism for lying.'

British politician to publicly advocate or admit the use of 'noble lies'. William Waldegrave did it, when under pressure from a cross-party committee to justify government conduct in the 'arms to Iraq' and 'Pergau Dam' affairs.[100] And much to the former prime minister's annoyance, he claimed that James Callaghan had lied to Parliament about devaluation of currency in order to try to avoid a run on the pound which would be caused by a truthful announcement.[101] Lying to Parliament about an intended devaluation has been something of a topos deployed by government representatives when asked whether it is ever justified to deceive MPs or the public in general.[102] Devaluation is an obvious candidate for justifiable deceit, not least because as soon as devaluation occurs, the lie and the good reasons for it are immediately revealed. But to use this example in relation to other areas of official deception, for example the 'arms to Iraq' issue, is clearly problematic. Interestingly, Waldegrave's implied application of the 'devaluation' example to the 'arms to Iraq' affair was not fully explored in public debate because Callaghan's indignation diverted attention away from it. But Callaghan's fury, and the controversy aroused by Waldegrave's comments demonstrate the sensitivity attached to the question of deceiving the public in a democracy, even where that deceit is clearly deployed in the interests of the citizen-majority.

[100] Reported in *The Guardian* 9 March (1994) 1. Ironically, Waldegrave was 'minister for open government' at the time. He told the committee that 'in exceptional circumstances it is necessary to say something untrue in the House of Commons'. But he then went on to say that there were 'plenty of cases', particularly those relating to diplomacy, when a minister 'will not mislead the House. But he may not display everything he knows about the subject'.

[101] *The Guardian* 9 March (1994) 1. Callaghan was chancellor in the Wilson government, and was questioned about devaluation of sterling in the House on 16 November 1967. Callaghan claimed that he had not lied, but had merely refused to comment when questioned about possible devaluation in the House. See *The Guardian* 10 March (1994) 6. Sir Robin Butler later backed Waldegrave up, when also under pressure from the cross-party committee about official deceit. On 13 November Wilson's inner cabinet had agreed to devalue, and when questioned three days later Callaghan had said 'I have nothing to add or subtract from anything I have said on previous occasions about devaluation.' Butler argued that the phrase 'nothing ... to subtract' took Callaghan into 'understandable' and 'defensible' lies. See *The Guardian* 27 April (1994) 6. Callaghan did not manage to avoid a run on the pound and resigned as chancellor. The Labour MP Robert Sheldon is traditionally blamed for asking Callaghan the compromising questions about sterling, but when appearing before the cross-party committee to shed light on the Callaghan episode, Sheldon insisted that it was Stan Orme who asked the fatal question.

[102] In addition to the arguments of Waldegrave and Butler, see Kerr (1990) 498 for Sir Robert Armstrong's use of devaluation as a justifiable context for deceit when he was testifying in the 'Spycatcher trial'. Paddy Ashdown agreed with Waldegrave that lying was justified when it came to 'sterling or soldiers' lives'. See *The Guardian* 10 March (1994) 6.

It would be foolish to go very far in using modern British democratic discourse as a comparative model for its classical Athenian counterpart; the differences between these two systems and cultures are too great to allow for such an assimilation.[103] But it should be clear that as models of 'the open society', neither the ancient nor the modern democracy exclude endorsement of 'the noble lie' from the arena of accountable public articulation. Andocides uses the Spartan connotations of official deceit (and of the general notion of lying to benefit the people) to convince his audience that he is speaking as an Athenian democrat. However, the rhetoric of Waldegrave and Demosthenes shows that 'the noble lie' in democratic politics can be endorsed in relation to specific contexts. For Demosthenes, lying to the demos is wrong and unAthenian, and yet, when it comes to the positive or negative representation of the demos of the historical past, an orator would appear 'uneducated', and it would be 'inappropriate' if he publicly proclaimed the negative picture, however true that picture proved to be. We do not know how Demosthenes' argument was received or whether it was contested. The fact that even a context-specific endorsement of a 'noble lie' occurs only once in extant Athenian oratory perhaps indicates that its enunciation was fraught with risks. But Demosthenes confidently frames his endorsement with appeals to education and appropriateness. Why would it be a mark of *paideia* to lie about the history of Athenian collective *charis*? And why would it be more seemly to do this than to tell the unpleasant truth?

On the evidence of the *Dissoi Logoi*, Xenophon's *Memorabilia*, and Plato's *Republic* it could be argued that Demosthenes equates *paideia* with 'sophistic' or 'Socratic' strands of ethical relativism on the question of lying and secrecy. Demosthenes' opponents lack *paideia* and *mathēsis* because they have failed to learn that it is *sometimes* justified to lie. To present openly a true picture of the demos as having been *acharistos*, is to fail to see that the truth can sometimes be damaging to friends or fellow citizens. It's worth recalling at this point that a relativistic approach to deceit is criticised by the Athenian in Plato's *Laws*. In the context of discussing deceit in the marketplace, the Athenian says that most people think that lies are often justified in certain circumstances (ἐν καιρῷ). He rejects this popular notion because it leaves the circumstances undefined (11.916d–917b).[104] But Demosthenes seems to be talking about the specific circumstance of narrating the

---

[103] See Ober (1989) 3–10; Farrar (1992); Cartledge (1993) 175f.; Roberts (1994) 47f. On questions of 'participation' see Osborne (1985a) and Carter (1986).
[104] See Powell (1994) 285–7.

(in)glorious past of the demos to the demos. I would suggest that he is not *primarily* concerned here with the teachings of elite intellectual *paideia*, or with a more popular acceptance that lying can sometimes be justified. Rather, the conjunction of his allusion to *paideia* or *mathēsis* and what is 'appropriate' suggest to me that Demosthenes is invoking the collective cultural education received by Athenians through the media of performed poetry and story-telling.[105] The poetry of Homer and Pindar, the verse of fifth-century thinkers and the lyrics of tragedy are all inscribed with an (often self-reflexive) engagement with the ethical status of what we would call 'fictional' narrative. Demosthenes is applying poetic assumptions about what constitutes an appropriate 'fiction' to the case of publicly representing the history of the ethical conduct of the democracy to itself.[106] In order to demonstrate this, I will briefly review the relevant secondary material. This review will also serve to introduce the next element in the complex picture I am attempting to draw of the democratic polis' negotiation with the concept of lying to benefit the demos or the polis.

A substantial body of recent research has concentrated on the relationship between lying and poetics in archaic and classical texts.[107] I am

[105] For knowledge of poetry as constituting Athenian collective *paideia* in oratory, see Aeschin. 1.141 where the orator attacks his opponents' patronising attitude in quoting Homer to the jury. See also Lyc. 1.102–4, where the orator praises the jury's ancestors for recognising Homer's didactic potential in the area of instilling collective martial *aretē*. At Pl. *Resp.* 10.606e1, Socrates speaks of Homer's wide reputation as the educator of Greece. For further evidence of archaic and classical perceptions of performed poetry as didactic and paideutic see Croally (1994) 17ff. The importance of poetry and song in Greek *paideia* is stressed by Detienne (1967); Svenbro (1976); Calame (1977). On the orators' engagement with archaic poetry and tragedy, see North (1952) and Perlman (1964). Ober and Strauss (1990) discuss the need for an orator to frame his citation of poetry as representing common *paideia* and the strategy of representing an opponent's use of poetry as a mark of elitism and sophistry. For the latter strategy see Dem. 19.245–50. Hall (1995) comprehensively explores the affinities between Athenian forensic and dramatic performance. Wilson (1996) demonstrates how fourth-century orators use fifth-century tragedy to 'explain, improve, exhort the present of the troubled city – and in the end to represent it' (324).

[106] I am not wishing to imply here that there is no overlap between elite theoretical conceptions of *paideia* involving a recognition of 'fiction' as good lying and the same recognition transmitted in Greek poetry and drama. A striking example of such an overlap is to be found in Isoc. 12.200–26 where Isoc.' praise of Athens is then subjected to critique by a young pro-Spartan pupil. The pupil offers a reading of the speech as an example of good *pseudologia* made possible by the speaker and the reader's *paideia*: the speech is actually ironically praising Sparta. For good discussion of this extraordinary passage see Von Reden and Goldhill (1999) 277–84. Isocrates markedly refuses to evaluate the pupil's 'reading against the grain'. But it is potentially significant that the identification of the speech as beneficially deceptive and oblique is represented as connected with a *Spartan* outlook.

[107] I am thinking especially of Pucci (1977), (1987); Rösler (1980); Ferrari (1988), (1989); Bowie (1993); Gill (1979), (1993); Belfiore (1985); Pratt (1993) 131ff. For discussion of Gorgianic *apatē* as 'fiction' see the bibliography cited above at n. 21.

not primarily concerned here with archaic representations and evaluations of 'fiction' but they will have a bearing on my discussion because classical texts are often explicitly or implicitly informed by them.[108] Furthermore, because Athenian cultural *paideia* included frequent and 'democratic' exposure to Homer and lyric poetry, their representation of 'fiction' must have informed popular thinking in the fifth and fourth centuries.[109] With regard to classical texts which address the issue of poetry as disseminating falsehoods, there is clearly a measure of consensus. Critics disagree as to whether the classical mind-set ever admits a notion which we would describe as 'fiction'. But they all seem to accept that fifth- and fourth-century writers do not have a problem with 'poetic' or 'mythological' lies *qua* lies.

It has recently been argued that classical, (and some would claim, archaic) texts do not criticise certain stories on the grounds that they are intentionally or unintentionally false. Rather, the criticism arises when narratives are deemed to be *ethically* false. Thus Socrates seems to suggest that the poets' representations of the gods are false in that they do not correspond to his notion that the divine is ethically perfect and unequivocally good.[110] But he argues that even if some stories were true, they should not be told because of their bad psychological effect on an audience, especially a young one. Gill argues that 'Plato regards lying as less ethically worrying than "falsehood in the psyche" or ethical ignorance.'[111] With respect to poetics in particular Gill argues that Plato's discussions 'seem to develop, and to give a theoretical framework for, a well established practice of understanding poetry in terms of the truth or falsehood of its *ethical* content'.[112] Gill appeals to evi-

---

[108] See Belfiore (1985), who argues that Plato's *Republic* polemically engages with the infamous line of the Hesiodic Muses where they claim that they sometimes speak *pseudē etumoisin homoia* (Hes. *Theog.* 27). Her article demonstrates how archaic representations of lies and falsehood can illuminate classical representations and vice-versa. This is not to say that classical texts simply borrow, copy or are 'influenced by' earlier representations as if the new context of the Athenian democracy and the development of dramatic and prose discourses could leave archaic models of truth unaffected. See Goldhill (1988a) 138ff. for a useful discussion of the workings of 'intertextuality' between Attic tragedy and earlier writings. See also Kristeva (1980) for an influential model of intertextuality, a model which can be fruitfully applied to the problem of classical texts' engagement with Homeric and archaic writing.

[109] For the Great Panatheneia as the occasion where the Athenian citizenry listened to performances of Homer, see Lyc. 1.102. For further discussion and evidence see Parke (1977) 34; Hurwit (1985) 262–4; Goldhill (1991) 167–73. As Goldhill points out there were, by the fifth century plenty of other opportunities for citizens to hear Homer. Cf. Xen. *Symp.* 3.5–6. It seems clear from Aristophanes' *Clouds* that recitation of lyric poetry (including Pindar) and tragedy was regular after-dinner practice in the household of the Attic *zeugite*.

[110] Pl. *Resp.* 377eff. See Page (1991) 8–12.

[111] Gill (1993) 55.

[112] Gill (1993) 73 (my italics).

dence in other fifth- and fourth-century writers to support his view that classical Athenian culture is not concerned that poetic or mythic narratives may be factually false. Pratt also conceives of classical writers as adhering to a distinction between *ethical* truth and falsehood. For her, Pindar, Stesichorus, Xenophanes, Herodotus, Thucydides and Plato all condemn poets and other story-tellers for 'lying not well' rather than for lying *per se*:

> That poets lie seems a truism of the culture. But it is possible for poets to lie either well or badly. These critiques are directed not at any and all forms of misrepresentation and invention, but only at those inventions that seem to the critic to promote harmful messages. Frequently the critic seems implicitly to accept that fictions (*pseudea*) may have positive functions as well. These critiques thus represent early attempts to come to terms with the strange and complex mix of true and false in fiction.[113]

Gill would refuse to translate *pseudē* as 'fictions'. Nevertheless, he seems to be in broad agreement with Pratt that in both the classical and archaic periods poetry and stories can be criticised as *pseudē* only on the grounds that such lies propagate paradigms and behaviours which are damaging socially and ethically. As I will demonstrate in my next section, Gill and Pratt are mistaken in their assumption that classical texts never treat the notion of socially or ethically good 'fictions' as problematic. But they usefully demonstrate that Homeric poetry, lyric and tragedy persistently evince a concern that stories and speeches, whether they contain *pseudē* or *alēthea* should be fitting, appropriate and useful in relation to religion, ethics and social order. It seems to me that it is precisely this popular notion of 'appropriate fiction' which Demosthenes assumes and applies in the passage cited above. In a speech which we saw consistently constructing deceit of the demos as ideologically incorrect, Demosthenes nevertheless endorses lying to the people when it comes to the issue of what representation a *rhētōr* should give to the history of the democracy. It is a mark of *paideia* to realise that only certain representations of Athens' past should be publicly articulated and in some cases that might involve the reproduction of representations that are not true. This one instance in Demosthenes' oratory does not mean that democratic ideology sanctioned 'official deceit' in the sense that Athens' elite could openly endorse the idea that they should be allowed to deceive the demos for their own good. Andocides flamboyantly stages his own rejection of precisely that idea. But Demosthenes clearly finds himself able to adumbrate the

---

[113] Pratt (1993) 156.

view that some lies about Athens are so useful ideologically that
they should not be exposed. We cannot know how far Demosthenes'
reasoning here was sharpened by Platonic reflections on the political
and educational value of lying well to your citizenry. But it is striking
that by invoking notions of education and learning (in my view, the
meta-poetic tradition), Demosthenes endorses a version of the 'noble
lie'.

Gill and Pratt have correctly identified an important strand of
thought. But there is material which questions the persistent notion
they have identified. In my next section, I want to analyse in detail a
fragment of drama which, in my view, explicitly interrogates the idea
that it is unproblematic to assess a referential lie in terms of its social and
ethical utility, 'goodness' or appropriateness. The fragment explores
the wisdom of even publicly singling out an item of traditional narrative discourse as a lie that is nevertheless socially or ethically beneficial.
Athenian drama makes it clear that (publicly proclaimed and performed) recognitions of poetic, mythological and 'pharmacological'
lies become implicated in broader questions concerning theology, theodicy, justice and the distinction between *nomos* (law, convention) and
phusis (nature) which arose during the fifth-century enlightenment in
Athens.

Fiction problematised: religion as 'noble lie' in the *Sisyphus*

In his scathing attack on Plato's political philosophy Karl Popper cites
what he regards as a significant precursor to the 'noble lie' of the *Republic*. The text he invokes is a fragment of the *Sisyphus*, a Satyr play of
disputed authorship.[114] Popper suppresses the context of the piece and
his assimilation of its content to the Platonic 'noble lie' is – and I hope
this will become apparent in my discussion – completely flawed. But in
a general sense the two texts do merit comparison and juxtaposition
precisely because they both deploy the notion of an ethically and socially beneficial lie. Sextus quotes the whole extant fragment of the
Sisyphus and attributes it to Critias, whom he describes as 'one of those

---

[114] Popper (1966) 140–5. He attributes the *Sisyphus* fragment to Plato's uncle Critias who
was a leading member of the oligarchic regime which overthrew the democracy in
404. Popper fails to address the problem of the fragment's disputed authorship and its
'dramatic' context – issues which I refer to below. For strong 'internal' arguments for
the fragment being from a satyr play see Dihle (1977) 37; Sutton (1981) 36; Davies
(1989) 29.

who held tyrannical power at Athens'.[115] But another doxographer, Aëtius, quotes three pairs of lines from what appears to be the same speech in the same play.[116] Aëtius attributes these lines to Euripides. For both doxographers the verses are testimony to the atheism of their author, although Aëtius argues that Euripides put his beliefs into the mouth of a dramatic character to avoid censure from the court of the Areopagus. It is necessary to quote the fragment in full:

> There was a time when human life had no order
> but like that of animals was ruled by force;
> when there was no reward for the good (*tois esthloisin*)
> nor any punishment for the wicked (*tois kakois*).
> 5 And then, I think, men enacted laws
> as punishments so that justice (*dikē*) would be tyrant (*turannos*)
> ... and *hubris* would be its slave,
> and whoever did wrong would be punished.
> Next, since the laws
> 10 only prevented people from using force openly
> but they continued to do so secretly, then I think
> for the first time some shrewd (*puknos*) and wise man (*sophos anēr*)
> invented fear of the gods for mortals, so that
> the wicked would have something to fear even if
> 15 they do, say or think something in secret.
> In this way, then, he introduced the divine (*to theion*)
> saying 'there is a divinity (*daimōn*), strong with eternal life,
> who in his mind hears, sees, thinks, and
> attends to everything with his divine nature.
> 20 He will hear everything said amongst mortals
> and will be able to see everything they do;
> and if you silently plot evil,
> this is not hidden from the gods, for our thoughts
> are known to them.' With such words as these
> 25 he introduced the most pleasant of lessons (*didagmatōn hēdiston*)[117]
> concealing the truth with a false account (*pseudēi kalupsas tēn
> alētheian logōi*).

---

[115] Sext. *Adv. Math.* 9.54: 'And Critias, one of the tyrants at Athens, seems to belong to the company of atheists when he says that the ancient law-givers invented god as a kind of overseer of the right and wrong actions of men, in order to make sure that nobody injured his neighbours secretly through fear of vengeance at the hands of the gods' (καὶ Κριτίας δὲ εἷς τῶν ἐν Ἀθήναις τυραννησάντων δοκεῖ ἐκ τοῦ τάγματος τῶν ἀθέων ὑπάρχειν φάμενος, ὅτι οἱ παλαιοὶ νομοθέται ἐπίσκοπόν τινα τῶν ἀνθρωπίνων κατορθωμάτων καὶ ἁμαρτημάτων ἔπλασαν τὸν θεὸν ὑπὲρ τοῦ μηδένα λάθρᾳ τὸν πλησίον ἀδικεῖν, εὐλαβούμενον τὴν ὑπὸ τῶν θεῶν τιμωρίαν. ἔχει δὲ παρ' αὐτῷ τὸ ῥητὸν οὕτως·).

[116] Aët. *Plac.* 1.6.7, 7.2. There are some minor differences between the two versions.

[117] Diggle (1998) reads *kudiston* for *hēdiston*. This would mean something like 'most glorious of lessons'.

And he claimed that the gods dwell in that place
which would particularly terrify (ἐξέπληξειεν) humans;
for he knew that from there mortals have fears
30 and also benefits for their wretched lives –
from the revolving sky above, where he saw
there was lightning and terrible crashes
of thunder and the starry body of heaven,
the fine embroidery (*kalon poikilma*) of Time, the skilled craftsman.
35 Thence too comes the bright mass of a star
and damp showers are sent down to earth.
With fears like these he surrounded humans,
and using them he established
the divinity well via discourse and in an appropriate place
(δι' οὓς καλῶς τε τῷ λόγῳ κατῴκισεν
τὸν δαίμον(α) οὗ⟨τος⟩ κἂν πρέποντι χωρίῳ).
40 and extinguished lawlessness with laws.
[(there is a gap of a few lines)]
thus, I think, someone first persuaded (*peisai*)
mortals to believe that there was a race of gods.
(DK 88 B25 [= *TrGF* fr. 19; Eur. fr. 19 N²]).[118]

Diels–Kranz place the fragment in the corpus of Critias the sophist, but Dihle has argued for Euripidean authorship.[119] Sutton and Winiarczyk have revived the claim that the fragment is by Critias.[120] Yunis has recently argued for the placement of a pair of previously dislocated Euripidean lines before those quoted above.[121] In these lines an unidentified speaker expresses a fear that the gods will punish some crime if it is carried out.[122] Yunis argues that the fragment is from a speech by the wily Sisyphus and represents an argument to persuade his interlocutor that a proposed crime will not be punished by omniscient gods.[123] As Dover and Davies have pointed out, there is no conclusive

---

[118] My translation is largely based on that of Gagarin and Woodruff (1995) 260–2 and has benefited from the commentary of Davies (1989) 18–24 and the new text of Diggle (1998) 177–9.

[119] Dihle (1977). Burkert (1985) 467, n. 22 points out that Dihle fails to take account of a fragment of Epicurus' *Peri Phuseōs* 11 (fr. 27.2 Arrighetti). This fragment associates Critias with atheism.

[120] Sutton (1981); Winiarczyk (1987). Parker (1996) 212 also attributes the fragment to Critias.

[121] Yunis (1988a).

[122] The two lines are quoted in the *Life of Euripides* by the third-century historian Satyrus (*POxy.* 1176, fr. 39, ii, 8–14 = Eur. fr. 1007c N²): one character says 'whom do you fear when these things are being accomplished secretly?' A second replies: 'the gods who see more than men' (– λ]άθρᾳ δὲ τούτων δρωμένων τίνας φοβῇ; | – τοὺς μείζονα βλέποντας ἀνθρώπων θεούς). Yunis argues that DK 88 B25 may begin one or two lines into Sisyphus' speech.

[123] Aëtius identifies the speaker of DK 88 B25 as Sisyphus and critics have generally accepted this identification.

evidence to settle the dispute over authorship.[124] But it is highly likely that the fragment represents a satyric Sisyphus' argument that a proposed crime will not be punished.

As Yunis and others have shown, the philosophical texts of the late fifth and fourth centuries suggest that the questions of divine omniscience and the advisability of committing undetected crime were much-debated topics.[125] While some thinkers maintained that the gods were the ultimate deterrent for crime, or attempted to argue that crime should be avoided regardless of legal or divine sanction, Antiphon advised that one should transgress laws if there are no human witnesses; he completely ignores the possibility of divine vigilance.[126]

The *Sisyphus* fragment posits the possibility of a socially and morally constructive context for deception. The speaker argues that belief in the gods' existence was fabricated in discourse in order to provide the ultimate deterrent to wrongdoing within society (11–42). The consensual institution of law still left room for disobedience. People could break the law with impunity because it was easy to escape detection (10–11). A *sophos anēr* convinced people of the existence of the gods in order to inspire fear of detection and punishment (14, 37). Sisyphus seems to praise the effectiveness and social benefits of the fiction (25–6). At the same time, if we accept the likely context of the fragment, he argues that there is nothing to fear in wrongdoing because the gods are no more than a social fiction to maintain and police a social contract.

Sisyphus is an emblematic figure of extreme cunning and trickery. Versions of myth surrounding him narrate Sisyphus' deceptions and punishments inflicted upon him by the gods.[127] Scodel speculates that

---

[124] Dover (1975) 46; Davies (1989) 24–8. Davies counters Yunis' arguments for Euripidean authorship by pointing to the fragment of Epicurus cited by Burkert (see above, n. 119). See also the stylistic arguments of Diggle (1981) 106.

[125] Yunis (1988a) 40ff. The main texts are Xen. *Mem.* 1.1.19, 1.4.18–21, 4.4.21; Pl. *Resp.* 2.359c–367e (Gyges' ring); Pl. *Leg.* 10.899d–905c. Although there are differences between the Xenophontic and Platonic 'Socrates' (or the 'Socratic' Athenian of the *Laws*), these texts always portray him as assuming or wanting to assume that the gods observe and punish all human crimes. In the *Republic*, of course, Socrates is not allowed to make this assumption and attempts to show that crime doesn't pay regardless of questions of detection. Democritus was unquestionably interested in the question of (a) whether the gods were invented; and (b) the notion of fear of gods and laws as (inadequate) reasons for not committing crimes. See Democritus DK 68 B30, 41, 181, 264 with Cole (1967); Lloyd (1979) 14; Farrar (1988) 230–48; Nill (1985) 54–8; Ostwald (1986) 283–4. See also the fourth-century Archytas of Tarentum DK 47 B3.

[126] Antiphon DK 87 B44, fr. A1. 12–2.23. This *'phusis'* view is also put forward by Callicles at Pl. *Grg.* 482c–486d and Thrasymachus at Pl. *Resp.* 1.343b–344e.

[127] See Hom. *Od.* 11.593 where Odysseus sees Sisyphus undergoing eternal punishment. His crime against the gods is not specified. At Hom. *Il* 6.153, Sisyphus is described as κέρδιστος ('most crafty' or 'sharpest'). See Thgn. 701–4 where Sisyphus cheats death.

the fragment comes from a play which narrated a version of a story in which Sisyphus steals Diomedes' horses when they were being delivered by Heracles to Eurystheus.[128] Several fourth- and fifth-century sources indicate that Sisyphus' name (and adjectives derived from it) were often deployed to connote individuals and behaviour as deceptive or cunning.[129]

As Scodel notes, there is an obvious irony that it is a trickster who comes out with an accusation of deception.[130] We have an habitual liar claiming to unveil the lies of another. It is possible that the rest of the drama plays out this irony. Many critics have argued that Sisyphus gets punished by the gods after this speech has been made.[131] It is more specifically ironic that a figure who, on Homer's account, was punished for wrongdoing by the gods should be advocating crime on the grounds that divine punishment is a lie. Scodel argues that the fragment comes from the satyr play which followed the 'Trojan Trilogy' of Euripides in 415.[132] She sees its interrogation of the existence of the gods and the uncertainties of its truth-value (a liar identifying a lie) as intertextual with the themes of the *Alexander*, the *Palamedes* and *Troades*.[133] In contrast to critics who have treated the fragment simply as a veiled manifesto of authorial atheism (be it Critias' or Euripides'), Scodel pushes the irony of Sisyphus' speech even further:[134]

Besides creating an amusing plot reversal, the juxtaposition of the speech of Sisyphus with an epiphany, whether a possible *deus* in the satyr play or the prologue of *Troades*, is just a further twist by which the irony is turned on the poet himself. The presence of the gods could convince the spectator that Sisyphus is wrong; it could also suggest that the device of the *deus* is one of the means by which the σοφοί have convinced men of the existence of the gods.

---

[128] See Scodel (1980) 122–3. The source for this story is 'Probus' on Vir. *Geor.* 3.267. However, as Scodel concedes, we can really have no idea what the plot of the play was.

[129] E.g. Ar. *Ach.* 391. See also Wheeler (1988) index s.v. 'Sisyphus'.

[130] Scodel (1980) 129–30. Sutton (1980) and Seaford (1984) note that the 'trickster figure' and a central act of deception appear to be recurring elements in the genre of the Athenian satyr drama.

[131] E.g. Guthrie (1971) 243; Scodel (1980) 136 thinks it 'more likely' that Sisyphus is punished.

[132] Scodel (1980) 122 and 128f. The source for a Euripidean *Sisyphus* in 415 is Ael. *Var. Hist.* 2.8. Scodel can't prove that DK 88 B25 comes from the same play but she argues that 'although it is a circular argument, the best reason for assigning this fragment to the Euripidean *Sisyphus* is its direct relevance to the issues raised in the tragic dramas of 415'. This view is supported by Ostwald (1986) 283.

[133] Scodel (1980) 128–37.

[134] For the 'atheist manifesto' view, see Popper (1966) 142; Guthrie (1971) 243. Others have assumed that the fragment comes from a play that was never publicly disseminated because of its atheistic content; Schmid and Stählin (1940) 180f.

The connection of poetry and religion was explicit. The speech thus becomes a piece of self-mockery by the poet: he too is among the deceivers.[135]

The way in which Sisyphus grounds his argument in the notion of a noble lie creates an undecidability about the authority and validity of institutional representations of the divine. The fact that it is Sisyphus who offers this cultural history makes for even more uncertainty. His comments about religion can be read as a critical engagement with the emotional and theological machinery of tragedy. And this engagement need not depend on the fragment being from the satyr play which followed Euripides' Trojan trilogy. All tragedy represents and proclaims the power of the gods. It disseminates fear of the gods through characters and audience alike. But this fragment raises the possibility that tragedy is merely an instantiation of the lying *logos* (26). If Sisyphus is right then civic drama can be seen as both constituting and perpetuating this false *logos* of divine existence and surveillance. The wise author of this noble lie did indeed 'establish the *daimon* well via discourse' (38–9), if Athens' prestige dramatic form constantly reproduces that discourse and perpetuates its emotional effects.

But this questioning of tragedy's truth value does not merely, simply or necessarily amount to 'self-mockery by the poet'. If Euripides/ Critias is among the deceivers, he is nevertheless among the deceivers who are *sophoi* (12). Furthermore, the fragment raises the question of the *nature* of the poet's deception. Is the playwright akin to the *puknos* and *sophos* ancestor who promotes a noble lying *logos* which benefits the community? Or does his decision to write verses like these cast the playwright in the role of a Sisyphean figure whose *sophia* lies either in his ability not to be duped or else in his arrogant and dangerous capacity to challenge the truth of established norms and beliefs and thus deceive the listener into transgression? Does the dramatist mirror the disruptive Sisyphean claim to 'know better' by virtue of the fact that he even dares to put that kind of claim into the mouth of one of his characters? The latter view approaches the judgement of the doxographers who preserved the fragment as an example of Euripides' or Critias' atheism.

However, the Sisyphus fragment does not only raise these unsettling questions and uncertain answers about polis religion and the civic dramatist's involvement in the (mis)representation of the gods. Many elements of the fragment express ideas which are closely paralleled in fifth- and fourth-century philosophical or 'sophistic' texts and

---

[135] Scodel (1980) 137.

fragments. The opening remarks in the speech are similar to ideas expressed in the history of civilisation which Plato attributes to Protagoras.[136] In Plato's *Republic*, Glaucon argues that men originally suffered violence from each other, and they set up laws and legal punishments to deter mutual aggression.[137] The idea that laws prevent civil strife born out of envy is also found in Democritus' writing.[138] Another fragment of Democritus describes the invention of religion by a group of ancient *logioi*.[139] Lines 29–32 also suggest an aetiology of religion which is strikingly similar to Sextus' summary of Democritus' thought and the doxography surrounding the views of Prodicus.[140] Xenophon's Socrates views god as capable of seeing all – even men's secret thoughts.[141]

For Scodel, the fragment's mingling, bowdlerising and 'misuse' of different theories are further evidence of Euripidean authorship.[142] For other critics, the fragment is informed by these theories, but it is essentially original and represents the views of the sophist Critias.[143] One notion which critics have not really stressed as a parallel for the *Sisyphus* fragment is that of the socially useful lie concerning religion and stories about the gods. Through its engagement with the arguments of several 'pre-Socratic' and 'sophistic' thinkers, Sisyphus' speech interrogates the morality and advisability of the notion of a 'noble lie'.

The danger of naming something as untrue, even if we accept that untruth as socially and morally beneficial, is that the reflection can be turned on its head. The chorus of Euripides' *Electra* do not believe a story that Zeus reversed the sun's course in response to Thyestes' theft of the golden lamb:

---

[136] See Pl. *Prt.* 324a–b, 325a–b, 326c–d. Kahn (1981) 98 warns that it would be dangerous to use this fourth-century dialogue to reconstruct the historical background of the *Sisyphus* fragment. Diogenes Laertius (9.55 = DK 80 A1) records that Protagoras wrote a treatise on 'the origin of the constitution' (περὶ τῆς ἐν ἀρχῇ καταστάσεως). It may be that this title was merely inferred from Plato's myth. See Dodds (1973) 9, n. 4.

[137] Pl. *Resp.* 2.359aff. See Kahn (1981).

[138] Democritus DK 68 B245.

[139] Democritus DK 68 B30; DK 68 A75.

[140] Sext. *Adv. Math.* 9.24; Phld. *De Pietate* 9.7; Cic. *Nat. D.* 1.42.118. On the similarities between the doxographical accounts of Democritus' and Prodicus' views on religion, see Henrichs (1975).

[141] Xen. *Mem.* 1.1.19, 1.4.18–21, 4.4.21.

[142] Scodel (1980) 136.

[143] See Guthrie (1971) 244: ' This is the first occurrence in history of a theory of religion as a political invention to ensure good behaviour, which was elaborately developed by Polybius at Rome and revived in eighteenth-century Germany.' Kahn (1981) 97ff. treats the speech as an early (perhaps the earliest) example of Greek 'social contract theory'. Sutton (1981) goes for Critian authorship but does not mistake the speech of a dramatic character for the beliefs of its creator.

These things are said, but
    small is the credit (*pistin smikran*) they hold with me
that the golden sun did turn
and alter its torrid position,
    to the misfortune of men,
because of a mortal's cause.
But fearful stories (*phoberoi muthoi*) are a gain (*kerdos*) for mortals:
they further the service of the gods.
Unmindful of such stories you
have killed your husband, sister of famed brothers.

(Euripides *Electra* 737–46)

The chorus do not doubt the existence of Zeus but they are sceptical that he intervened directly. Nevertheless, they argue that such a tale can be profitable for mortals and Clytemnestra should have listened to such stories.[144] It is clear that Xenophanes, Democritus and Prodicus viewed the Greek pantheon and its mythology as fabrications, though they seem to differ on the intentionality behind them. An elegiac fragment of Xenophanes implies that certain tales of the exploits of the traditional gods are socially useful and beneficial, whilst others are ethically pernicious and inappropriate (DK 21 B1).[145]

If we set this evidence against Sisyphus' description of the *sophos anēr* and his 'noble lie' we can see that a similar assumption about theistic *logoi* is at work. The phrase 'and using them he established the divinity well via discourse and in an appropriate place' (καλῶς τε τῷ λόγῳ κατῴκισεν τὸν δαίμον(α) οὗτος κἀν πρέποντι χωρίῳ: 38–9) appeals to the ideas of ethical good, persuasive efficacy and appropriateness which Pratt and Gill find in archaic and classical texts' characterisations of mythological story-telling.[146] Sisyphus apes the assumptions about good lying which we find in (among others) Xenophanes, Plato and the chorus in Euripides' *Electra*. But the *context* of his words and the manner in which he deploys the notion of a noble lie constitute a disturbing interrogation of the very assumptions which Gill and Pratt regard as so

---

[144] See Yunis (1988b) 98–9. Here, I follow the interpretation of Cropp (1988) 152 on *El.* 745 rather than Stinton (1976) 88, n. 53. Stinton argues that ὧν refers to the 'gods' rather than 'such stories' *about* the gods because it is perverse for the chorus to attack Clytemnestra for forgetting tales which are probably untrue. But this does not seem to follow so well from the chorus' mention of the value of *muthoi* and as Cropp points out, they are recommending 'fearful, piety-inducing tales *in general*'.

[145] On this see Pratt (1993) 136–40.

[146] I am not implying that πρέποντι χωρίῳ denotes the appropriate nature of the entire lie. Rather it suggests the appropriateness of saying that the gods live in a place which mortals associate with frightening meteorological phenomena. I thank Dr Andrew Ford for this point. However, the καλῶς τε τῷ λόγῳ κατῴκισεν τὸν δαίμον(α) οὗτος does suggest appropriate, effective and ethically sound qualities.

prevalent in ancient Greek writing. Firstly, Sisyphus can invoke the traditional and 'enlightenment' notions of narrative *pseudē* and the ethical relativity of lying whilst extending the usual limits of their application. That is, he goes one better than any pre-Socratic critique by characterising the very idea of the divine as a deliberate invention.[147] Secondly, he concedes that the invention was ethically and socially beneficial and that it was appropriately established. But it is clear that Sisyphus is not deterred from wrongdoing by the threat of divine punishment. For him the notion of divine surveillance may be a socially beneficial lie, but it is a lie nonetheless. He does not feel bound by the deeper ethical 'truth' or social utility of the lie. The *logos* of omniscient divinity is effective because human society regards it as referring to reality. It is this reference to divinity and its nature which engenders fear and deterrence. Take away the reality of god and wrongdoing becomes a choice without consequences. The only threat of punishment comes from human authority, but, as the *sophos anēr* realised, human sanctions can be avoided through cunning and secrecy.

When Plato's Socrates endorses the fabrication of a myth to maintain the structure of Kallipolis, his deployment of the noble lie is geared towards a (dubious) utopian future (we will lie to them and they will believe). The character of Sisyphus posits the socially beneficial lie along the lines of a completely different trajectory. He reads a noble lie into the past (we believed but it wasn't true). The Democritian argument that the traditional gods are no more than cultural constructs is manipulated in order to unearth a 'truth': if no mortal catches you, you can get away with murder. By contrast Socrates places himself in the position of Sisyphus' *sophos anēr*; he is the social engineer who disseminates lies in order to establish and maintain higher social and ethical goods and 'truths'. The chorus of the *Electra* admit their disbelief, but that lack of faith is local. They are unsure of the veracity of a particular story of divine intervention in human affairs. But they are convinced that the lying tale represents a deeper moral 'truth'. Like Plato's Socrates, they regard the lies of myth as importantly paradigmatic and crucial in the enforcement of norms. The underlying assumption that referential lies can nevertheless represent and promote deeper 'truths' was already being articulated implicitly and explicitly in the fifth century. Xenophanes had a conception of god and it seems likely that Democritus was not an atheist in the modern sense. But their

---

[147] See Ostwald (1986) 283. As Ostwald puts it, Sisyphus 'undermines belief even in philosophical gods, for which the doctrines of Democritus and Prodicus may still have left room'.

insistence that conventional myth and religion constituted a socially convenient lie necessarily called the notion of divine punishment into question. Divine surveillance and punishment were ideas which underpinned Athens' political and legal institutions. More importantly, they were ideas which lent weight to those institutions' performed rhetoric of 'policing' – a rhetoric which is powerfully articulated in Lycurgus' speech *Against Leocrates*:

> There is a further point which you should understand, gentlemen. The power which keeps our democracy together is the oath. For there are three things of which the political constitution (*politeia*) is built up: the archon, the juror and the private citizen (*idiotēs*). Each of these gives this oath as a pledge (*pistin*) and rightly so. For many have often deceived men (τοὺς μὲν γὰρ ἀνθρώπους πολλοὶ ἤδη ἐξαπατήσαντες). Many criminals evade them, escaping the dangers of the moment, yes, and even remaining unpunished for these crimes for the remainder of their lives. But the gods no one who broke his oath would evade. No one would escape their vengeance. If the perjured man does not suffer himself, at least his children and all his family are overtaken by great misfortunes. (Lycurgus 1.79)

What we have in the *Sisyphus* fragment is a questioning of questioning itself. The idea that the *sophos anēr* lies for good social and ethical reasons is not good enough. To simply *say* that the idea of the divine is a lie, regardless of whether it is a 'good' or a 'bad' lie, is to undermine the religious beliefs that authorise Lycurgus' invocation of divine punishment. Sisyphus will exploit what he sees as the fact of fabrication and encourage others to do the same. The *Sisyphus* fragment implies that some noble lies and good 'fictions' must maintain their appearance as referential truths if they are to maintain their ethically 'true' effect. It thereby stages the danger of characterising certain forms of traditional knowledge or 'truth' as noble lies.

The *Sisyphus* fragment demonstrates that the medium of public drama was alive to the moral complexities of the notion of a 'noble lie'. But the orientation of the fragment is firmly directed towards the specific argument that religious belief may be a 'noble lie' and the consequences that such an argument might have. In the next section I will return to a more general conception of the 'noble lie'. How does Athenian drama approach the possibility that it might sometimes be good to lie to your own people?

War's first casualty: deception in Sophocles' *Philoctetes*

The most detailed and complete exploration of the complexities of the 'noble lie' in extant Athenian drama is to be found in Sophocles' *Phil-*

octetes.[148] This tragedy was performed at the City Dionysia in 409 BC. This secure dating means that *Philoctetes* has been heavily 'contextualised' by critics: it responds, in one way or another, to the contemporary intellectual milieu of sophistic teaching, display and inquiry.[149] It conveys a crisis of moral, military and political values which mark it as speaking to an Athenian audience who had experienced oligarchic revolution in 411 and who were still recovering from reverses in the war with Sparta.[150] Its three main characters have all been read (with different levels of sophistication and plausibility) as ciphers for Alcibiades, a political 'problem child' for Athenians who had been recalled in 411.[151] *Philoctetes* concerns the return of an exiled hero who will save his former comrades and this has been regarded as allegorical for Alcibiades' return.[152] Neoptolemus' youth and ambition and Odysseus' ruthless cunning have also been related to Alcibiades' portrayal in fifth- and fourth-century historiography. Odysseus' emphasis on trickery and ultimate victory for his enterprise has reminded critics, not only of Alcibiades or a general 'sophistic' approach to morality but also of an entire class of post-Periclean politicians with disreputable qualities.[153] The play has also been seen to be informed by Athenian civic and religious institutions. Neoptolemus is of ephebic age and persuaded by Odysseus to use *dolos* and *apatē* on Philoctetes. The action takes place in the 'liminal' space of the wild island of Lemnos. These factors have led Vidal-Naquet to read the play as an ephebic narrative.[154] Goldhill stresses that Philoctetes' extreme heroism, Neoptolemus' dilemma of loyalties and the play's abrupt 'solution' problematise the ideological force of the hoplite oath and the opening ceremonies of the City Dionysia.[155]

---

[148] See Blundell (1989) 184: '*Philoctetes* is the most ethically complex of all Sophocles' plays.'

[149] For *Philoctetes* as a 'thinking through' of sophistic anthropology in relation to notions of aristocratic birth and inherited excellence, see Rose (1992) 266–330. For the play's engagement with the sophistic interest in language and rhetoric, see Craik (1980); Goldhill (1997) 141–5. See also Nestle (1910); Knox (1964) 164.

[150] See Thuc. 8.47, 81–2.

[151] See Bowie (1997) 56–61 for the most convincing arguments in favour of an 'Alcibidean' reading. Bowie argues that Philoctetes, Odysseus and Neoptolemus all display different characteristics of Alcibiades as recorded by the historians. See also Jameson (1956); Calder (1971); Craik (1980); Vickers (1987).

[152] See Jebb (1898) xlii–xliii; Webster (1970) 7; Bowie (1997) 56.

[153] See Jameson (1956) 219 who cites a scholion (Σ *Phil.* 99) in support of his view that Odysseus' viewpoint conjures up the ruthless reputation of figures such as Cleon, Alcibiades, Antiphon, Peisander and Theramenes.

[154] Vidal-Naquet (1988). For critique of the 'ephebic' reading see Di Benedetto (1978); Winnington-Ingram (1979); Goldhill (1990).

[155] Goldhill (1990).

Exactly how far one should go in regarding *Philoctetes* as a response to specific political events, individuals and institutions remains open for debate and I will not be arguing over such specificities here.[156] But few would deny that the tragedy prominently parades concerns which reflect those of a democracy during a period of warfare and intellectual interest in the nature of language, truth and communication.[157] Furthermore this play clearly explores the nature of the relationship between the divine and human understandings of it. Evaluation of the three main characters cannot be divorced from their (differing) understandings of divine will and theodicy.[158] Though Odysseus' justifications for tricking Philoctetes and Neoptolemus' reactions to this strategy have attracted a wealth of (often fruitful) critical interpretation, there has been little discussion of the possible relationship between Odysseus' ruse and the discourse of the 'noble lie' which I have already presented. This must largely be due to a prevalent view that the representation of Odysseus in *Philoctetes* is almost completely negative: Odysseus represents his deception-plan against Philoctetes as 'noble' and justifiable but this is self-serving rhetoric and cruel, hypocritical sophistry.[159] It is true that Odysseus often represents himself (and is often represented by Philoctetes and Neoptolemus) as preoccupied with success and has little thought for Philoctetes' own wishes. Furthermore, Odysseus' moral vocabulary is far from consistent: for example, he implies that his scheme is unjust but later asks Neoptolemus how it can be just to frustrate the same scheme (82, 1246).[160] But if we start with the idea that an Athenian audience would recognise his arguments as relating to a specific strand of contemporary intellectual debate, then the play's fostering of sympathies and antagonisms for its characters takes a more complex shape.

As many commentators have noted, Odysseus justifies his past and present behaviour towards Philoctetes in terms of achievement of

---

[156] See Rose (1992) 327–30 for pertinent critique of readings which tie the play closely to specific events and personalities.

[157] On warfare, see Philoctetes' bitter conclusions at 435–7 and 446–52. His view that war destroys good men whilst sparing those who are worthless and criminal can be taken as having contemporary resonances. See Jebb (1898) on 435; Webster (1970) on 436; Calder (1971), Jameson (1956). On language and truth, see Goldhill (1997) 145: 'Sophocles gives a central place to the problem of communication between men, of words in action of words as action.' See also Rose (1992) 319–30; Buxton (1982) 118–32; Garvie (1972); Podlecki (1966).

[158] See especially Hinds (1967); Segal (1995) 95–118.

[159] E.g. Knox (1964) 124: 'The Odysseus of this play has no heroic code which binds him, no standards of conduct of any kind, he is for victory by any and every means.' See also Rose (1992) 309; Blundell (1987).

[160] This and other inconsistencies in Odysseus' moral vocabulary are traced by Blundell (1987).

'safety' (*sōtēria*) for the Greek army ranged against Troy.[161] How far does the play make this justification plausible and understandable for an audience? Does Odysseus' argument that Philoctetes must be deceived to achieve a greater good have any moral force for a fifth-century audience? Let us look, first of all at the reasons Odysseus gives for treating Philoctetes' own views and wishes with contempt. At the opening of the play Odysseus explains to Neoptolemus that Philoctetes' foul and incurable wound made it impossible to keep him on the expedition to Troy:

> This is the place where, many years ago,
> Neoptolemus son of Achilles –
> Your father was the best among the Greeks –
> Acting on the orders of our overlords,
> I left Philoctetes the Malian, Poeas' son,
> Lamed by a festering disease in his foot,
> At which he would moan and howl incessantly
> Our camp was never free of his frantic wailing –
> Never a moment's pause for libation or prayer,
> But the silence was desecrated by his savage cries.
>
> (Sophocles *Philoctetes* 3–10)

According to Odysseus, Philoctetes is abandoned because he disrupts the silence necessary for the correct conduct of religious ritual. By threatening to pollute the libations and prayers of the Greek army, he jeopardises the success of the military operation. In explaining the reasons for the abandonment of Philoctetes, Odysseus embarks on a self-justification which he will repeat when explaining his plan to trick Philoctetes into returning to Troy. He acts 'under orders' and the safety and success of the military expedition is paramount. Later in the play, Philoctetes will claim that Odysseus has equal responsibility with the Atreidae for his abandonment (1028). He also claims that he was left behind on the *pretext* that his disease threatened the army. If this threat was a genuine motivation for abandonment, it makes no sense for Odysseus to now be willing to take Philoctetes back to Troy on his ship (1031–4): 'You, most hated by the gods, how is it now that I am not lame and foul-smelling? How can you burn your sacrifices to the gods if I sail with you? How can you pour libations? This was your excuse (*prophasis*) for casting me away.' Philoctetes' aspersions must be taken seriously and it is certainly the case that his abandonment is a violation of the 'help friends' ethic.[162] But Philoctetes sustained his

---

[161] See Rose (1992) 309; Blundell (1989) 187–90.
[162] See Blundell (1989).

wound because he violated Chryse's sacred ground and was punished by her snake (191–200, 1326–8). For the Greek expedition, Philoctetes' wound marks him as a pollution: he is subject to divine disapproval and a threat to their sacrifices.[163] While Philoctetes views these religious difficulties as a mere excuse, I think an Athenian audience would understand why the Greek leadership would want to put distance between the polluted hero and their expedition.[164]

Furthermore, Odysseus' willingness to have Philoctetes on board again only renders his stated reasons for abandoning him insincere if we ignore the changed religious circumstances brought about by Helenus' prophecy, an unreliable version of which is told to Philoctetes during his deception (610–13), and eventually presented in concrete form by Neoptolemus and (in a different form) by Heracles at the end of the play (1324–42, 1421–44). The gods have made it clear that Philoctetes and his bow are required at Troy for the Greeks to prevail. If, at the beginning of the play, Odysseus knows this divine decree, then it can be argued that his deception-plan is a *necessity*, because it is only through deception that Odysseus can get closest to fulfilling the prophecy's requirements. But can it be established that Odysseus does understand the prophecy fully and that deception is the only course of action he can take?

When the deception-plan has failed and Philoctetes cannot be persuaded, Odysseus makes to leave with just the bow (1054f.). Critics argue as to whether Odysseus *really* intends to use the bow without Philoctetes or is simply bluffing in an attempt to change Philoctetes' mind.[165] And one of the fundamental ambiguities surrounding this play's presentation of Odysseus concerns the extent to which he understands that Philoctetes must return *willingly* to Troy *with* the bow in order for the divine prophecy to be fulfilled (Neoptolemus swears by this version of the prophecy at 1329–42). Why try tricking Philoctetes into returning and why decide to leave with just the bow, if success can only be achieved if the hero brings the bow willingly? It has been argued that Odysseus' decision to trick Philoctetes rather than attempt

---

[163] Segal (1995) 97 stresses that Philoctetes' cries 'destroy one of the fundamental ways in which humankind acknowledges and communicates with the gods'.

[164] On the seriousness of divine disapproval and pollution, see Parker (1983) 191–206.

[165] In favour of the 'bluff': Linforth (1956) 135–6; Calder (1971) 160–2; Hinds (1967) 177ff.; Gellie (1972) 151. Against the 'bluff': Wilamowitz (1917) 304; Robinson (1969) 45. For the hint that he is bluffing but the impossibility of knowing for sure, see Webster (1970) on 1055; Winnington-Ingram (1980) 293. Segal (1995) 100–1 argues that the most important point about Odysseus' departure with the bow is the way in which it emphasises his disregard of the spirit and the letter of the prophecy and his instrumental view of human beings.

the persuasion which is required by the prophecy is actually an indication of Odysseus' flawed character: he is so concerned to achieve an end, regardless of the means deployed, that he focuses on getting the *bow* to Troy and the question of whether Philoctetes accompanies the bow or not becomes subordinate to that focus.[166] This makes sense if we regard Odysseus as a character who is cunning but not wise. Neoptolemus will make a similar charge against him when his sympathy for Philoctetes gets the better of him: 'Wise (*sophos*) as you are, you do not say what is wise (*sophon*)' (1244). But if Odysseus knows the same prediction as that presented by Neoptolemus, then how could he not understand that his mission is to secure Philoctetes' willing return with the bow? It may be that Odysseus believes that it is enough to have Philoctetes persuaded by a false promise to take him home. This would be a characteristically sophistic interpretation of the prophecy's requirement that Philoctetes' return to Troy be voluntary: through the deception, he will be 'willing' to get on the boat and that is enough to fulfil the prophecy. Perhaps he believes that Philoctetes can be persuaded once he is dumped back at Troy. Philoctetes may be happy to shoot Odysseus or the Atreidae rather than be persuaded or forced by them, but will he be so impervious to the persuasion of heroes like Nestor for whom he retains admiration (421–2)?

These speculations should be resisted, however, for they take us away from the evidence for a definitive account of the prophecy or Odysseus' thinking as presented in the text. Most scholars argue that the information contained in the prophecy is unclear throughout the play and that this obscurity suits the requirements of character, action and plot. When Odysseus arrives on Lemnos, he fails to make it clear that *both* Philoctetes and Neoptolemus are required to wield the bow at Troy. Neither Neoptolemus nor Odysseus address the requirement that Philoctetes return willingly. It could be that Neoptolemus does not realise that Philoctetes' voluntary return is required until he hears the messenger's version of the prophecy at 610ff. If this is the case, then Odysseus perhaps omits Philoctetes' essential role because he has to win Neoptolemus around to his plan with the promise that the hero will win glory for the enterprise (115–20). Neoptolemus' Achillean *phusis* might make him unwilling to execute the plan if glory has to be shared.[167] But it is more likely that Odysseus sidelines the need to persuade Philoctetes because such persuasion is an impossibility. Odysseus knows that Philoctetes' resentment towards him and the Greek

---

[166] Linforth (1956); Nussbaum (1976) 35; Gill (1980) 140; Segal (1995) 102.
[167] This is the explanantion of Hinds (1967) 179.

leadership will make it impossible to persuade the wounded hero to return to Troy of his own free will (103). Nor is physical force a viable strategy – Philoctetes has the formidable bow to protect him (105). To achieve his mission Odysseus mobilises his own secret weapon, namely deception. It is easy to view this tactic as a cruel misunderstanding of the prophecy's requirements and to overlook the strategic bind that confronts Odysseus. Philoctetes will not listen to anything which Odysseus could say to him face-to-face. For Neoptolemus to use genuine persuasion would not work on Philoctetes either. To fight him openly would be honourable, but his bow is invincible and there is no point in either Neoptolemus or Odysseus getting themselves killed for nothing. In this sense, any requirement that Philoctetes be persuaded and willing is impossible for Odysseus to fulfil. The closest Odysseus can get to such a requirement is to use deception, and to hope that such deception will get the bow and the man onto his ship.[168] As Odysseus points out to Philoctetes: 'whatever the occasion demands, such a one am I' (οὗ γὰρ τοιούτων δεῖ, τοιοῦτός εἰμ' ἐγώ: 1049). By this, we can understand Odysseus to be emphasising that he makes the best of any situation he is in. Odysseus' 'noble lie' is not activated out of *choice* but necessity. In this respect, his deception-plan has a circumstantial resemblance to the examples of noble lying which were put forward by Plato, Xenophon and Andocides. To save an insane friend, to preserve your troops' morale, to maintain the structures of your ideal polis it is *necessary* to use deception. I believe an audience could have entertained the argument that Odysseus had no choice but to use deceit. The play makes it clear that Philoctetes would never be persuaded by any articulation of that prophecy from Odysseus or anybody else who admitted that Odysseus was with them. And it is crucial to realise that both the philosophical and 'common-sense' discourse of the 'noble lie' (alongside Andocides' lying *stratēgos*) share the notion that lies can be necessary when there is no other available means of achieving an outcome which is generally agreed to be desirable. An audience might suspect Odysseus of manipulating a prophecy in a manner which reminded them of Spartan practice and he certainly presents as a cynical sophist and politician. But on my reading, their familiarity with a notion that good ends can sometimes *only* be achieved through lies would substantially affect their evaluation of Odysseus' behaviour. This is not to say that they would 'side' with

---

[168] See Easterling (1978) 28: 'Odysseus is approaching the prophecy in the pragmatic spirit that you do the best you can towards fulfilling what is foretold, crossing your fingers that whatever is beyond your control will somehow fit into place.'

Odysseus: rather, Odysseus' predicament and arguments would have more weight than is generally assumed.

But if Odysseus' course of action can be viewed as a necessity, to what extent does the play vindicate the goals of that action? Is his 'noble lie' really 'noble' when it is directed towards bringing a man (against his will) back to Troy to serve those who are now his sworn enemies? In his opening speech Odysseus describes his plan to capture Philoctetes as a *sophisma* ('scheme': 14), a word which conjures up the suspicious world of sophistic teaching and rhetoric.[169] Of course, an Athenian audience would associate Odysseus with trickery, not least because of his portrayals in Homeric epic and these portrayals are particularly important for understanding the character of his deception in *Philoctetes*. During the embassy of the *Iliad* Achilles is suspicious of Odysseus' diplomacy: 'As much as I detest Hades, I detest a man who says one thing whilst hiding another in the depths of his heart' (9.312). The Homeric Achilles' contempt for Odyssean cunning provides an important backdrop for the action of the *Philoctetes* and the whole play can be read as a reworking of the Iliadic embassy to Achilles.[170] For it is Achilles' adolescent son, Neoptolemus who has accompanied the trickster to Lemnos. He will be required to execute Odysseus' plan to trick the wounded bowman. Achilles and Philoctetes were good friends. Achilles is dead but Odysseus knows that Neoptolemus can win Philoctetes' trust. If Odysseus stays out of sight, the young man can tell Philoctetes that he has fallen out with the Greek leadership and is returning home from Troy. He can get Philoctetes and his bow onto a ship with the false promise that they will both return to Greece. How will the son of Achilles be persuaded to deceive his father's old friend? And what would an Athenian audience make of the ensuing debate about the rights and wrongs of trickery?

Odysseus knows that Neoptolemus will find deceit repulsive. But he argues that the end justifies the means. He tells Neoptolemus that if he is 'shameless' for one day, he will be the 'most pious' of mortals for the rest of his life (83–5). Odysseus seems to be claiming that the fall of Troy is willed by the gods and that the dishonest acquisition of the bow, while 'shameless' from Neoptolemus' point of view, is nevertheless a pious act. Odysseus appeals to Neoptolemus' noble nature: 'Son of Achilles, it is necessary for you to be *gennaios* in your mission, not just by bodily exertion' (50–1). Here, it seems that Odysseus is glossing

---

[169] See Rose (1992) 307–8; Craik (1980) 251. At Eur. *Hec.* 238, *sophisma* connotes trickiness and is also associated with Odysseus.

[170] See Beye (1970).

gennaios to mean 'loyal' or 'dependable'.[171] But the adjective carries with it the sense of having qualities which one inherits from one's ancestors and it is precisely in this sense that Philoctetes uses the term in appealing to Neoptolemus to take him home (475–6).[172] This is interesting, because Neoptolemus will reply that 'evil craft' is not in his nature nor that of his father (88–9). He says he prefers force to deceit and argues that he would rather lose by noble means than win through base tactics (86–95). Odysseus replies that he took the same view as Neoptolemus when he was young. But he has learnt from experience that 'words count more than deeds in the world of mortals' (96–9). Neoptolemus asks if persuasion will work. When Odysseus explains that Philoctetes must be deceived because he cannot be forced or per-suaded to return to Troy, Neoptolemus asks if it is not 'shameful' (*aischron*: 107) to lie. Odysseus replies: 'not if the lie brings safety' (οὐκ εἰ τὸ σωθῆναί γε τὸ ψεῦδος φέρει: 108). So, at this point, Odysseus re-futes the suggestion that his plan is shameful. As Nussbaum puts it, his position 'is not simply that a good end justifies the use of questionable means, but that actions are to be assessed only with reference to those states of affairs to which they contribute'.[173] Much later in the play, when Neoptolemus has been moved by shame and pity to admit to Philoctetes that he has lied, Philoctetes produces a torrent of abuse against Odysseus. The chorus of sailors respond to the wounded hero's vitriol in the following manner:

> It is the business of a man (*andros*), you know,
> to say that what turns out expedient (*to eu*) is just (*dikaion*)
> and, having said so, not to give vent to spiteful bitterness of speech.
> He was given a command as one from many,
> and at their mandate achieved a common benefit (*koinan arōgan*)
> for his friends (*philous*).
>
> (Sophocles *Philoctetes* 1140–5)

The first line of this response is fraught with textual problems and dif-ficulties of interpretation.[174] And it is far from clear whether the person

---

[171] See Calder (1971) 170.

[172] See Blundell (1988) 138.

[173] Nussbaum (1976) 33.

[174] I have followed the OCT of Pearson. Even the reading I follow can be translated in more than one way: see Webster (1970) on 1140ff. and Jebb (1898) on 1140. It may be that 'man' does not primarily refer to Odysseus but to Philoctetes and his vitriol: 'it is a man's part fairly (*eu*) to urge his plea (*dikaion*)'. The Teubner edition of Dawe reads οὖ instead of εὖ and Ussher (1990) translates his text as 'it's a man's duty, you know, to speak when it is justified ...' The new OCT of Lloyd-Jones and Wilson has ὅν, proposed by Kells (1963), which they justify in Lloyd-Jones and Wilson (1990) 207 on the grounds of 'easier syntax' to give the translation: 'It is the part of a man to put his own case.'

who achieves the 'common benefit' is Odysseus or Neoptolemus.[175] But, on any reading, the chorus stress that Odysseus/Neoptolemus is a representative of the entire army and is attempting to aid the collective of his friends. Of course, the chorus are not an independent or disinterested voice in this play: they help with Neoptolemus' deception of Philoctetes and then falsely deny any part in the ruse to Philoctetes (507–18, 1116–17). But they emphasise the moral rationale which guides the deception-plan. Odysseus/Neoptolemus is a servant of the army and as such is motivated by what critics have called a 'hedonistic calculus': 'Odysseus' position is a form of utilitarianism ... a consequentialism aimed at promoting the general welfare.'[176] Now this approach leaves little room for respecting what we might call 'the rights' and 'integrity' of the individual. Odysseus' utilitarian lie undeniably undermines notions of individual freedom and dissent. But it is equally difficult to maintain that late fifth- and fourth-century Athenians would be unequivocally hostile to the idea that success and survival in warfare might entail the curtailing of individual integrity. We have seen how Andocides carefully distinguishes between a noble lie told to one's own troops in wartime as a necessity and a noble lie told to the democratic assembly as a means of circumventing debates and disputes that would waste valuable time. Xenophon's Socrates similarly points out that it is just to lie to one's own troops to boost morale. Demosthenes implies that it would be preferable to maintain a false image of Athens' benefactors as motivated by love of the polis rather than the expectation of material rewards than to tell the truth that those benefactors did expect and receive substantial returns. The Platonic Socrates distinguishes between the lie in words and the lie in the soul. His *gennaion pseudos* is a 'lie in words' writ large in that he believes that it will establish and perpetuate happiness and harmony amongst all classes of his ideal city.

In his hatred of deceit and his preference for open confrontation, Neoptolemus is articulating views he has inherited from his heroic father. But for an Athenian audience, the young man's viewpoint was directly relevant to their own value-system. And Odysseus' promotion of deceit was equally pertinent to their experience of the war with Sparta which was raging at the time of the play's performance. Deceit and trickery were opposed to the military and democratic ideals which

---

[175] Kamerbeek (1980) ad loc. (157) and Lloyd-Jones and Wilson (1990) 207 have good arguments for making these lines refer to Neoptolemus rather than Odysseus (as is usually assumed).

[176] Nussbaum (1976) 39.

we find in Athenian public oratory and which I outlined in my first two chapters. Neoptolemus' hatred of deceit and his preference for victory by open confrontation is strikingly paralleled in the Thucydidean Pericles' attack on Spartan *apatai* and in Demosthenes' contrast between Conon's victory and Themistocles' *apatē*.[177] But I have also described how, in contrast to Pericles' ideals of military behaviour, Thucydides frequently records occasions when Athenian land-troops were tricked and ambushed in the war against Sparta. Furthermore, he tells us that Athenian generals soon learnt to use trickery and ambushes.[178] This was to be a 'dirty war' where the honourable and chivalrous ideals of 'open' hoplite confrontation would be useless in mountainous terrain or against a more mobile and cunning enemy. When Sophocles' Odysseus argues that safety can sometimes only be achieved through trickery, then there must have been citizens in the audience of this play who understood what he meant from bitter experience.

It is clear that Odysseus has little thought for Philoctetes' personal wellbeing when he asks Neoptolemus to deceive him. At the end of the play the intervention of the divine Heracles makes it clear that if Philoctetes returns to Troy with the bow he will be healed and win glory. But Odysseus does not have Philoctetes' rehabilitation in mind when he hatches his plot. In this sense, Odysseus can hardly be equated with Socrates' example of the man who can only help his *philos* by deceiving him. But the philosophical and democratic invocations of noble lying which I have discussed all imply that a 'noble lie' can be justified by the requirements of *necessity*. Furthermore, these invocations argue that the polis or its army can be sometimes be better served if its citizens believe something that is untrue. Thus Odysseus' argument that there are cases where an army can only be saved by deceiving a comrade could not have seemed unreasonable to everybody. For some citizens, no doubt, it sounded like a dubious rhetorical ploy and gave off the stench of anti-democratic, anti-hoplitic values and self-serving sophistry. For others, Odysseus' justification of this particular trick would come across as the kind of wise, patriotic and realistic strategy which they would expect their own military and political leaders to deploy in the tight situations which a war can create.

Odysseus' reliance on *dolos* and *apatē* when faced with a cave-dwelling foe on a wild island echoes the manner in which he tricks the Cyclops in order to save himself and his surviving comrades in the *Odyssey*.[179] Philoctetes' curse on Odysseus (314–16) echoes the Cyclops' invoca-

---

[177] See above, pp. 26–51.   [178] See above pp. 97–9.   [179] See Bowie (1997) 59–62.

tion of Poseidon. And this curse condemns Odysseus to the same cave-dwelling existence that Philoctetes has suffered. Odysseus is 'seeing his own future'.[180] Odysseus' predicament with the Cyclops in *Odyssey* 9 has come about because he failed to heed the advice of his crew. His use of deception against Achilles in the embassy of *Iliad* 9 is similarly involved in failure. Achilles is not persuaded. In the *Philoctetes*, Odysseus gets the result he wants, but Philoctetes returns with his bow to Troy at the behest of the divine Heracles rather than through the trickster's schemes. The play's intertextual relationship with Odyssean trickery in Homer suggests that the ruse against Philoctetes is far from wise or laudable. But the late fifth- and fourth-century discourse of the 'noble lie' should not be neglected as a frame of reference for interpreting this Odysseus and his predicament. The *Philoctetes* can thus be seen to confront the moral and ideological dilemmas which various contemporary articulations of the 'noble lie' provoked for the democratic city in military and political crisis.

We can gain an added sense of the way in which *Philoctetes* opens up the possibility of a positive appraisal of Odysseus' trick by comparing it with a ruse in a very different Sophoclean tragedy. In Sophocles' *Electra*, Orestes sends his *paidagogus* to deceive Clytemnestra with a long and false account of his death in a chariot race. Like Odysseus, Orestes uses the language of profit when he explains and justifies his deception: 'I think that nothing that is spoken for profit (*sun kerdei*) is bad' (*El.* 61). But this deception also takes in Electra, thereby prolonging and deepening her already considerable grief and agony. This is a play where Orestes cruelly deceives his own loyal sister and where both siblings seem to deceive themselves with respect to the nobility of their planned matricide. In contrast to *Philoctetes*, the *Electra* characterises Orestes' ephebic-style deceit as unequivocally dark and callous.[181] Even if we view the deception of Clytemnestra as a tactical necessity for the achievement of righteous vengeance, the play's lack of discussion concerning the rights and wrongs of deception, alongside Orestes' willingness to have his sister believe the falsehood, mark its representation of trickery as very different to that of *Philoctetes*. In the latter play, the 'noble lie' is given a voice with which to justify and defend itself through appeals to collective salvation. In the intra-familial setting of the *Electra*, tactical lying is stripped of any nobility.

We have seen, then, that the notion of the 'noble lie' in Athens' democratic, civic and public arenas of performance and competition is

---

[180] Bowie (1997) 61.   [181] Here, I follow the interpretation of Kells (1973) 1–12.

complicated and nuanced. It is almost wrong-headed to ask whether Demosthenes' claim about deceit's incompatibility with a 'system based on speeches' is ever challenged by positive public representations of the 'notion' of the noble lie. For the texts I have discussed severely undermine the explanatory potential of such an abstract 'notional' category. It may be convenient terminological shorthand to ask how the 'noble lie' or the notion of 'fiction' are treated in a range of Athenian texts. But it is clear that the 'noble lie' which Andocides rejects (for what I have argued to be shrewd ideological reasons) is not identical to the category of 'noble lie' which Demosthenes endorses. Demosthenes could hardly have disagreed with Andocides' abstract assertion that it is wrong to lie to the demos for its own good and yet, when it comes to a specific argument with opponents who have claimed that the demos has a history of ingratitude to Athens' benefactors, he believes it is strategically advantageous and ideologically acceptable to invoke an idea of 'appropriate fiction'. It seems that the discourse of this 'open society' had a very negotiable framework for the endorsement or rejection of lying to the people for 'noble' ends.

This complex picture is further enhanced by the satyric fragment I have analysed. In the text we saw that popular conceptions of fiction and 'sophistic' or 'philosophical' construals of conventional religious belief as a 'noble lie' are interrogated. The interrogation does not primarily consist in a claim that the traditional gods really exist, although the entire plot of the *Sisyphus* possibly implied such a claim. Nor does it constitute an assertion that the lie is not noble, although the suggestion that generations of men have been slaves to a clever deception might provoke an audience to question the morality of such paternalistic manipulations, be they real or imagined.[182] Rather, the fragment explores the pernicious consequences of publicly and persistently reassessing the truth-status of socially beneficial beliefs and stories. The field of discussion which the fragment inhabits has little to do with the field of political ideology in which Popper seeks to place it; it is not part of an oligarchic tract which seeks either to endorse or undermine the social and religious fiction it describes. But it has everything to do with Athens' public discourses of legal and moral enforcement and the threat which certain rationalist construals of the divine as a beneficial fiction might pose to the continued effectiveness of those discourses.

Plato's 'noble lie' was seen to be imbricated with the need to distance his grand myths of origin from Athenian presumptions that such

---

[182] On the general hostility to 'paternalistic' ethical behaviour in classical Greek sources see Blundell (1989) 36–49.

official lies were the hallmark of Spartan oligarchy. Plato draws on certain 'common-sense' and traditional notions of good lies and fiction in order to achieve this distance. In doing so, he also relies on a view of discourse which sophistic and archaic texts celebrate, namely the material power of words to cure, poison or charm.

Within this democratic and intellectual scene of suspicion and support for various versions of 'good lying', Sophocles offers an Odyssean rendition of the 'noble lie', a difficult articulation of deceit's powers and perils which serves to focus its audience's attention on the ways in which a 'noble lie' can be viewed as necessary, communitarian (even democratic), authoritarian, life-saving, selfish, destructive (of trust and freedom), effective or disastrous.

In this chapter, I have attempted to outline and explore responses to the problem of speech's 'ambiguity' in the competitive spaces of Athens' lawcourts, *ecclēsia* and theatre which do not primarily implicate the teaching and execution of public speaking as a *technē*. We have seen that 'deceiving the demos' can be represented as inimical to Athenian national character and can be described as a unique threat to the deliberative processes of democracy. We have also seen that an orator of Demosthenes' stature can dare to hint that a litigant should lie to the demos for the 'good end' of preserving an ideologically acceptable version of its own history. My reading of the *Sisyphus* fragment was primarily intended to demonstrate the issues at stake in (and the complexity of) Athenian public culture's response to notions of 'good lying'. But this reading also serves to illustrate the extent to which intellectual discourses and inquiries which have been placed under the rubric of the late fifth-century 'enlightenment' can crucially inform Athenian public representation and anxious discussion of deceit's connotations and consequences. The recognition of what Detienne calls 'the ambiguity of speech' must be traced in these public texts as well as the 'enlightenment' texts which so often form the frame against which such texts are to be understood. It is with this point in mind that I now return to Athenian orators' condemnations of their opponents as liars.

4   The rhetoric of anti-rhetoric: Athenian oratory

This morning, I listened to some of the comments that the Labour party was spinning in the media. I understand that it is in the nature of politics to oppose. By opposition, one questions, and by questioning one elicits for the common good knowledge that can make policies work better. To mislead the country and paint a picture that is not true is not to oppose but to spin yarns. Spinning yarns is not the traditional role of the Opposition. To spin yarns in the media is to mislead the public and the business community. Yarn spinning wrecks confidence in the country; it makes the country look inadequate and international investors become suspicious. To spin yarns is not clever. It is too self-interested and too self-serving. When the election comes, the electorate will not be fooled.[1]

Before the hon. Member for Cunninghame North (Mr Wilson) leaves with his electronic device, could you confirm, Madam Speaker, that there is a ban, enforced by yourself, on electronic devices? When an hon. Gentleman has a message from Mr Mandelson on his electronic device, which he reads at the Dispatch Box, I suspect that that is a new departure for the House.[2]

The Labour Party under Tony Blair is the party of 'soundbites' and 'spin-doctors'. The Conservative Party under John Major was revealed to be the party of 'sleaze'. Or at least, these are the images of political deceit, trickery and corruption which emerged and informed the arguments and analyses of politicians and journalists in the last two years of Major's government. Recent workers in political science have shown how different countries and different political climates defy any attempt to write a monolithic account of how and why political skulduggery occurs, increases or becomes an 'issue'.[3] But individuals or institutions which take up stances *against* corruption (or, more rarely, are happy to

---

[1] Nirj Deva (Conservative MP for Brentford and Isleworth) quoted in *Hansard*, 26 November 1996.
[2] Ian Bruce (Conservative MP for South Dorset) quoted in *Hansard*, 11 March 1997.
[3] See the following collections of essays: Ridley and Doig (1995); della Porta and Mény (1997); Levi and Nelken (1996); Ridley and Thompson (1997). For important observations on 'bribery' in Athenian politics and its representation in the orators, see Harvey (1985).

admit to *being* corrupt) are often doing so for strategic reasons of self-legitimation and self-promotion in a variety of competitive environments.[4] In this sense, the exposure and pursuit of scandals is crucially implicated in processes of political *performance*. Today's political scientists soberly reflect that corruption and deceit can no longer be regarded as tools exclusive to totalitarian regimes, 'developing' democracies or a few rotten apples in the 'developed' democratic barrel. They could also add that 'show trials' can take place in 'developed' democracies too.[5]

But if political scientists have started to examine actual instances of democratic 'sleaze' and (to a much lesser extent) the 'discourse' of corruption, they are not doing the same for 'spin'. To be sure, we have had countless books and television programmes which document how 'spin' works and what a 'spin-doctor' does.[6] But these accounts are *part* of a phenomenon or 'discourse' which requires explanation. Why is 'spin' now a key topos in the rhetoric of politicians or the assessments of the Fourth Estate? There have always been press officers and political statements designed for mass communication in the media. So why have 'spin' and 'soundbite-politics' suddenly become objects of scrutiny and vexed argument? And what does it mean for modern democratic culture that it has apparently become so concerned with its own processes of performance and communication?

I do not intend to answer these questions about modern democracy seriously. But I have raised them in order to provide a clarifying frame for the real concerns of this chapter.[7] I want to argue that the democratic oratory of classical Athens is crucially concerned with its own modes and techniques of performance in general and deceptive performance

---

[4] See Levi and Nelken (1996) 2.

[5] The strategic and theatrical quality of recent anti-corruption campaigns was most recently and blatantly demonstrated in Britain when Labour and the Liberal Democrats encouraged the television journalist Martin Bell to stand as an independent 'anti-sleaze' candidate against the Tory MP for Tatton, Neil Hamilton. Hamilton was under investigation for having taken bribes. Bell held a press conference on Tatton Common but as the cameras and reporters arrived, he was confronted by Hamilton and his wife. A surreal argument between the two candidates was performed in the midst of a scuffling *corona* of media personnel. The television image was of two men and a woman duelling in an empty field for the benefit of attending journalists. Thanks to Dr Neil Reynolds for reminding me of this piece of theatre.

[6] The BBC screened a *Panorama* documentary on (predominantly Labour) techniques of 'spin' on the eve of the 1996 Labour Conference. Earlier in the same year, Channel 4 screened an American documentary about Democratic and Republican techniques. For insider accounts of Westminster 'spin' and 'soundbite' techniques and media collusion with them, see Jones (1995). See below pp. 243–7 for a novelistic account of 'spin' in the United States.

[7] The particular examples of 'sleaze' and 'spin' rhetoric will no doubt soon fade from the memory, but newly topical examples will readily come to readers' minds.

in particular: in other words, Athenian oratory is meta-discursive and self-conscious.[8] The orators deploy reflections on rhetorical performance which, when we listen to them, help us to understand what was seen to be at stake in the legal and political contests which constituted Athenian democracy. Indeed, these anti-rhetorical reflections help to explain why the Athenian democracy preserved itself for so long. Here, I will be indebted to the excellent work of Josiah Ober, but I hope to raise some further issues which he does not address.[9]

Spin and anti-spin: rhetoric as the technology of lies

Before I turn to the Athenian texts, I need to make some more remarks about 'spin' in contemporary British politics because they clarify my argument. The second of my opening quotations refers to an incident which occured in the House of Commons during the weeks running up to the 1997 General Election. The Labour MP Brian Wilson was caught receiving information on an electronic pager. This information was then deployed by him to make an allegation of 'sleaze' in the form of a 'point of order'. Ian Bruce made out that Wilson was receiving messages from Peter Mandelson (then perceived to be Labour's most powerful and ruthless 'spin-doctor').[10] Another Tory MP accused Wilson of receiving electronic messages from Labour's 'Dirty Tricks Department' and demanded to know on whose behalf Wilson was 'merely the messenger boy'.[11]

It is clear that the notion of 'spin' provided the Tory party with a useful network of images with which to undermine the Labour Party's developing self-representation as a modernised party. My first quotation is just one example of the way in which the Conservative Party and its supporting agencies sought to counteract Labour's 'anti-sleaze' strategy by representing Labour as an organisation which had em-

---

[8] For 'self-consciousness' as a defining feature of Athenian democratic culture see Goldhill (1999) 10: 'Democratic culture proceeds in a symbiotic relation with (democratic) theorizing (a theorizing that goes beyond the narrowly defined political theory of constitutional matters). The citizen's self-representation and self-regulation are formulated within this self-reflective critical discursive system.'

[9] See Ober (1989), (1994).

[10] Mandelson initially became 'Minister without Portfolio' in the Labour administration. Journalists worried that his lack of 'Portfolio' made him unaccountable to Parliament. *Private Eye* magazine nicknamed him 'The Spinning Minister'. Mandelson had to resign as minister for Trade and Industry following allegations of 'sleaze'. Alistair Campbell currently attracts the most attention as Labour's chief unelected 'spin-doctor'.

[11] Nicholas Winterton (Conservative MP for Macclesfield) quoted in *Hansard*, 11 March 1997.

braced the modern environment of technology and high-speed media communications in order to manipulate it with lies and hollow rhetoric. The trivial spats over the use of mobile phones and pagers were a brief side-show. But these exchanges were reported in the news media and, taken with the first quotation, they demonstrate a number of important points.

Firstly, to identify and attack 'spin' is not simply another way of accusing an opponent of lying or using fancy rhetoric. It is a rhetorical and strategic response which provides a negative 'gloss' on Labour's attempt to represent itself as 'New Labour'; a born-again centrist party of the nineties. It attempts to redescribe Labour as 'new' only insofar that it will utilise modern technology and the rhetorical armatures of corporate public relations and the advertising industry. 'Spin' gets its currency as a term of abuse precisely because 'new' techniques and technologies are seen as aids to the Labour party's public performance. And here 'performance' must mean two things. There are the 'first-order' performances; Commons speeches, television interviews and battle-bus tours. But the *technai* of 'spin' are also seen more generally as the manipulative and disingenuous means by which Labour enhances its 'second-order' performance in polls and public opinion. Thus 'anti-spin' rhetoric is reliant on a perceived presence of new *technai* and their effect on modes and standards of political performance. Even the apparently unimportant exchange about electronic pagers constitutes an element in a significant set of attacks, debates and counter-strategies about performance. And this discursive focus on performance translates into an argument about how democratic politics should be conducted and who is fit to serve in its offices.

Crucially, the 'anti-spin' rhetoric glosses this use of modern modes of communication and performance as politically bankrupt. The use of 'spin' means a party that will do and say anything to get into power. It means a party that will lie and smear its way towards the short-term goal of victory rather than argue on the basis of the long-term goals of national interest and collective prosperity. As Nirj Deva puts it, to 'spin' is to opt out of doing 'democracy' fairly, properly and traditionally.

In addition to this, accusations of 'spin' are similar to allegations of 'sleaze' in that they raise concerns about accountability and deception. 'Spin' often seems to make the elected representative the 'mere messenger boy' of unelected men who control strategy and policy decisions from the wings of the political theatre. And as in the first quotation, 'spin' can itself be 'spun' in order to connote the artful dissemination of untruths and evasions of the truth.

Indeed, Nirj Deva's gloss on 'spin' as 'the spinning of yarns' illustrates a further point I will be making in connection with Athenian oratory. The gloss may not seem very clever or original. And if one has the patience to trawl through *Hansard*, one finds that attacks on Labour 'spin' are predominantly a Tory topos. An association between 'spin' and outright deception is also a recurring theme. And yet, Deva's pun is unique. His particular *way* of identifying 'spin' and glossing it as lies is an original intervention. We may still wish to describe this as a topos but it is not *formulaic*. We might rather describe Deva's attack as unique but not idiosyncratic. I will argue that it is crucial to understand that Athenian democratic culture's topoi of 'anti-rhetoric' are often similarly to be characterised as *both* commonplaces at one level *and* as creative, unique strategies at another. At other times, speeches deploy completely unique strategies to 'unmask' an opponent's tricks. And it is the requirements and dynamics of a *performed* contest between individual elite actors in a democratic setting which motivate this interplay between topology and originality.

Finally, while this concern to gloss an opponent's political performances as amounting to a new and dangerous mode of deceptive communication is undoubtedly a *strategic* gloss (a 'spin' on 'spin') it is not to be viewed as the invention of a few party strategists at Tory Headquarters. 'Spin' has developed meanings and currency in British political exchange because our Media have identified its operations and introduced them to us. The notion of political 'spin' was named and identified by journalists in the United States long before we had heard of the term here. But at the same time as Blair was described as subjecting his party to 'Clintonisation', so the British Media focused on Labour's new penchant for something called 'spin'.[12] Contrived political manipulation of the Media has been happening in Britain for decades. But it is important to realise that the public representation of 'spin' as something 'new' goes hand in hand with a perception that Labour have harnessed performative techniques which are in some sense 'alien' to British political discourse. Despite the presence of American products and culture in all aspects of British life, and despite 'the special relationship' between the two countries, Britain's political and Media elite continue to identify certain modes of behaviour as

[12] Although Labour are now in power, the identification between technology, spin and 'New Labour' persists. Labour's Deputy Prime Minister John Prescott is generally regarded as closer to 'Old' Labour's ideology. Lobby journalists report his antipathy to Mandelson's power and tactics. In August 1997, Prescott appeared to express that antipathy publicly and one television reporter summed up the situation in these terms: 'All the pagers, lap-top computers and the like are clearly powerless when faced with the "Prescott Factor."'

'American' and then exploit deep-seated British fears or prejudices concerning 'Americanisation'.

Athenian democracy bore little resemblance to modern Western democracies and I will not rehearse all the differences between them here.[13] Suffice it to say that I will make no attempt to equate British democracy with the very different conditions at Athens. But it is striking and potentially helpful to note that the extant Athenian legal orations exhibit self-reflexive concerns which have similarities with the topoi concerning 'spin' that I have been discussing.

The idea of an opponent dangerously and deceptively harnessing a *technē* of speech and performance is explicitly raised by Aeschines in his speech *On the Embassy* – a speech which, like the oration of Demosthenes to which it responds, is replete with meta-discursive strategies concerning rhetoric and deception:

> You hear the witnesses under oath and their testimony. But these unholy arts of speech (*tas d' anosious tautas tōn logōn technas*), which this man offers to teach our youth and has now employed against me … (Aeschines 2.56)

Demosthenes teaches *technai* of speech to Athens' youth and Aeschines goes so far as to represent this technology as 'unholy'. Here he perhaps invokes the same sense of public deceit as a religious transgression which I discussed in the context of the curse against *apatē* and the *Sisyphus* fragment.[14] Aeschines goes on to mimic one of Demosthenes' attacks on him, referring to his shrill and unholy voice (157). So often it is Aeschines' career as an actor and his trained voice which Demosthenes attempts to disparage.[15] But here, Aeschines attempts to trope Demosthenes' deceptive *technai* of rhetoric as akin to a mimetic

---

[13] For good accounts of the differences and similarities between Athenian and modern Western democracy see Finley (1973); Ober (1989) 3–10; Farrar (1992); Cartledge (1993) 175f.; Roberts (1994), 47f. See also the essays collected in Ober and Hedrick (1996).

[14] See above pp. 63–4 and pp. 179–88.

[15] See Dem. 18.129, 209, 232, 261–2, 308 with Rowe (1966) and the comments of Wänkel (1976) ad loc. On Aeschines' career as an actor see Dorjahn (1929); Ghiron-Bistagne (1976) 158–60, 191–4; Kindstrand (1982) 20; Wilson (1996) 321–4; Easterling (1999) 154–61. The denigration of an opponent as a theatrical performer falls in line with Aristotle's displeasure at having to admit *hupokrisis* ('delivery') as an important element of rhetoric. See Arist. *Rh.* 3.1403b35–1404a13. See also 3.1403b20–35 where he states that *hupokrisis* is a matter of how the voice should be used in expressing emotion. He then points out that those who use vocal techniques properly nearly always carry off prizes in dramatic contests and as in his own time actors have greater influence on stage than poets, so it is with political contests (*politikous agōnas*), owing to the corruption/moral bankruptcy of forms of government (*dia tēn mochthērian politeiōn*). On this, see Lord (1981) 331; Garver (1994) 247–8.

theatrical performance and he implicitly connects these *technai* with the paideutic practice of sophistry and the industry of logography.

This kind of 'self-reflexivity' where the orator foregrounds his opponent as a technologist of performance has a *strategic* and *antagonistic* quality.[16] As Ober and others have noted, the forensic orators frequently represent themselves as innocent of various procedures associated with rhetorical training and preparation.[17] Often this self-representation will correlate with an attack on the speaker's opponent on the grounds that he, by contrast, is heavily implicated in rhetorical procedures. Ober rightly stresses that such claims to innocence or ignorance of rhetorical preparation describe a 'dramatic fiction'. No speech in our extant corpus could possibly be described as the spontaneous creation of a semi-educated man who was 'unfamiliar with public speaking'. A Lysian speech may well be beautifully crafted to match the character and social status of the client who was to deliver it.[18] But it can hardly have escaped the notice of jurors or opponents that such a speech had indeed been *crafted*. Although he does not characterise them as 'meta-discursive' or 'self-reflexive', Ober views extant oratory's strategies concerning speaking ability and rhetorical training as germane to the continued existence of the democracy.[19] Alongside other topoi (for example, those concerned with wealth), these strategies show that 'the members of the educated elite participated in a drama in which they were required to play the roles of common men and to voice their solidarity with egalitarian ideals'.[20] This drama policed the political

---

[16] There has been a (sometimes justified) recent tendency to attack critical works which concentrate on texts' apparent elements of 'self-reflexivity' or 'meta-discursive' aspects as ahistorical or banal. See Seaford (1994b) who in the context of criticism on tragedy expresses 'the vain hope that self-reflexivity is an idea whose time is up'. My analysis in this chapter should go some way towards demonstrating that this hope is misguided when 'meta-discursive' elements in prose and poetic texts are approached with certain questions and contexts in mind.

[17] See Dem. 27.2–3, where a young Demosthenes asks for a fair hearing having proclaimed his own youth and inexperience and the cleverness, ability and preparedness (*paraskeuē*) of his opponents. Other examples of this combination of topoi ('plea for a hearing' and 'I am unskilled') in extant speeches; Ant. 3.2.b2, c3; Andoc. 4.7; Lys. 19.2; Isoc. 8.5; Dem. 18.6–7, 37.5, 38.2, 57.1. For further examples of these two topoi and the 'my opponent is a skilled speaker' topos see Ober (1989) 170–7. See also Dover (1974) 25–8; Ostwald (1986) 256–7.

[18] On Lysias' particular aptitude for *ēthopoiia* see Kennedy (1963) 135f.; Usher (1965), (1976); Carey (1994) 40–3.

[19] See, however, Ober (1998) 96 where he uses the term 'meta-rhetoric' in connection with Thucydides' Mytilinean debate.

[20] Ober (1989) 190–1. See also 153–4, where Ober argues that regular mass participation in the Athenian dramatic festivals educated the citizenry in the process of colluding in these 'dramatic fictions'. See also Ford (1999) for an account of the orators' performances of Homeric and dramatic poetry as strategic engagements with mass and elite conceptions of poetic performance and education.

ambitions of the elite. At the same time as the Athenians gained the benefit of having educated men serve in advisory roles of the state, they kept these advisors on a tight leash and restrained the tendency of the educated elite to evolve into a ruling oligarchy.

In the lawcourt, the speaker attacks his opponent as a deceptive sophist, a 'clever speaker', a logographer (or reliant on one), a magician with words and so on. And in Ober's terms, the 'logical corollary' of this is the self-representational claim to be 'inexperienced' in speaking.[21] In order to keep the disingenuous and strategic quality of these self-representations or invectives firmly in mind, I want to designate them with the phrase 'the rhetoric of anti-rhetoric'.[22] At the same time, my loose analogy with modern 'anti-spin' rhetoric only goes so far. I will discuss the orators' attacks on opponents as 'types' of rhetorical technician – sophist, logographer and so on. But I will also address oratory's focus on 'rhetoric' in a much broader sense of the word. My fourth section will show how a speaker can expose the deceptive 'rhetoric' of a citizen's presentation of body and self in everyday life.[23] My fifth section returns to the sense of 'rhetoric' as a dangerous *technē* in Athens' lawcourts. But here the orator's 'anti-rhetoric' will be seen to expose, not the opponent's conformity to a deceptive 'type', but rather his deceptive manipulation of common strategies of argument (topoi). My final section examines Aeschines' and Demosthenes' engagement in an antagonistic meta-discourse which scrutinises the fabrication of truth (*alētheia*) in terms of imitation (*mimēsis*) and detectability.

Sophistry and logography, witchcraft and 'cleverness' in Athenian oratory

In his speech *Against Meidias*, Demosthenes anticipates the charge that he has written and practised his oration.[24] He argues that it would be foolish of him not to prepare himself and adds that it is effectively Meidias who has written the speech for him through his crimes:

Perhaps too he will say something of this sort; that my present speech is all carefully thought out and prepared. I admit, Athenians that I have thought it

---

[21] Ober (1989) 174.
[22] I have borrowed this phrase from Valesio (1980).
[23] Here I have deliberately purloined the title from Goffman (1969). For Goffman's reading of self-presentation in modern western society as a 'theatrical' and 'performative' process and its relevance to Athens, see Cohen (1991); Goldhill (1999) 13–14.
[24] There is some doubt as to whether this speech was ever actually delivered. For the evidence and the arguments see MacDowell (1990) 23–8; Wilson (1991) 187. See also Ober (1994).

out and I should not dream of denying it; yes, and I have spent all possible care on it (*memeletēkenai*). I would be a wretched creature if all my wrongs, past and present, left me careless of what I was going to say to you about them. Yet the real composer of my speech is Meidias. The man who has furnished the facts with which the speeches deal ought in strict justice to bear that responsibility, and not the man who has devoted thought and care to lay an honest case before you today. (Demosthenes 21.191–2)[25]

A rhetorical treatise attributable to Anaximenes of Lampsacus indicates that it was a common tactic to deride speakers for writing their oration and for intensive training or preparation.[26] However, Anaximenes does recommend a suitable reply to such derision: 'we must come to close quarters about suggestions of that sort, in a tone of irony, and about writing the speech to say that the law does not forbid one to speak a written speech oneself any more than it forbids one's adversary to speak an unwritten speech'.[27] As to the charge of having learnt and practised a speech, Anaximenes recommends the following:

If they say that we study and practise (*meletan*) speaking, we shall admit the charge and say: 'We who study speaking are not litigious (*philodikoi*), whereas you who do not know how to make a speech are proved to be making a malicious prosecution (*sukophantōn*) against us now and have done so before.' So we make it appear to the advantage of citizens if he too learnt to be a *rhētōr* as he would not be such a wicked blackmailer (*sukophantēn*) if he did. (Anaximenes *Ars Rhetorica* 36.39–40 (p. 88, 14–20))

Interestingly, Anaximenes claims that even a charge of teaching others how to plead or of composing their dicanic speeches can be deflected

---

[25] Although Demosthenes is happy to use it of himself here, the verb μελετάω and its cognates, meaning 'to practise oratory', is elsewhere used in a derogatory sense to characterise opponents as manipulative and skilled speakers. See the attack on Aeschines' oratorical *meletē* at Dem. 18.308 and 19.255.

[26] Anaxim. *Ars Rhet.* 36.37 (p. 88, 3–5) in the text of Fuhrmann (1966): 'If they try to slander us by saying that we read out written speeches or practise them beforehand . . .' (ἐὰν δὲ διαβάλλωσιν ἡμᾶς, ὡς γεγραμμένους λόγους λέγομεν ἢ λέγειν μελετῶμεν . . .). On the disputed dating and authorship of what is more commonly known as the *Rhetorica ad Alexandrum*, see Kennedy (1963) 114–24. Kennedy follows the majority view that the treatise was written in the late fourth century.

[27] Anaxim. *Ars Rhet.* 36.37 (p. 88, 5–10): χρὴ πρὸς τὰ τοιαῦτα ὁμόσε βαδίζοντας εἰρωνεύεσθαι καὶ περὶ μὲν τῆς γραφῆς λέγειν, μὴ κωλύειν τὸν νόμον ἢ αὐτὸν γεγραμμένα λέγειν ἢ ἐκεῖνον ἄγραφα · τὸν γὰρ νόμον οὐκ ἐᾶν τοιαῦτα πράττειν, λέγειν δὲ ὅπως ἄν τις βούληται συγχωρεῖν. The sophist Alcidamas implies that speeches were learnt by heart when written out and not read from a text held in the hand during proceedings. See Alcid. 15.11, 18, 21, 34, in the text of Radermacher (1951). For the possibility of a logographer advising on delivery as well as, or instead of actually writing the speech, see Dover (1968) 151. See also Lavency (1964).

by replying that everyone, as far as he can, helps his friends with in-struction and advice (36.42 (p. 89, 4–8)).

This last piece of advice is not taken up in any of our extant public speeches. Nobody admits to having written speeches for others or having taught them. Nor does anyone ever admit to buying a written speech. But there are occasions when orators openly or tacitly admit their opponents' abusive labels of 'cleverness at speaking' (*deinotēs legein*) or 'being a *rhētōr*'. In these instances (some well documented by Ober) the speaker draws a contrast between a rhetorical activism which is deceitful and harmful to the polis and the honest, beneficial activism which (of course) he has always adhered to.[28] In his speech *On the Crown*, Demosthenes rejects Aeschines' charges of deception (*apatē*), sophistry and wizardry (*goēteia*) as applicable to Aeschines rather than himself (18.276). But he admits to Aeschines' charge of *deinotēs*: 'I am also sure that my cleverness – well, be it so' (κἀκεῖν᾽ εὖ οἶδ᾽ ὅτι τὴν ἐμὴν δεινότητα – ἔστω γάρ). He goes on to make it clear that unlike Ae-schines, he always uses his skill in the public domain and for the good of the demos (277–84). In his speech *Against Ctesiphon*, Aeschines tacitly admits that he is an able speaker by nature (*phusis*) when he 'anticipates' Demosthenes' claim that his *phusis* is like that of the Sirens whose charming voices bring destruction (3.228–9).[29] Aeschines de-flects this picture by arguing that, while strictly unfounded, such an accusation would be understandable coming from an inarticulate gen-eral (*stratēgos*) who was jealous of his ability. But, he continues, it is intolerable to hear this attack from a man who 'is made up of words' (*ex onomatōn sunkeimenos*) and who 'takes refuge in "simplicity" and the "facts"'. He concludes that Demosthenes would be as useless as a reed-less *aulos* if you took out his tongue (3.229).[30] This is just one example of Demosthenes' and Aeschines' constant tussle over the

---

[28] Ober (1989) 187–91.

[29] On the significance of the Sirens comparison see Easterling (1999) 154–5. Although Demosthenes' extant speech (18) in reply frequently accuses Aeschines of being a clever and deceptive speaker, he never likens him to the Sirens. Adams (1919) 487 suggests that Demosthenes omitted his comparison when he revised his speech for publication. See also Dover (1968) 178. The difficulty (I would say impossibility) of determining the relationship between published speeches and their performed 'origi-nals' has generated much discussion; see Kennedy (1963) 206; Adams (1912); Dover (1968); Usher (1976); Hansen (1984); Harris (1995) 10–15. Ober (1989) 49 suggests that orators and logographers would not revise speeches substantially for fear of being mocked by opponents or losing clients.

[30] The *aulos* was a wind-instrument (like an oboe or clarinet) which was used in a variety of performance contexts in Athens. For the ambiguous cultural status of the *aulos* in Athenian texts, see Wilson (1999) 85–95.

training, quality and effects of their voices and I will have cause to return to their focus on vocal performance below.

Cleverness and ability in speech and preparation: these are notions which the speaker *can* admit as applying to himself. Demosthenes admits to having written out his speech for *himself* but no extant oration follows Anaximenes' recommendation that a speaker should admit to having trained others or to having written their speeches.[31] And on the evidence we have, it seems that admissions of preparation and rhetorical skill are confined to high-profile *rhētores* such as Demosthenes or Aeschines, spoken *in propria persona*. Legal speeches written for clients do not seem to contain such admissions, despite (or perhaps because of) Anaximenes' recommendations. In the case of well-known career politicians, their standing was perhaps so high and the 'fiction' of their inexperience so obviously fragile, that the demos gave them the licence to attempt the reassurance that their transparent involvement with the *technai* of speech was all in a just cause.

Alongside the accusation of writing for others, there was another charge levelled at any elite speaker, whatever the extent of his involvement in political and legal discourse, which could not be admitted, even implicitly. This was the accusation of being a sophist, with all its apparent connotations of cunning and deceit. It seems that whoever you were, this label could not be admitted or given a positive colouring. Like the accusation of sycophancy and writing for others, a charge of sophistry had to be ignored or denied and turned back on the opponent who tried to pin it on you.[32] Aeschines and Demosthenes constantly accuse each other of being sophists in the five speeches relating to the trial of Timarchus, the embassy to Philip and the crowning of Demosthenes.

They also abuse each other, in the context of alleged rhetorical abil-

---

[31] It seems likely that Anaximenes' recommendation that these particular charges be admitted is polemical. Scholars have generally viewed the *Ars Rhetorica* as a 'sophistic' text. See Kennedy (1963) 115f. Whilst I would argue that anyone teaching rhetoric or writing speeches for others could be labelled 'a sophist' (hence Isocrates' and Aristotle's anxieties to attack and distance themselves from sophistry), Anaximenes is attempting to find and promote a topos which admits and neutralises accusations of sophistry and logography. For him, such practices should not be taboo. This would explain why he promotes this topos when (as we will see below), unlike admissions to preparation and writing one's own speech, admissions to sophistry and writing for others are not found in extant oratory.

[32] See Aeschin. 1.125, 175, 3.16 and 202: Demosthenes 18.276, 19.246–8 and 250. For a variation on 'he's a sophist' see Lys. fr. 1.5 in the text of Thalheim (1901) with the translation and discussion of Millett (1991) 1–3. An alleged ex-pupil of Socrates is accused of systematically cheating a range of creditors. The speaker glosses this behaviour as 'the life of the sophist'.

ity or sophistry, with names denoting witchcraft and magic.[33] Demosthenes is described as a *goēs* ('wizard') several times by Aeschines. The term implies trickery and delusion of an audience through magic arts but, as Burkert and Bowie have emphasised, it is also associated with unAthenian identity and behaviour.[34] It is thus a perfect term of abuse to connote sophistry since many notable 'sophists' were foreigners. The public texts of Athens can be seen to be identifying a technique of performance as 'deceptive communication' and classifying it as alien to normative Athenian identity.

Just as the Spartans are castigated for their dishonesty and deceptive speech in late fifth-century Athenian drama and historiography, so the oratory of the fourth-century tropes 'sophistic' technique in public trials and debates as the infiltration of 'unAthenian' activity. But if this aspect to the representation of 'sophistry' reminds us of the Tory exploitation of the American associations of 'spin', there is also a peculiarly ancient Greek resonance to this connection between rhetoric and witchcraft. Dinarchus, Aeschines and Demosthenes all utilise a cultural analogy between the deceits of sophistry or rhetoric and the spell-binding effects of magic which we see theorised in the writings of Gorgias, Plato and Isocrates.[35] Again these terms (*goēs* and *baskanos*) are non-negotiable; neither Aeschines nor Demosthenes can admit to being 'wizards' of speech.

Where the label 'sophist' crops up as a term of abuse throughout extant oratory, Aeschines and Demosthenes often offer extended vignettes of the other's sophistry. Demosthenes tells his jury that Aeschines never acted in a play from which he quoted in a previous

---

[33] Demosthenes is described as a *goēs* at Aeschin. 2.124, 153, 3.137 (in conjunction with *magos*) and 207. *Goēs*, *pharmakeus* and *sophistēs* are used of Eros at Pl. *Symp.* 203d. Demosthenes prefers a different word for a magician against Aeschines – *baskanos*; see 18.132 and adjectivally at 119, 139, 242, 317. See also 21.209, 25.80, 83. No other orator uses it. Whereas *goēs* seems to be a general term connoting trickery and working magic, *baskanos* more specifically connotes malevolence. It is derived from the verb βασκαίνω which can mean 'to bewitch' or 'give the evil eye'. As at Dem. 18.242, Aristophanes uses *baskanos* in relation to sycophancy and slander; see Ar. *Eq.* 105, *Plut.* 571. It would seem that Demosthenes attempts to trump Aeschines' deployment of *goēs*, by using an analogous, but more specifically loaded term. At Dem. 18.257-9 Aeschines is mocked for reading texts during his mother's shady nocturnal rituals, and it is implied that his howling voice was trained in this context. Perhaps *baskanos* is meant to evoke this past.

[34] Burkert (1962) 55; Bowie (1993) 114-15.

[35] See Din. 1.66, 92 where, again, Demosthenes is the *goēs*. On the link made between magic and rhetoric in Gorgias, Plato and Isocrates see de Romilly (1975). For the specific links made by Plato between *apatē*, sophistry, rhetoric and *goēteia* see Burkert (1962) 50-1.

legal clash. He 'hunts up' quotations thereby demonstrating that *he* is the sophist and the last person who should accuse others of sophistry (19.246–50). Demosthenes is responding to Aeschines' speech *Against Timarchus*, in which he is compared to the 'sophist' Socrates. In that speech, Aeschines reminds the jury that they put 'the sophist Socrates' to death for being the teacher of the oligarch Critias (1.173). If Socrates was executed for teaching Critias, the jury should not sanction Demosthenes' advocacy: for this is a man who takes vengeance on *idiōtai* ('private citizens') and *dēmotikoi* ('friends of the people') for their *isēgoria* ('freedom of speech'). Aeschines then draws a vivid picture of Demosthenes the sophist:

So I do beg you by all means not to furnish this sophist with laughter and patronage at your expense. Imagine that you see him when he gets home from the court-room, putting on airs in his lectures to his young men, and telling how successfully he stole the case away from the jury: 'I carried the jurors off bodily from the charges brought against Timarchus, and set them on the accuser, and Philip, and the Phocians, and I suspended such terrors before the eyes of the hearers that the defendant began to be the accuser, and the accuser to be on trial; and the jurors forgot what they were to judge and what they were not to judge, to that they listened.' But it is your business to take your stand against this sort of thing, and following close on every step, to let him at no point turn aside nor persist in irrelevant talk; on the contrary, act as you do in a horse-race, make him keep to the track – of the matter at issue. (Aeschines 1.175–6)

Demosthenes uses his lawcourt performances as object-lessons in deceptive rhetoric for his young students. Aeschines imagines him boasting about his successful displays of deception to his pupils and urges the jury to keep strict control of him, as if he were a race-horse. Ober analyses this passage well, highlighting the way in which Aeschines warns the jury that sophistry is a threat to the democratic ideal of *isēgoria*.[36] It should also be emphasised that Aeschines represents a vote for Demosthenes as a vote for his intention to transform the people's court into his private school for rhetorical deception.

These vignettes derive their force from an interplay between commonplace and creative strategy. Both Demosthenes and Aeschines mobilise the 'he's a sophist' topos but they often extend and 'particularise' the commonplace. This creative 'spin' on an opponent's techniques of 'spin' serves a double purpose. It distinguishes its author's performance. The jury has heard all these anti-rhetorical topoi before but *this* speaker is doing something different. He knows the 'script' but he departs from it and develops it. At the same time, the departure

---

[36] Ober (1989) 172.

from the 'script' serves to make the speaker's attack more authoritative. The opponent is a sophist, but a creative vignette of his activities appears to raise the attack above the level of conventional name-calling. Aeschines wants to convince the jury that he is not just tapping into a set of commonly-held prejudices which have worked well in the past. He makes his accusation sound 'truthful' by describing what *this particular sophist* does at the demos' expense.

While we have examples of anti-rhetorical charges being admitted and given a positive colouring, the charge of being a sophist was *non-negotiable*. It seems that the charge of being a logographer, in the sense of writing for others, was similarly impossible to admit. Thucydides represents Cleon criticising his audience for listening to *ecclēsia* speeches as if they were spectators of sophistic displays rather than deciding on national and international policy (3.38.7). And, as we will see in the next chapter, Aristophanes certainly portrays sophistic teaching and logography as a threat (albeit laughable) to honest and just legal and political transaction.[37] We can see that the cultural image of the sophist connoted the display of, and instruction in self-serving deception at the same time as 'sophistry' became identifiable as a new technology and a distinctive form of education.[38]

Whilst Ober does observe that an orator can admit to *deinotēs* or being a *rhētōr* and write those roles positively, he does not mark a difference between terms connoting rhetorical deceit which can be neutralised and those which cannot. The distinction is not important for Ober because he is primarily concerned to demonstrate that the subgroup of the citizen elite who are perceived to be *rhētores* have a licence to admit and defend their own eloquence and experience at the same time as they are attacked for it. He does not ask himself why an orator can admit to being *deinos legein* but not to being a *sophistēs*. I now turn to that question.

Speaking democratically and the response of Plato and Aristotle

We saw that Demosthenes had no trouble in redefining his *deinotēs* positively and democratically. And Aeschines was able to turn the

---

[37] For the most pertinent references and limited discussion, see Murphy (1938) 71–8. A mass of bibliography could be given. See Dover (1970) xxviii–xxvii, (1972) 109ff.; Cartledge (1990b) 35–8; O' Regan (1992); Bowie (1993) 112–24; MacDowell (1995) 125ff.

[38] On the history of the word *sophistēs* and its increasingly pejorative connotations in the classical period, see Guthrie (1971) 24–37.

charge that he had the *phusis* of a Siren into a modest admission that his eloquence was indeed a matter of *phusis* – a positive *phusis* with all its implications of an ability which has not been acquired artfully or artificially. Other speakers who go to court can be subject to the full range of meta-discursive abuses, but unlike *rhētores* they have to maintain the 'inexperience' topos at all times. However the *rhētōr* can and must deny that he writes speeches for others, teaches and uses the *technai* of rhetoric as a sophist, or transforms the courtroom or *ecclēsia* into a sophistic laboratory of deception. The *rhētōr* is allowed to be more 'rhetorical' than anyone else but he is constantly subject to the suspicion that his 'rhetoric' exceeded the limits imposed by *isēgoria*. One of Ober's fundamental questions is why, given the obvious dangers and deceptions which rhetorical expertise brought to the democracy, *rhētores* were allowed to operate at all. The answer is not simply (as Ober formulates it) that egalitarian suspicion of rhetoric's deceptive potential kept a useful elite's deployment of rhetoric in check. Rather, the inadmissibility of being a peddler or a recipient of logography and sophistry reveal and reinforce the limits of democratic rhetorical licence.

The terms *sophistēs* and *logographos* are not abusive, inadmissible terms just because they describe elitist occupations. In their strategies of suspicion and denigration the orators represent sophistry and logography as practices which valorise the end of winning an argument over and above the means and motives through which that end is achieved. Aeschines even represents 'Demosthenes the sophist' as using the legal process as a forum for the didactic display of his powers of deception. In the speech *Against Lacritus*, Demosthenes' client similarly accuses his opponent of being a 'perfidious sophist' (*ponēros sophistēs*) who considers himself a great deceiver of juries and takes money for teaching others to do the same (35.40–3).[39]

When we set these attacks on sophistry against the orators' definitions of what makes a good upstanding *rhētōr*, it becomes clear that sophistry and logography are demonised because they are perceived as lacking an ideological priority of commitment to the demos. In the speech *Against Ctesiphon*, Aeschines warns his jury that they will be deceived by Demosthenes if they focus on the pleasing sound of his speech rather than the obvious defects of his *phusis* and the real 'truth' (*alētheia*) (3.168). Aeschines goes on to outline some predictable qualities for the *dēmotikos rhētōr*; he must be freeborn, he must have an

---

[39] On this see Ober (1989) 170–1.

ancestrally inherited love of democracy, he should be 'moderate' (*metrios*) and 'self-controlled' (*sōphrōn*), have 'manly courage' (*andreia*) and never desert the demos (169–70). He should also be of good judgement (*eugnōmōn*) and an able speaker (*dunatos eipein*). For his disposition (*dianoia*) should prefer what is best and both the *paideia* of the *rhētōr* and the *paideia* in *logoi* should persuade his listeners. But, Aeschines continues, if the *dēmotikos rhētōr* cannot have both, good judgement (*eugnōmosunē*) should always be preferred to *logos* (170). This check-list of attributes is of course introduced in order to demonstrate that Demosthenes does not match up to any of them; amongst other failings Aeschines contrasts his initial status as a trierarch with his eventual emergence as a logographer, and a corrupt one at that. Furthermore, Demosthenes may be *deinos legein* and produce 'fine words' (*kaloi logoi*) but his life is base (*kakos*) and his deeds are disgraceful (*phaula*) (174–5).

Sophistry and logography produce a speaker whose valorisation of winning a case or an argument by any means (especially deceptive ones) makes him antithetical to the democratic ideal of the speaker whose speaking ability is subordinate to his political *eugnōmosunē*. This speaker is allowed to deploy a *paideia* in rhetoric to articulate his good advice, but if a speaker moonlights as a paid teacher or consultant himself, then it is assumed that any apparent *eugnōmosunē* is simply a dishonest rhetorical effect of his priority to display the invincibility of his *deinotēs* and successful deployment of *apatē* through the arts of rhetoric. To be sure, Aeschines' invocation of Socrates indicates that the sophist and his deceits can be associated with 'oligarchic tendencies'. But oratory's consistent demonisation of the logographer and the sophist constitute an ideological isolation of practices which are deemed to privilege self-serving rhetorical deceit of juries and assemblies over and above any other concern. Rhetoric must only be harnessed in the service of articulating wisdom, good judgement and genuine democratic commitment. One is reminded of Deva's distinction between proper 'opposition' for the 'common good' and mere 'yarn-spinning'.

The ideological terrain mapped out by these anti-rhetorical topoi and the areas of negotiation and inadmissibility which that terrain reveals, can help us to assess the force and contextual significance of Plato and Aristotle's discussions of rhetoric. It is clear, although too infrequently observed, that many of Plato's grounds for condemning contemporary rhetorical theory and practice develop meta-discursive reflections on political and legal discourse which had already been articulated in Thucydidean speeches and Aristophanic comedy.[40] Plato's characterisation of contemporary rhetoric as a form of deceptive flattery analogous to cookery and cosmetics is a theoretical development of late fifth-century democratic culture's own anti-rhetorical critiques and self-authorisations.[41] But where Plato attempts to carve out a 'true' or 'philosophical' *technē* of rhetoric in the *Phaedrus*, or where (as his detractors gleefully point out) he appropriates the seductive operations of *peithō* for the maintenance of law and social order in his ideal polis, he effectively proposes the same subordination of rhetoric to the articulation and achievement of 'the good' which is implied by the orators' definitions of acceptable *deinotēs* and the good *rhētōr*.[42] This is not to say that the orators share the same definition of wisdom, or the same political ideals or goals as Plato. Nor can we argue that Plato's complex arguments against contemporary rhetoric and in favour of a 'philosophical' rhetoric are doing the same 'work' as the meta-discourse of the orators. But the notion that rhetoric's deceptive and destabilising potential can only be contained if it is kept subordinate to knowledge, wisdom and a constitutional status-quo is a notion which is shared between the strategies of *rhētores* and Plato's philosophy. Plato wishes to expose contemporary rhetoric and sophistry as false discourses of knowledge and subordinate the art of persuasion to dialectical wisdom and self-knowledge.

The orators authorise their commitment to democracy by legitimating a notion of rhetoric which is subordinate to, and in the service of, good judgement and advice. For both the orators and Plato, sophistry presents as a discourse which has no prior commitment to 'truth' or agreed moral and political ends: it is only concerned with achieving victory for an individual in any debate and demonstrating that it can do so. Where the orator represents himself as having a prior knowledge and political commitment which shapes and delimits his use of rheto-

---

[40] Yunis (1996) provides a refreshing, if limited, account of the ways in which Plato takes up the images of the flattering, deceptive demagogue and the fickle, easily-led demos which are projected by Aristophanes and Thucydides.

[41] See Pl. *Grg.* 463a–c, 464c–d, 481d, 521a. For the comic image of the demos as misled by the flattering deceits of demagogues see Ar. *Eq.* 763–1110, 1340–4 and below pp. 255–8. At Ar. *Ach.* 370–8 and 634–5 we have the ironic, 'didactic' representation of the demos as prone to the deceptive demagogic flattery. On this, see below pp. 258–74. See also Thuc. 2.65.8–10, where Pericles is praised for not resorting to flattering rhetoric and his successors are condemned for it.

[42] See Pl. *Phaedr.* 259e1–261a5. On the *Phaedrus*' complex subordination of rhetoric to philosophy and ethical goals, see Ferrari (1987), especially 39–45 and 204–32; Murray (1988); Halliwell (1994); Yunis (1996) 172–210. On the role of rhetoric in the *Laws* and *Republic*, see above pp. 160–1 and Popper (1966) 138–46, 270–2; Vickers (1988) 143f.; Yunis (1996) 211–36.

ric, Plato represents all orators as lacking in 'true' knowledge or as practitioners of sophistry. But both Plato and the individual orator mobilise their model of good subordinated rhetoric and contrast it with the false, falsifying and insubordinate rhetoric of everybody else.

The orators' demonisation of sophistry and their self-representation as harnessing *deinotēs* and speaking ability for good political and moral ends also finds its analogue in Aristotle's attempt to carve out a theory of legitimate civic rhetoric. Aristotle argues that what distinguishes the sophist from (his vision of) the rhetorician is not a 'difference in faculty (*dunamis*) but in moral purpose (*prohairēsis*)'.[43] For Aristotle the faculty of public speaking only becomes sophistry when its intentions and effects are deemed to be politically and morally undesirable.[44]

My qualification to Ober's characterisation of anti-rhetorical topoi demonstrates that Athenian democracy's legal discourse does not straightforwardly associate *technai* and powers of rhetoric with *apatē*. Rather, the two related practices of logography and 'sophistry' are singled out as deceptive practices because they are seen to represent the prioritising of personal victory over and above commitment to the values and integrity of the demos and a concomitant disregard for legitimate methods of persuasion. The Athenians both utilised rhetorical skill and fostered continuing articulations of its powers to deceive, bewitch and stupefy. According to Ober, they reaped rhetoric's benefits and kept its threat to their constitutional system in check. I would add that this was not simply a process of articulating what Ober calls 'ambivalence and balance'.[45] There is no ambivalence surrounding the orators' representations of sophistry and logography. Rather, the elite orator develops and responds to an ideological demand that rhetorical skill be subordinated to a regime of political and moral 'truth'. The sophist and the logographer are imagined and invoked as inadmissible actors because they stand for rhetorical practice unchecked by long-term commitment to this regime.

The physiognomics of deception: Demosthenes' *Against Stephanus 1*

Ober focuses on Attic oratory as evidence for answering questions about how Athens maintained and reproduced its democracy and the

---

[43] Arist. *Rh.* 1.1355b18–21 in the text of Kassel (1971). Garver (1994) 206–31 unpacks this distinction with reference to Aristotle's ethical philosophy.

[44] This is not to dispute the controversial but attractive view that Aristotle's *Rhetoric* 'time and again subordinates truth to victory' (Wardy (1996a) 81). See also Garver (1994) 208.

[45] Ober (1989) 187.

apparent sovereignty of mass over elite. But there is another perspective on Athenian oratory which is stressed by those critics who seek to use these speeches as 'evidence' for the 'sociology' or 'discursive practices' of Attic society.[46] If we are to give a full account of Athenian culture's confrontation with the possibility of deception – what Detienne calls the 'ambiguity of speech' – we need to address political and legal discourse's involvement in the negotiation of disputes between individuals. High-profile politicians and lower-profile litigants participated in 'democratic discourse' but at the same time they were using the lawcourts and the *ecclēsia* to fight each other for status and recognition in the wider community. Of course, in many private cases it is clear that large sums of money were at stake. But wealthy individuals also used the courts to seek redress and renewed gains in an elite contest of manhood and honour.[47] Here, the citizen performs in court in order to enhance or rehabilitate his general 'performance' in the eyes of the city.

It is from this perspective that we must view some highly individual strategies and counter-strategies through which speakers expose an enormous variety of lies and tricks on the part of their opponents. These strategies cannot be described as topoi, and I suspect that their force derived from their relative novelty and singularity; their particularity served to highlight and isolate the singular (often exceptional) 'dishonesty' of the individuals against whom they were directed. They all invoke cultural norms and accepted paradigms of behaviour but, unlike the anti-rhetorical arguments I have just discussed, they are not even recognisable as commonplaces. While these strategies focus on the dishonesty of the opponent, and they are certainly 'meta-discursive',

---

[46] Here I am thinking particularly of the following studies: Dover (1974), (1978); Nouhaud (1982); Humphreys (1985); Foucault (1987); Halperin (1989); Millett (1991); Cartledge (1990a); Osborne (1990); Winkler (1990b); Todd (1990), (1993); Cohen (1991), (1995); Hunter (1994); Hall (1995); Wilson (1991).

[47] Recent studies have highlighted the use of the lawcourts as a forum for feuding and competition over public status and reputation. Our extant Athenian forensic speeches participate in, or else draw on the language and protocols of, what has been termed a 'zero-sum' game. In accordance with this model of social rivalry, the male citizen elite (and mainly the inner wealth-elite of the liturgical class) extend their rivalries and squabbles as high-profile citizens to the public stage of the lawcourts. This extension occurs, as Cohen (1995) 141 puts it, in order to 'avenge dishonour or outmanoeuvre an enemy'. See Winkler (1990b) 178ff.; Cohen (1991) 171–202; (1995) 63–70. See Arist. *Rh.* 2.1382b where Aristotle articulates a zero-sum principle of social competition in his treatment of fear. See also the sophistic extract *Anonymus Iamblichi* DK 89 B17–20, where it is stated that nobody likes to give honour to someone else because they think that they are themselves being deprived of something.

they cannot all be described as 'anti-rhetorical' strategies in the narrow sense which I have been using. In the remainder of this chapter, I will discuss examples of this broader 'rhetoric of anti-rhetoric'.

My first example of a non-standard, meta-discursive strategy comes from the Demosthenic speech *Against Stephanus 1*. This strategy does not interrogate the opponent's honesty with respect to his involvement in *technai* of public speaking. This time it is the nascent formation of 'physiognomic' inquiry (the ancient 'meta-discourse' of performance *par excellence*) at Athens during the late fifth and fourth centuries which provides an important frame for thinking about the strategy's force and the social behavioural assumptions which give it a foundation.[48] Whether directly informed by the theory and practice of this new 'science' or simply an inevitable product of Athens' 'surveillance culture', the peroration of the Demosthenic *Against Aristogeiton 1* makes it clear that legal oratory could make good use of physiognomic assumptions:

One more thing I have to say before I sit down. You will soon be leaving this court-house, and you will be watched by the bystanders, both aliens and citizens; they will scan each one as he appears, and detect by their looks (*phusiognōmonēsousi*) those who have voted for acquittal. What will you have to say for yourselves, Athenians, if you emerge after betraying the laws? With what expressions and with what looks will you return their gaze? (Demosthenes 25.98)[49]

---

[48] Winkler (1990b) 199–200, defines the ancient 'science' of physiognomics as 'the informal practice of reading people's "natures" by the observation of their physical characteristics and style'. For a succinct account of the problems of defining certain ancient practices as 'scientific' see Lloyd (1970) 125ff. This kind of practice, and the assumptions on which it rests, can be traced back to Homeric epic. See Hom. *Il.* 13.275–87, where Idomeneus offers instructions for spotting a coward from his physical appearance before a battle. Evans (1969) lists passages informed by physiognomic assumptions in Homer, and other archaic poets. Most of our surviving physiognomic texts date to the second century AD and after (Förster (1893), Gleason (1995) and Barton (1994) 95–131). However, two pseudo-Aristotelian treatises on human physiognomy are datable to the fourth century BC. See Lloyd (1983) 18–26; MacC. Armstrong (1958) 52f. Galen *Anim. mor. corp. temp.* 7 claims that Hippocrates invented physiognomics, and the Hippocratic corpus certainly contains physiognomic material. See, for example Hippoc. *Epid.* 2.5.1, 16, 23, 2.6.1. Porph. *Vit. Pythag.* 13 claims that Pythagoras used physiognomic analysis. Cic. *De Fato* 5.10 and *Tusc.* 4.37 relate a story of Zopyrus' physiognomic diagnosis of Socrates as stupid and fond of women. A *Zopyrus* is listed at D. L. 2.105 as a treatise written by Socrates' pupil Phaedo. D. L. 6.16 (= Caizzi fr.1), lists a *Peri tōn sophistōn phusiognōmonikos* as a work by Antisthenes.

[49] This speech may not be by Demosthenes. Kennedy (1963) 207–8 and Ober (1989) 358 regard it as genuine.

This passage is an outrageous spin on the topos of reminding a jury that their decision will be judged by bystanders or the rest of the demos.[50] This speaker actually warns the jury that when they leave the court, onlookers will even be able to distinguish which of them has voted for an acquittal through physiognomic scrutiny. He even attempts to make them self-conscious about what facial expression those who vote for Aristogeiton will adopt when confronted with this scrutiny. Physiognomy was clearly a strategic resource for the fourth-century litigant.[51]

It is with this resource in mind that I turn to the speech *Against Stephanus 1*. This oration was delivered by Apollodorus in an indictment against a witness in a previous trial.[52] Stephanus is alleged to have given false testimony on behalf of his friend Phormio who had been involved in a previous legal battle with Apollodorus. At one point in the speech, Apollodorus accuses Stephanus of greed, money-seeking flattery, covetousness and insolence (45.65-7). He then makes the following observations concerning Stephanus' behaviour in everyday public life:

Neither should the appearances which this man fashions as he walks with a sullen face along the walls be properly considered as signs of self-control, but rather as signs of misanthropy. In my opinion, a man whom no misfortune has befallen, and who is in no lack of the necessaries of life, but who none the less habitually maintains this demeanour, has reviewed the matter and reached the conclusion in his own mind, that to those who walk in a simple and natural way and wear a cheerful countenance, men draw near unhesitatingly with requests and proposals, whereas they shrink from drawing near in the first place to affected and sullen characters. This demeanour (*schēma*), then, is nothing but a

---

[50] Surprisingly, this passage is not mentioned by Winkler (1990a) or Gleason (1990), (1995). Nor is the passage discussed by Cohen (1991) or (1995) which both cite other parts of speech extensively. Hunter (1994) 232, n. 41 does cite the passage in her list of references to the perceived importance of bystanders as witnesses to events which have a bearing on trials and as viewers of the courtroom conduct of litigants and juries. Din. 1.30, 66 and 2.19 remind the jury of the judgemental surveillance of bystanders. See also Bers (1985) 8 on the *thorubos* of bystanders at trials.

[51] See Barton (1994) 99 on the relationship between physiognomics and rhetoric at Rome: '... the basic elements of the system were morally persuasive. The methods of physiognomics reveal themselves as developments of traditional τόποι of praise and blame which worked to persuade the audience to identify with the speaker against the categorised Other'.

[52] This speech is generally held to be the work of Demosthenes and written for delivery by Apollodorus. See Trevett (1992) 50-76. There seems to be a difficulty in giving this speech to Demosthenes when other 'Apollodoran' speeches in the Demosthenic corpus have been ascribed to a previously unknown orator, namely Apollodorus himself. Why did Apollodorus write the other speeches and not this one?

cover for his real character, and he shows therein the wildness and bitterness of his disposition. (Demosthenes 45.68–9)[53]

Apollodorus believes that the demeanour (*schēma*) of his opponent in public life is relevant to the case in question. The term *schēma* is a fundamental expression in Athens' agonistic culture of rhetoric, performance and surveillance – not least because it develops technical senses which connote the learning and composition of 'postures' and 'figures'.[54] Apollodorus makes it clear from the outset that he believes Stephanus' appearance to be manufactured or affected. Stephanus is described as walking by the city walls with a sullen facial expression (ἐσκυθρωπακώς) and he fashions appearances (*ha peplastai*). Apollodorus assumes (perhaps deliberately and falsely) that this spectacle is familiar to the audience. The ascription of the adjectives σκυθρός, σκυθρωπός or the verb σκυθρωπάζω to a subject or subject-group seems to connote a range of emotions manifested in a frowning facial expression; solemnity, sadness, sullenness and anger.[55] It is hard to determine exactly what sort of expression Apollodorus is seeking to convey with 'ἐσκυθρωπακώς'. However, it is clear that Stephanus is represented as having some kind of fixed countenance of gravity. Apollodorus thinks that the audience would be likely to interpret this expression and other unspecified airs and graces as 'signs of self-control' (*sēmeia sōphrosunēs*). Stephanus gives the appearance of being self-controlled, moderate and modest; his body-language is easily correlated with a moral and political disposition which was greatly valorised by Athenian culture.[56]

According to Apollodorus, everybody is likely to infer from a person's facial and bodily signs to an internal character or disposition. Of course, this is a rhetorical move on Apollodorus' part and can give us only partial insight into the extent to which Athenians deployed a 'folk' physiognomics as an embedded social practice. Nevertheless, there is a

---

[53] οὐ τοίνυν οὐδ' ἃ πέπλασται καὶ βαδίζει παρὰ τοὺς τοίχους οὗτος ἐσκυθρωπακώς, σωφροσύνης ἄν τις ἡγήσαιτ' εἰκότως εἶναι σημεῖα, ἀλλὰ μισανθρωπίας. ἐγὼ γάρ, ὅστις αὑτῷ μηδενὸς συμβεβηκότος δεινοῦ, μηδὲ τῶν ἀναγκαίων σπανίζων, ἐν ταύτῃ τῇ σχέσει διάγει τὸν βίον, τοῦτον ἡγοῦμαι συνεορακέναι καὶ λελογίσθαι παρ' αὑτῷ, ὅτι τοῖς μὲν ἁπλῶς, ὡς πεφύκασι, βαδίζουσι καὶ φαιδροῖς, καὶ προσέλθοι τις ἂν καὶ δεηθείη καὶ ἐπαγγείλειεν οὐδὲν ὀκνῶν, τοῖς δὲ πεπλασμένοις καὶ σκυθρωποῖς ὀκνήσειεν τις ἂν προσελθεῖν πρῶτον. οὐδὲν οὖν ἄλλ' ἢ πρόβλημα τοῦ τρόπου τὸ σχῆμα τοῦτ' ἔστι, καὶ τὸ τῆς διανοίας ἄγριον καὶ πικρὸν ἐνταῦθα δηλοῖ.
[54] See Goldhill (1999) 4–5.
[55] See Eur. *Hipp.* 1152 (sadness or solemnity); Ar. *Lys.* 7 (anger or sullenness); Aeschin. 2.36 (anger or sourness), 3.20 (solemnity); Pl. *Symp.* 206d5 (discontented frowning).
[56] On *sōphrosunē*, see North (1966), especially 85–149.

case to be made for Apollodorus raising the issue precisely *because* he knows that he must deal with a general perception of Stephanus' appearance as connotative of an upright moral character. Stephanus does not look or behave like a cheat and, for his prosecutor, there is a lot riding on these conclusions – conclusions surely derived from the collective practice of a social semiotics of the body. There can be no certainty of the extent to which Athens was truly a 'face-to-face' society where everyone in the jury had heard about Stephanus or had seen him going about his daily business.[57] But Apollodorus' staged scrutiny of Stephanus' facial expressions and demeanour evokes the notion of a 'surveillance culture' (whether it be a rhetorical myth or an oppressive social reality) which Winkler, Cohen and Hunter all detect as crucial to Athenian legal discourse.[58]

Having set up Stephanus as a man who looks upright, Apollodorus offers his audience a different interpretation of his opponent's physical appearance. Stephanus has suffered no personal misfortune and is not lacking in life's necessities. This biography somehow debars Stephanus from the honest deployment of the physical signs of *sōphrosunē*. Apollodorus explains that those who walk simply and *naturally* and maintain a cheerful or bright expression are often approached by others with requests and proposals. However, people will not approach those who appear affected or sullen/solemn. Apollodorus infers that Stephanus has represented himself in this way so that he can deter any demands from other citizens. And he will go on to claim that Stephanus has never performed a single act of private or civic generosity in his life (69–70). The demeanour commonly associated with *sōphrosunē* is nothing more than a cover (*problēma*) for a very different internal dis-

---

[57] See Ober (1989) 148–51 on rumour as a democratic and acceptable form of proof in the orators and their use of the 'you all know' topos. On the question of whether the notion of Athens as a 'face-to-face' society was reality or ideality see Finley (1973) 17–18, (1983) 28–9 (reality); Osborne (1985a) 64–5 and Ober (1989) 31–3 (ideality). Recent work on the unlikeliness of a real face-to-face society at the level of polis structures would suggest that gossip and rumour about a litigant might not always filter from deme communities to the mixed-deme audiences of the assembly and lawcourt juries. For the impact of Athenian law enacting a shift from face-to-face relations in villages to the polis where such relations no longer existed in reality see Humphreys (1985) 350f. The possibility that, at the level of social reality, there could rarely have been anything like an absolutely 'common report' concerning all but the most prominent political individuals seems to follow from the following observation of Ober (1989) 32: 'When a rich Athenian entered the people's court as a litigant, he could not count on having a single fellow demesman on the jury, and the rest of the jurors were likely to be strangers.'

[58] See Winkler (1990b) on elite 'surveillance culture'. On neighbourhood gossip, rumour and surveillance, see Cohen (1991) 49–55, 64–9, 90–5. On gossip and rumour as a means of social control in Athens, see Hunter (1994) 96–119.

position; in reality it confirms Stephanus 'misanthropic' temper (*misanthrōpias*) and the 'wildness and bitterness of his disposition' (*to tēs dianoias agrion kai pikron*). Apollodorus' argument here dovetails uncannily with a section of the Aristotelian *Physiognomics* which explores the drawbacks of an 'expression method' of physiognomic interpretation; this is a method which the author distinguishes from an equally flawed 'zoological' approach.[59] The *Physiognomics* soberly points out that two men with radically different dispositions (*dianoiai*) can exhibit the same facial expression; there is often nothing to tell the difference between the expression of a courageous man and that of an impudent one. Similarly, a man of generally gloomy disposition can have a good day and therefore look cheerful.[60]

Apollodorus destroys any unequivocal link between a specific set of physical signs and the character-type which they are commonly held to signify. But he does not disrupt the workings of the assumptions which ground physiognomic interpretation. Apollodorus is very careful to provide a plausible causal account of how the signs of *sōphrosunē* could also connote a completely different (in this case, totally antithetical) moral disposition. Stephanus is not simply held to have hidden his misanthropy and malignity behind a mask of moderation and modesty. Rather, the commonly recognised signs of *sōphrosunē* are given a functional role in the practice of misanthropy. To appear unapproachable is to *be* unapproachable; to want to be unapproachable without mitigating personal circumstances is to be misanthropic and rude. Hence the signs of unapproachability, which happen to be the same as those of *sōphrosunē*, are often proof that a man does not wish to take part in the 'give-and-take' of everyday public life. The misanthrope can perpetuate his disposition by warding off demands from others with his sullen looks. At the same time he can hide that disposition because its physical manifestation usually signifies a positive character-type. In short, Apollodorus exposes Stephanus' public self-representation as a clever but disingenuous theatrical performance.

Athenian oratory does not abound with physiognomic-style assumptions and interpretations.[61] But we have seen that, within their specific battles, Demosthenes and Aeschines are fond of diagnosing an inner disposition, *phusis* or *ēthos* from the quality and strength of each other's public-speaking voice.[62] They also mock, mimic and analyse

[59] See MacC. Armstrong (1958) 53–5.
[60] Arist. *Physiognomics* 3 in the text of Förster (1893).
[61] However, Evans (1969) is too pessimistic in claiming that Attic oratory is virtually silent in relation to physiognomic assumptions or strategies.
[62] See Aeschin. 2.34–5, 3.228–9; Dem. 18.308–10, 19.336.

each other's physical gestures within the performative context of the lawcourt. They even mock and imitate (through words and gestures) each other's strategies of (verbal and gestural) mockery and imitation.[63] Often the opponent's quality of voice or use of mimicry and gesture is represented as leading an audience away from the truth or the real issues at hand. Demosthenes makes particular play of Aeschines' career as an actor.[64] Demosthenes also claims that Aeschines' voice and articulation signify dishonesty and hidden criminality (19.207–10).

There are one or two occasions where the litigant has to deny the negative character-trait which is implied by the way he walks and talks about town. A plaintiff in a Demosthenic speech has to explain that his habit of 'fast walking and loud talking' is not, as his opponents claim, a sign of bad character but an unavoidable natural trait, and he appeals to his general reputation for support (37.52, 55–6). And at the same time as Apollodorus exposes the fraudulence of Stephanus' outward appearance in the manner I have just discussed, he later asks the jury to excuse his own 'fast walking and loud talking' as an unfortunate affliction of *phusis* (45.77). He may partly have embarked on his extraordinarily detailed 'physiognomic' exposure of Stephanus' deliberately misleading appearance in order to distract the jury from his own 'physiognomic reputation'.[65]

In his analysis of Stephanus' everyday *schēmata* before the trial and outside the confines of the lawcourt, Apollodorus does not simply give his opponent a permanent disposition of mean misanthropy. He also represents Stephanus as habitually dishonest and duplicitous in his relationship with other citizens. This was obviously a good argument to deploy against a man accused of having given false testimony. An implied probability argument and an implied argument from character are rolled into one. The argument has no near parallel in extant oratory. And yet, at the same time as it is highly unusual, it is very 'typical' in terms of its appeal to ideologically and morally charged notions of *sōphrosunē*, wildness (*agriotēs*) and reciprocity.[66] It is also a classic (and classically manipulative) example of the interrelationship between a culture of surveillance and the strategic articulation of physiognomic

---

[63] See Dem. 18.232–3. See also Aeschin. 2.156–8. For more on Demosthenes and Aeschines' focus on performance see Ford (1999) and Easterling (1999).

[64] See above n. 15. Aeschin. 2.156–8 tropes Demosthenes' shrill voice and mimicry as tools of slander.

[65] 'Physiognomic reputation' is also at work at Dem. 54.32ff. and Lys. 16.18f. For the physiognomics of 'walking' in Greek culture see Bremmer (1991).

[66] See North (1966) on *sōphrosunē*; Cartledge (1993) 50–5 on savagery and 'wildness'; Von Reden (1995) on reciprocity.

assumptions. Finally, and most importantly for my purposes, the passage demonstrates how a speaker can confront and represent the problem of the citizen who lies to the demos with a meta-discursive strategy that is strikingly unusual, thereby creating the impression that the strategy is not a strategy at all. Apollodorus creates the impression that the conventional topoi of anti-rhetoric are both inadequate as descriptions of Stephanus and unnecessary as typical strategies of invective. With Stephanus, we have a man who lives and breathes dishonesty in order to remain true to his socially unacceptable self. He is able to *be* misanthropic by hoodwinking everyone into assuming that he is *sophrōn*. There is, Apollodorus implies, no need for the name-calling ('sycophant', 'sophist' and so on) which juries hear every day, and such name-calling would fail to capture the extraordinary truth of Stephanus' life of deception. Apollodorus' physiognomics of deceit attempts to authorise its truth-status by virtue of its distinctive distance from the standard topoi of invective used against 'dishonest' opponents.

The lying topos: the orators deconstruct the commonplace

Apollodorus conjures up an image of his opponent's dishonesty by focusing on his (strategic) performances in Athens' thoroughfares and meeting places. This is not an attack on Stephanus' use of rhetorical *technai* in the limited domain of the lawcourt and as such it is a marked departure from the anti-rhetorical topoi which I have already discussed. But there are occasions where a speaker actually distances himself from the deceptive connotations of rhetorical *technē* by foregrounding his opponent's use of commonplaces and by 'unmasking' the lies which such topoi conceal. There are several examples of this anti-rhetorical strategy in extant oratory but I will only discuss two in detail.[67] They all deal with different topoi and they all serve to undermine an opponent by representing an argument he has used (or will use) as a mere commonplace which has *become* a commonplace precisely because it has proved itself an effective means of disguising guilt. As Ober has argued, topoi were the means by which mass and elite colluded in dramatic fictions. But the orators occasionally argue that topoi constitute the fiction of an opponent's innocence.

The 'as you all know' topos is a particularly frequent commonplace

---

[67] Other examples: Ant. 5.4–5 (on the 'plea for a hearing' topos) with Usher and Edwards (1985) 70; Dem. 21.136–7 (on the 'have you ever seen me doing this' topos) and 141–2 (on the 'inexperience' topos).

which is introduced through a recurring set of phrases.[68] The topos is used to represent a piece of information about an individual as truthful by common report or rumour.[69] It is also used to introduce exemplifying lines of poetry, legal statutes or historical events.[70] In the *Rhetoric*, Aristotle claims that speech-writers use this topos to drum up assent from everyone, including those who do not really know the information being expressed as common knowledge, because the latter would be too ashamed to reveal their ignorance.[71] The topos' function and effectiveness has also been associated with 'the fiction that the entire polis was the sort of face-to-face community that in reality existed only at the level of the demes' and the fact that *phēmē* (rumour) was regarded as expressive of a highly democratic and egalitarian mode of proof.[72] But in their analysis of the topos as a recurrent fictionalising and authorising strategy, critics have failed to remark on an occasion when the topos' fictionalising function is interrogated within practical Athenian rhetorical discourse itself.[73] In the second speech *Against Boeotus*, Demosthenes' client Mantitheus issues this warning concerning the rhetorical tactics of his opponent:

And he is such a criminal that, if he has no witnesses to prove a fact, he will say that it is well known to you, men of the jury. This is something which is done by all those who do not have a clean argument. If he should try any such device (*technazēi*), do not tolerate it; expose him. What anyone of you does not know, let him assume that his neighbour does not know it either. Let him demand that Boeotus prove clearly whatever statements he may make, and not run away from the truth by declaring that you know things about which he will have no just argument to advance; since I, for my part, men of the jury, although you all know the way in which my father was compelled to adopt these men, am none the less suing them at law, and have brought forward witnesses responsible for their testimony. (Demosthenes 40.53–4)

---

[68] See Ober (1989)147–9 for discussion and examples. The most interesting creative expansion of the 'as you all know' topos has to be Aeschin. 1.127–30. For this appeal to *phēmē* see the discussion of Ford (1999).

[69] See above nn. 57 and 58.

[70] On the orators use of 'as you all know' for history see Pearson (1941); Perlman (1961); Nouhaud (1982). On orators using the topos to introduce citations and references to drama and poetry, see North (1952); Perlman (1964); Ober and Strauss (1990) 250–5.

[71] Arist. *Rh.* 3.1408a32–6. Ober (1989) 149 connects this interpretation of the topos' manipulation of the masses with Hyp. 4.22 where the orator claims that even children know which of Athens' *rhētores* had taken bribes.

[72] Ober (1989) 150–1. On the question of whether the notion of Athens as a 'face-to-face' society was reality or ideality see above n. 57.

[73] See, however, Dorjahn (1935) 291 who gives a passing reference to my passage as evidence that the 'as you all know' topos was 'finally turned into an abuse'.

Mantitheus anticipates Boeotus' possible use of the 'as you all know' topos and represents it as something crafted (*technazēi*) by all those who have nothing to say that is fair or sound. The topos is viewed in terms of a contrivance deployed by a non-specific mass of speakers who use it as a veil for 'reality'. The speaker explicitly connects his opponent with 'the many' who use the topos and describes his opponent's likely deployment of it as a method of 'running away from the truth' (*apodidraskein tēn alētheian*). Mantitheus associates the topos with the failure to provide supporting witnesses. As with Demosthenes' depiction of Aeschines' histrionic rhetoric an opponent's rhetoric is marked as deceptive through its representation as a substitution for the provision of testimony.[74] In this instance, however, a specific strategy is being dismantled.

Furthermore, Mantitheus does not simply gloss the 'as you all know' topos as a cover for the presentation of unsubstantiated lies as common facts; he offers a methodology to the audience for interpreting the legitimacy of any occurrence of information represented as common knowledge. He asks each jury-member to consider whether Boeotus' 'commonly knowns' are known to him personally. If they are not, the juror is to assume that his ignorance is not private to himself but shared by the rest of the jury and therefore deduce that the 'as you all know topos' has been used to present a fiction or an unsubstantiated claim in terms of a common rumour which is actually non-existent. In asking the jurors to infer from their own ignorance to that of their fellow judges, the speaker attempts to demolish any possibility that an individual will not be party to a body of communally held knowledge. He therefore takes advantage of a democratic notion that common report is necessarily defined as knowledge held by *all* individuals in the polis without any exception. This passage could be read as a deliberate playing off between a social reality on the one hand and an ideality on the other. If it was actually possible, at polis level, for a citizen not to be party to a particular item of *phēmē*, then Mantitheus destroys that possibility by introducing the ideal conception of *phēmē* as something which has to be known by absolutely everyone for it to count as forensically and civically legitimate; 'real' *phēmē* as opposed to Boeotus' plans for a topologically contrived *phēmē*.[75]

---

[74] See Dem. 19.120 where he suggests that Aeschines' rhetorical and theatrical skill can render the need for witnesses redundant and, by implication, can be effective in masking the fact that he has no witnesses.

[75] See above n. 57 on the likelihood that not everybody was party to a particular item of *phēmē*.

Mantitheus' meta-discursive interrogation of the 'as you all know' topos can be compared instructively with Andocides' summing up of a defensive account of his part (or lack of it) in the profanation of the Mysteries in 415 BC. In his speech *On The Mysteries*, which was delivered in 399, Andocides rounds off his long narrative of events that occurred some sixteen years previously with this request: 'Gentlemen, recollect as to the truth of my words and those of you who know must teach the rest who do not' (Andocides 1. 69). In this instance the speaker is unafraid to admit that not everyone will know his story of events that occurred some years before. He actually instructs those jurors who know and remember to inform those who do not. He still adheres to the spirit of the 'as you all know' topos, because he constructs an image of a group of cognoscenti, implying that there are younger jurors who would not have been old enough in 415 to know details of the events in question. But he is careful to take the diverse competence of his audience into account and as such, provides an example of the way in which orators did not always simply repeat topoi or feel a necessity to play along with the 'dramatic fictions' which they both reflected and reproduced.

Mantitheus' deconstruction of the 'as you all know' topos is explicitly characterised as an anticipation of his opponent's arguments. Lysias varies this strategy of anticipation in *Against Eratosthenes*. He is accusing Eratosthenes of having been a member of the Thirty and being responsible for the execution of his brother Polemarchus. Lysias argues that there are certain arguments which are not available to Eratosthenes:

And note that he cannot even resort to the expedient, so habitual (*eithismenon*) in this polis, of saying nothing in answer to the accusations but making other statements about oneself which at times deceive you; they represent to you that they are good soldiers, or have taken many of the enemy's ships while in command of triremes, or have won over cities from hostility to friendship. Why, only tell him to show where they killed as many of our enemies as they have our citizens, or where they took as many ships as they themselves surrendered, or what city they won over to compare with yours which they enslaved. (Lysias 12.38–9)

Here, Lysias foregrounds the various topoi whereby elite litigants demonstrate that they have performed valuable military and diplomatic services for the state.[76] These commonplaces have often deceived the

---

[76] For examples of such topoi, and valuable discussion, see Ober (1989) 226–47.

demos. He does not say that Eratosthenes *will* attempt to rehearse such topoi: Lysias' point is that these strategies are simply not open to a member of the Thirty. By focusing on the commonplaces which elite speakers use to deceptively promote their patriotic character, Lysias encourages his audience to be suspicious of any attempt by Eratosthenes to use such commonplaces. But he also frames any recourse to these commonplaces as an absurdity in Eratosthenes' case. It is as if Eratosthenes' crimes are so blatant and heinous that rhetorical topoi cannot perform their usual role of misleading a jury. Here, the 'rhetoric of anti-rhetoric' serves to highlight Eratosthenes' exceptional villainy: his actions are so beyond the pale that the formal and habitual language of rhetorical self-defence and misrepresentation is useless to him.

Lysias attacks his opponent on the grounds that his past behaviour is not amenable to the norms of rhetorical deception. If rhetorical topoi constituted certain fictions of innocence, inexperience, public duty, and democratic character, it was sometimes advantageous for speakers to stage an exposure of such fictions (to show *how* an opponent was using established rhetorical elements to deceive) as part of their *own* self-representing strategy.

Deceptive *mimēsis*: 'lie detection' in Aeschines and Demosthenes

The orators seem to have developed *creative* strategies which mobilised a self-consciousness concerning the rhetorical exchanges in which they participated. This staged awareness of public rhetoric's power to use deceitful and artful techniques which were so self-disguising or commonplace that they could slip past a jury unnoticed, is well illustrated in the four speeches which represent the clash between Aeschines and Demosthenes concerning an embassy to Philip and the crowning of Demosthenes.

In his defence speech *On the Embassy*, Aeschines complains about his involvement with Demosthenes: 'In public affairs, I have become excessively entangled with a *goēs* and a villain who cannot even say something true by accident' (συμπέπλεγμαι δ᾽ ἐν τῇ πολιτείᾳ καθ᾽ ὑπερβολὴν ἀνθρώπῳ γόητι καὶ πονηρῷ, ὃς οὐδ᾽ ἂν ἄκων ἀληθὲς οὐδὲν εἴποι: 2.153). He claims that Demosthenes starts his lies by swearing oaths (using his 'shameless' eyes as well as words) and then not only presents things that never happened as facts, but even tells of the day on which they occurred. He 'fabricates' the name of someone who was supposed to be there (τινος ὄνομα πλασάμενος). Aeschines describes his opponent's 'precision-lying' as 'imitating those who speak the truth' (*mimoumenos tous talēthē legontas*: 153)

This formulation of Demosthenes' deceit as a *mimēsis* of those who speak *alētheia* is peculiar to Aeschines. He expands this character-isation of Demosthenes' lies in his later speech *Against Ctesiphon*. The main focus of this oration is the past political conduct of Demosthenes and the inappropriateness of his receiving a crown or any other public honours. As part of his narrative on his opponent's career, Aeschines describes the guarantees and promises that Demosthenes made in the spring of 340 concerning the securing of allies and troops in prepara-tion for a campaign against Philip (3.97–8). He details the very specific nature of Demosthenes' statements; he apparently claimed that all of the Peloponnesians could be counted on, and that he had brought all the Acarnanians into line. He told the *ecclēsia* that there was enough money contributed to provide for the manning of one hundred swift ships, ten thousand foot-soldiers and a thousand cavalry. He even provided a date for the completion of these and other specific military arrangements (98). Having outlined the specific nature and fine detail of Demosthenes' claims, Aeschines goes on to give the following assessment:

> For this is his own personal (*idion*) and uncommon (*ou koinon*) way of doing things. Other charlatans (*alazones*), when they are lying, try to speak in vague and unclear terms (*aorista kai asaphē*), afraid of being convicted. But De-mosthenes, when he is cheating you (*alazoneuētai*), first lies with an oath, call-ing down destruction on himself; and secondly, predicting an event that he knows will never happen, he dares to tell the date of it. And he dares to tell the names of men, when he has never so much as seen their faces, stealing your hearing and imitating men who tell the truth (*mimoumenos tous talēthē legontas*). And this is another reason for hating him, that he is not only a villain (*ponēros*) himself, but destroys even the signs of honesty (*tōn chrēstōn sēmeia diaphtheirei*). (Aeschines 3.98–9)[77]

David Harvey cites Aeschines' observation to support his argument that the orators often use vague and ambiguous terms which might (or might not) connote bribery, in the course of their verbal assassinations

---

[77] καὶ γὰρ τοῦτο ἄνθρωπος ἴδιον καὶ οὐ κοινὸν ποιεῖ. οἱ μὲν γὰρ ἄλλοι ἀλαζόνες, ὅταν τι ψεύδωνται, ἀόριστα καὶ ἀσαφῆ πειρῶνται λέγειν, φοβούμενοι τὸν ἔλεγχον· Δημοσθένης δ' ὅταν ἀλαζονεύηται, πρῶτον μὲν μεθ' ὅρκου ψεύδεται, ἐξώλειαν ἐπαρώμενος ἑαυτῷ, δεύ-τερον δέ, ἃ εὖ οἶδεν οὐδέποτε ἐσόμενα, τολμᾷ λέγειν εἰς ὁπότ' ἔσται, καὶ ὧν τὰ σώματα οὐχ ἑώρακε, τούτων τὰ ὀνόματα λέγει, κλέπτων τὴν ἀκρόασιν καὶ μιμούμενος τοὺς τἀληθῆ λέγοντας. διὸ καὶ σφόδρα ἄξιός ἐστι μισεῖσθαι, ὅτι πονηρὸς ὢν καὶ τὰ τῶν χρηστῶν σημεῖα διαφθείρει.

of legal and political opponents.[78] In his *Rhetoric* Aristotle counsels that the orator avoid the use of ambiguity (*amphibolē*) unless he intends to mislead.[79]

But Aeschines' discussion of deceptive ambiguity is much more than a useful commentary on standard Athenian techniques of rhetorical misrepresentation. It is introduced as a foil to Demosthenes' radically contrasting and unique style of deception. Demosthenes' lies are characterised here as 'uncommon' and individual, marking their transgressive quality and their incompatibility with the 'normal' behaviour of Athenian speakers. Aeschines significantly characterises the *mimetic* mode as exceptionally unusual and transgressive. Demosthenes is described as actually robbing the audience of their hearing (κλέπτων τὴν ἀκρόασιν) with his truthful-sounding discourse. Furthermore, such perverse and peculiar oratorical piracy must brand Demosthenes as doubly disgraceful. For Demosthenes' behaviour has done more than mark him as a *poneros* and a liar. The employment of a mimetic mode of deception has the more far-reaching consequence of destroying the integrity of the signs (*sēmeia*) by which good and honest people or things (*hoi chrēstoi*) are to be unequivocally identified. The words and phrases of orators who hide behind ambiguities are characterised as signalling their own deceptive quality. Ambiguity and vagueness actually offer a signpost to an audience that lies are being told. According to Aeschines, then, the ambiguous form of speech employed by the average *alazōn* is self-exposing. But Demosthenes has a far more dangerous method of telling lies because they imitate the signs of truth so accurately.[80]

---

[78] Harvey (1985) 79: 'The Attic orators, then, may be deceptively vague: liars generally use undefined and unclear words as Aeschines points out ... and he should know.'

[79] See Arist. *Rh.* 3.1407a32–4: 'thirdly, avoid ambiguous terms, unless you deliberately intend the opposite, like those who, having nothing to say, yet pretend to say something' (τρίτον, μὴ ἀμφιβόλοις · ταῦτα δέ, ἂν μὴ τἀναντία προαιρῆται. ὅπερ ποιοῦσιν ὅταν μηδὲν μὲν ἔχωσι λέγειν, προσποιῶνται δέ τι λέγειν). See also 3.1407b1–6 where Aristotle explains why prophets and soothsayers use vague and ambiguous expressions: 'And as there is less chance of making a mistake when speaking generally, diviners express themselves in general terms on the question of fact; for in playing odd or even, one is more likely to be right if he says "even" or "odd" than if he gives a specific number, and similarly one who says "it will be" than if he says "when." This is why soothsayers do not further define the exact time. All such ambiguities are alike, wherefore they should be avoided, except for some such reason.' See Garver (1994) 153.

[80] It is interesting to note in passing that the rhetorical theorist Hermogenes also emphasised that Demosthenes' rhetorical style was geared towards creating an enhanced impression of veracity (*alētheia*), sincerity and clarity. See Wooten (1989) for references and discussion.

Earlier in this speech, Aeschines has deployed a series of arguments which elucidate the alleged illegality of Ctesiphon's proposal to crown Demosthenes at the City Dionysia for services rendered to the state. In accordance with the thrust of the opening remarks of his speech, Aeschines claims that the laws relevant to public crownings are coherent and he emphasises that they were specifically drawn up as safeguards against the abuse or compromise of the Athenian political and juridical processes. Aside from the question of whether or not Demosthenes was worthy of such public honours, Aeschines sets out to show that Ctesiphon has flouted a law which was designed to ensure the absolute accountability of public officials to the demos. He starts with an account of the 'bad old days' when certain men who held the highest offices in government and administered the state's finances would devise a clever ruse to ensure that they avoided prosecution for acts of bribery and corruption they had committed (3.9–11). Long before they submitted to their public accounting (*euthunē*), they would buy the services of *rhētores* in the *boulē* and the *ecclēsia*. These speakers would introduce many votes of thanks and proclamations in praise of the officials such that 'when the time came for them to render their account, those who had charges to prefer fell into very great embarrassment, and this was even more the case with the jurors' (9–10).[81] Many who were found to have stolen public funds during their *euthunai* nevertheless went from the courtroom acquitted. Aeschines explains that the jurors were ashamed to see the same man in the same city proclaimed and crowned on one day and then convicted of theft a little later. They were forced to acquit the men in question in order to avert the shame of the demos.

Aeschines goes on to argue that 'some lawmaker' (νομοθέτης τις) remedied this situation by passing a law which forbade the crowning of any man who had not yet passed his final *euthunai*. 'And yet', he continues, 'in spite of this wise provision of the framer of the law, forms of statement have been invented which circumvent the laws; and unless you are warned of them you will be taken unawares and deceived' (11).[82] Aeschines literally says that *logoi* which are stronger (*kreittones logoi*) than the laws have been found, and in using such phraseology he perhaps wishes to associate the authors of these deceptive arguments

---

[81] ὥστ' ἐν ταῖς εὐθύναις εἰς τὴν μεγίστην μὲν ἀπορίαν ἀφικνεῖσθαι τοὺς κατηγόρους, πολὺ δὲ ἔτι μᾶλλον τοὺς δικαστάς.

[82] καὶ ταῦτα οὕτως εὖ προκατειληφότος τοῦ νομοθέτου, εὕρηνται κρείττονες λόγοι τῶν νόμων, οὓς εἰ μή τις ὑμῖν ἐρεῖ, λήσετε ἐξαπατηθέντες.

with a sophistic training in relativistic argument.[83] In representing those who employ *logos* to circumvent *nomos* in such a way as to connote sophistry, Aeschines prepares the jury for the pejorative assessments of Demosthenes as a *sophistēs* and a *goēs* which he puts forward later in the speech.[84] But if these men who employ powerful *logoi* to pass illegal proposals are like sophists, Aeschines goes on to point out that they do at least display a sense of shame and he hints that the form of their proposals signify a level of political and ethical propriety:

For among those men who illegally crown officers who have not yet submitted their accounts, some, who are by nature moderate (*phusei metrioi*) – if anyone is really moderate who proposes illegal measures – at any rate some do try to cloak their shame (*tēs aischunēs*); for they add to their decrees the proviso that the man who is subject to audit shall be crowned 'after he shall have rendered account and submitted to audit of his office'. The injury to the polis is the same, for the hearings for accounting are prejudiced by previous praises and crowns. But the man who makes the motion does show (*endeiknutai*) to his hearers that while he has made an illegal motion, he is ashamed of the wrong he has done. But Ctesiphon, fellow citizens, overleaping the law that governs those who are subject to audit, and not deigning to resort to the pretext of which I have just spoken, has moved that before the accounting, you crown Demosthenes in the midst of his term of office. (Aeschines 3.11–12)[85]

Having set up this picture of certain men who deceptively argue for illegal crowning proposals and pay lip service to the prohibitions of the law in the forms of their statements, Aeschines immediately declares

---

[83] Protagoras was notorious for supposedly teaching people how to make the 'weaker' argument into the 'stronger' argument. See Kerferd (1981a) 100–10 and Arist. *Rh.* 2.1402a5–28 on false enthymemes of probability, esp. 22–5: 'And this is what 'making the worse appear the better argument' means (καὶ τὸ τὸν ἥττω δὲ λόγον κρείττω ποιεῖν τοῦτ' ἐστίν). Wherefore men were justly disgusted with the promise of Protagoras. For it is a lie (ψεῦδός τε γάρ ἐστίν), and is not true (οὐκ ἀληθές) but apparent probability (ἀλλὰ φαινόμενον εἰκός), not found in any *technē* except rhetoric and eristic (καὶ ἐν οὐδεμιᾷ τέχνῃ ἀλλ' ἐν ῥητορικῇ καὶ ἐριστικῇ). See also Ar. *Nub.* 112–18 where Strepsiades describes the *phrontistērion* as the place where they keep the *kreittōn logos* and the *hēttōn logos* not to mention the parodic contest between these two personified *logoi* at 888f. Kerferd (101) regards these as parodies of Protagorean doctrine.

[84] See above n. 33.

[85] τούτων γὰρ τῶν τοὺς ὑπευθύνους στεφανούντων παρὰ τοὺς νόμους οἱ μὲν φύσει μέτριοί εἰσιν, εἰ δή τις ἐστὶ μέτριος τῶν τὰ παράνομα γραφόντων, ἀλλ' οὖν προβάλλονταί γέ τι πρὸ τῆς αἰσχύνης. προσγράφουσι γὰρ πρὸς τὰ ψηφίσματα στεφανοῦν τὸν ὑπεύθυνον 'ἐπειδὰν λόγον καὶ εὐθύνας τῆς ἀρχῆς δῷ'. καὶ ἡ μὲν πόλις τὸ ἴσον ἀδίκημα ἀδικεῖται· προκαταλαμβάνονται γὰρ ἐπαίνοις καὶ στεφάνοις αἱ εὔθυναι· ὁ δὲ τὸ ψήφισμα γράφων ἐνδείκνυται τοῖς ἀκούουσιν, ὅτι γέγραφε μὲν παράνομα, αἰσχύνεται δὲ ἐφ' οἷς ἡμάρτηκε. Κτησιφῶν δέ, ὦ ἄνδρες Ἀθηναῖοι, ὑπερπηδήσας τὸν νόμον τὸν περὶ τῶν ὑπευθύνων κείμενον, καὶ τὴν πρόφασιν ἣν ἀρτίως προεῖπον ὑμῖν ἀνελών, πρὶν λόγον πρὶν εὐθύνας δοῦναι γέγραφε μεταξὺ Δημοσθένην ἄρχοντα στεφανοῦν.

that Ctesiphon has not even used these forms of pretext; he has not twisted the law or compromised with its wording as others have done. Rather, he has completely overleapt the law (ὑπερπηδήσας τὸν νόμον).

The immediate implication of this contrast between those who twist the law on the one hand, and the individual Ctesiphon who completely flouts it on the other, is ethical and political in tone. The former group still feel their actions constrained by a *metrios phusis* and a characteristically Athenian sense of *aischunē*. These political and ethical qualities are what prevent them from proposing a wholesale violation of the law. By contrast, Ctesiphon's proposal is represented as a complete break with established legislation. Aeschines thereby implies that Ctesiphon's approach displays none of the traces of moderation and shame which could be found in the 'half-way house' deceptions deployed by the other proposers. He is thus represented as completely lacking these two central ethical and political qualities.

Ctesiphon's proposal sets him apart, not only from the law-abiding community *per se* but even from a constructed group of speakers who edge around the law with their rhetoric; the proviso in *their* proposals acknowledges and negotiates the text of the law. Ctesiphon has acted as if the text of the law did not exist. He is thereby made to look far worse than the average proposer of illegal motions. But Aeschines is also at pains to emphasise that the 'usual' articulation of the proviso *shows* something to the audience. Despite his initial warning that these new forms of statement might deceive the listener into overlooking their illegality, he seems now to be maintaining that such provisos actually *signify* an illegality and a sense of concomitant shame. *These* forms of proposal draw attention to their own distorted quality. They mark themselves as transgressive by signposting their difference to cited law. They are deceptive proposals, and yet markedly so. It is this markedness which, according to Aeschines at least, makes them prone to identification as distortions. By contrast, Ctesiphon does not mark his trick as a trick in the customary manner.

In Demosthenes' speech *On the False Embassy*, the orator makes a characteristic statement of his own patriotic opposition to the supposedly corrupt 'faction' of Aeschines (19.207–10). He claims that at every *ecclēsia* whenever there is any discussion of this faction and its activities, the demos hears Demosthenes denouncing and incriminating these men, and declaring roundly that they have been taking bribes and making traffic of all the interests of the polis (207). Demosthenes points out that these declarations are met by an incriminating silence from those he accuses:

And none of them ever contradicts me, or opens his mouth or lets himself be seen. How is it, then, that the most impudent men in the polis, and the loudest speakers, are overborne by me, the most timid man, who can speak no louder than another? Because truth is strong (*talēthes ischuron*), and consciousness of corruption is weak (*asthenes*). This paralyses their audacity. This cripples their tongues, closes their mouths, stifles them, puts them to silence. (Demosthenes 19.207–8)[86]

Demosthenes does not make a distinction between 'ordinary' and *extra*ordinary mimetic forms of deception here, but his discussion of conscience does articulate and expand on the same basic assumption as that found in Aeschines: in normal circumstances, you can detect a liar from the *way* he speaks and reacts. Truth, argues Demosthenes, has a strength which sustains those who speak it (ὅτι τἀληθὲς ἰσχυρόν). But the consciousness that one has uttered the opposite of truth necessarily engenders a weakness. Demosthenes implies that the corrupt deceiver's weakness can stifle speech altogether. The metaphors of physical constraint on the mouth and tongue portray the conscience of the liar as inducing a kind of aphasia whenever a full and strong response is to be expected. Demosthenes goes on to detail a specific instance of this in the response of Aeschines after his exclusion from an embassy. Aeschines' conscience supposedly reduces him to the briefest of accusations, to inaudibility, to threats and slanders (209–10). The inherent weakness of the liar destroys the possibility of lengthy proofs or arguments. Demosthenes is careful not to impute to Aeschines any sense of shame at his acts of corruption and deceit. But his attack definitely articulates the idea that a deceptive orator's self-awareness causes his speech to be markedly distinct in form from that of a truthful speaker.

It is precisely this idea that we see Aeschines adopting in his description of *kreittones logoi* and the ambiguous or vague speech of most deceptive orators in his speech *Against Ctesiphon*. Vestiges of shame and moderation cause the authors of the *kreittones logoi* to display their deviance *from* the law by partially citing the law. And other orators' consciousness of their own culpability causes them to moderate and yet draw attention to their lies through techniques of vagueness, ambiguity and indirect insinuation. For the attentive listener, the deceptive

---

[86] καὶ τούτων οὐδεὶς πώποτ' ἀκούων ταῦτ' ἀντεῖπεν οὐδὲ διῆρε τὸ στόμα, οὐδ' ἔδειξεν ἑαυτόν. τί ποτ' οὖν ἐστι τὸ αἴτιον ὅτι βδελυρώτατοι τῶν ἐν τῇ πόλει καὶ μέγιστον φθεγγόμενοι τοῦ καὶ ἀτολμοτάτου πάντων ἐμοῦ καὶ οὐδενὸς μεῖζον φθεγγομένου τοσοῦτον ἡττῶνται; ὅτι τἀληθὲς ἰσχυρόν, καὶ τοὐναντίον ἀσθενὲς τὸ συνειδέναι πεπρακόσιν αὐτοῖς τὰ πράγματα. τοῦτο παραιρεῖται τὴν θρασύτητα τὴν τούτων, τοῦτ' ἀποστρέφει τὴν γλῶτταν, ἐμφράττει τὸ στόμα, ἄγχει, σιωπᾶν ποιεῖ.

speech signals itself and the formal elements that give rise to such a signalling are notably absent from the speech of the truth-teller. Only the mimetically deceptive speeches of Demosthenes provide an exception to this rule, and therein, argues Aeschines, lies their danger. According to Demosthenes, the speech of those who are consciously corrupt and deceitful is similarly distinctive in form; conscience produces weak, feint, elliptical expression. Thus the weak speech of the liar is easy to spot and directly contrasts with the 'strong' speech of the truth-teller. Ctesiphon is not attacked for *mimēsis* as Demosthenes is, but Aeschines' inscription of two levels of deceit (the detectable, and the undetectable) is striking. Clearly, Aeschines authorises himself here as a *rhētōr* who can act as a watchdog for, and educator of the demos – a common strategy in extant oratory, and particularly so in the legal/political battles between Aeschines and Demosthenes which engage with policy towards Macedonia.[87] He offers his juries a methodology for detecting 'normal' liars at the same time as he stages an analysis of exceptionally dangerous 'super-liars'.

Doubtless, Aeschines' isolation of Demosthenes as a 'mimetic' liar is a countering ploy to deflect Demosthenes' meta-discursive attacks on his own previous career as an actor and the vocal, imitative and gestural skills which he brings into the *ecclēsia* and the courtroom.[88] But the explicit characterisations of Demosthenes' lying *mimēsis* also constitute two moments where a meta-discourse on the relationship between rhetoric, representation (of truth or lies) and imitation which occurs in the works of Plato and Isocrates finds an (albeit limited and crude) expression in practical rhetoric itself.[89] Here, as with the other anti-rhetorical arguments which I have discussed (the vignettes of sophistry, the deployment of physiognomics, the deconstruction of

[87] For the self-representation as 'watchdog' and 'educator' see Kennedy (1963) 239; Pearson (1976) 198; Montgomery (1983) 58–60; Ober (1989) 182ff. For a good account of political in-fighting in relation to Athens' attitude towards Macedonia see Montgomery (1983), especially 68–94 on Aeschines' political and legal battles with Demosthenes and their cultural, institutional and historical context.

[88] See above p. 207 for references and bibiography. See also Hall (1995).

[89] At Pl. *Grg.* 501d1–502d8 Socrates describes poetry as rhetoric with metre and rhythm. At. Pl. *Resp.* 3.393b1–c11 Socrates regards poetry's *mimēsis* as dangerous because of its capacity to pass off falsehood as truths. At Pl. *Resp.* 10.596d1 an imaginary craftsman who can make perfect copies of objects is described as 'a most amazing sophist' and this kind of imitation is described in terms of *apatē and goēteia* at 10.598c1–d6. See Murray (1996) 200–1. At Pl. *Soph.* 233e–235a the sophist is compared to the painter. On Plato's theories of *mimēsis* see Ferrari (1989) 114–18; Murray (1996) 3–6, 168–82, 237–8. On the use of the term in the fifth century see Else (1958). For Isocrates' discussions and valorisation of *mimēsis* as a tool in rhetorical pedagogy see Too (1995) 184–94.

'topology' . . .), the democratic orator can be seen to represent himself as a 'master of truth' through the antagonistic theorisation of the opponent as a master of lies. In many cases the opponent is represented as a technician of rhetoric: public and persuasive speech is figured as the product of sophistic pedagogy or as infected with dissembling commonplaces. But Demosthenes' deceptive 'wizardry' makes him capable of a *technē* which conceals itself. The resources of *mimēsis* make his lies indistinguishable from the truth. Both Aeschines and Demosthenes argue that lies *can* often be detected in the lawcourts or the *ecclēsia*: vagueness, ambiguity, a feint voice, and silence all signal deceit. The truth is strong but lies are weak and riddled with shameful equivocation. And yet there are those deceptions (Stephanus' physiognomic *sōphrosunē*, Demosthenes' *mimēsis*) which are undetectable without special knowledge of the individual who perpetrates them.

The orators' rich taxonomy of detectable and undetectable lies, their strategic portraits of sophistic deception, physiognomic trickery and topological beguilement constitute a significant episode for our understanding of how and why the notion of 'rhetoric' has had such a negative reception in western political thought and practice. It may be that some of the orators' attacks on rhetorical deception are directly influenced by Plato's anti-rhetoric.[90] For my inquiry such questions of influence are not particularly important. What *is* important, however, is the fact that *democratic* discourse entertained the 'rhetoric of anti-rhetoric'. The idea of a distinctive specialised and formal 'rhetorical' discourse may be the product of democracy and an ideology of 'free speech', but the ensuing *evaluation* of that discourse *within* the democracy's culture and institutions is decidedly negative: rhetoric is always likely to be the handmaiden of the kind of deception which is inimical to the health of the polis. In this sense, Athenian democratic speech 'theorises' the deceptive powers of contemporary rhetoric in a similar fashion to Plato's and Aristotle's (differing) critiques. In Detienne's terms, democratic culture inhabits the realm of *doxa/apatē* and the realm of *alētheia* at the same time: this culture relies on the efficacious, antagonistic world-view of the sophist (there are two sides to every story and the trick must work on the *doxa* of your audience more successfully than your opponent). But the *representation* which the orator actually produces in the exercise of the democratic *agōn* is very much in line with the 'philosophico-religious' logic of contradiction:

---

[90] For the difficult question of the extent to which Platonic ideas can be shown to inform fourth-century oratory, see the comments and bibliography of Ober (1998) 369–70.

truth must be praised, nurtured and opposed to deception. Only very rarely (as we saw in the last chapter) could the orator endorse a 'true lie'. The democratic orator's valorisation of truth is hardly surprising, but the way in which he exposes a deliberate falsehood (lurking beneath the disguise of a sophistic flourish, or a reassuringly familiar topos, or a respectable *schēma*, or the *mimēsis* of precision and accuracy) demonstrates that the opening fanfare for the anti-rhetorical tradition cannot simply be attributed to the antidemocratic thought of Plato. Contrary to the polemic of Popper and Vickers, the first democracy quickly became rhetoric's critic.

As spaces for the contest and performance of *logoi*, Athens' lawcourts provoke strategic constructions of, confrontations with and 'solutions' to what Detienne calls 'the ambiguity of speech'. A fragment of the orator Hyperides articulates this 'ambiguity' and the anxiety it generates: 'There is no stamp of men's intention on their face' (*charaktēr oudeis epestin epi tou prosōpou tēs dianoias tois anthrōpois*: fr. 226). With its stress on the absence of an external marking (*charaktēr*) for determining inner disposition, this dislocated phrase reads like a gnomic warning from the *Theognidea* and even more like the many reflections on the impossibility of detecting lies and 'true' character from words and external appearances which we find in Euripidean tragedy.[91] As we saw in the last chapter, Demosthenes represents the dangers of deceit's undetectability as peculiarly threatening to democracy: 'for in a political system based on speeches, how can it be safely administered if the speeches are not true?' (19.184). For the orators, the threat of deception is a fundamental stumbling-block for the conduct of democracy which they must constantly address and resolve in their own favour.

The need for the democratic speaker to disambiguate speech, to stamp himself as honest and his opponent as a liar, gives rise to a proliferation of meta-discursive strategies which invoke the manifold possibilities and techniques of deception. Some of these strategies are frequent and standardised enough to be called topoi. Others are commonplaces with unique and creative descriptions coming out of them. Others still are highly original for the extant corpus. It may be no accident that many of the exceptional strategies which I have described are deployed against citizens whom we could not class as *rhētores*. Stephanus and Boeotus are not recognisable or plausible as 'professional' technicians of deceit and it is therefore important that their dishonesty

---

[91] See Thgn. 119–28; Eur. *El.* 367f., *Hipp.* 927f. At Eur. *Med.* 515–19 the heroine asks Zeus why he has not offered a clear *charaktēr* on the human body which would be a mark of counterfeit virtue. On these texts see below, pp. 277–89.

be constituted by distinctive strategies rather than conformity to 'types' of deceptive performer.

The agonistic nature of democratic public discourse generated its own 'theory' of (mis)representation and performance. The orators assess the recently formed *technai* of rhetorical pedagogy and consultancy in political theoretical terms and find them to be inappropriate to 'democratic' performance. They warn of speech's 'ambiguity' and at the same time offer (albeit self-interested) reflections on the ways in which deceptive communication (whether verbal or physical) should be detected, policed and classified. As we will see in my final chapter, fifth-century dramatists and historians highlighted the dangers and opportunities which rhetorical performance and 'the ambiguity of speech' presented.[92] In the fourth century, the orators seem to sustain and develop this atmosphere of self-consciousness and suspicion amongst their audience. Undoubtedly they did so to compete, curry favour and fulfil democracy's ideological requirements. But in doing so they also kept the demos aware of the ways in which dissembling and manipulative performances throughout the various spaces of the city could rob them of their apparent sovereignty. In this sense, 'the rhetoric of anti-rhetoric' was more than a *strategic* meta-discourse. It was a meta-discourse which heightened mass vigilance and suspicion over the very individuals who used it as rhetorical strategy. When British Conservatives accuse Labour of 'spin', they are in a glass house throwing stones. But instead of falsely blaming America for inventing 'spin', British citizens should perhaps thank American journalists for first identifying its performances and subjecting them to surveillance.

[92] Most recently, Halliwell (1997) stresses that tragedy engages with rhetoric's powers and perils, rather than simply harnessing its new formulae and strategies as creative resources.

5   Thinking with the rhetoric of anti-rhetoric

Fuck all this lying look what I'm really trying to write about is writing not all this stuff.[1]

> The rhetorician would deceive his neighbours,
> The sentimentalist himself; while art
> Is but a vision of reality.[2]

The study of how to uncover deceptions is also by and large the study of how to build up fabrications ... one can learn how one's sense of ordinary reality is produced by examining something that is easier to become conscious of, namely, how reality is mimicked and/or how it is faked.[3]

Primary Colors: metafiction and metarhetoric

One of the interesting features of modern literary fiction is its propensity for self-consciousness – critics call this 'metafiction'. Such self-consciousness is hardly new: Homer's *Odyssey* contains many representations of song and story-telling which make it a self-reflexive epic. But the modern metafictional novel is often an explicit departure from the 'classic realism' of nineteenth-century fiction. Modern novelists like to make you aware that they are *not* representing reality or 'truth'. Their metafiction sometimes comes close to the old tenets of so-called 'Romantic Irony': reality is beyond theirs or anybody's representation.[4] They can also evoke the Shakespearean suggestion that 'all the world's a stage': social life involves the adoption and discarding of quasi-theatrical roles, the manipulation of one's self-representation according to context, the realisation that cherished realities are in fact illusions or illusions in fact. Patricia Waugh offers a succinct appraisal of the effects of

---

[1] B. S. Johnson (1964) *Albert Angelo* 163.
[2] W. B. Yeats (1917) 'Dominus Tuus'.
[3] Goffman (1974) 151.
[4] For the link between postmodernism and Romantic Irony, with good bibliography and application to ancient texts, see Fowler (1994).

metafiction in relation to John Fowles' (highly metafictional) novel *The French Lieutenant's Woman*:

... it can be argued that metafictional novels simultaneously strengthen each reader's sense of an everyday real world while problematizing his or her sense of reality from a conceptual or philosophical point of view. As a consequence of their metafictional undermining of the conventional basis of existence, the reader may revise his or her ideas about the philosophical status of what is assumed to be reality, but he or she will presumably continue to believe and live in a world for the most part constructed out of 'common sense' and routine. What writers like Fowles are hoping is that each reader does this with a new awareness of how the meanings and values of that world have been constructed and how, therefore, they can be challenged or changed.[5]

There are some novels which use 'metafiction' to focus on the ways in which specifically 'political' realities, meanings and values are 'constructed'. *Primary Colors* is a fine example, though its explicit metafictional frame is only a brief prefatory note. The novel reads as an insider's documentary on Bill Clinton's campaign to become the Democratic presidential candidate: its central characters Jack Stanton and his wife Susan are obviously Bill and Hillary Clinton. Nevertheless, the anonymous author's note at the beginning of the novel claims that (apart from a few 'cameos' by real and well-known journalists) the book 'is a work of fiction and the usual rules apply. None of the characters are real. None of these events ever happened'. This is a common novelistic strategy, and the reader is not deterred from an inference that this must be a first-hand account of the Clinton campaign. At the same time as the reader makes this inference, however, she is always wondering whether this account is historically or factually accurate. Anyone who followed the Clinton campaign closely might be able to identify events which definitely did not happen or were not reported, but the novel's focus on secret and 'behind-the-scenes' discussions and practices in the Stanton camp makes it difficult to know how far our insider-narrator ('Henry') is making things up. How much of this story is 'fiction' and how much 'reality'? How far is the prefatory note to be taken at 'face value'? Furthermore, the novel stages debates between Jack, Susan, their aides and their spin-doctors which reveal that their world is fraught with conflicting representations both of fact and morality: the politics depicted in *Primary Colors* is crucially concerned with distinguishing between 'false' and 'genuine' character, truth and lies, decent and indecent strategy, appearance and reality. In the middle of his campaign, Stanton is accused by his political opponents of having

[5] Waugh (1984) 33–4.

an affair with his wife's hairdresser. The affair was real but the evidence put forward by his opponents is fabricated. They produce a 'taped phone conversation' between Stanton and the hairdresser. Henry realises that this conversation is a cleverly constructed collage of different 'bugged' telephone calls: innocent banter between himself and Stanton has been spliced with the hairdresser's voice in order to concoct the evidence they need. The Stanton camp bug and record the calls of a television news anchor in order to concoct a similarly false and incriminating conversation. One of Stanton's aides gets an on-air interview with the anchor and plays him the tape. This (diversionary) stunt demonstrates how easy it is to fabricate the relevant incriminating evidence: the truthful accusation against Stanton is thus substantially discredited.

Primary Colors is subtitled 'a novel of politics'. It paints the Stantons in a morally ambiguous light. Stanton is ambitious, ruthless, sexually promiscuous and ultimately prepared to 'play dirty' with his opponents and mislead his electorate. But he is also a man of ideas and conviction who convinces everyone around him that he is the 'genuine article' who really thinks and cares about 'the folks' of America. When Henry realises that his boss is far from perfect, he decides to leave the campaign. Stanton tries to keep Henry on board with the following speech:

Two thirds of what we do is reprehensible. This isn't the way a normal human being acts. We smile, we listen – you could grow calluses on your ears from all the listening we do. We do our pathetic little favors. We tell them what they want to hear – and when we tell them something they *don't* want to hear, it's usually because we've calculated that's what they really want. We live an eternity of false smiles – and why? Because it's the price you pay to lead. You don't think Abraham Lincoln was a whore before he was president? He had to tell his little stories and smile his shit-eating backcountry grin. He did it all just so he'd get the opportunity, one day, to stand in front of the nation and appeal to the 'better angels of our nature'. That's when the bullshit stops. And that's what this is all about . . . because you know as well as I do there are plenty of people in this game who never think about the folks, much less their 'better angels'. They just want to win.[6]

Henry subsequently tells us (on the book's last page) that Stanton could 'talk all he wanted about an eternity of "false" smiles: his power came from the exact opposite direction, from the *authenticity* of his appeal, from the stark ferocity of his hunger. There was very little artifice to him. He was truly needy. And now he truly needed me'. Thus *Primary Colors* presents the reader with an 'exposé' of the corruption,

---

[6] Anonymous (1996) 364.

trickery, manipulation and deceptive rhetoric which lie beneath the surface of American politics. But it also seeks (through the arguments of the Stantons) to pose the question of whether all of this really matters if the 'good guy' gains power. Further to this, the reader is left pondering Henry's description of the 'genuineness' of his boss. Stanton looks and sounds as though he 'really cares' but he is prepared to admit that his self-presentations in the campaign are disingenuous. And Henry talks in terms of the 'power' of his 'authenticity'. Stanton is good at being authentic and that opens up the possibility that his political sincerity is itself another ruse. Does he *really* care about the 'folks' or is he one of the 'bad' guys who only cares about winning? Stanton's moral and political ambiguity (real ideas or calculated sound-bites? conviction or empty ambition? noble liar or profound hypocrite?) even makes the reader wonder whether it makes sense to carve up political reality in terms of good and bad guys. Furthermore, the novel offers the reader a deeply personal and tragic dimension to the Stantons' ambiguity. When Jack and Susan show that they are prepared to dig up and publicise 'dirt' about their main rival's private life, their old friend and adviser, Libby, commits suicide. She ends her own life because she is so disappointed by their apparent moral hypocrisy and lack of integrity.

A final 'twist' of uncertainty generated by this novel derives from its brief prefatory note. For this creates a sense of oscillation between an eye-witness 'warts-and-all' account (which is evoked by the author's anonymity and the thinly-disguised name-changes) and the claim that the whole story is nothing more than a complete fiction. Perhaps this novel is a 'fabrication' in the same way that Stanton's camp splice and recontextualise real speech in order to (pretend to) make a false allegation. In this case, the novel is not so much an exposé of the 'truth' as another fabricated 'spin' on reality. If the Stantons are a 'cut and paste' image which is as distorted as those faked telephone conversations, then the novel's commentary on what real politicians and politics are like becomes suspect. But the metafictional preface also allows us to read the novel as a lie based on reality: Stanton's opponents may have fabricated the evidence but the accusation of an affair is presented as truthful. Perhaps *Primary Colors* is dishonest about the details, but gets across the underlying truth about what American political life is like. Either way, the novel's metafictional preface and its metarhetorical and metadiscursive content invite us to understand that political 'reality' is or *may* be constructed through countering fabrications, false claims to authenticity, expedient lies which allow the 'authentic' to win through, and so on. The novel offers no solid conclusion to these various possibilities: the narrative ends before Stanton gets the chance to make good his claim that the 'bullshit' will stop when he is in power. It is all rather unsettling.

I have chosen to begin this final chapter with a discussion of *Primary Colors* because this modern novel illustrates a number of ways in which fiction or documentary narrative can productively represent the problems which deception, rhetoric and what I have already termed 'the rhetoric of anti-rhetoric' pose for a democracy. The novel mixes four modes of representing rhetoric and deception which are pertinent to my ensuing discussion of Thucydides, Aristophanes and Euripides and their engagement with deception, rhetoric and anti-rhetoric in the democratic polis: the historical, the comic, the tragic and the metafictional. If we treat *Primary Colors* as an historical account of the Clinton campaign, it offers an analysis of the ways in which democracy and its ideals are strained or undermined by an elite political and media culture of smear and counter-smear campaigns, corruption, devious strategies of rhetorical misrepresentation and the temptation to tell the electorate what they want to hear. The novel also has a comic, even satirical, strain: it represents Stanton's struggle for nomination as a series of rhetorical wrestling bouts where policy issues become absurdly and often hilariously obscured by superficial processes of image-making and tabloid revelation. Then there is the distinctly serious and tragic side: Stanton fails to live up to the moral expectations of his camp-followers and that failure destroys individuals. The business of democratic representation is stripped of nobility as Stanton's honesty and integrity become more and more questionable. But the metafictional preface disturbs the import of these historical, comic and tragic modes. This is 'just' a work of novelistic fiction: the Stantons are not 'real' and 'none of these events ever happened'. As the novel describes a campaign race in contemporary America as a mad and, in many ways, bad business where 'spin' and countering misrepresentations leave the electorate very much in the dark about who or what they are voting for, the suggestion that this is just a good (funny, sad or 'plausible') story makes it difficult to assess. The comic and tragic plot-making of the novelist, alongside the 'reality effects' of first-hand witnessing and historical recollection may amount to a penetrating interpretation of American politics, but do these fictional devices make that interpretation truthful or do they make it distorted, unfair and partial? Is this just another 'spin' on 'spin'? The metafictional preface makes you realise that novels can lie too. Thus the novel's depiction of rhetoric, lies, spin and counter-spin can be read in several different ways depending on which modes (the historical, comic, tragic, metafictional) we choose to emphasise as we read. I hope to show that Thucydides, Aristophanes and Euripides offered their Athenian readers and audiences a similar range of responses. When taken together, these responses can be seen to have given Athens' democratic citizenry some important interpretive equipment with which they could enter their rhetoric-based and 'logocentric' institutions.

I have been anxious to characterise Athenian oratory's rhetoric of anti-rhetoric as a collection of 'strategies'. I have done so, not simply because I believe that it would be impossible to show (for example) that Aeschines is telling the truth about Demosthenes' mimetic mode of lying, but also because I suspect that an Athenian audience must have found it difficult to assess two opposing speakers who both provided them with (sometimes sophisticated) accounts of the other's techniques and strategies of deceit. How were mass audiences to evaluate such claims and counter-claims? We cannot know how they did so or even whether they paid much attention to these countering accusations of deceit. But I will end this book by arguing that in the late fifth century, Thucydidean historical narrative, Aristophanic comedy and Euripidean tragedy foreground the problem of detecting deception in forensic and political contests of speech. More specifically, Thucydides and Aristophanes confront the possibility that the anti-rhetorical strategy is just another deceptive strategy of self-authorisation and self-representation. In the case of Aristophanes, this confrontation accepts and underlines the further possibility that comedy and tragedy are themselves forms of rhetorical representation which may themselves be implicated in a deceptive 'rhetoric of anti-rhetoric'. Here, metatheatre, metafiction and metarhetoric are fused to produce an unsettling (if comical) picture of accusations of deception and claims to 'truth' and 'justice' as *always* potentially deceptive and disingenuous – even comedy's supposed political, didactic and anti-rhetorical diatribes cannot be taken at face value. The tragedies of Euripides can also be read as self-reflexively questioning their own integrity as representations. Most famously, the female chorus of *Medea* point out that women's reputation for deviousness would be replaced by accounts of men's faithlessness if *women* had been given the power of poetry and song.[7] In this section, however, I will focus on a moment in Euripidean tragedy

---

[7] Eur. *Med.* 410–45. On this remarkable piece of 'metatragedy' see Walsh (1984) 113–26; Hall (1997) 121. Despite this chorus, Rabinowitz (1993) 125–54 stresses the negative portrayal of Medea in the play.

where anti-rhetorical thinking and a specifically *forensic* context are used to highlight the difficulties which rhetoric and deceptive communication pose for the fulfilment of justice.

In making this claim, I do not want to elide the differences of genre, representation and 'world-view' which exist between these three authors. Nor do I wish to ignore the difficulty of understanding how their texts are to be read. They have all been characterised as adopting a critical or even *polemical* stance in relation to Athenian democracy and my argument supports this characterisation. The interpretation of Thucydides' history as an attack on the workings of the post-Periclean democracy is reasonably uncontroversial. But there is no consensus concerning Euripidean tragedy's engagement (or lack of it) with the 'here and now' concerns of its democratic audience. There is even less agreement over the relationship between Attic comedy and the 'real' individuals, politics, institutions and ideologies which it (mis)-represents. So far, I have argued or implied that Thucydidean history, tragedy and comedy have serious things to say about the connotations and consequences of deception in Athenian democratic culture. I hope that this chapter will complete this argument for seriousness.

Who can you trust? Thucydides' *Mytilenean debate* and Aristophanes' *Knights*

In his third book, Thucydides recounts the course of the Mytilenean revolt against the Athenian empire and its aftermath.[8] The demagogue Cleon had successfully urged a meeting of the *ecclēsia* to execute Mytilene's entire adult male population and to enslave the women and children. But with a ship dispatched to do the job, the demos had second thoughts about the cruelty of wiping out an entire city as opposed to executing only the ringleaders who were chiefly responsible for the revolt. A second meeting was convened for renewed debate. Thucydides introduces Cleon's speech against revoking the previous decision by describing him as 'the most violent man among the citizens and by far the most persuasive in the demos' (... βιαιότατος τῶν πολιτῶν τῷ τε δήμῳ παρὰ πολὺ ἐν τῷ πιθανώτατος: 3.36.6). The Thucydidean Cleon is furious that the Athenians have called another *ecclēsia* to reconsider their original decision. He tells the *ecclēsia* that anyone who speaks for a reversal of the decision must *either* be extremely confident in their ability to argue against what has been universally established *or*

[8] Thuc. 3.2.3–4, 3.3.4–5, 3.6–18, 3.25–49.

else, because he has been offered a bribe, attempts to mislead the *ecclē-sia* with 'an elaborate display of specious oratory' (38.2).[9]

Cleon goes on to criticise his audience's management of debates: 'you are responsible for setting up contests badly' (αἴτιοι δ' ὑμεῖς κακῶς ἀγωνοθετοῦντες: 38.4). As spectators (*theatai*) of speeches and hearers of deeds, they pay little attention to accomplished facts and are swayed by eloquent speakers' accounts of what is feasible in the future rather than the sight of what has actually been done (38.4). 'You are the best', he continues, 'at being deceived (*apatasthai*) with novelty of argument and at refusing to follow established opinion, always slaves to paradox (*atopōn*) and scorners of what is familiar' (38.5).[10] Cleon then accuses the Athenians of all wanting to be orators themselves, or failing that, to compete with those dealers in paradox and novelty by seeming not to lag behind them in wit but to applaud a smart saying before it is out of a speaker's mouth (38.6). Cleon concludes that the Athenians are as quick to anticipate what is said as they are slow to foresee the consequences of such words. They treat deliberation as if it were an epideictic *agōn*: 'you are in thrall to pleasure (*hedonei*) of the ear and are more like men who sit as spectators (*theatai*) of sophists than men who deliberate about the polis' (38.7).[11] Later in his speech, Cleon reiterates his warning concerning a hedonistic impulse in both the speaker and his audience. He tells the *ecclēsia* not to reverse their decision through pity (*oiktos* and *eleos*) or through delight in eloquence (*hedonēi logōn*). As for orators who give pleasure through speech (*hoi terpontes logōi rhētores*), they will have other opportunities for display, where for a brief pleasure the polis will not pay a heavy penalty while they themselves get a fine fee for fine speaking (40.3).

The man who does get up to speak in favour of clemency towards Mytilene opposes Cleon's rhetoric of anti-rhetoric with a countering rhetoric of anti-rhetoric. Diodotus implies that Cleon is wrong to attack the Athenians' decision to reopen debate about the right course of action. Haste and anger will result in acts of folly and anyone who

---

[9] καὶ δῆλον ὅτι ἢ τῷ λέγειν πιστεύσας τὸ πάνυ δοκοῦν ἀνταποφῆναι ὡς οὐκ ἔγνωσται ἀγωνίσαιτ' ἄν, ἢ κέρδει ἐπαιρόμενος τὸ εὐπρεπὲς τοῦ λόγου ἐκπονήσας παράγειν πειράσεται.

[10] καὶ μετὰ καινότητος μὲν λόγου ἀπατᾶσθαι ἄριστοι, μετὰ δεδοκιμασμένου δὲ μὴ ξυνέπεσθαι ἐθέλειν, δοῦλοι ὄντες τῶν αἰεὶ ἀτόπων, ὑπερόπται δὲ τῶν εἰωθότων ...

[11] ἁπλῶς τε ἀκοῆς ἡδονῇ ἡσσώμενοι καὶ σοφιστῶν θεαταῖς ἐοικότες καθημένοις μᾶλλον ἢ περὶ πόλεως βουλευομένοις. As Macleod (1978) 68, n. 18 points out, a similar contrast between epideictic and deliberative oratory is found at Isoc. 5.12–13 and Dem. 14.1–2.

contends that words should not be guides for actions is either stupid or anxious to conceal his own inability to speak well for a cause which he knows to be discreditable (42.1–2). Diodotus implies that Cleon is concealing bad advice and self-interest by engaging in slander. Using a verb which is often used (by Gorgias, Plato, and Aristophanes) to describe rhetoric and poetry's power to dumbfound, deceive and paralyse cognition, he says that such slanders 'unhinge' (*ekplēxai*) his opponents and audience (42.2).[12] Given Gorgias' deployment of the term *ekplēxis* to describe the effects of rhetoric and representation, Diodotus is perhaps signalling that Cleon's figures and tropes constitute the very displays of cleverness and sophistry which the demagogue condemns.[13] As Ober has put it most recently: 'Diodotus reveals the obvious flaw in Cleon's anti-public speech meta-rhetoric: Cleon's attack on clever speech is embedded in a clever speech, and thereby demonstrates the impossibility of communicating complex meanings through the medium of words.'[14]

Diodotus maintains that slanders and imputations of bribery of the sort that Cleon has uttered create an unacceptable climate of suspicion in the political arena (42.3–6). The orator who has been accused of taking a bribe to make a deceptive speech becomes an object of suspicion if he is successful, and if he fails he is regarded as dishonest as well as stupid. Diodotus sees this climate of prejudice and suspicion as detrimental to the polis because good advisers become afraid to speak out. Diodotus implies that the eloquence of slanderers like Cleon causes the demos to make mistakes under their influence. He also implies that the current political climate is unhealthy because the people bestow rewards and honours on the speakers whose advice they approve and they punish the orators whose advice they reject. Diodotus argues that this climate of reward and punishment makes it more likely that orators will speak insincerely in an effort to curry favour with their audience. Returning to the theme of suspicion, he then makes the bizarre claim that speakers have to deploy deception in order to gain acceptance with their audience:

---

[12] For the connotations of *ekplēxis* in drama, philosophy and rhetorical theory see the references and excellent discussion of Lada (1993) 97–8 and 127, nn. 26–34. On the term in Thucydides, see Hunter (1986) 415–21.

[13] See Gorg. *Hel.* 16 (= DK 82 B11.16). On the Gorgianic style of Cleon's speech, see Yunis (1996) 90–1.

[14] Ober (1998) 98. I only read Ober's analysis of the Mytilenean debate during the final stages of completing this book. His characterisation of the debate as a 'substantial "meta-rhetoric"' (96) which offers a critique of the democracy's capacity to make good policy is close to my own and I have tried to incorporate it where relevant.

καθέστηκε δὲ τἀγαθὰ ἀπὸ τοῦ εὐθέος λεγόμενα μηδὲν ἀνυποπτότερα εἶναι τῶν κακῶν, ὥστε δεῖν ὁμοίως τόν τε τὰ δεινότατα βουλόμενον πεῖσαι ἀπάτῃ προσάγεσθαι τὸ πλῆθος καὶ τὸν τὰ ἀμείνω λέγοντα ψευσάμενον πιστὸν γενέσθαι. μόνην τε πόλιν διὰ τὰς περινοίας εὖ ποιῆσαι ἐκ τοῦ προφανοῦς μὴ ἐξαπατήσαντα ἀδύνατον· ὁ γὰρ διδοὺς φανερῶς τι ἀγαθὸν ἀνθυποπτεύεται ἀφανῶς πῃ πλέον ἕξειν.

And it has come to pass that good advice frankly given is regarded with just as much suspicion as the bad, and that, in consequence, a speaker who wants to carry the most dangerous measures must resort to deceit in order to win the people to his views, precisely as the man whose proposals are good must lie in order to be believed. And because of this excessive cleverness Athens is the only polis where a man cannot do a good service to his country openly and without deceiving it; for whenever he openly offers you something good you requite him by suspecting that he will secretly profit by it. (Thucydides 3.43.2–4)

Diodotus concludes his excursus on the nature of contemporary political debate by attacking his audience. He tells them that they would be more prudent in their decisions if they had to suffer the same dangers and risks as those who advise them. 'But as it is', he says, 'whenever you meet with a reverse you give way to your first impulse and punish your adviser for a single judgement instead of yourselves, the multitude who shared in the error' (43.5).

Gomme remarks that the quarrel between Cleon and Diodotus is 'as much about how to conduct debate in the *ekklesia* as about the fate of Mytilene'.[15] These reflections on the character and reception of political rhetoric are located within an acrimonious rhetorical *agōn* and, as Ober points out, this agonistic quality is emphasised by Thucydides' introduction and conclusion to the debate, as well as Cleon's own terminology.[16] Cleon's attack on orators and audiences alike is clearly part of a strategy to discredit the whole idea of calling for a second debate when it had already been decided to mete out a severe punishment to the Mytileneans. Diodotus' interpretation of the dynamics of contemporary political debate leads off from a need to neutralise Cleon's claim that the second discussion is driven by deception, bribery and an Athenian penchant for over-cleverness, sophistic display and rhetorical hedonism.[17] In the wake of Cleon's charge that anyone who speaks for Mytilene has been bribed, his rejection of the use of *logos*, and his at-

---

[15] Gomme (1956) 315. See also Croally (1994) 56–7: the Mytilenean debate and Plataean debate 'both reveal a (sophistic) concern with the possibilities of language; both betray the idea that *logos* must deceive to be effective and that it is dependent on paradox and contradiction for its power'.

[16] See Ober (1998) 103 for references and discussion.

[17] See Macleod (1978) 75–7 for Diodotus' verbal and thematic echoes of Cleon's arguments.

tack on pity, Diodotus is compelled to spend 'a good third of his time establishing his right to speak at all'.[18]

Cleon and Diodotus' substantive arguments concerning the rights and wrongs of punishing the Mytileneans are both internally inconsistent.[19] Both speakers argue on the basis that a decision over the fate of Mytilene must be dictated by longer-term considerations of how to maintain the Athenian empire. Cleon claims that it is just and expedient to punish the Mytileneans because their revolt is unjust. But he follows the Thucydidean Pericles in characterising the Athenian empire as a tyranny and admits that the empire is itself unjust. In the end he can only argue for the expediency of punishment. Diodotus argues for rational deliberation based on expediency rather than anger. However he also has to admit to the injustice of the empire and the consequent inevitability of allied revolt. Like Cleon, he can offer no long-term solution for this inevitability. Thucydides relates that the Mytilenean population was spared by a barely discernible majority of votes. Nevertheless, Croally is perhaps right to question Macleod's extreme conclusion that these two speeches demonstrate a truth that 'all advice is futile'.[20]

However, these inconsistencies and *aporiai* of argument, when taken together with the countering anti-rhetorical charges, must have provoked a deep sense of bafflement and insecurity in the Athenian reader. To illustrate this evocation of insecurity, I want to consider Diodotus' claim that Cleon's slandering strategies create so much suspicion that even the good honest speaker has to 'persuade by deceit' in order to gain trust and avoid censure and his claim that this absurd situation is unique to Athens. Critics have rightly argued that this argument must strike the reader as precisely the kind of rhetorical paradox and novelty which Cleon condemns both speakers and the demos for deploying and enjoying.[21] Diodotus' claim here is indeed unique in Athenian literature. The notion of deceiving the demos nobly in order to overcome suspicion is not paralleled in the orators. Even Andocides' consideration and rejection of benefiting the demos through deceit, or Demosthenes' hypothetical endorsement of lying about Athens' past do not come near Diodotus' particular formulation of justifiable deceit as a response to suspicion. However, my third chapter's presentation of these and other texts makes it clear that the 'paradox' of the lie which

---

[18] Andrewes (1962) 71.
[19] On the inconsistencies of argument see Macleod (1978) 68–78; Croally (1994) 58–9; Ober (1998) 94–104.
[20] Croally (1994) 59; Macleod (1978) 78.
[21] See Hornblower (1991) 433, following Andrewes (1962) 74.

achieves or maintains a deeper social or ethical 'truth' or 'good' is neither unique nor Thucydides' invention.

The paradoxical quality of Diodotus' claim has led commentators to mark it as absurd. Andrewes describes the paradox as 'close to the border of nonsense' and asks 'what should the honest man do? Convey just a flavour of spurious dishonesty, enough to gratify suspicion but not wreck his proposal?'[22] Given Aeschines' discussion of 'normative' liars who are tolerated because their lies are self-signalling, it is tempting to answer Andrewes with a simple 'yes'. But Diodotus' complaint does not have to envisage the orator's *gratification* of suspicion through 'spurious' deceit. It merely states that a speech containing good advice which is genuinely *open* and lacking in *apatē* will provoke suspicion that the speaker is secretly profiting from the 'good actions' he recommends.

Diodotus does not explain exactly *how* the orator uses *apatē* to overcome suspicion. But his argument that (thanks to slanderers like Cleon) the *ecclēsia* is so gripped by suspicion that the good adviser must deploy deceit suggests that Diodotus himself will have to use *apatē*.[23] Macleod and Johnson have shown that his arguments concerning justice, expediency and anger contain tricks of argument, slides of premise and sops to the audience's illusions about the attitude of their allies. Given that these tricks, slides and indulgences achieve the decision which Diodotus wants, they can be said to exemplify his own model of good and just advice which, through the essential ingredient of *apatē*, successfully overcomes suspicion and is acted upon by the demos.[24] On this reading, Diodotus' paradox can hardly be described as 'nonsensical'.

But both speakers fail to come up with the long-term 'good' of a solution to the problems of empire, despite their explicit claim to be addressing that wider question. And an attentive reader could not feel secure that a short-term 'good' (the sparing of the Mytileneans) has prevailed as a result of 'good' motives and fair, honest or rational argument.[25] For Thucydides' design emphasises the *strategic* nature of Cleon's and Diodotus' rhetoric of anti-rhetoric and the consequent

---

[22] Andrewes (1962) 74 and 74, n. 25. See also Hornblower (1991) 433: 'the thought here is close to absurdity'. Macleod (1978) 74 and 74, n. 47 is more sensitive, simply noting the 'disturbing' quality of the argument, the oxymoronic ψευσάμενον πιστὸν γενέσθαι (43.3) and the fact that there was a curse against deceitful speakers at the opening of assemblies.

[23] On Diodotus articulating a version of the 'Cretan liar paradox' (where a Cretan says 'all Cretans are liars'), see Ober (1998) 99.

[24] See Macleod (1978) 76–7; Manuwald (1979), *passim*; Johnson (1991), *passim*.

[25] See Winnington-Ingram (1965) 77–9 on Diodotus' skilful, as opposed to rational, arguments.

difficulty of deciding which of these speakers recommends the best policy. Gomme and Macleod have detailed the elements of sophistic rhetorical style and argument which demonstrate that Cleon (ironically) utilises the kind of rhetoric which he condemns.[26] His attacks on clever speakers and the motives of anyone who wants to reopen the debate seem to be designed to undermine Diodotus' credibility. Diodotus attempts to confirm this by arguing that such attacks are mere slanders designed to instil suspicion and fear. But his use of a novel and a paradoxical conceit concerning deceit itself invites the suspicion that Diodotus has indeed carried his audience away by activating the hedonistic propensities for paradox and novelty which Cleon emphasises.

It should be noted here that Cleon explicitly connects the Athenians' tendency to be deceived through their love of a new *logos* and an unfamiliar paradox with their tendency to depart from previously established decisions. If Diodotus enacts his own paradox by using deceit to put forward his 'good' advice, then perhaps the audience has been misled into changing their minds through their love of novelty. And perhaps this change of heart is not a 'good' outcome achieved through the 'unfamiliar' notion of deceit used with 'good intentions', but a 'bad' outcome achieved through the all too familiar notion of deceit used with 'bad' motives. Has Cleon slandered maliciously and deceitfully or is his anti-rhetoric a timely and justified warning to the audience?

Diodotus may have used *apatē* with sincere motives to successfully steer the demos towards a good decision. But his failure to adequately address the long-term problem of empire and revolt invokes the countering suspicion that he has indeed been bribed to secure the short-term end of Mytilenean salvation. On that suspicious reading, Diodotus' failure to tackle the long-term problem effectively is a symptom of a self-interested and hidden agenda to secure the short-term goals of his paymasters. Furthermore, Diodotus fails to offer his audience or a reader any solution to the paradox which he himself presents. Although Diodotus is in favour of long-term forethought in political decision-making (3.34.4) he does not make it clear how the need to deceive the demos will allow good long-term policy to be communicated and adopted. As Ober puts it: 'What techniques will the speaker use to gauge the likely course of future events? Why should listeners believe that an acknowledged liar is sincere when he claims to seek the public good rather than private advantage?'[27]

It has been argued that such a suspicious reading is illegitimate be-

---

[26] Gomme (1956) 304–7; Macleod (1978) 71.   [27] Ober (1998) 99.

cause Thucydides offers no evidence (outside the disreputable accusations from Cleon) to suggest that the reader should *not* take Diodotus' argument at 'face value'. For Harvey Yunis, Diodotus and Cleon both exaggerate the truth and use trickery, but Diodotus' praise of deliberation puts him closer to Pericles' vision of 'taming democracy' through legitimate techniques of instruction and rhetoric. Thucydides' (not to mention Yunis') admiration for Pericles therefore means that Diodotus' motives and arguments are not to be viewed with suspicion.[28] Yunis also points out that unlike Cleon, Diodotus is an obscure figure. Like Agoracritus (the sausage-seller) in Aristophanes' *Knights*, Diodotus therefore represents the transforming possibilities of an individual who offers a different model of political rhetoric and decision-making to the established *équipe* of corrupt, flattering *rhētores*.[29] For Yunis, Diodotus' obscurity means that he is exempt from Thucydides' comments in the previous book that post-Periclean Athens declined because of the infighting and flattering rhetoric of this *équipe* (2.65.10).

Thucydides makes no explicit appraisal of Cleon's and Diodotus' speeches. As I have already noted, he does introduce Cleon as 'the most violent of the citizens and by far the most persuasive of the demos' (3.36.6). And in his second book he has offered his opinion that post-Periclean politicians competed with each other for supremacy but, in contrast to Pericles' manifest hegemony, they were always on a par with each other (2.65.9–10). This is apparently confirmed by the historian's claim that despite a prevalent mood of leniency prior to the second debate, Cleon's and Diodotus' speeches were so equal to each other in force that the demos was as good as equally divided in its show of hands (3.49.1). Even if Diodotus' speech *is* only his second ever delivered to the *ecclēsia*, Thucydides' marking of his ability to be equal to the demagogue Cleon surely raises a problem for Yunis' confidence that Diodotus is not to be viewed as one of the demagogues whom Thucydides despises.

Aristophanes' representation of Agoracritus in *Knights* (whom Yunis invokes as a parallel for a 'face-value' assessment of Diodotus) actually highlights the problem of securely assessing motives of a previously unheard-of speaker who emerges to challenge the deceptive rhetoric of established demagogues. Agoracritus certainly appears from nowhere and apparently transforms the old man Demos, a character who is clearly an allegorical personification of the Athenian demos. Ago-

---

[28] Yunis (1996) 92–101. Yunis also points to the Protagorean flavour of Diodotus' arguments. On this, see also de Romilly (1956) 180–239.

[29] Yunis (1996) 93.

racritus also usurps the Paphlagonian slave (a thinly veiled cipher for Cleon). But his methods (of trickery, theft and flattery, not to mention his social and sexual background) are marked in the play as identical to those of Cleon. Indeed the comic premise of the play is that Cleon can only be defeated by a man who can beat him at his own game.[30]

Agoracritus' acts of 'exposing' Cleon and of 'boiling down' Demos so that he supposedly becomes less manipulable through gratification and flattery are explicitly represented as making the old man grateful, attentive and loyal to the sausage-seller (1335–6, 1404f.). Agoracritus tells the rejuvenated Demos that if he knew what he was like in his previous incarnation, he would call Agoracritus a god for transforming him (1337–8). And Agoracritus does indeed tell Demos how he was easily deceived by the flattering rhetoric of politicians. Demos is ashamed for his former errors. But Agoracritus then reassures him that he is *not* to blame – the blame lies with the speakers who deceived him (1340–54, 1355–7). Demos then advocates policies which illustrate his new-found sense and his rejection of the temptations of short-term gratification. But Agoracritus rewards him with a well-hung boy to have sex with. Then he brings out two or three women who personify a thirty-years peace treaty with Sparta claiming that Cleon has been hiding them away. Demos checks that he will be allowed to κατα-τριακοντουτίσαι them. This is a coined word which means both 'to thirty yearise up them' and can be etymologised as 'to pierce them three times with a long pole from below' (1391).[31] This association between returned peace and sexual gratification is typical of Aristophanic comedy.[32] And it is indisputable that the play was performed when Cleon was pressing for continuation of the war despite the fact that the Spartans had recently suffered reverses and were offering a peace treaty.[33] But in the context of the *Knights* where Cleon's deceptive rhet-

---

[30] See Sommerstein (1981) 2: 'At the moment of the sausage-seller's rise to power we are encouraged to believe that he will rule in the same way as his predecessor, by deception and robbery of the "Open-Mouthenian" people (1263), and by malicious prosecution of his political rivals (in which Demosthenes begs to be allowed to assist: 1255–6).' See also Ar. *Eq.* 125–44, where the oracle predicting Agoracritus' rise states that a sausage-seller will usurp a leather-seller (i.e. Cleon). See also 211–19 and 178–93. At 266–99 Cleon and Agoracritus compete over their skills in shouting, thieving and denunciation. At 844ff. they compete in counter-accusations of deceiving Demos and attempt to outdo each other in flattering him. At 1151–1226 they steal from each other in a competition to satisfy Demos' appetite. The parallels (at the level of imagery as well as theme) between the Paphlagonian and Agoracritus in terms of their tricks, rhetoric and low social background are discussed by Edmunds (1987) 1–37; Bowie (1993) 54–8; MacDowell (1995) 89–103.

[31] See Sommerstein (1981) ad loc. (219).

[32] See Gomme (1938); Heath (1987b); Newiger (1980).

[33] See Sommerstein (1981) 2.

oric of flattery is constantly troped as the immediate gratification of Demos' insatiable appetites, Agoracritus' motives for offering peace and Demos' unconsidered and hedonistic response allow for a suspicious interpretation of the 'transformation' of democratic politics which has supposedly occurred.

The conclusion of *Knights* is not, or need not be, a *clear-cut* utopian fantasy of a democratic politics freed of flattery, deceit and the damaging short-term desire (coming from both the *rhētōr* and the demos) for immediate gratification.[34] I am not arguing that the 'utopian' interpretation was not entertained by Aristophanes' audience. Rather, the play's action and its conclusion raises disturbing and unsettling possibilities which encroach on the utopian reading.[35] Perhaps Agoracritus has simply enacted a new strategy of manipulating the demos by convincing it that Cleon is its enemy rather than its friend. By making the demos feel that it has now mended its gullible ways, and by claiming credit for the transformation, he has perhaps done nothing more than inherit and deepen the process of manipulation from Cleon. After all, for most of the play, Agoracritus is explicitly represented as a dead ringer for Cleon.

Aristophanes' presentation provokes the suspicion that, instead of achieving a utopian form of democracy, Agoracritus has made the current political climate even worse for his own ends. This is the dystopian nightmare (as Thucydides would see it) of a post-Periclean demagogue who actually *does* manage to achieve total supremacy and control of the demos through flattering rhetoric, gratification of his audience and the slandering of an opponent. The uncertainty over whether Agoracritus has made changes for the better or for the worse emphasises the difficulty and danger of feeling secure about the newly emerged speaker who claims to have exposed the corrupt rhetoric of his adversary and offers the people an 'instructive' vision of a politics without manipulation.

Thucydides has argued that post-Periclean politicians were prepared to flatter and indulge the pleasures (*hēdonas*) of the demos in their at-

---

[34] For the 'utopian fantasy' view see, for example, Sommerstein (1981) 2–3; MacDowell (1995) 104–7. For a more sophisticated reading of Demos' 'boiling down' and Agoracritus' agency as connoting mythic and ritual reversals and transformations, see Bowie (1993) 45–77. Brock (1986) posits a 'double plot' where the unsatisfactory situation of a defeated Cleon and an as yet 'unreconstructed' Demos is juxtaposed with the 'second ending' of Demos' fantastic 'boiling down'.

[35] Dover (1972) 99 does entertain the possibility of an 'ironic' reading of Demos' transformation. On the difficulty of approaching 'irony' in Aristophanic comedy and the need to entertain competing readings which mark or ignore possible ironies, see Hesk (2000).

tempts to gain favour over and above their rivals (2.65.10). He claims that one of the consequences of this un-Periclean subordination of sound arguments to flattery and self-interested intrigue is the disaster of the Sicilian expedition. It is also clear that he regards the conduct of politics after Pericles as a major cause of Athens' 'decline' (2.65.11–13).[36] But Aristophanes' unsettling representation of Agoracritus (is this a new Pericles or a new Cleon in the making?) suggests that Diodotus' apparent emergence from obscurity is no guarantee that an Athenian reader could not view him as a manipulative demagogue in the making.

Given these frames for interpreting Thucydides' representation of post-Periclean debate, alongside the ironies and countering accusations generated by Cleon and Diodotus' speeches it seems impossible to sustain a 'face-value' attribution of sincerity and good motives to Diodotus' speech. And I hope that the preceding analysis has shown that the impossibility or difficulty of feeling secure about either Cleon or Diodotus' motives and advice is achieved through the combination of their substantive arguments and the ironies generated by their countering strategies of anti-rhetoric. Thucydides seals this response of uncertainty and insecurity by signalling the self-interested and corrupt quality of post-Periclean debate and by refusing to provide any clear approval or endorsement for either speaker. For Thucydides, 'the rhetoric of anti-rhetoric' is both a symptom and a cause of the post-Periclean democracy's decline. And while we would expect a writer who was out of sympathy with radical democracy to present a negative image of its decision-making process, it is noteworthy that he does so by inculcating a sense of irony and insecurity in the reader. In this respect, Thucydides shares his technique (if not his outlook) with Aristophanes and Euripides.

'Trust me, I'm a comedian!' Aristophanes' *Acharnians*

My brief discussion of Aristophanes' *Knights* as a play which can usefully frame Thucydides' Mytilenean debate suggests a need to explore other comedies' uses and representations of a rhetoric of anti-rhetoric. A complete exploration cannot be conducted here. But there is one comedy in which the Aristophanic concern to 'think with' deception and rhetoric in the democracy is particularly acute. It may be no accident that this play, *Acharnians*, has become the focus of intense critical

[36] See Yunis (1996) 67–72.

disagreement: it is difficult to interpret in itself and its form and content make it the text most often referred to in more general arguments over the extent to which Aristophanic comedy had a 'serious' political role to play in the Athenian democracy.[37] Recent studies of (and disputes about) this play have focused on the difficulty of determining the morality of its main character's autarchy and the justice of his rhetorical arguments, not to mention the slippery tropes of the 'authorial voice' which Aristophanes playfully inserts.[38] In this section I want to discuss the play's provocation of reflection and uncertainty through its representation of rhetorical advocacy as a process of theatrical consultation, disguise and deception. This will also involve analysis of its characters' appropriations of anti-rhetorical topoi and their association with the play's metafictional or metatheatrical themes.[39]

The protagonist of *Acharnians* is called Dicaeopolis. His name is not revealed until line 406 but it is significant because it is a compound of the words 'just' and 'city'. It is impossible to know quite what this compound name means: it could be 'just towards the city' or 'having a just city' or 'making the city just'.[40] Dicaeopolis appears at the beginning of the play in a disgruntled mood. He is waiting alone for a meeting of the *ecclēsia* though (significantly) it is not at first clear where he is or what he is waiting for. Having expressed antipathy for Cleon and delight at (either a real or theatrical) come-uppance at the hands of the Knights (5–8), he goes through the various poets whose performances have vexed him (9–17).[41] Up to this point, the audience might

---

[37] Discussions which enlist *Acharnians* for various 'serious' or 'political' readings of Aristophanes: de Ste Croix (1972) appendix 29; Cartledge (1990b) 54–8; Henderson (1990), (1993); Hubbard (1991); MacDowell (1983), (1995). Various forms of denial of seriousness or 'serious effects': Gomme (1938); Halliwell (1984), (1993); Heath (1987a), (1990), (1997). See also Goldhill (1991) 188–201, for a reading of *Acharnians* which seeks to collapse the 'serious'/'unserious' polarity.

[38] For a flavour of these disputes, with good analyses and further bibliography, see Bowie (1982); Bowie (1988); Foley (1988); Cartledge (1990b) 54–8; Goldhill (1991) 176–201; MacDowell (1995) 47–79.

[39] Some of these appropriations were actually highlighted a long time ago by Murphy (1938) although his commentary on them is limited. Foley (1988) has argued that the play's meta-theatrical deployment of tragedy's resources is linked to reflection on the process of rhetorical communication and the possibilities of deceptive communication in the Athenian democracy. See also Goldhill (1991) 188–201. On Aristophanes' persistent concern with disguise and theatricality see Muecke (1977) and Zeitlin (1981).

[40] On Dicaeopolis' name, see MacDowell (1983) 162, n. 37, (1995) 78–9; Goldhill (1991) 184.

[41] For the attractive possibility that Dicaeopolis is referring to Aristophanes' own attack on Cleon in his *Babylonians*, see Slater (1993) 398. On the play's subsequent reference to *Babylonians* see below pp. 263–4. On the inconclusive evidence that lines 5–8 refer to a real legal or political set-back for Cleon see Sommerstein (1981) ad loc.

think that Dicaeopolis is waiting for a play to begin.[42] But it then becomes clear that he is on the Pnyx. The lateness of everyone's arrival
for the *ecclēsia* is what *really* vexes Dicaeopolis: 'that there shall be
peace they don't care a jot' (26–7). He tells us that he is 'absolutely
prepared to shout, interrupt and abuse these speakers (*rhētoras*) if anyone speaks on any topic other than peace' (38–9). Dicaeopolis wants
the war with Sparta to end.

When a herald appears and the *ecclēsia* finally convenes, Dicaeopolis
is frustrated to discover that peace will not be on the agenda. A character called Amphitheus arrives, claiming to be immortal and to have
been entrusted by the gods with the task of securing peace with the
Spartans (46–53). He is summarily silenced and ejected by a herald
despite Dicaeopolis' protests that the presiding Prytaneis do an injustice to the *ecclēsia* by arresting a man who is prepared to make peace for
Athens (54–60). The herald then announces the arrival of Athenian
ambassadors returning from negotiations with the king of Persia.
Dicaeopolis immediately signals that these ambassadors may not
be entirely straight with the *ecclēsia* by saying that he is tired of their
alazoneumata (ἄχθομαι ... ἀλαζονεύμασιν: 62–3). When one of the
ambassadors starts to recount the luxurious lifestyle they have been
'forced' to lead (at Athens' expense) in the Persian court, he again
bewails their *alazoneumata* (87). This noun, meaning 'impostures' or
'false pretensions' and its cognate verb are often used (along with the
more common noun *alazōn*: 'impostor') to denote deceptive sophistry
in Aristophanes, Plato and Xenophon.[43] Dicaeopolis also draws attention to the lavish clothing of the ambassadors (obviously corrupted by
Persian luxury): 'Ectabana, what a get-up' (64). Here he uses the word
schēma for their appearance or 'get-up'. This term can mean 'theatrical
costume' in Aristophanes.[44] But (as we saw in the last chapter) it also
connotes the outward form of what is presented to a viewer in extra-
theatrical contexts and sometimes carries with it the general implication of 'semblance or concealment of true nature'.[45] Thus the play's
subsequent association between deceptive self-representation in politics and the techniques of theatrical illusion is established early on.

The ambassador continues to brag about the gastronomic and alco-
holic excesses that he and his colleagues have endured in Persia while
Dicaeopolis attempts to gloss their report as making fools out of the

---

[42] On the initial suggestion that Dicaeopolis might be either a theatrical spectator or
waiting for the *ecclēsia*, see Goldhill (1991) 186; Slater (1993) 398–9.
[43] See Ar. *Nub.* 102; Xen. *Cyr.* 2.2.12, *Mem.* 1.7.5; Pl. *Chrm.* 173c.
[44] See Ar. *Eq.* 1331, *Ran.* 463, 523.
[45] Goldhill (1999) 4.

Athenian demos. The ambassador flaunts his corruption by using the language of deception: he says that the Persian king served them with a bird 'three times the size of Cleonymus: it was called a "fooler" (*phenax*)' (89). As well as being a joke at the expense of the Athenian politician Cleonymus, the pun (*phenax*: 'impostor'; *phēnē*: 'eagle'; *phoinix*: mythical eastern bird) is 'detected' and continued by Dicaeopolis: 'so that is why you were fooling (*ephenakizes*) us and drawing two drachmas a day for it' (90). The ambassador's knowing selection of this pun and Dicaeopolis' lonely comprehension of the flaunted deceit serve to authorise the latter's assessment that the returned delegation is 'mocking' (*katagelōn*) the polis (75).

The presentation of deceptions which are transparent (but only to Dicaeopolis and the play's audience) continues when the ambassadors bring on the Persian king's representative ('the King's Eye'). This character is called Pseudartabas – another give-away clue (*Pseud*artabas) which only Dicaeopolis comprehends. In pidgin Greek, the King's Eye makes it clear to Dicaeopolis and the play's audience that the ambassadors have failed to secure financial aid from the Persians: 'You not vill get goldo, you open-arsed Iaonian' (104: Sommerstein's fine rendition).[46] The ambassador attempts to translate the pidgin Greek as 'open carts full of gold' (108) but Dicaeopolis calls him an 'impostor' (*alazōn*) and decides to interrogate the Persian envoy himself. Under the threat of physical violence from Dicaeopolis, Pseudartabas and his retinue of eunuchs confirm (with suspiciously Greek nodding: 115) that the ambassadors are indeed deceiving the *ecclēsia* about the gold (ἄλλως ἄρ' ἐξαπατώμεθ' ὑπὸ τῶν πρέσβεων;: 114). The Greek nodding leads Dicaeopolis to unmask the retinue of eunuchs as 'from this very city' (116). He exposes two of these supposedly foreign eunuchs to be none other than the Athenians Cleisthenes and Strato (118–22). These men (particularly the former) are lampooned as pathic effeminates both here and elsewhere in Aristophanes.[47] Dicaeopolis' unmasking of lies and disguise in this scene develops the initial verbal accusations of deception against the ambassadors: 'this is the first use of a major theme of the play, that of putting on and stripping off costumes'.[48]

Dicaeopolis' revealing cross-examination does nothing to affect the credulity of the *ecclēsia* and its presiding officials: Dicaeopolis is silenced by the heralds and the King's Eye (with his 'Persian' delegation)

---

[46] Sommerstein (1980) 49.
[47] E.g. Ar. *Eq.* 1373–4; *Nub.* 355; *Thesm.* 325, 574–654; fr. 407.
[48] Slater (1993) 400. See also Goldhill (1991) 192–3. See Muecke (1977) for disguise and fictionality as Aristophanic themes.

is invited to be entertained in the Prytaneum (123–5). This is the last straw for Dicaeopolis and he immediately asks the reappeared Amphitheus to take eight drachmas and make peace with the Spartans for himself, his wife, and his children (130–3). He bitterly abuses the *ecclēsia*: 'You lot can have your embassies and your gaping mouths!' (134). The last phrase here (*kechēnete*: literally, 'you gape') recalls Dicaeopolis' self-description in his opening speech as having been open-mouthed when anticipating Aeschylus (*kechēnē*: 30), his yawning whilst waiting for the *ecclēsia* to convene (*kechēna*: 30) and (less closely) the Persian envoy's description of the Athenians as 'gaping-arsed' (*chaunoprōkt' Iaonau*: 104). This ascription of 'gaping' to Athenian audience-behaviour and gullibility will return in the play's parabasis (see below).[49]

After another envoy appears to hoodwink the *ecclēsia* ('another *alazōn*' in Dicaeopolis' words: 135) the comic hero decides to halt proceedings by pretending that he has felt an ill-omened drop of rain (171). Amphitheus returns from Sparta with a set of peace-treaties for Dicaeopolis to choose from. Naturally, he picks the thirty-year vintage and prepares to celebrate his own private rural Dionysia (195–202). But a group of angry citizens from the deme Acharnae are in hot pursuit. The chorus of old Acharnians are furious that Dicaeopolis has made peace with the Spartans because their territory has suffered considerably at the hands of the enemy (219–36). When they intercept Dicaeopolis in the midst of his Dionysiac celebrations, they call him shameless (*anaischuntos … kai bdeluros*: 287) and a 'betrayer of the fatherland' (*prodota tēs patridos*: 289). Dicaeopolis wants to explain why he made peace (294) but the old men are not interested in hearing his defence: they want to kill him, claiming that they hate Dicaeopolis even more than Cleon (295, 297–302). Dicaeopolis provokes the chorus even further by claiming that, if only he had the opportunity to speak, he could demonstrate that the Spartans 'have often in some ways actually been the wronged party' (*ekeinous … kadikoumenous*: 314). Here, Dicaeopolis introduces the theme of justice for the first time: the question of whether this character and the comic playwright can and do articulate *to dikaion* concerning affairs of the polis becomes the play's main focus.

By seizing a charcoal basket and threatening to 'kill' it, Dicaeopolis manages to persuade his assailants to lay down their weapons and listen to a speech of self-justification (326–48). This comic 'hostage-scene' is the first in a series of parodic references to Euripides' tragedy,

---

[49] On the play's imagery of 'gaping', see Bowie (1982).

Telephus.[50] In another parodic realisation of this tragedy, Dicaeopolis says that he is prepared to proclaim his defence of the Spartans over a butcher's block (355) and this is duly brought out as a visible sign that Dicaeopolis is now on trial (*dikēn*: 364) and fighting for his life. It is crucial to understand that Dicaeopolis' defence-speech engages in parody of the *Telephus*. But that parody is itself a means of parodying three other forms of democratic performance: forensic defence and procedure, deliberative oratory in the *ecclēsia* and the specific scenario of a comic playwright justifying his comedy's content in the face of political and legal censure.

Before Dicaeopolis prepares for his defence he offers the audience some clues as to how that speech might be interpreted. He swears he will not 'hide behind any shield' (368). Nevertheless (*kaitoi*: 370) he has much cause for fear:

I know the ways of the country folk: they are extremely pleased if some fraud of a man (*alazōn anēr*) spouts eulogies on them and the polis, just or unjust (*dikaia kadika*); that's how they can be bought and sold and they are never aware of it. And I know the minds of the old jurors as well, that they look to nothing other than biting with their vote. And I know about myself, what I suffered at Cleon's hands because of last year's comedy. He dragged me into the council chamber, began slandering me and telling glib-tongued lies about me (*pseudē kateglōttize mou*), roaring at me like the Cycloborus and bathing me in abuse, so that I very nearly perished in a sewer of troubles. So now, first of all, before I speak, please let me dress myself up as piteously as I can. (Aristophanes *Acharnians* 370–84)

Dicaeopolis stresses the Athenians' gullibility in the face of rhetorical deception. Ostensibly he is afraid that his audience will be unfavourably disposed towards a speech which will not exploit that gullibility. A speech in defence of the Spartans is not likely to approximate the flattering rhetoric of the *alazōn* which he describes. But his decision to adopt a pitiable disguise recalls the use of dissembling costume which the Persian delegation had used in the play's opening parody of the democracy's deliberations. And his claim that country folk can be hoodwinked by 'unjust' oratory raises the question of how far Dicaeopolis' speech will be different from the deceptive and 'unjust' *alazōneia* which was exposed in the opening scene.

There has been much critical discussion of Dicaeopolis' remarks concerning Cleon's attack on him 'because of last year's comedy'

---

[50] See Sommerstein (1980) 171; Handley and Rea (1957) 36–7. The *Telephus'* 'hostage-scene' (whether on-stage or reported off-stage action) is also parodied at Ar. *Thesm.* 689–761.

(378).[51] He is probably identifying himself with Aristophanes and he may be referring to some political or legal move made by Cleon in response to the content of Aristophanes' *Babylonians* of the previous year.[52] Having said this, it is difficult to know what this identification amounts to with any clarity: the 'I' in 'I know what I suffered at Cleon's hands' could make Dicaeopolis the 'mouthpiece' of Aristophanes as a sincerely aggrieved comic playwright. But it could equally represent a *persona*: the 'fiction' of a persecuted poet who is (obviously and ironically) making exaggerated claims for his own precarious position as a satirist of the city and its prominent politicians. In another sense, Dicaeopolis' reference to his treatment at the hands of Cleon could be a more general identification with the genre of comedy as a whole: the protagonist of a comedy equates himself with comedy's vulnerable status as 'topical' drama. Perhaps Dicaeopolis is not Aristophanes but *any* poet who has suffered or might suffer political attacks. When he again adopts the role of the poet at the beginning of his defence, Dicaeopolis is anxious to maintain that he is not 'slandering the city' and he underlines the fact that there are no foreigners present. *Acharnians* was performed at the Lenaia festival, whereas *Babylonians* took place at the City Dionysia, an occasion when representatives of Athens' allies would have been among the audience. This is an indication that Cleon had claimed that *Babylonians* had in some sense slandered Athens in the presence of non-Athenians. It is open to debate whether or not Cleon *really* attempted to prosecute Aristophanes: Dicaeopolis could be exaggerating or manufacturing Cleon's attack in order to make (comic) claims for Aristophanes' ability to affect political reality. For my purposes, the precise force of this self-reflexive strand in the play is less important than the general point that Dicaeopolis the character equates his speech of 'justice' and self-defence with the comic playwright's (comic or serious) self-image as an artist whose drama has been regarded as politically provocative.

In response to Dicaeopolis' request that he be allowed to don pitiable clothing, the chorus articulate their suspicion that their opponent is scheming: 'Why do you twist things and craft (*technazeis*) and con-

---

[51] See, for example, Forrest (1963) 8–9; Dover (1963); de Ste Croix (1972) app. 29; Halliwell (1980); Bowie (1982); Goldhill (1991) 190–201; MacDowell (1995) 30–5.

[52] Bowie (1988) argues that Dicaeopolis is identifying himself with the comic poet Eupolis at *Ach.* 377–9. For arguments against this thesis see Parker (1991) and Storey (1993) 388–92. In my view, Bowie's arguments must be taken seriously: it is possible that Dicaeopolis could be seen as a composite character: if Eupolis' play(s) had raised similar 'anti-war' themes to *Acharnians* or had been subject to Cleon's censure along with Aristophanes' *Babylonians*, then Dicaeopolis could remind audiences of both playwrights.

trive delays?' (385). They feel sure that no tragic disguise will mask his 'Sisyphean contrivances' (*mēchanas tas Sisuphou*: 391) because Dicaeopolis' case admits no 'plea of evasion' (*skēpsin*: 392). In this context, *skēpsis* has a rich resonance. It is found in tragedy and forensic oratory with the meaning 'pretext' or 'excuse'. But it also has more technical legal senses: it can be used to mean a 'plea that one is exempt or disqualified from performing what would ordinarily be a legal duty, such as carrying out a compulsory public service (liturgy) ... or appearing as a defendant on the date named in a summons'.[53] The chorus can thus be seen to characterise Dicaeopolis' use of deception either as a means of avoiding their accusations altogether or else as a tactical attempt to claim exemption from public duty. Both characterisations add to the contemporary forensic flavour of the scene, while the latter force of *skēpsis* implies that Dicaeopolis' defence of his private peace will resemble liturgy-avoidance. The Acharnian men regard their opponent as a dishonest defaulter in civic duty.

Dicaeopolis decides that he must visit the tragic playwright Euripides in order to equip himself for his defence. It transpires that Dicaeopolis will not only use the ragged costume of the disguised Euripidean Telephus, but will also purloin or adapt lines from this tragic character's own speech of self-justification. Dicaeopolis quotes from the *Telephus* as he explains his needs to Euripides:

> 'For this day I must seem to be a beggar,
> Be who I am and yet appear not so.'
> The audience must know who I am, but the chorus must stand there like fools, so that I can give them the long finger with my neat little utterances (*rhēmatiois*). (Aristophanes *Acharnians* 440–4)

Here, Dicaeopolis makes it clear that he wishes to deceive the Acharnians. The Euripidean Telephus' adoption of a beggar's disguise to defend his past actions before an internal audience of Greeks is a very appropriate model of deceptive communication for Dicaeopolis and this appropriateness has been well discussed by critics.[54] The disguise of a tragic figure (himself in disguise) who defends the Trojans to the Greeks befits the situation of Dicaeopolis as a citizen who is trying to defend his sympathy for his audience's enemy in the face of their hostility. But it also enhances the play's sense of Aristophanes' precarious position in the face of Cleon's previous attacks. Dicaeopolis says that

---

[53] Sommerstein (1980) 172.
[54] See Foley (1988); MacDowell (1995) 53–8. Bowie (1993) 27–32 points out that the *Telephus* parody extends beyond the parabasis and is particularly important in Dicaeopolis' exchange with Lamachus at *Ach.* 1094–1234.

the play's audience must know who 'he' is while the chorus are deceived. Dicaeopolis has identified himself with the 'voice' of the comic poet but it is not entirely clear 'who' this character is beneath the tragic disguise: is he Dicaeopolis the farmer, Dicaeopolis the representative of comedy, Dicaeopolis the cipher for a seriously aggrieved Aristophanes ... ? The protection of disguise is further bolstered through the adoption of the mask of tragic parody – a parody which itself involves the adoption of deception and disguise.

As Foley and other critics have pointed out, it is significant that the speech which Dicaeopolis will make is purloined from Euripides' storeroom of tragic speeches and characters: 'by linking his comedy and Euripidean tragedy ... [Aristophanes] claims for it the moral authority, literary prestige and latitude that audiences have always given to more pretentious genres'.[55] At the beginning of the speech, Dicaeopolis again addresses the role of comedy within civic affairs:

Be not indignant with me, members of the audience, if though a beggar, I speak before the Athenians about the polis in a comedy (*trugōidian*). *Trugōidia* too knows about justice (*to dikaion*). And what I have to say will be shocking, but it will be just. This time Cleon will not allege that I am slandering the polis in the presence of foreigners; for we are by ourselves and it's the Lenaean competition ... (Aristophanes *Acharnians* 497–504)

Here, Dicaeopolis deliberately coins a word for 'comedy' (*trugōida*) which sounds like 'tragedy' (*tragōida*).[56] Much debate concerning the entire comedy's meaning centres on the relationship between the claim of this proem ('my speech is just and comedy speaks justice as much as the higher genre of tragedy') and Dicaeopolis' subsequent defence of himself and the Spartans. This defence involves a causal account of the Peloponnesian war: Dicaeopolis argues that the Spartans have behaved understandably and claims that the Athenians would have reacted in exactly the same manner as their enemies (507–39). Alongside parody of Euripides and (possibly) Herodotus, Dicaeopolis' speech offers what Goldhill calls a 'hilariously trivializing account of the processes of war and diplomacy'. Critics have been unable to agree on the import of this account: 'is this lengthy and brilliant parody of rhetoric and history to be seen through, like Dicaeopolis' rags, to reveal a kernel of the serious expression of truth? Or does the parodic narrative comically undercut the (self-important) truth-telling claims of comedy in the proem?'[57]

It is difficult (and perhaps undesirable) to determine the import of

---

[55] Foley (1988) 43.
[56] See Taplin (1983). *Trugōida* is probably derived from *trux*, meaning 'wine lees'.
[57] Goldhill (1991) 195.

Dicaeopolis' defence-speech and there are similar problems involved when we try to gauge the tenor of Dicaeopolis' enactment of his 'private peace' in the rest of the play. Several commentators have argued that Dicaeopolis' unwillingness to share the fruits of that peace with others must be read as selfish (even treasonable) and unjust.[58] But there are also grounds for arguing that where Dicaeopolis refuses to share, he is making the point that 'anyone wanting the advantages of peace must himself make the appropriate effort'.[59] Angus Bowie may be closest to the mark when he suggests that Dicaeopolis' autarchy would provoke differing responses and continuing debate amongst a citizenry that would have been divided by tensions between demes, rural deme and 'urban' polis, and age-groups.[60]

One feature of Dicaeopolis' self-defence which has a bearing on the question of evaluating Dicaeopolis' actions and the 'seriousness' of his claims concerning 'trugedy' and justice is its engagement with contemporary rhetorical strategy. Dicaeopolis can only make his speech after he has consulted Euripides. He knows that he must get Euripides to loan him some deceptive (and yet see-through) Telephean rags, but the terms in which the consultation are presented imply that Euripides is playing a double role. He provides the appropriate paratragic disguise, but in doing so he fulfils the role of a sophist or *logographos*. The exchange between protagonist and playwright emphasises the latter's penchant for sophistic language-games. When Euripides' slave answers the door to Dicaeopolis he answers with the kind of repetitive paradox which had made his master so notorious: οὐκ ἔνδον ἔνδον ἐστίν, εἰ γνώμην ἔχεις (396: 'he is at home and not at home, if you understand me').[61] When the slave explains the paradox, Dicaeopolis remarks that Euripides is blessed to have a slave who answers so 'cleverly' (*sophōs*: 401). Dicaeopolis expects that the disguise of Euripides' Telephus will allow him to deceive the chorus and trump them with 'phraselets' (*rhēmatiois*: 444). The sophistic connotation of *rhēmatia* is made clear in Aristophanes' *Clouds*: the sophistic 'Worse Argument' promises that he will shoot down his opponent with 'new phraselets' (*kainois rhēmatiois*: 944). Once Euripides gives him his Telephus, Dicaeopolis remarks that he is already 'filling up' with *rhēmatia* (447). Euripides

---

[58] See Dover (1972) 87–8; Newiger (1980) 223–4; Foley (1988) 45–6; Fisher (1993) 39–41.

[59] MacDowell (1995) 76. Parker (1991) also argues that Dicaeopolis is not selfish.

[60] See Bowie (1993) 32–44.

[61] Sommerstein (1980) 173 offers the following Euripidean paradoxes as close parallels: *Alc.* 521, *IT* 512, *Ph.* 272. At Ar. *Ran.* 101–2, 1471 and *Thesm.* 275 Aristophanes makes fun of Hippolytus' 'my tongue is sworn but my mind is unsworn' (Eur. *Hipp.* 612).

agrees to loan him the disguise because he feels that Dicaeopolis is lacking in resources: 'I'll give it to you; for thin-spun (*lepta*) are the contrivances (literally, 'you contrive': *mēchanai*) of your rich intelligence' (445).

The consultation scene as a whole is one instance of Aristophanes' comic isolation of Euripides' sophistic style and tone, an isolation which finds its fullest expression in *Thesmophoriazusae* and *Frogs*.[62] But the joke in this scene does not simply consist in the lampooning of Euripides' fondness for imbuing his characters with sophistic turns of phrase and thought. The point is that Dicaeopolis is treating Euripides as his rhetorical consultant. In doing so, Dicaeopolis enacts a comic oscillation between category-mistake and appropriateness. Euripides is *not* a logographer or a sophist. But he possesses characters who make great and clever rhetorical defence-speeches. What is more, these characters and their playwright exhibit the sophistic and fashionable rhetorical training which can both hoodwink and delight a contemporary audience. In this sense, Euripides *is* the appropriate consultant because he can provide the right character and speech for Dicaeopolis and his embattled playwright. The appropriation of tragic rhetoric may constitute a claim that comedy can rival tragedy's authority, but that claim is itself comically undercut by the implication that Dicaeopolis is seeking the services of tragedy's premier sophist and *logographos* so that the Acharnians can be fooled. Dicaeopolis' need for the resources of 'new fangled' rhetorical consultation is elaborated upon by the play's parabasis. Here, the chorus bewail the fact that old men have to face 'stripling orators' in Athens' lawcourts (680):

We stand by the stone, so old we speak in a mumble, seeing nothing but the gloom of justice. Then the young man, who has intrigued to speak for the prosecution against him, rapidly comes to grips and pelts him with hard round phrases (*strongulois rhēmasin*). Then he drags him out and questions him, setting verbal man-traps, tearing a Tithonus of a man in pieces, harrying him and worrying him. The defendant replies in a mumble, so old is he, and then off he goes convicted. (Aristophanes *Acharnians* 683–9)

In the light of these remarks, Dicaeopolis' visit to Euripides' house can be seen as an attempt to acquire the rhetorical equipment which is needed for an adequate 'modern' legal defence. This can be seen as another element underpinning the play's celebration of Dicaeopolis' individualism: he knows he must learn new tricks if he is to pacify the Acharnians and bring about his private peace. But the implication that Dicaeopolis has adopted the unscrupulous rhetorical techniques of the

---

[62] See Walsh (1984) 80–106.

younger generation must lead the audience to question whether his claim to speak 'justice' should be believed. Just as we saw later orators offering a jury anti-rhetorical vignettes of their opponents' 'behind-the-scenes' sophistry, so Aristophanes presents a vignette of Dicaeopolis' own backstage preparations for trickery as he raids the rhetorico-theatrical closet of a sophist-tragedian.

The sense of suspicion surrounding Dicaeopolis' tactics is enhanced by the rhetorical device with which Dicaeopolis opens his defence. As the play's *real* audience spies the comic character beneath tragic rags, they can see a standard forensic topos beneath the tragic parody. Dicaeopolis asks the Acharnians and the audience not to be indignant with him if he speaks about the polis in a 'trugedy' when he is a mere beggar (497–8). This is an adaptation of the Euripidean Telephus' words (Eur. fr. 703). But it also apes the topoi of inexperience and humility which we find in the proems of Attic oratory. Dicaeopolis' explicit decision to deceive the Acharnians with the pitiable garb of a beggar highlights the potential duplicity of his opening topos. The play's concern to stage and foreground visual and verbal techniques of rhetorical deception is thus linked with Dicaeopolis' claims for comedy's capacity to 'know justice' and speak about the polis. Is this profession of comedy's integrity the 'truth' which the audience must see beneath a topos designed to deceive the Acharnians? Or is it disingenuous rhetoric masquerading as the 'underlying truth'?

The difficulty of determining comedy's relationship with dissembling public rhetoric is made more acute by the play's parabasis. At first, it seems as if the chorus step forward to represent Aristophanes as a playwright who reminds the Athenians of the ever-present threat of deception in the *ecclēsia*:

Our poet says he deserves a rich reward at your hands for having stopped you being too easily deceived by the words of foreigners (παύσας ὑμᾶς ξενικοῖσι λόγοις μὴ λίαν ἐξαπατᾶσθαι), taking pleasure in flattery, being gaping citizens (*chaunopolitas*). Previously, when the ambassadors from the allied states were trying to deceive you, they began by calling you 'violet-crowned'; and when someone said that, at once that word 'crowned' made you sit on the tips of your little buttocks. (Aristophanes *Acharnians* 633–8)

Here, Aristophanes draws a parallel between the function of his comedy and Dicaeopolis' role as an exposer of flattery and fraudulence in the play's opening scene. The chorus go on to argue that Aristophanes had shown 'what democracy meant for the peoples of the allied states' (642). This suggests that Aristophanes had dealt with the nature of democratic government in the cities of the Athenian empire in *Babylonians*. That play may also have contained a scene which was similar to the opening scene of *Acharnians* with the difference that it specifically staged flattering speeches from allied envoys.[63] The parabasis claim that the allies are now keen to bring their tribute to Athens so that they can see 'that superlative poet who took the risk of talking justice (*ta dikaia*) to the Athenians' (644). The chorus go on to make an even more fantastic claim for the positive political effects of their poet's didactic prowess: even the king of Persia, when he questioned a Spartan embassy, first asked them which side (the Spartans or Athenians) had the more powerful navy, and then which side received plenty of abuse from Aristophanes (647–9). The king is reported to have said 'for those people have been made much better men, and they will win the war decisively with him for an adviser' (650–1). The chorus then argue that Aristophanes' reputation has caused the Spartans to ask for peace and demand the return of Aegina (Aristophanes' native island): 'they're not concerned about that island, they're concerned to take away this poet' (653–4). The chorus advise the audience never to let Aristophanes go because 'in his comedies he'll say what is just' (*kōmōidēsei ta dikaia*: 655). Aristophanes will make Athenians happy by teaching what is good, 'not flattering you, nor dangling rewards before you, nor deceiving you (*exapatullōn*), nor playing knavish tricks nor drenching you with praise' (656–8).

Aristophanes' self-representation here mimics the rhetorical adoption of the role of the city's 'watchdog' and 'adviser' which we have seen at work in the Athenian orators.[64] Significantly and specifically, Aristophanes appropriates deliberative and forensic oratory's anti-rhetorical topoi whereby the demos is warned against the deceitful and/or flattering speech of an opponent or other speakers in general.[65] But this self-positioning as the anti-rhetorical orator is quickly undermined by ironic exaggeration: the comic poet's didactic role has a fantastic and unbelievable effect on the allies, the Persians and Spartans. This is the comedy of 'wilfully distorting self-aggrandisement'.[66] And such

---

[63] As suggested by MacDowell (1995) 32.

[64] See Halliwell (1984) 17 and Goldhill (1991) 198; Heath (1997) 232–4 and 246, n. 11.

[65] Heath (1997) 232–4 and 246, n. 11 adduces the following parallels as illustrative examples: Aeschin. 2.124, 153, 3.99; Dem. 16.3, 18.276, 282, 19.43–4, 23.188; Din. 1.91, 99, 110–11 (opponents deceive). Aeschin. 1.178; Dem. 18.159, 23. 145, 185 (*ecclēsia* susceptible to deception). Aeschin. 2.177; Dem. 3.13, 8.34, Din. 1.103; Isoc. 12.140 (opponents flatter). Aeschin. 3.234; Dem. 3.21–4, 8.34, 9.4 (*ecclēsia* susceptible to flattery). Dem. 3.3, 6.31, 8.24, 9.3–4 (I am not a flatterer).

[66] Goldhill (1991) 198. Foley (1988) 38 seems to find a more serious point behind Aristophanes' exaggerations: 'How absurd, the parabasis implies, that only Athens's enemies and allies can see the poet's virtues; has the fickle audience forgotten the reception it gave to the *Babylonians*?' This point works for me, if it is interpreted to mean that the parabasis is affirming Aristophanes' satirical prowess – a prowess which includes the process of ironising his own claims to 'speak justice'.

wilful distortion makes it difficult to take seriously Dicaeopolis' early claim that 'trugedy' knows justice. For it is precisely Aristophanic 'justice' which has such laughably unbelievable effects on Athens' allies and enemies. Thus the parabasis' rhetoric of anti-rhetoric is foregrounded as the kind of language which can be harnessed to make deceptive claims to honesty, integrity and effectiveness in the sphere of political advice. As Todorov remarks, 'invocation of truth is a sign of lying'.[67]

But how does the parabasis' comic framing of anti-rhetoric as a disingenuous metafictional strategy relate to the play's representation of Dicaeopolis' own exposures and appropriations of deception and rhetoric? Helene Foley argues that Dicaeopolis uses the 'mesmerising persuasiveness of tragic dramaturgy and rhetoric' in order to deceive the chorus into accepting his 'treasonable secession'.[68] But she stresses that Aristophanes is different: his comedy plays fair by its audience 'by exposing all its tricks and stratagems'. Niall Slater draws a similar conclusion:

Ironically, he must defend his private peace with theatrical means (i.e., the parody of *Telephus*) every bit as fraudulent as those in the assembly. The Euripides scene, however, shows us how to see through the rags and tricks of the tragic stage. It forms the basis of Aristophanes' defence of his own art; comedy is politically useful, because it teaches the citizens to see through political frauds.[69]

The problem with this appraisal (though undoubtedly perceptive and commonly held) is that it removes Aristophanes' comedy from the potential field of 'political fraud'. The 'Aristophanes' of the parabasis proclaims his usefulness as an exposer of rhetorical flattery and deception on the part of those who address the demos. But that anti-rhetorical proclamation is explicitly and comically framed as a deceptive and distorted exaggeration. The play explicitly confuses the distinction between legal or political orator, comic playwright and 'ordinary' private citizen. Dicaeopolis is Aristophanes, Telephus *and* a legal defendant *and* a political *rhētōr*. He is also himself: a frustrated citizen-farmer who has made a private peace and sees the Spartans' point of view. When

---

[67] Todorov (1977) 61 who is commenting on Odysseus' claim that he will tell the truth at Hom. *Od.* 14. 192, before he embarks on one of his lying 'Cretan tales'. See also Goldhill (1991) 40.

[68] Foley (1988) 44.

[69] Slater (1993) 415. Reckford (1987) 179 has a similar formulation. See also Henderson (1990) 312: 'comic poets particularly wanted the demos to look through the lies, compromises, self-interest, and general arrogance of their leaders and to remember who was ultimately in charge'.

Dicaeopolis uses deception for dubious ends, the claim that this play simply celebrates comedy's didactic political role becomes highly dubious too. Dicaeopolis and the parabatic Aristophanes share a rhetoric of anti-rhetoric. The fact that the audience can *see through* Dicaeopolis' deception does help them to detect deception in the *ecclēsia* or law-courts. It may heighten their awareness and develop their suspicion of rhetoric in general and the rhetoric of anti-rhetoric in particular. But Aristophanes the 'trugedian' self-consciously raises the possibility that his comic didactics are also a self-aggrandising strategy of misrepresentation. However many deceptions and disguises are 'stripped away' by the play's protagonist, the manifest deceptiveness of Dicaeopolis–Aristophanes fosters the sense that the comedy itself may be a misrepresentation of these misrepresentations. What if all this 'unmasking' of other people's deceptions is itself a distortion of democratic discourse? If you leave this play thinking that Aristophanes has taught you to 'see through political frauds', you may be Aristophanes' dupe. The play's vertiginous staging of anti-rhetorical rhetoric only tells you that an accusation of deception may itself be deceptive. It is all rather unsettling.

Malcolm Heath has also argued that it is impossible to 'drive a wedge' between Dicaeopolis and Aristophanes on the grounds that the two are associated in the Telephean speech and that this association is reinforced by the parabasis: 'Would it not be reasonable to infer from this association that Aristophanes' claims on his own behalf deserve as much scepticism as those made for Dicaeopolis?'[70] Quite so, but Heath puts this argument in the service of an agenda which also has its problems. He rightly maintains that in *Acharnians* and other plays, we must always reckon with deception when Aristophanes is laying claim to a serious and distinctive advisory or didactic role. After all, Aristophanes' chorus and characters often make general claims about the originality of his comedy (in opposition to that of his rivals) which are subsequently (and comically) undermined through corresponding enactments of the very sorts of 'unoriginal' strategy which have been impugned.[71] But (both here and in a subsequent essay) Heath also wishes to argue that the impossibility of 'driving a wedge' between Dicaeopolis and Aristophanes makes it consequently impossible to regard the *Acharnians* as either offering serious political advice about the war,

---

[70] Heath (1990) 236.
[71] Heath (1990) 237. For this sort of self-undermining irony, see Ar. *Nub.* 537–44 with 1297–1300, 1490ff. Aristophanes is particularly audacious when his parabases claim that he does not recycle material from one play to the next. See *Nub.* 546 in a play which is certainly substantially recycled from its first version and *Pax* 751–60 which itself repeats *Vesp.* 1029–37. On Aristophanes not taking his advisory role seriously see Halliwell (1984) 17–19. On his comic disingenuousness, see Murray (1987).

political life or politicians. He concedes (with impressive illustration) that the language of the parabasis and Dicaeopolis' speeches are closely paralleled in the topoi of the orators, but this 'closeness' between political discourse and its comic appropriation is actually the means by which Aristophanic political didacticism ironically and comically undercuts itself.[72] For Heath, the citizens watching *Acharnians* did not need to be reminded (*contra* Slater, Foley and Henderson) of the dangers of deception or to be told not to forget their sovereignty in the face of demagogic manipulation: 'the frequency with which the Athenians deposed, fined, and even executed their leaders proves that it was not in fact forgotten'.[73] He goes on to argue that there is really no way to determine the extent of Aristophanic comedy's effect on its original audience: we lack the necessary evidence for reconstructing the presuppositions and strategies of reception that Aristophanes' audiences brought to comedy and to which Aristophanes addressed himself. For Heath then, the Aristophanic rhetoric of anti-rhetoric only tells us *Acharnians* cannot be 'political' in any of the senses in which this adjective is usually applied to the play. He accepts Aristophanic comedy was perhaps 'political' in the sense that it told its citizen-audience what they already knew about their democracy, but even this is open to speculation.

Heath seems to me to be too sceptical about reconstructing assumptions which Athenians might have brought to the *Acharnians* but this question of 'context' cannot be explored here. Heath does make some contextual assumptions of his own: it could be argued that the fact of the demos' continued control over its leading politicians was in no small part due to comedy's insistence on criticising Athens' political elite. To be sure, there is no correlation between named individuals (like Cleon) who are attacked and their subsequent career: Cleon continued to prosper politically after *Knights* was performed. But Aristophanic comedy's sustained attacks on individuals in positions of power over the demos might well have helped to isolate the elite as a definable group whom the masses must constantly police.

The idea that Aristophanes' self-implication in the rhetoric of deception and anti-rhetoric makes the *Acharnians* mere 'entertainment' devoid of any meaningful political import is also difficult to sustain. Even if an audience *expected* Aristophanes to self-consciously undermine his own rhetoric of anti-rhetoric, such an expectation and its fulfilment can be understood as a highly 'political' negotiation between play and audience. *Acharnians* construes (or restates a construal of) discourse from those with special licence to speak to the demos (elite

---

[72] Heath (1997).   [73] Heath (1997) 241.

litigants and politicians, tragic and comic playwrights) as potentially misleading. Perhaps Athenians knew this already. But the idea that they could not trust anybody's representation of their political society, of the 'reality' of how far they were being lied to or who was 'really' doing the lying to whom, was (at the very least) an important vision of Athenian democracy to be kept in place. Athenians may not have even looked to comedy to provide the 'truth'. The *Acharnians* reminded them that the 'truth' is hard to establish from *any* source in the city. And the act (just an act?) of 'exposing' the lies and rhetoric of other speakers, other sources of authority is no guarantee that *this* act is genuine. The *Acharnians* thinks with the rhetoric of anti-rhetoric to emphasise the fictive, constructed and potentially misleading quality of the democracy's political, legal and dramatic rhetorics. It is appropriate, I think, to call this comedy 'political' just as *Primary Colors* is aptly subtitled 'a novel of politics'. But this appropriateness derives, not simply from *Acharnians*' exploration and exposure of the way in which the rhetoric of anti-rhetoric can conceal truth, but also from the comic (and yet unsettling) suggestion that such explorations and exposures (political, legal, comic or tragic) may constitute another layer of deceptive rhetoric.

'Men should have two voices': Euripides' tragedy of (anti-)rhetoric

In my first chapter, I offered a reading of Euripides' *Andromache* which highlighted that tragedy's representation of deception as a category of communication with a crucial bearing on notions of ideal and transgressive identity. For me, this play was concerned both to diagnose deceptive behaviour as unmanly, anti-hoplitic and (implicitly) un-Athenian, whilst at the same time suggesting that dishonesty might be infectious amongst the elite rulers of any Greek polis. In the previous section of this chapter, we saw that Aristophanes was able to imagine Euripidean tragedy as a resource for rhetorical deception and a mode of representation whose claims to speak 'justice' to the polis were to be reckoned with in his own rival genre of comedy.

In this section, I want to set Euripides' interest in deception next to the ancient and modern recognition that his tragedy exhibits a keen concern with rhetoric and agonistic argumentation.[74] A thoroughgoing

---

[74] For modern accounts of the rhetorical and sophistic features of Euripidean themes and characters' speeches, see Winnington-Ingram (1969); Buxton (1982) 170–86; Walsh (1984) 80–106; Ostwald (1986) 229–90; Goldhill (1988a) 222–42, (1997) 145–50; Lloyd (1992); Croally (1994) 134–62; Conacher (1998).

study of deception and rhetoric in Euripides would require a book to itself: here, I will discuss several plays but my discussion will be anchored to one tragedy which is exemplary in some senses but also (in my view) unique in the extent to which it addresses the problem of deception in a specifically rhetorical and forensic context – and in a manner which would speak very directly to its audience's experience and identity as democratic citizens.

Euripides' *Hippolytus* was perfomed in 428. It was a rewritten and a restructured version of a play which now survives only in fragmentary form.[75] The play is breathtakingly rich in interwoven themes: it stages sexual desire, self-control (*sōphrosunē*), violence, misogyny, male arrogance and anxiety, female cunning and madness, divine cruelty, religious transgression and ritual aetiology, the inadequacies and excesses of language and much more besides. It has thus attracted much fruitful analysis and commentary.[76] The play charts the destruction of Hippolytus, the bastard son of Theseus, and Hippolytus' step-mother Phaedra. Hippolytus' concern for *sōphrosunē* leads him to reject the goddess Aphrodite altogether. In the play's prologue Aphrodite states that she has plotted to punish Hippolytus' rejection of *erōs* by causing his step-mother Phaedra to conceive sexual desire for him (1–57). Theseus will also be an instrument in his son's downfall (41–6). The action takes place in Trozen, where Theseus is king. Theseus himself is absent on a trip to consult an oracle. We soon learn that Phaedra would rather die of her 'sickness' than reveal its cause or confront her step-son with her lust for him. But her nurse wrenches the truth from her and, in a misguided effort to save her mistress from her own sense of shame, she tells the young man of Phaedra's secret passion. Hippolytus is horrified and unleashes a scathing attack on womankind. Despite his rejection of the nurse's overture, he agrees to swear an oath that he will not reveal his step-mother's shameful desire to anyone. Phaedra overhears the exchange between Hippolytus and the nurse. She decides it is better to kill herself than risk the shame and infamy of revelation. To ensure that her reputation will remain intact after her death, she leaves a written suicide-letter for her absent husband to read on his return. The letter falsely accuses Hippolytus of raping her. Theseus is meant to assume that Phaedra has killed herself because she has been raped by his own son.

[75] For the details of the first version see Barrett (1964) 11–12, 18–22. For fuller discussion and translations of the surviving fragments see Halleran (1995) 25–37.

[76] For exemplary studies of the play, see Knox (1952); Zeitlin (1985); Luschnig (1988); Goldhill (1988a) 107–37; Gill (1990); Goff (1990); Gregory (1991) 51–84; Segal (1986), (1988); Rabinowitz (1993) 155–88; Cairns (1993) 314–40.

The entrance of Theseus marks the emergence of certain polis-based concerns. As Goff puts it, 'the first part of the play is concentrated on those whose exclusion defines the polis, namely women, slaves and youths. Theseus is thus the only figure that remotely resembles the Athenian males who gather to watch the dramatic performances at the festival of Dionysos'.[77] Theseus is Athens' most prominent and ideologically important mythical king: in other tragedies, his entrance goes hand-in-hand with a positive image of Athens as a site for the resolution of conflict, a haven for suppliants and the transcendence of blood-guilt through pity and compassion.[78] In *Hippolytus*, Theseus' Athenian associations are much less prominent.[79] But he is described as king of Athens as well as Trozen and when he pronounces his banishment of Hippolytus, he makes it clear that this includes exile from Athens (974, 1093f., 1158). Furthermore, when the messenger enters to tell Theseus of Hippolytus' mortal wounding, he describes his report as of concern to the 'citizens of both Athens' and 'those within the boundaries of the Trozenian land' (Θησεῦ, μερίμνης ἄξιον φέρω λόγον σοὶ καὶ πολίταις οἵ τ' Ἀθηναίων πόλιν ναίουσι καὶ γῆς τέρμονας Τροζηνίας: 1157–9). It may be true that Theseus is 'never linked with Athens as its representative as he is in all the other extant Theseus plays' and that 'the *Hippolytus* could have been a radically disturbing play if, say, in the *agon* scene with his father, Hippolytus had begged Theseus to show the pity that an Athenian should naturally show and Theseus had explicitly denied that he cared for the reputation of his city'.[80] But Theseus clearly holds sway over Athens (974–5) and Trozen is only his temporary home. It would be hard for the play's Athenian audience not to see themselves implicated in the tragedy's closing scenes through the figure of Theseus and the references to their city and its *politai*.[81]

The Athenian audience's implication in Theseus' discovery of Phaedra's body, her letter and his confrontation with Hippolytus is further enhanced by forensic and theatrical structure and tone. Theseus twice describes himself as a *theōros* ('spectator': 792, 807) and in

---

[77] Goff (1990) 116. On the vexed question of whether women attended the Great Dionysia, see Goldhill (1995) with further bibliography cited therein.
[78] See Mills (1997) 87–164 on the role of Theseus and the projection of Athenian identity, democracy and empire in Euripides' *Suppliants*, *Heracles* and Sophocles' *Oedipus at Colonus*. For Theseus in Athenian myth, art and civic ideology, see Neils (1987); Walker (1995); Mills (1997) 1–86.
[79] See Mills (1997) 193–4.
[80] Mills (1997) 193 and 194.
[81] Goff (1990) 116.

discovering the body, he sees a *pikra thea* ('bitter sight': 809).[82] Goff argues that Theseus' exclamation, 'look!' (*skepsasthe*: 943) and his proclamation, 'I speak to all' (*prophono pasi*: 956) are 'theatrical gestures that must in some sense include the audience'.[83] The possibility and extent of Theseus' words here being inclusive of the audience is controversial.[84] But there is little doubt that his scene with Hippolytus would focus the audience's attention on their own (actual or potential) role as citizen-jurors in Athens' lawcourts. Both characters use forensic terminology and the language of legal rhetoric.[85] Both use probability arguments to accuse and defend (962–70, 1007–20). Theseus' probability arguments also constitute the forensic topos of 'anticipation' of the opponent's defence (962–70). He refers to Phaedra's body as the 'clearest witness' to Hippolytus' guilt (*marturos saphestatou*: 972). The letter itself 'accuses' Hippolytus convincingly (*hē deltos . . . katēgorei sou pista*: 1057–8). Hippolytus has been 'convicted' of wickedness by the dead woman (*ex elenchetai*: 945); he has been 'caught' (*elēphthēs*: 955) and 'found out' (*haliskēi*: 959).

When Theseus has read Phaedra's letter and Hippolytus comes on stage, he bewails the fact that men have taught 'countless crafts' (*murias technas*: 917), have devised and discovered everything, but they 'do not know . . . to teach good sense (*phronein*) to those who have no wits' (920). Hippolytus replies that it would be a 'clever sophist' (*deinon sophistēn*: 921) who could teach good sense (*eu phronein*) and asks his father to stop being subtle at an inappropriate moment (921–4). Theseus responds with the following reflection:

---

[82] Noted by Goff (1990) 116. It should be pointed out that Theseus' use of *theōros* primarily means here 'a visitor to an oracle'. But the meaning 'spectator' would surely also have a resonance, given that Theseus arrives to hear of his wife's death and then views the catastrophic spectacle of her corpse wheeled out of the palace doors. On the visual impact of such revelatory stagecraft see Taplin (1977) 442–3. Halleran (1995) on 809 (219) notes the possibility of 'grim word play' between *dustuchēs theōros* ('unfortunate visitor/spectator') and *pikran thean* ('bitter sight').

[83] Goff (1990) 116.

[84] For the implications and issues see Bain (1975) who is sceptical about the possibility of 'audience address' in tragedy. See also Taplin (1985), though Taplin (1996) is more generous.

[85] See Goldhill (1988a) 233–4; Goff (1990) 38–9, 78–80; Lloyd (1992) 32, 46–8. Mills (1997) 215 points out that Theseus may use legal language but he 'perverts forensic practice': he has already decided that his son is guilty of the letter's accusations before Hippolytus makes his defence. His 'witnesses' are a corpse and 'just a letter'. Hippolytus certainly feels that he has been banished before a proper trial (1055–6): 'Without examining (*elegxas*) oath or pledge or the words of prophets, will you throw me out of this land without a trial (*akriton*).'

Alas, mortals ought to have established a clear sign/touchstone (*tekmērion*) of friends (*philoi*) and a means of distinguishing their minds, to tell who is a true (*alēthes*) friend and who is not, and all men should have two voices (*dissas phōnas*): the one just (*dikaian*) voice, the other how it happened to be, so that the one thinking unjust things might be refuted/convicted (*exēlencheto*) by the just voice, and we should not be deceived (*kouk an ēpatōmetha*). (Euripides *Hippolytus* 925–31)

Critics vary in their interpretation as to whether these words are specifically directed against Hippolytus, who has shown him no previous indications of base intent, or more generally express the difficulty of determining which 'of those dear to him, either his son or his wife, is false and counterfeit'.[86] There has also been much discussion as to what Theseus means by the 'two voices'.[87] What they *do* express is a desire for a distinguishable and transparent form of true speech to supplement the always potentially deceptive voice which mortals normally employ. In her study of the *Hippolytus*, Barbara Goff points out that the lack of transparency which Theseus bemoans 'can be seen in linguistic events such as Phaidra's letter, or the gulf between word and intent which Hippolytus threatens when he tells the Nurse that his tongue swore but his mind remains unsworn (612)'.[88] Theseus' second transparent voice is an impossibility (the rhetorical and literary trope of the *adunaton*); 'there is no point at which language can achieve such an identity with the world as would exclude the possibilities of fiction. The "deviations" that Theseus seeks to abolish are the very conditions of the existence of language'.[89] And she goes on to produce an interesting reading of the play's dramatisation of the ways in which both desire and language 'introduce disruptive differences and thwart human longings for stability and containment'.[90] Of course, Theseus mistakenly and ironically believes the written voice of the suicide letter and its absent author as opposed to the living voice of Hippolytus. He fails to apply his insight into the potential fiction of his son's *spoken* evidence to the *written* evidence of his dead wife.

Jones notes the 'unconsciously ironical' flavour to Theseus' words – he is falsely accusing Hippolytus almost at the very moment in which

---

[86] DuBois (1991) 13.
[87] See Musurillo (1974) for a survey.
[88] Goff (1990) 46.
[89] Goff (1990) 46. Here Goff glosses Theseus' *adunaton* as a reflection on what Umberto Eco has observed to be a very condition of all linguistic and extra-linguistic signification: 'the definition of a "theory of the lie" should be taken as a pretty comprehensive program for a general semiotics' (Eco (1976) 7). See also Eco (1985).
[90] Goff (1990) 46.

he discourses on the impossibility of identifying liars.[91] He also describes these words as 'the nearest approach to a characteristic attitude in this most diverse writer' because, as I noted in the last chapter, Euripides' tragedies contain several similar reflections on the impossibility of distinguishing truth and trustworthiness from deception and faithlessness or else the difficulty of determining someone's moral character because of misleading external evidence. I will examine some of these similar instances because they provide an important frame for reading Theseus' wish for transparency and the *Hippolytus*' *agōn* as a whole.

Theseus' words seem to have been carried over from a similar formulation in the first version of the *Hippolytus*, though we can only speculate that the speaker and context were the same:

Alas, alas, that the facts (*pragmata*) have no voice for humans, so that those who are clever at speaking (*deinoi legein*) would be nothing. But as things are, they conceal (literally 'steal': *kleptousin*) with glib tongues (literally 'wide mouths': *eurooisin stomasi*) what is truest (*alēthestata*), so that what ought to appear to be so (*dokein*) does not. (Euripides Fragment 439 [= N Barrett])[92]

Wherever these lines appeared in the first version, they actually connect the *adunaton* of a transparent 'second voice' with the specific discourse of rhetoric.[93] The speaker uses the same gloss for rhetorical skill (*deinos legein*) which we saw deployed in forensic orations of the late fifth and fourth century. But they also offer an image of truth being 'stolen' by rhetoric, as if it were a physical commodity. In the place of truth rhetoric leaves no room for 'what ought to appear so' (*ha chrē dokein*). Here, Euripides' speaker stresses that rhetoric is in the business of establishing *to dokein* or *doxa*: 'appearance', 'seeming' or 'opinion'.

The connection between the effects of deceptive communication and the mortal condition of *doxa* is vehemently made in Euripides' *Andromache*. When Menelaus announces that he intends to kill Androm-

---

[91] Jones (1962) 252.
[92] The translation here is that of Halleran (1995) 30 with my own literal translations in parentheses.
[93] Halleran (1995) 27 calls F 439 'a lament over clever rhetoric'. The lines could well be Theseus' initial response to Hippolytus' self-defence speech in the first play's *agōn*. See Eur. *Hipp.* 1038–40. But they could also be part of Hippolytus' proem: see Eur. *Hipp.* 986–9. Given that the first version probably included a direct confrontation between Phaedra and Hippolytus, the lines could be the latter's response to the former. They could even be Phaedra's response to the Nurse's arguments in favour of breaking her silence and approaching Hippolytus: see Eur. *Hipp.* 670f.

ache and her child, the heroine replies with an outburst on the subject of false appearances and undeserved reputation:

ὦ δόξα δόξα, μυρίοισι δὴ βροτῶν
οὐδὲν γεγῶσι βίοτον ὤγκωσας μέγαν.
[εὔκλεια δ᾿ οἷς μέν ἐστ᾿ ἀληθείας ὕπο
εὐδαιμονίζω· τοὺς δ᾿ ὑπὸ ψευδῶν ἔχειν
οὐκ ἀξιώσω, πλὴν τύχῃ φρονεῖν δοκεῖν.]
σὺ δὴ στρατηγῶν λογάσιν Ἑλλήνων ποτὲ
Τροίαν ἀφείλου Πρίαμον, ὧδε φαῦλος ὤν;
ὅστις θυγατρὸς ἀντίπαιδος ἐκ λόγων
τοσόνδ᾿ ἔπνευσας καὶ γυναικὶ δυστυχεῖ
δούλῃ κατέστης εἰς ἀγῶν᾿· οὐκ ἀξιῶ
οὔτ᾿ οὖν σὲ Τροίας οὔτε σοῦ Τροίαν ἔτι.
[ἔξωθέν εἰσιν οἱ δοκοῦντες εὖ φρονεῖν
λαμπροί, τὰ δ᾿ ἔνδον πᾶσιν ἀνθρώποις ἴσοι,
πλὴν εἴ τι πλούτῳ· τοῦτο δ᾿ ἰσχύει μέγα.]

Reputation! Reputation (ō doxa doxa)! You do indeed puff up countless no-bodies to greatness. [Those who have fame by truth I congratulate; but those by falsehoods (hupo pseudōn), I will not consider that they have, except by chance to seem wise (phronein dokein).] Was it really you, who are so petty, who once led the chosen men of Greece and seized Troy from Priam? You, who breathed such rage as a result of the words of your child-like daughter, and entered into a contest with an unfortunate slave-woman: I no longer regard you as worthy of Troy, or Troy of you. [Those who have the reputation of being wise (hoi dokountes eu phronein) are outwardly illustrious, but inwardly the same as everybody else; except perhaps in wealth; that has great power.] (Euripides Andromache 319–32)[94]

This reply picks up on Menelaus' earlier claims to intellectual prowess (phronousa: 313) by comparing the false reputation of men who *seem* to be wise (phronein dokein: 323) through the benefit of good fortune with those who have *truly* earned their 'good fame' (eukleia: 321–3).[95] An-

---

[94] The translation is that of Lloyd (1994) 44–5.
[95] Some scholars bracket lines 321–3 and 330–2 as corrupt. The grounds for bracketing 321–3 are (1) improbably compressed syntax (τοὺς δ᾿ ὑπο ψευδῶν, ἔχειν οὐκ ἀξιώσω); and (2) that φρονεῖν is intrusive to the context. The recent OCT of Diggle brackets the lines on these grounds. However, see Stevens (1971) 136 who offers good arguments for accepting the lines. Ground (2) is clearly weakened if read as a retort to Menelaus' boast at 313 (see Lloyd (1994) ad loc.). On 330–2, Diggle's OCT and Lloyd (1994) ad loc. follow Stevens (1971) 137. See also Kovacs (1980) 29 who endorses the OCT of Murray. Stevens argues that 'it is odd that E. should insert here another generalisation on the same lines as 319–23'. Secondly, Stobaeus 104.14 cites 330 and 331 (with the substitution of εὐτυχεῖν for εὖ φρονεῖν) as from Menander, and Stevens argues that all three lines were written in the margin of a manuscript as a parallel to 319f. and were then incorporated into the text. Of course, he cannot rule out the possibility that Menander might have copied from Euripides. Stevens also has a difficulty with 332 as

dromache 'emphasises the gap between the true and the false, appearance and reality, and the great difficulty of distinguishing between them'.[96] But the terms in which Andromache formulates her critique of indiscriminate *doxa* are important for the play's negotiations of political representation.[97]

Andromache's remarks on *doxa*, with its connotations of seeming, appearance, repute, belief and opinion, bear resemblances to the concerns of Eleatic and sophistic thought which I discussed in my third chapter.[98] The writings of Parmenides and Gorgias both stress that mortals suffer from the possession of incomplete knowledge; they are confined to the realm of *doxa*.[99] Andromache is specifically discussing the realm of opinion in relation to the attribution of positive *kleos* to men in general and Menelaus in particular. She does not address the possibilities or impossibilities of absolute knowledge *per se*. Like Parmenides, however, she claims for herself a level of enlightenment when she implies that she can discern the difference between truly and falsely earned *eukleia*.

For the sophist Gorgias, the positive and negative charming effects of linguistic and visual representations are due primarily to the vulnerable condition of *doxa* in which mortals find themselves. In his ironic *Encomium of Helen*, Gorgias lays particular emphasis on the persuasive power that *logos*, especially false *logos*, exerts over mankind because

---

an idea following on from the contrast in 330–1, since wealth can hardly be counted as among τὰ ἔνδον. To make 330–2 cohere as one interpolation, Stevens glosses 332 as 'it's only in wealth (which is external) that they differ'. But Andromache's sarcastic point is precisely that wealth instils great strength and power (τοῦτο δ' ἰσχύει μέγα: 332). If Menelaus' glory is superficial in that it derives from a false reputation, he is nevertheless not 'equal' to other men because he still has the wealth which gives him power over others. And such reflections on the workings of wealth are not simply 'on the same lines as 319–23' since these previous lines do not address the separate issue of the way in which money confers power and hierarchy regardless of moral legitimacy or genuine reputation. Furthermore, this separate issue is hardly an anomalous theme for the play; Andromache's comments in these disputed lines can be related to the exchanges and representations concerning wealth in her earlier confrontation with Hermione.

[96] Boulter (1966) 55.
[97] It could also be argued that Andromache's critique of *doxa* and Menelaus' *eukleia* also introduces a questioning of poetic and specifically Homeric representations of the past. This questioning of Homer is perhaps developed by Peleus' attack on Menelaus' military conduct at 616–18. For Euripidean interrogation of Homeric tradition in other plays see Walsh (1984) 107–26; Goldhill (1988a).
[98] I can find no specific discussion of this speech's engagement with pre-Socratic or sophistic ideas. For the connection between ideas expressed elsewhere in the play by Hermione and Andromache and the texts of Gorgias and Antiphon, see Saïd (1978) 251–9.
[99] See Parmenides DK 18 B1, B6 and B19; Gorg. *Hel.* 11–14 (= DK 82 B11.11–14), *Pal.* 24–35 (= DK 82 B11a.24–35).

nobody has certain knowledge or memory. Most have only *doxa* (belief) to rely on and yet, as Gorgias puts it, '*doxa*, being slippery and unreliable, brings slippery and unreliable success to those who employ it'.[100] Among his examples of persuasive *logoi* which mould the mind are poetry and the 'compulsory contests in which a single speech pleases and persuades a large crowd, because written with skill, not spoken with truth'.[101] His reflections have started from the premise that Helen may have gone to Troy with Paris because 'speech persuaded and deceived her mind'.[102] Critics disagree as to whether Gorgias sees *all* speech as a kind of *apatē*.[103] It is clear, however, that he represents the condition of belief and opinion as rendering the human soul extremely vulnerable to misrepresentations and deceptive persuasion. As we have seen already, he even compares the power of speech to the power that drugs have on the body: 'some speeches cause sorrow, some cause pleasure, some cause fear, some give hearers confidence, some drug and bewitch the mind with a certain evil persuasion'.[104]

Like Gorgias, Andromache connects the operation of lies (τοὺς δ' ὑπὸ ψευδῶν ἔχειν οὐκ ἀξιώσω) and the effects of *doxa* (ὦ δόξα δόξα, μυρίοισι δὴ βροτῶν οὐδὲν γεγῶσι βίοτον ὤγκωσας μέγαν).[105] She goes on to question the very possibility that one so base as Menelaus could have led those who took Troy from Priam (σὺ δὴ στρατηγῶν λογάσιν Ἑλλήνων ποτὲ Τροίαν ἀφείλου Πρίαμον ὧδε φαῦλος ὤν;). The implication is that Menelaus' political and military power are founded on a lie. Comparison with Gorgias' *Encomium of Helen* suggests that the terms in which she formulates the dissemination of that false reputation are recognisable from a specifically late fifth-century discourse on the

---

[100] Gorg. *Hel.* 11 (= DK 82 B11.11): ἡ δὲ δόξα σφαλερὰ καὶ ἀβέβαιος οὖσα σφαλεραῖς καὶ ἀβεβαίοις εὐτυχίαις περιβάλλει τοὺς αὐτῇ χρωμένους.

[101] Gorg. *Hel.* 13: δεύτερον δὲ τοὺς ἀναγκαίους διὰ λόγων ἀγῶνας, ἐν οἷς εἷς λόγος πολὺν ὄχλον ἔτερψε καὶ ἔπεισε τέχνῃ γραφείς, οὐκ ἀληθείᾳ λεχθείς.

[102] Gorg. *Hel.* 8: Εἰ δὲ λόγος ὁ πείσας καὶ τὴν ψυχὴν ἀπατήσας . . .

[103] Discussions of Gorgias' theory of *apatē* and *doxa*: Detienne (1967) 121ff.; Guthrie (1971) 192–9; Kerferd (1981a), ch. 8; Rosenmeyer (1955); Segal (1962); Untersteiner (1954) 108–39; Verdenius (1981). MacDowell (1982) 12–16, takes issue with Verdenius' view that Gorgias sees all speech as involving *apatē*.

[104] Gorg. *Hel.* 14 (= DK 82 B11.14): ὥσπερ γὰρ τῶν φαρμάκων ἄλλους ἄλλα χυμοὺς ἐκ τοῦ σώματος ἐξάγει, καὶ τὰ μὲν νόσου τὰ δὲ βίου παύει, οὕτω καὶ τῶν λόγων οἱ μὲν ἐλύπησαν, οἱ δὲ ἔτερψαν οἱ δὲ ἐφόβησαν, οἱ δὲ εἰς θάρσος κατέστησαν τοὺς ἀκούοντας, οἱ δὲ πειθοῖ τινι κακῇ τὴν ψυχὴν ἐξεφαρμάκευσαν καὶ ἐγοήτευσαν.

[105] Gorgias was from Leontini in Sicily but evidence suggests that he became a familiar figure in Athens. According to Diodorus 12.53 he was sent as an envoy to Athens in 427. See Thuc. 3.86. Plato's *Gorgias* represents him as a well-known and much-admired teacher of rhetoric. Engagement with Gorgianic style and ideas has been detected in other plays of Euripides. See Scodel (1980) 94–104; Walsh (1984) 62–132; Goldhill (1988a) 236–8; Croally (1994) 222–3.

power of languages (including the language of legal and political rhetoric) to shape belief through its (mis)representations.

Theseus' wish for transparency in the second *Hippolytus* contains no
specific reference to 'clever speaking' or the slipperiness of *doxa*. But
the presence of these concerns in the first *Hippolytus* and the *Andromache* shows how Euripidean tragedy repeatedly represents the problematic 'ambiguity of speech' as significantly exacerbated by 'sophistic'
and 'rhetorical' discourse. Of course, such anti-rhetorical reflection
does not translate into an 'anti-rhetorical' message for a play as a
whole. In Euripides' *Hecuba*, there is a tense *agōn* between the play's
heroine and Polymestor. Hecuba and the Trojan women have killed
Polymestor's children and blinded him. They lured him to their tents
at Troy in order to take revenge on him for killing Hecuba's son Polydorus. Polymestor seeks Hecuba's punishment at the hands of Agamemnon. He gives a speech of self-defence in which he claims that he
did not kill Polydorus for gold (as Hecuba alleges) but in order to destroy an enemy of the Greeks. Hecuba's speech in reply opens with an
anti-rhetorical flourish:

Agamemnon, men never ought to have a tongue more powerful than their
deeds; rather, just as a man ought to speak nobly if he acted nobly, so, con-
versely his words should ring false (*tous logous einai sathrous*) if he has done
wicked things, and he should never be able to speak well (*eu legein*) about
wrong-doing. Now there are indeed clever men (*sophoi*) who do that to precision, but they cannot be clever all through, and they meet a miserable end; no
one has escaped yet. (Euripides *Hecuba* 1187–94)

Like Theseus in the second *Hippolytus*, Hecuba wishes for an *adunaton*
that dishonest speech be easily detectable. In this instance, she wants
dishonest words to be *sathroi*: 'unsound' like a cracked pot.[106] The desire is for human speech to be testable for quality and authenticity like
a physical object and I will return to this longing for deception to approximate debased materials below. But at the same time as Hecuba
laments the power of deceptive rhetoric, she expresses confidence that
it never ultimately pays off. Furthermore, her own speech of accusation
and defence is a masterpiece of rhetoric in itself.[107] Agamemnon does
not believe Polymestor (1240–51). Indeed, he had already sanctioned
Hecuba's plans for revenge in a previous exchange (785–904). There,
as Hecuba attempts to persuade Agamemnon to delay her daughter's
sacrifice and permit the vengeance, she articulates the value of rhetoric:

---

[106] For the metaphor of the earthenware jar (*pithos*) which is unsound (*sathros*) in a moral
context, see Pl. *Grg.* 493e7. For *sathros* used of speech and deception see Eur. *Rh.* 639,
Supp. 1064. See also Dodds (1960) on Eur. *Bacc.* 267–71.

[107] See Buxton (1982) 181f.; Collard (1991) on 1187–1237 (194); Mossman (1995) 134.

Why then do we mortals labour in search of all other kinds of learning as we ought, but make no further effort, by paying fees, to learn persuasion (*peithō*) thoroughly, the only *turannos* of men, so that it might sometimes be possible to persuade about one's wishes, and gain them too? (Euripides *Hecuba* 814–19)

Again, Hecuba's metarhetoric (this time a depreciation of her own rhetorical ability) comes in the midst of a highly proficient display of persuasive argument: Collard calls it 'a model of calculated pleading' and 'a text-book show-piece, an *epideixis*'.[108] Interestingly, Hecuba's version of the 'I am unskilled' strategy makes a commendation which I believe no real Athenian demagogue or litigant could have dared to make. She advocates a sophistic rhetorical education even as she demonstrates that she has no need of such an education. Her representation of *peithō* as a *turannos* is close to the sophist Gorgias' depiction of speech as a powerful *dunastēs*.[109] Thus, through Hecuba's comments on the difficulties of seeing through specious rhetoric and her ironic desire to learn the art of persuasion, Euripides presents his audience with two views of rhetoric: it is the positive means by which individuals may be enabled to gain their own wishes or a negative medium of deceptive communication. But Euripides also places these comments in the framework of powerful rhetorical speeches. Their *strategic* quality is thus underlined as Hecuba disingenuously positions herself as unschooled in rhetoric's arts and as the potential victim of its deceptions.

Theseus' wish for a means of distinguishing truth from lies is paralleled in other Euripidean tragedies too. In *Heracles Furens*, the chorus wish for the *adunaton* that men be granted a 'second youth' to distinguish 'those whose lives were virtuous' (655–68). The Old Man of Euripides' *Electra* reflects that nobility may be counterfeit (*kibdēlos*: 550): for many who are of noble birth (*eugeneis*) may be bad (*kakoi*: 551). In the same play, Orestes begins a speech on the difficulties of distinguishing good from bad character by observing that 'nothing is precise (*akribes*) when it comes to virtue (*euandrian*: 367)'.[110] In the *Medea*, the heroine reflects on Jason's faithlessness in the following terms:

Oh Zeus! Why have you given us clear signs/touchstones (*tekmēria*) to tell true gold from counterfeit (*kibdēlos*); but when we need to know bad men from good, the body reveals no mark/stamp (*charaktēr*)? (Euripides *Medea* 516–19)

---

[108] Collard (1991) on 787–847 (170). See also Buxton (1982) 178–80; Heath (1987a) 145–7; Mossman (1995) 126–7.

[109] Gorg. *Hel.* 8 (= DK 82 B11.8).

[110] Nobody has doubted the authenticity of this line but most other parts of the speech (368–400) have been suspected. On the question (a rather ironic one, given the speech's content) of how much of the speech is to be regarded as genuine, see Reeve (1973); Basta Donzelli (1978) 229–42; Goldhill (1986); Cropp (1988) ad loc. (123–5).

Like Theseus, Medea wishes for *tekmēria*. The word *tekmērion* can be used in Athenian forensic oratory to mean 'proof' of an argumentative kind (as opposed to direct evidence).[111] Antiphon opposes *tekmērion* to arguments from probability (*eikota*) but also speaks of *tekmēria* which are not probable (2.4.10, 4.4.2). It need not have a specifically forensic flavour: it can simply mean a definite 'sign' or 'token', a sure medical symptom or, in Aristotelian logic a demonstrative proof as opposed to a fallible *sēmeion* or probability argument (*eikos*).[112] Medea clearly uses *tekmērion* in the context of a monetary metaphor: unlike coins, human bodies display no stamp (*charaktēr*) to guarantee moral goodness.

Given that Hippolytus has already used the language of monetary debasement to describe women (*kibdēlon kakon*: 619), critics have seen Theseus' wish for 'clear *tekmēria*' as a further deployment of the 'counterfeit coin' metaphor.[113] Theseus certainly directs his comments towards the specific question of how to distinguish between true and false *philoi*. This question is couched in monetary terms in the aristocratic elegy of the *Theognidea* (640–479 BC). In the paranoid world of the Theognidean symposium and polis, it is best not to reveal one's intentions to *philoi* because few are trustworthy (73–4).[114] Theognis stresses that nothing is more difficult to know than the real nature of a *kibdēlos* ('counterfeit') man (117–18). And the counterfeit *philos* who deceives your mind has to be tested out like an animal (119–28). Because people conceal their counterfeit character (*kibdēlon ēthos*) it is best not to praise a man until you truly know him (963–70). In a couplet which strongly prefigures Andromache's remarks discussed above, Theognis also points out that *doxa* (reputation) is inferior to experience (*peira*) concerning a man's character (571–2). It is also wise to be deceptive and cunning oneself (359–64) and to have a 'variegated character' (*poikilon ēthos*) among one's *philoi* (213–14, 1071–2). Whether or not we see Theseus' 'second voice' speech as reliant on the metaphor of 'debased coinage', he clearly speaks in the Theognidean mode of the paranoid *sententia*. Indeed, his words are similar to an Attic drinking-song preserved by Athenaeus:

Would that, to see what sort of man each is, we could open up his breast, and look at his mind (*noun*) then locking it up once more, regard him surely as our friend. (Athenaeus *Deipnosophistae* 694d–e [= *PMG* 889])

---

[111] See Isoc. 4.12, 8.6.
[112] Sign or token: Hdt. 2.13; Aesch. *Ag.* 1366; Soph. *El.* 774, 1109; [Eur.] *Rh.* 94. Medical symptom: Hipp. *Prog.* 25, Sor. *Vit. Hippocr.* 12; Aristotelian proof: Arist. *Pr.* 70b2, *Rh.* 1.1357b4, 2.1402b19.
[113] See Goff (1990) 45; DuBois (1991) 13–14.
[114] See the excellent analyses of Levine (1985); Cobb-Stevens (1985); Ferrari (1988).

Of course, in aping the aristocratic and suspicious *sententiae* of Theognis and sympotic songs, Euripides' Theseus might be regarded as unsympathetic to a democratic audience: on reading Phaedra's letter he is too quick to find authority for his first conclusions in the maxims of elitist poetic tradition and the culture of aristocratic and oligarchic faction.[115] It is certainly poignant that Theseus' recognition of the difficulty of detecting false friends and deception tragically misses the right target. Mills has recently noted that the Theseus of *Hippolytus* is much more tyrannical in word and action than the Theseus of other extant Euripidean tragedies.[116]

But at the same time as an Athenian audience see their mythical king at a greater distance in this play, his bitter plea for transparency conveys a problem which was very close to their own situation as democratic citizens. As with many of the other Euripidean, Theognidean and sympotic *sententiae* which I have discussed, Theseus longs for truth and falsehood to have a distinguishable and demonstrable materiality. If only words and faces could be like coins or pots, then we could distinguish honesty and moral integrity from falsity and deception. Here, through his ironic comments and his mistaken interpretation of the scene which confronts him, Theseus articulates the inescapable problem posed by deception in a forensic context. Speech, writing and rhetoric may have an 'independent materiality' with the power to bewitch, persuade, deceive and ultimately destroy. Goff notes the many instances in the *Hippolytus* where spoken and written words are represented as having a negative material force.[117] But the sophistic celebration or anti-rhetorical condemnation of this materiality cannot resolve the fact that words are *not* amenable to the same tests as certain material objects. In a crucial respect, the play highlights deceptive communication's *lack* of materiality as an insurmountable problem. As a spectator, accuser and judge Theseus' predicament in the face of such immaterial lies mirrored that of an Athenian audience as they viewed, judged or themselves became litigants in the people's courts.

The representation of rhetorical argument in the *agōn* between Hippolytus and Theseus exacerbates the disturbing ramifications of Theseus' failure to uncover the truth for an Athenian audience. As I noted at the beginning of this section, Hippolytus produces a defence full of rhetorical flourishes. He will not break his oath to the Nurse and so is

---

[115] As Figuera and Nagy (1985) 1 point out, Theognis was imitated in the elegies of Critias (leader of the Thirty Tyrants at Athens) and was also the subject of treatises and citations by the likes of Antisthenes, Xenophon and Plato.

[116] Mills (1997) 195.

[117] See Goff (1990) 54 for discussion and references.

unable to speak of Phaedra's desire for him. Instead, he relies on a version of the 'I am unskilled' topos, a series of probability arguments and sworn oaths. Like Hecuba's professed lack of rhetorical ability, his claim to inexperience seems disingenuous: Hippolytus' speech is packed with classic rhetorical moves. But, in contrast to Hecuba, Hippolytus' use of rhetoric comes across as tactless and misjudged. He couches his lack of skill in terms which connote arrogance and aloofness:

I am unaccomplished at giving speeches before a crowd (*eis ochlon*), but more skilled (*sophōteros*) before a few of my peers, and this too is natural: for those who are inadequate in the presence of the wise are more eloquent at speaking before a crowd. (Euripides *Hippolytus* 986–9)

In Hippolytus' mouth, a topos which Attic oratory typically deploys as a means of begging indulgence from the crowd and distancing the speaker from 'cleverness' is twisted into a profession of superior wisdom and contempt for the masses.[118] In the main body of his speech, Hippolytus asks Theseus what motive he would have for raping Phaedra. He rather tactlessly implies that there were more beautiful women available should he have wanted to break his chastity (1009–10). Did he hope to usurp Theseus' power by taking an heiress as a wife (1010–11)? Hippolytus dismisses this possibility by arguing that no one in his right mind would want the dangers of being a monarch (1012–20). This was perhaps not the best way to confront an angry king.

Theseus responds to Hippolytus' speech by calling him an 'enchanter' (*epōidos*) and a 'sorcerer' (*goēs*) who is 'confident that he will master my soul with an easy disposition, when he has dishonoured the one who begot him' (1038–9). Hippolytus' attempts at rhetorical persuasion have only led Theseus to conclude that his son is indulging in lazy and specious sophistry. In using a commonplace analogy between deceptive rhetoric and witchcraft, Theseus demonstrates that Hippolytus' rhetoric (and his 'anti-rhetoric') has had the opposite effect to that which his son intended. The analogy also constitutes the potential hollowness of anti-rhetorical clichés and stances. Just because someone *sounds* like a sorcerer-sophist doesn't mean they are lying. Of course, Theseus' error of judgement and fatal curse on Hippolytus are understandable: father and son are unable to communicate properly because Hippolytus is sworn to silence and Phaedra cannot be questioned. And

---

[118] The turning of 'indulgence' to 'contempt' is noted by Halleran (1995) on 983–91 (234). Michelini (1987) 304–10 notes the parallels between Hippolytus' contempt for 'the many' and preference for 'the few' and the attitude of Socrates in Plato's *Apology*.

Aphrodite has ensured that Hippolytus will be killed by his father's curse. But the understandable nature of the chain of events and misunderstandings which lead to Hippolytus' death also serve to heighten the destructive power of Phaedra's deception and the consequences of Theseus' misplaced confidence.

For a citizen audience who were actual or potential dicasts and litigants, Theseus (the king of Athens) is to some extent a reflection of themselves in the guise they were called upon to adopt in the juridical context of the people's courts. Before a knowing audience of citizen jurors, Theseus misinterprets the case evidence before him and dismisses the 'clever oratory' of Hippolytus the defendant. And in the midst of this forensic process, Theseus bemoans the ever-present potential duplicity of outward appearances and speech acts. The audience find themselves gazing on a man coming to a verdict which they know to be wrong. But Theseus' wish that man had two voices *during* this stage trial foregrounds the dangers inherent in juridical interpretation. It wasn't just Theseus who was vulnerable to deceptive evidence and the duplicitous manipulations of spoken or written testimony – the audience were too. And their vulnerability can only have been exacerbated by the accusations and counter-accusations of calumny and the deceptive rhetoric which defendants, plaintiffs and politicians levelled at each other on a daily basis. Hippolytus' death following the forensic scene suggests that the business of working out who is lying and who is telling the truth in a lawcourt could be much more than an institutional game.

Euripides stages the personal tragedy that can result from forensic deception and misinterpretation. But in this and other plays, there is no suggestion of a 'solution' to speech's 'ambiguity'. From Euripidean tragedy, the audience only (re)learns the lesson that all evidence and arguments (written, spoken, 'rhetorical', 'anti-rhetorical') can lie or tell the truth. This is not to underestimate the power of Euripides' differing and complex stagings of deception, rhetoric and anti-rhetoric: such stagings surely helped the citizenry to be self-aware and cautious as they listened to litigants or the (anti-)rhetoric of advisers like Cleon or Diodotus. Euripidean tragedy may even have prompted more critical responses to Thucydides' vision of the democratic process. Noteworthy here is the manner in which Euripidean tragedy articulates an equivocation on deceptive rhetoric's relationship with notions of 'materiality'. Deceptive speech is described and used in the Gorgianic (and Foucauldian) sense of an independent and narcotic material force. But Euripides' characters also bemoan speech's capacity to deceive us successfully by virtue of its immaterial nature.

Theseus' predicament also speaks to us. Like Hippolytus who calls in vain on the silent palace to bear witness to the truth (1074–5), there are a number of women and men who have spent years in prison wishing that British and American juries could have heard some transparent testimony to their innocence and the duplicity of writing and speech. And if Euripides teaches us that rhetorical skill can help the disempowered and the oppressed to be successful in their pursuit of justice, he also reminds us that slick rhetoric and pernicious deception can enslave and destroy lives.

Postscript: the deceptive demos

In this study I have largely discussed Athenian representations of deceit between individuals, deceit of an enemy or deceit of a community by individuals. But there is one further twist in Aristophanes' *Knights'* representation of political and rhetorical deception which I have not yet discussed and which will serve to conclude my exploration of public Athens' extensive and strategic metadiscourse concerning deceptive communication and rhetoric.

Agoracritus 'rescues' a demos which is not in control of its own affairs and which is very much manipulated by elite *rhētores*. However, prior to his supposed rehabilitation Demos engages in a lyric exchange with the cavalry chorus. Demos responds angrily to their suggestion that he is gullible. They accuse him of being easily flattered, deceived and overawed by every speaker (1111–20). The action of the play up to this point has seemed to corroborate their accusation. But Demos' reply problematises the chorus' (and Agoracritus') assessment (1121–30, 1141–50). He tells the Knights that they have no brains if they think he is witless. He deliberately acts like a fool because he takes pleasure in his daily feed (1125–6). He deliberately 'fattens up' (*trephein*) a 'thieving political leader' (*kleptonta prostatēn*) and when the thief is full, Demos strikes him down (1127–30). The chorus are impressed (or are they humouring him?) that Demos is shrewd enough to deliberately fatten up politicians until he needs some meat for a sacrifice and dinner. Demos then describes himself as wisely (*sophōs*) ensnaring men who think they can deceive him (*exapatullein*: 1145). He watches them all the time, while seeming not to (1145–7). He lets them steal from him and then uses the funnel of a voting urn to make them vomit up what they have stolen (1147–50). As Demos finishes this revelation Cleon and Agoracritus re-enter, falling over each other to feed him.

After his 'rehabilitation' Demos cannot remember anything about his former life and accepts that he was manipulated by the politicians

(1135–55). Critics have dismissed Demos' claims to have been the manipulator all along as unconvincing, the mark of senility, absurd or a sop to the audience which is bracketed off from the rest of the plot.[119] Landfester argues that Demos is deceiving *himself* here and remains in the power of the demagogues.[120] Brock insists that his lyrics must be taken at 'face-value: Demos' cunning *pretence* to gullibility is the most optimistic 'solution' which Aristophanes can reach on the premise of the play's 'first plot', a plot which centres on the destruction of Paphlagon but which must be superseded by the more satisfactory solution of a rejuvenated Demos.[121] But it is precisely by raising and not coherently answering the question of whether the demos deceives the orator or vice versa, that Aristophanes makes his audience ponder the relationship between deception and sovereignty in their political system. Demos is a comic personification of Aristophanes' audience. Demos' reply to the Knights could be senile self-deceit with the implication being that their sovereignty over Athens as members of the demos is a delusion. Or are they being told of Demos' (their own) maintenance of sovereignty through countering surveillances and deceptions of elite politicians. Perhaps then, Demos' 'transformed' state is a pretence on his part. Agoracritus *thinks* he has 'boiled down' Demos, but the old man has resisted the process, choosing to *appear* to be transformed in order to maintain his 'daily feed' and begin the process of 'fattening up' another dubious politician.

By claiming (with indeterminate levels of sanity and honesty) that, like Agoracritus, he also fights deception with counter-deception, Aristophanes' Demos invites the audience to consider the uncertain limits and powers of their sovereignty. Ober argues that, excepting the events of 411 and 404, the demos was not cheated out of its sovereignty. This may be a correct assessment, but Aristophanes articulates the difficulty of determining who has had the last laugh and the last lie in a democracy. His and Euripides' vertiginous and unsettling portrayals of deception, rhetorical self-representation and counter-accusation must have helped citizens to remain alert to the 'ambiguity' of any speech – especially the speech which professed its honesty and its insulation from techniques of deception. If the *Acharnians* empha-

---

[119] Sommerstein (1981) 2 sees Demos' claim as a crude calculation of self-interest and offering 'little comfort, even if we believe it'. Bowie (1993) 75 sees a link between the lyrics and Demos' subsequent description of the defeated Cleon as a *pharmakos* (1405) but also describes Demos' claim to cleverness as implausible. MacDowell (1995) 106–7 reads Demos' claims as 'wishful thinking, attractive to a complacent audience'. Edmunds (1987) makes no mention of the passage.

[120] Landfester (1967) 68–73.

[121] Brock (1986) 22–5.

sises the vulnerability of the demos to deception by highlighting comedy's own dissembling rhetoric, the *Knights* invites its democratic audience to consider its own manipulative power as *both* a mark of ultimate sovereignty and a dangerous delusion. Thucydides' portrayal probably had a very different impact: his representation of deceptive democratic rhetoric and counter-rhetoric may well have fuelled the development of anti-democratic dissent and critique which emerged in the writings of Plato and Aristotle. In this sense, the problem of deceptive communication in the democracy (and the discursive scrutiny of that problem which that democracy's institutions allowed) contributed to the birth of Western political thought. One wonders whether political thought will ever resolve the problems which deception poses for democracy.

Epilogue

Among today's adept practitioners, the lie has long since lost its honest function of misrepresenting reality.[1]

Athenian democratic culture sought to locate deceit elsewhere; for example in the upbringing, political organisation and military customs of the Spartan enemy. According to the Athenian imaginary, the Spartans exhibited and promoted a category of communication and behaviour which ran counter to the lineaments of hoplite excellence and inherent excellence. At the same time however, we have seen that the Athenian representation of military deceit was always open to public re-negotiation and anxious theoretical consideration of its problematic social and ethical connotations and consequences. It seems that the ideology of 'la belle mort' could countenance the welding of *mētis* and/or *apatē* to ideal hoplite agency. Thus Vidal-Naquet's influential description of *apatē* has to be framed with a much more nuanced model of deceit's negotiability in public projections of identity and ideal military endeavour.

The problematisation of military trickery at Athens perhaps stems from the way in which the city puts deceit to work ideologically. The Athenian is to define himself in opposition to the enemy who is 'other' because that enemy trains and prepares for military deceit. How is this opposition to be maintained if the 'ideal' Athenian citizen entertains such training himself? Only the ephebe can do this temporarily. And yet the need to entertain military deceit did become more pressing because of the changed operational demands thrown up by the Peloponnesian War. Thus the negotiability of military trickery becomes less surprising.

A discourse of 'othering' is also apparent in the orators' strategies of anti-rhetoric and self-authorisation. The democracy has to be, as

---

[1] Theodor Adorno, *Minima Moralia: reflections from a damaged life*, cited in Norris (1992) 5.

Demosthenes puts it, 'a system based on speeches'. The threat of deceptive rhetoric is paradoxically acknowledged, classified and theorised by the orators. The sophist and the logographer are demonised as the deceptive other, and are then strategically imagined to lie inside and behind every political opponent. Just as Euripides' Andromache and Peleus trope Menelaus' lies as typically Spartan *and at the same time* as typical of *any* Greek general, Demosthenes imagines dishonesty to be inconsistent with Athenian national character *and at the same time* to be present within his Athenian adversary Leptines.

We found that Athenian representations of deceit within the city's spaces of law, politics and government often conform (very broadly speaking) to the Popperian account of official deceit and noble lies as the provenance of oligarchy and its apologists. But Demosthenes seemed to entertain a notion of 'good fiction' when claiming that his opponents shouldn't have attacked the demos of the past – even if the attack proved to be grounded in the truth. And yet (alongside even Socrates' embarrassment and Glaucon's shock over the *gennaion pseudos*) we saw a fragment of satyr drama which actually represents the ethical and legal dangers of characterising traditional religious beliefs as nothing more than noble lies. As with the anxious narrative of the *Cyropaedia*, this material on 'good lying' demonstrates the range of ways in which justified deceit can be construed at Athens and attests, not to complete rejection of the notion as a purely oligarchic, but to a tentative debate as to where noble lies and good fictions are appropriate. The *Sisyphus* fragment explores the dangers of using the notion at all in the field of religious observance (with all its implications for public discourses of 'divine' policing and legal enforcement). Sophocles' *Philoctetes* offers its Athenian audience some space from which to view Odysseus' lying as justifiable and necessary as it sets the claims of collective safety against the right of the individual to assert his freedom and disillusionment with the rhetoric of collective goals. Again, we have seen that recent accounts of the Athenian representation of 'good lies' require a deeper recognition of nuance, anxiety and debate.

Above the proliferating strategies of invective and negotiations of deceit's morality, we can see mass and elite attempting to carve out a theoretical (imaginary, strategic and ideological) distinction between a deceptive use of rhetoric which is centred on winning at all costs, and a harnessing of *technē* and *deinotēs* in the service of responsible, honest advocacy which benefits the polis. The orators draw a strategic line between the (always deceptive) sophist and the (sometimes honest) speaker who is *deinos*. But they also exploit the depressing opacity of deceit to stage a wide variety of dramatic detections and exposures (always distinguishing and classifying forms and degrees of deceit in the process). Stephanus and Demosthenes are able to enact perfect imitations of honesty or moderation. Aeschines is able to distract and deceive through his abilities as an actor. Some speakers actually show you that they are lying, if you watch them closely. Others use a commonplace, which if you think about it, is *always* a cover for lies. I have argued that these aspects of strategy and representation concerning the workings of *apatē* and *pseudē* in democratic discourse supplement and modify Detienne's history of laicised 'truth'. They also build on and modify Ober's account of public discourse's role in perpetuating democracy.

These proliferating anti-rhetorical strategies lend a dynamic quality to rhetorical exchange at Athens which we would miss if we simply focused on the exchange of commonplaces. The metadiscursive possibilities of the notion of rhetoric and the threat of deception provide the orator with original material to promote himself as a particular individual and to condemn his opponent as a (particularly devious) particular individual. These strategic possibilities simply place the threat of deceit at another remove. Why trust the 'rhetoric of anti-rhetoric' any more than 'rhetoric' itself?[2] And it is this difficulty which Thucydides, Euripides and Aristophanes foreground in their representations of anti-rhetorical mudslinging. The novel strategy for proclaiming innocence alongside an attack on another's use of deceptive novelty is no escape from the threat of speech's ambiguity: 'invocation of truth is a sign of lying'. Aristophanes' *Acharnians* was seen to take these reflections one step further: this play wickedly trumpets the possibility that comedy is just 'rhetoric' too. There may be no way to escape the 'loop' of countering rhetorical (mis)representations of countering rhetorical (mis)representations of countering rhetorical (mis)representations ...

The Athenian use and representation of 'the rhetoric of anti-rhetoric' seems to offer a depressing picture of democracy. But it can become comforting if we take it to be a sign that democracy did not need a figure like Plato to see and (perhaps quite effectively) monitor what was dangerous about an industry and practice of rhetoric in a

---

[2] The example of Athenian legal discourse's 'rhetoricity' and the *strategic* quality of its 'meta-discourse' shows how difficult it would be for modern legal procedure to formally recognise its own 'rhetoricity' without that recognition itself becoming another rhetorical resource for the litigant or advocate. For recognition of modern legal discourse's rhetoricity, see the following 'critical legal studies' approaches: White (1985), esp. 33–125; Dalton (1985); Unger (1986); Goodrich (1987). For pertinent, but conservative, critique of these attempts to introduce recognition of legal rhetoricity, see Fish (1994) 174f.

context of 'free speech' (*parrhēsia*). Vickers characterises the practice of rhetoric in a context of 'free speech' as its finest hour. The rhetoric of anti-rhetoric can perhaps teach us that however 'free' our political circumstances are, we should never *defend* rhetoric any more than we attack it. If we love our 'freedoms' we should never let ourselves be so unsuspicious of rhetoric that we allow it to take those freedoms away or else render them meaningless through its capacity to stifle the possibility of ever grasping certain political 'realities' in order to make informed democratic decisions.

The Athenian representation of deceit has the potential to be politically instructive for modern Western democracy. Like Euripides' Hippolytus, our own citizens have been wrongly convicted by lies or the misapprehension of *who* is doing the lying. Like Demosthenes, our government ministers have attacked the dishonesty of some and yet justified deceit in certain contexts. Like Pericles, our representative elites *do* construct our national identity with reference to notions of 'honesty and openness' and contrasting stereotypes of duplicitous 'foreign' nations. And this construction helps to justify all manner of dubious adventures in foreign policy and to conduct even well-intentioned adventures in an imperious manner. Popper's connection between honesty and democracy is undoubtedly Athenian in origin. But the contrast between the Thucydidean Pericles' ideals of openness and the double-dealing of Paches or the unedifying depiction of the Mytilenean debate shows how tenuous such a connection can become.

Of course, Thucydides had his own agenda in representing Athenian democracy as failing to live up to its articulated ideals. But the voices of critique which emerge from Thucydides, Xenophon, Aristophanic comedy and Attic tragedy demonstrate that the public representation of deception and rhetoric (as deception) did not pass unexamined in literature and civic drama. I have tried to suggest that these authors provided a focus for education and debate on the problems and opportunities which deceptive communication presented for Athens' citizens. Ideals of honesty are tested and placed under strain. Accusations of deception and sophistic trickery are shown to be falsely grounded or deliberately duplicitous. Lies are exposed but perhaps only in the service of a new regime of distortions and false claims. The consequences of deception are staged as leading to personal triumph, human tragedy, collective salvation or social breakdown. Rhetoric is represented both as a technology of pernicious lying and as a means of securing justice. The advantages of using deceit on enemies are set against the dangers of training future citizens to be tricksters. In these and many other ways, Athenian literature formulates a discourse which makes the threats and opportunities of deception a fundamental concern for democratic citizenship.

To my mind, the problems posed by deception for modern democracy are not given a discursive focus comparable to that which I have traced for Athenian culture. To be sure, our news media report and comment on scandals and 'spin'. But there is little public discussion or imaginative representation of the morality and mechanisms of deceit in politics, law, business or education. However, certain episodes bring deception to the fore of public consciousness: 'Iran-Contra', 'Watergate', 'Lewinsky', the Scott Inquiry, 'Cash for Questions' and so on. These sorts of episodes are often the source of much fruitful investigative journalism and politically charged academic analysis. One thinks of Arendt on the Pentagon papers, Eco on Nixon's face, Pilger on British and American lies and hypocrisy from Vietnam to the present day and Chomsky on the 'manufacturing of consent' through the media's complicity with government.[3] One also thinks of the way in which the politics of representing reality to electorates has become a focus for critical theoretical debates about the relationship between representation and reality *per se*. The way in which the lead-up to the Gulf War was beamed into our living rooms prompted Baudrillard to make the now infamous claim that the war would not take place.[4] Once it *had* taken place, he maintained that it hadn't *really*.[5] For Baudrillard, the machinery of 'war games rhetoric', Public Relations and media manipulation meant it made no sense to think of the Gulf War as real. There was simply no way in which this war could be verified. This claim caused something of a storm – except, perhaps, in the places where Desert Storm had left families in no doubt as to the truth of the war's effects. Baudrillard saw the war as demonstrating that the Western powers' hold on the way in which we receive information was now so complete that we had no way of being able to distinguish reality from simulations of reality. In short, everything had become unverifiable: everything was now equally true or equally false. It was an act of stupidity to uphold a distinction between truth and falsehood at all.

Baudrillard's claims were in many ways obscene. But they prompted some Western intellectuals to discuss the implications of living in a world where the 'truth' is so very hard to establish with certainty. While

---

[3] See Arendt (1972); Eco (1985); Pilger (1994); Herman and Chomsky (1988); Chomsky (1987), (1989).
[4] Jean Baudrillard, 'The Reality Gulf', *The Guardian*, 11 January 1991.
[5] Jean Baudrillard, 'La guerre du Golfe n'a pas eu lieu', *Liberation*, 29 March 1991.

Baudrillard maintained that there was no longer a 'truth' to be found, Christopher Norris pointed out that the difficulty of establishing certain facts and truths should not be mistaken for their non-existence.[6] It was also argued that the investigative work of the kind conducted by Chomsky, Pilger and Hitchens could get beyond the field of 'representation' in order to establish certain facts about why the Gulf War happened and where propaganda and lies had supplanted the truth of the situation.[7] The 'postmodernist' claim that there were only differing rhetorics of reality and competing 'truths' actually helped the cause of the propagandists because it announced that there was no point in attempting to test or verify media reports or government statements. And many thinkers of radical left-wing persuasion felt that the 'there is no truth' argument was complicit with a process of media censorship whereby the anti-war case was side-lined in public debate.

It was, and still is, important for someone like Baudrillard to highlight the possibility that the truth/falsehood distinction has become meaningless. It would not only be undemocratic to censor such ideas. It would also cut off an important stimulus for artists and intellectuals to provoke debate about how we ensure that lies are brought to light, evaluated and deemed to be central to our conception of what democracy is and should be like. It would not be surprising if the spirit of Baudrillard's ideas motivates many tyrants, spin doctors and democratic politicians. It is good to see this form of relativism out in the open where its moral and political consequences can be scrutinised.

But it is equally important that Baudrillard's outlook be challenged. In looking at the way in which Athenian oratory, drama, historiography and philosophy discuss deception, one thing is striking. Despite Gorgias' observation that mortals inhabit a realm of uncertain opinion (*doxa*) and despite the Athenian dramatists' concern to articulate the difficulties of detecting deception, there is no sustained insistence that truth and lies do not exist. There is an acceptance that lies might sometimes be useful or that lies will be mistaken for truth. There is also the sophistic observation that certain moral or social 'truths' are conventional and contingent. But there is no serious recommendation that it is a waste of time to search for the deceiver as opposed to the truth-

---

[6] See Norris (1992).
[7] See, for example Noam Chomsky, 'The weak shall inherit nothing', *The Guardian*, 25 March 1991; John Pilger, 'Alternative Reality: why don't we hear about what is happening in the Gulf', *New Statesman*, 29 May 1991; Christopher Hitchens, 'Realpolitik in the Gulf' *New Left Review* 186 (March 1991) 89–101. For fuller discussion of the issues traced here, see Norris (1992).

teller or to understand the difference between a truth and a falsehood. As Demosthenes says, a system based on *logoi* cannot function without entertaining a real distinction between deception and truth-telling. We may now inhabit a world where *logoi* are transmitted and doctored electronically but we still need to be aware that those *logoi* can lie and engage in the struggle to determine which *logos* is lying to us. Without that struggle, we may as well give up on democracy altogether.

Bibliography

Adam, J. (1963) *The Republic of Plato*, 2nd edn, 2 vols., Cambridge.

Adams, C. D. (1912) 'Are the Political "Speeches" of Demosthenes to be Regarded as Political Pamphlets?', *TAPA* 43: 5–22.

(1919) *The Speeches of Aeschines*, Cambridge, Mass. and London.

Adcock, F. E. (1948) 'The Cleverness of the Greeks', *PCA* 45: 7–20.

Adkins, A. W. H. (1960) *Merit and Responsibility: a Study in Greek Values*, Oxford.

(1972) 'Truth, Κόσμος and Ἀρετή in the Homeric Poems', *CQ* 22: 5–18.

Andrewes, A. (1962) 'The Mytilene Debate: Thucydides 3. 36–49', *Phoenix* 16: 64–85.

Anonymous (1996) *Primary Colors. A Novel of Politics*, London.

Anti, C. (1952) 'Il vaso di Dario e i Persiani de Frinico', *Archaeologia Classica* 4: 23–45.

Arendt, H. (1972) 'Lying in Politics: Reflections on the Pentagon Papers', pp. 1–35 in *Crises of the Republic*, New York.

Arthur, M. B. (1973) 'Early Greece: Origins of the Western Attitude toward Women', *Arethusa* 6. 1: 7–58.

Babut, D. (1974) 'Xénophane critique des poètes', *AC* 43: 83–117.

Bain, D. (1975) 'Audience Address in Greek Tragedy', *CQ* 69: 13–25.

Bambrough, R., ed. (1967) *Plato, Popper and Politics*, Cambridge.

Barnes, J. A. (1994) *A Pack of Lies: Towards a Sociology of Lying*, Cambridge.

Barrett, M. (1991) *The Politics of Truth: from Marx to Foucault*, Cambridge.

Barrett, W. S. (1964) *Euripides' Hippolytos*, Oxford.

Barthes, R. (1972) *Mythologies*, New York.

Barton, T. (1994) *Power and Knowledge: Astrology, Physiognomics and Medicine Under The Roman Empire*, Ann Arbor.

Basta Donzelli, G. (1978) *Studi sull' Electra di Euripide*, Catania.

Bekker, I. (1814) *Anecdota Graeca*, vol. I, Berlin.

Belfiore, E. (1985) '"Lies Unlike the Truth": Plato on Hesiod *Theogony* 27', *TAPA* 115: 47–57.

Benjamin, A., ed. (1988) *Post-Structuralist Classics*, London and New York.

Bergren, A. (1979) 'Helen's Web: Time and Tableau in the *Iliad*', *Helios* 7: 19–34.

Bers, V. (1985) 'Dikastic *Thorubos*', pp. 1–15 in Cartledge and Harvey eds.

Beye, C. R. (1970) 'Sophocles' *Philoctetes* and the Homeric Embassy', *TAPA* 101: 63–75.

Blass, F. (1887–98) *Die attische Beredsamkeit*, vols. i–iii, Berlin and Leipzig.

Blass, F., and Fuhr, C., eds. (1913) *Andocides, Orationes*, Leipzig.

Blundell, M. W. (1987) 'The Moral Character of Odysseus in *Philoctetes*', *GRBS* 28: 307–29.

(1988) 'The Phusis of Neoptolemus in Sophocles' *Philoctetes*', *G&R* 35: 137–48.

(1989) *Helping Friends and Harming Enemies: a Study in Sophocles and Greek Ethics*, Cambridge.

(1992) 'Character and Meaning in Plato's *Hippias Minor*', pp. 131–72 in *Methods of Interpreting Plato, Oxford Studies in Ancient Philosophy Supplementary Volume*, Klagge J. C. and Smith N. D., Oxford.

Bok, S. (1978) *Lying: Moral Choice in Public and Private Life*, New York.

Bond, G. W. (1981) *Euripides' Heracles*, Oxford.

Bonner, R. J. (1905) *Evidence in Athenian Courts*, Chicago.

(1927) *Lawyers and Litigants in Ancient Athens: the Genesis of the Legal Profession*, Chicago.

Bonner, R. J., and Smith, G. (1930–8) *The Administration of Justice from Homer to Aristotle*, 2 vols., Chicago.

Borthwick, E. K. (1967) 'Trojan Leap and Pyrrhic Dance in Euripides' *Andromache*', *JHS* 87: 18–23.

(1970) 'P. Oxy. 2738: Athens and the Pyrrhic Dance', *Hermes* 98: 318–31.

Boulay, J. du (1974) *Portrait of a Greek Mountain Village*, Oxford.

(1976) 'Lies, Mockery and Family Integrity', pp. 389–406 in *Mediterranean Family Structures*, Peristiany, J. G., ed., Cambridge.

Boulter, P. N. (1966) 'Sophia and Sophrosyne in Euripides' *Andromache*', *Phoenix* 20. 1: 51–8.

Bourdieu, P. (1966) 'The Sentiment of Honour in Kabyle Society', pp. 193–241 in *Honour and Shame: the Values of Mediterranean Society*, Peristiany, J. G., ed., Chicago.

(1977) *Outline of a Theory of Practice*, trans. Nice, R., Cambridge.

Bowie, A. M. (1982) 'The Parabasis in Aristophanes: Prolegomena, *Acharnians*', *CQ* 32: 27–40.

(1987) 'Ritual Stereotype and Comic Reversal: Aristophanes' *Wasps*', *BICS* 34: 112–25.

(1993) *Aristophanes: Myth, Ritual and Comedy*, Cambridge.

(1997) 'Tragic Filters for History: Euripides' *Supplices* and Sophocles' *Philoctetes*', pp. 39–62 in Pelling ed.

Bowie, E. L. (1988) 'Who is Dicaeopolis?', *JHS* 108: 183–5.

(1993) 'Lies, Fiction and Slander in Early Greek Poetry', pp. 1–37 in Gill and Wiseman eds.

Bowra, C. M. (1963) 'Simonides or Bacchylides?', *Hermes* 91: 257–67.

Bradford, A. (1994) 'The Duplicitous Spartan', pp. 59–86 in Powell and Hodkinson eds.

Bremmer, J. (1991) 'Walking, Standing and Sitting in Ancient Greek Culture', pp. 15–29 in *A Cultural History of Gesture*, Bremmer, J. and Roodenburg, H., eds., Cambridge.

Brisson, L. (1982) *Platon: les mots et les mythes*, Paris.

Brock, R. (1986) 'The Double Plot of Aristophanes' *Knights*', *GRBS* 27: 15–27.

Burian, P., ed. (1985a) *Directions in Euripidean Criticism: a Collection of Essays*, Durham.

(1985b) '*Logos* and *Pathos*: the Politics of the *Suppliant Women*', pp. 129–55 in Burian ed.

Burkert, W. (1962) 'Γόης: sum griechischen "Schamanismus"', *RhM* 105: 36–55.

(1985) *Greek Religion: Archaic and Classical*, trans. Raffan, J., Oxford.

Burn, L. (1989) 'The Art of the State in Fifth-Century Athens', pp. 62–81 in *Images of Authority: Papers Presented to Joyce Reynolds on the Occasion of her Seventieth Birthday*, Mackenzie M. M. and Roueché C., eds., Cambridge.

Busolt, G. (1897) *Griechishe Geschichte bis zur Schlacht bei Chaeroneia*, vol. III.1, Gotha.

Buxton, R. G. A. (1982) *Persuasion in Greek Tragedy: a Study of Peitho*, Cambridge.

(1994) *Imaginary Greece: the Contexts of Mythology*, Cambridge.

Cairns, D. L. (1993) *Aidōs: the Psychology and Ethics of Honour and Shame in Ancient Greek Literature*, Oxford.

Caizzi, F. D. (1966) *Antisthenis Fragmenta*, Milan.

Calame, C. (1977) *Les Choeurs de jeunes filles en Grèce archaïque*, 2 vols., Rome.

Calder, W. M. (1971) 'Sophoclean Apologia: *Philoctetes*', *GRBS* 12: 153–74.

Campbell, J. K. (1964) *Honour, Family and Patronage: a Study of Institutions and Moral Values in a Greek Mountain Community*, Oxford.

Carey, C. (1994) 'Rhetorical Means of Persuasion', pp. 26–45 in Worthington ed.

Carey, C., and Reid, P. A. (1985) *Demosthenes: Selected Private Speeches*, Cambridge.

Carson, A. (1992) 'Simonides Painter', pp. 51–68 in Hexter and Selden eds.

Carter, L. B. (1986) *The Quiet Athenian*, Oxford.

Cartledge, P. A. (1979) *Sparta and Lakonia: a Regional History 1300–362 B.C.*, London.

(1987) *Agesilaos and the Crisis of Sparta*, London.

(1990a) 'Fowl Play: a Curious Lawsuit in Classical Athens', pp. 41–62 in Cartledge, Millett and Todd, eds.

(1990b) *Aristophanes and his Theatre of the Absurd*, Bristol.

(1993) *The Greeks: a Portrait of Self and Others*, Oxford.

Cartledge, P. A., and Harvey, F. D., eds. (1985) *CRUX: Essays in Greek History Presented to G. E. M. de Ste. Croix on his 75th Birthday*, London.

Cartledge, P. A., Millett, P. and Todd, S., eds. (1990) *Nomos: Essays in Athenian Law, Politics and Society*, Cambridge.

Casson, L. (1971) *Ships and Seamanship in the Ancient World*, Princeton.

Cave-Brown, A. (1976) *Bodyguard of Lies*, London.

Cawkwell, G. (1972) 'Epaminondas and Thebes', *CQ* 22: 254–78.

(1989) 'Orthodoxy and Hoplites', *CQ* 39: 375–89.

Chomsky, N. (1987) *On Power and Ideology*, Boston.

(1989) *Necessary Illusions: Thought Control in Democratic Societies*, London.

Christ, M. (1992) 'Ostracism, Sycophancy and Deception of the Demos: [Arist.] *Ath. Pol.* 43.5', *CQ* 42: 336–46.

Clairmont, C. (1983) *Patrios Nomos: Public Burial in Athens During the Fifth and Fourth Centuries B.C.*, Oxford.

Clavaud, R. (1974) *Démosthène: Prologues*, Paris.

Clay, D. (1988) 'Reading the *Republic*', in *Platonic Writings, Platonic Readings*, Griswold, C. ed., New York.

Cobb-Stevens, V. (1985) 'Opposites, Reversals and Ambiguities: the Unsettled World of Theognis', in Figuera and Nagy eds.

Cohen, D. (1978) 'The Imagery of Sophocles: a Study of Ajax's Suicide', *G&R* 25: 24–36.

(1991) *Law, Sexuality and Society: the Enforcement of Morals in Classical Athens*, Cambridge.

(1994) 'Classical Rhetoric and Modern Theories of Discourse', pp. 69–82 in Worthington ed.

(1995) *Law, Violence and Community in Classical Athens*, Cambridge.

Cole, T. (1967) *Democritus and the Sources of Greek Anthropology*, Boston.

Collard, C. (1972) 'The Funeral Oration in Euripides' *Suppliants*', *BICS* 19: 39–53.

(1975) *Euripides' Supplices*, Gröningen.

(1991) *Euripides' Hecuba*, Warminster.

Conacher, D. J. (1967) *Euripidean Drama: Myth, Theme, and Structure*, Toronto.

(1998) *Euripides and the Sophists*, London.

Connor, W. (1971) *The New Politicians of Fifth-Century Athens*, Princeton.

Conomis, N. (1970) *Lycurgus: Oratio in Leocratem*, Leipzig.

(1975) *Dinarchi: Orationes*, Leipzig.

Cornford, F. M. (1907) *Thucydides Mythistoricus*, London.

(1953) *Microcosmographia Academica. Being a Guide for the Young Academic Politician*, 5th edn, London.

Craik, E. (1980) 'Sophokles and the Sophists', *L'Antiquité Classique* 48: 15–29.

Croally, N. T. (1994) *Euripidean Polemic: The Trojan Women and the Function of Tragedy*, Cambridge.

Cropp, M. (1988) *Euripides' Electra*, Warminster.

Cruickshank, C. (1979) *Deception in World War II*, Oxford.

Dalton, C. (1985) 'An Essay on the Deconstruction of Contract Doctrine', *Yale Law Review* 94: 1007–87.

Davies, J. K. (1978) *Democracy and Classical Greece*, London.

Davies, M. (1989) 'Sisyphus and the Invention of Religion ('Critias' *TrGF* 1 (43) F 19 = B 25 DK)', *BICS* 36: 16–32.

De Jong, I. J. F. (1991) *Narrative in Drama: The Art of the Euripidean Messenger-Speech*, Leiden.

Derrida, J. (1981) *Dissemination*, trans. Johnson, B., Chicago.

Detienne, M. (1967) *Les Maîtres de vérité dans la Grèce archaïque*, Paris.

(1996) *The Masters of Truth in Archaic Greece*, trans. Lloyd, J., New York.

Detienne, M. and Vernant, J.-P., (1978) *Cunning Intelligence in Greek Culture and Society*, trans. Lloyd, J., Hassocks.

Di Benedetto, V. (1978) 'Il *Filottete* e l'Efebia secundo P. Vidal-Naquet', *Belfagor* 33: 191–207.

Diggle, J. (1981) Review of Scodel (1981), *CR* 31: 106.

(1998) *Tragicorum Graecorum Selecta*, Oxford.

Dihle, A. (1977) 'Das Satyrspiel "Sisyphos"', *Hermes* 105: 28–42.

Dilts, M. R., ed. (1986) *Scholia Demosthenica*, vol. II, Leipzig.

Dobrov, G., ed. (1997) *The City as Comedy: Society and Representation in Athenian Drama*, Chapel Hill and London.

Dodds, E. R. (1960) *Euripides' Bacchae*, Oxford.

(1973) *The Ancient Concept of Progress*, Oxford.

Donlan, W. (1980) *The Aristocratic Ideal in Ancient Greece: Attitudes of Superiority from Homer to the End of the Fifth Century B.C.*, Kansas.

(1985) '*Pistos Philos Hetairos*', pp. 112–31 in Figuera and Nagy eds.

Dorjahn, A. P. (1929) 'Some Remarks on Aeschines' Career as an Actor', *CJ* 25: 223–9.

(1935) 'Anticipation of Arguments in Athenian Courts', *TAPA* 66: 274–95.

Dougherty, C. (1993) *The Poetics of Colonization: from City to Text in Archaic Greece*, Oxford and New York.

Dover, K. (1963) 'Notes on Aristophanes' *Acharnians*', *Maia* 15: 6–21.

(1968) *Lysias and the Corpus Lysiacum*, Berkeley.

(1970) *Aristophanes: Clouds*, Oxford.

(1972) *Aristophanic Comedy*, Oxford.

(1974) *Greek Popular Morality in the Time of Plato and Aristotle*, Oxford.

(1975) 'The Freedom of the Intellectual in Greek Society', *Talanta* 7: 24–54.

(1978) *Greek Homosexuality*, London and Ithaca.

Drews, P. (1983) *Basileus. The Evidence for Kingship in Geometric Greece*, New Haven.

Dreyfus, H., and Rabinow, P. (1982) *Michel Foucault: Beyond Structuralism and Hermeneutics*, London and New York.

DuBois, P. (1991) *Torture and Truth*, London and New York.

Due, B. (1980) *Antiphon: a Study in Argumentation*, Copenhagen.

(1989) *The Cyropaedia: Xenophon's Aims and Methods*, Copenhagen.

Eagleton, T. (1991) *Ideology: an Introduction*, London and New York.

Easterling, P. E. (1978) '*Philoctetes* and Modern Criticism', *ICS* 3: 27–39.

ed. (1997a) *The Cambridge Companion to Greek Tragedy*, Cambridge.

(1997b) 'Constructing the Heroic', pp. 21–37 in Pelling ed.

(1999) 'Actors and Voices: Reading Between the Lines in Aeschines and Demosthenes', pp. 154–66 in Goldhill and Osborne eds.

Eco, U. (1976) *A Theory of Semiotics*, Bloomington.

(1985) 'Strategies of Lying', pp. 3–11 in *On Signs*, Blonsky, M., ed., Oxford.

Eden, K. (1986) *Poetic and Legal Fiction in the Aristotelian Tradition*, Princeton.

Edmunds, L. (1975) *Chance and Intelligence in Thucydides*, Cambridge, Mass.

(1980) 'Aristophanes' *Acharnians*', *YCS* 26: 1–41.

(1987) *Cleon, Knights and Aristophanes' Politics*, Lanham and London.

Else, G. (1958) '"Imitation" in the Fifth Century', *CPh* 53: 73–90.

Emlyn-Jones, C. (1986) 'The Reunion of Penelope and Odysseus', *G&R* 31: 1–18.

Erbse, H. (1966) 'Euripides' *Andromache*', *Hermes* 94: 276–97.

Evans, E. C. (1969) *Physiognomics in the Ancient World*, Philadelphia (= *TAPS* 59. 5).

Farrar, C. (1988) *The Origins of Democratic Thinking: The Invention of Politics in Classical Athens*, Cambridge.

(1992) 'Ancient Greek Political Theory as a Response to Democracy', pp. 17–46 in *Democracy: the Unfinished Journey, 508 B.C. to A.D. 1993*, Dunn, J., ed., Oxford.

Femia, J. V. (1981) *Gramsci's Political Thought: Hegemony, Consciousness and the Revolutionary Process*, Oxford.

Ferrari, G. R. F. (1987) *Listening to the Cicadas: a Study of Plato's Phaedrus*, Cambridge.

(1988) 'Hesiod's Mimetic Muses and the Strategies of Deconstruction', pp. 45–78 in Benjamin ed.

(1989) 'Plato and Poetry', pp. 92–148 in *The Cambridge History of Literary Criticism, Vol. I: Classical Criticism*, Kennedy, G., ed., Cambridge.

Figuera, T., and Nagy, G., eds. (1985) *Theognis of Megara: Poetry and the Polis*, Baltimore and London.

Finkelberg, M. (1998) *The Birth of Literary Fiction in Ancient Greece*, Oxford.

Finley, M. (1973) *Democracy Ancient and Modern*, London.

(1983) *Politics in the Ancient World*, Cambridge.

Fish, S. (1994) *There's No Such Thing as Free Speech, and it's a Good Thing Too*, Oxford.

Fisher, N. R. E. (1993) 'Multiple Personalities and Dionysian Festivals: Dicaeopolis in Aristophanes' *Acharnians*', *G&R* 40: 31–47.

(1994) 'Sparta Re(de)valued: Some Athenian Public Attitudes to Sparta Between Leuctra and the Lamian War', pp. 347–400 in Powell and Hodkinson eds.

Flynn, T. (1994) 'Foucault as Parrhesiast: His Last Course at the Collège de France', pp. 102–18 in *The Final Foucault*, Bernauer, J. and Rasmussen, D., eds., Cambridge, Mass.

Foley, H. P. (1981a) 'The Concept of Women in Athenian Drama', pp. 127–69 in Foley ed.

ed. (1981b) *Reflections of Women in Antiquity*, London, Paris and New York.

(1988) 'Tragedy and Politics in Aristophanes' *Acharnians*', *JHS* 108: 33–47.

(1995) 'Tragedy and Democratic Ideology: the Case of Sophocles' *Antigone*', pp. 131–50 in Goff ed.

Ford, A. (1993) 'The Price of Art in Isocrates', pp. 26–34 in Poulakos ed.

(1999) 'Reading Homer from the Rostrum', pp. 231–56 in Goldhill and Osborne eds.

Forrest, W. G. (1963) 'Aristophanes' *Acharnians*', *Phoenix* 17: 1–12.

Förster, R. (1893) *Scriptores Physiognomici Graeci*, Leipzig.

Foucault, M. (1975) *The Birth of the Clinic: an Archaeology of Medical Perception*, trans. Sheridan Smith, A. M., New York.

(1980) *The History of Sexuality. Volume 1: an Introduction*, trans. Hurley, R., New York.

(1981) 'The Order of the Discourse', pp. 51–77 in *Untying the Text: a Post-Structuralist Reader*, Young, R., ed., London.

(1982) 'Afterword: the Subject and Power', pp. 208–26 in Dreyfus and Rabinow.

(1987) *The Use of Pleasure*, Vol. 2 of *The History of Sexuality*, trans. Hurley, R., London.

Fowler, D. (1994) 'Postmodernism, Romantic Irony and Classical Closure', pp. 231–57 in *Modern Critical Theory and Classical Literature*, de Jong, I. and Sullivan, J. P., eds., Leiden.

Friedl, E. (1962) *Vasilika: A Village in Modern Greece*, New York.

Fuhrmann, M., ed. (1966) *Anaximenis Ars Rhetorica*, Leipzig.

Gagarin, M. (1989) 'The Nature of Proofs in Antiphon,' *CPh* 85: 22–32.

Gagarin, M., and Woodruff, P. (1995) *Early Greek Political Thought from Homer to the Sophists*, Cambridge.

Garver, E. (1994) *Aristotle's Rhetoric: an Art of Character*, Chicago.

Garvie, A. F. (1972) 'Deceit, Violence and Persuasion in the *Philoctetes*', pp. 213–36 in *Studi classici in onore di Quintino Cataudella*, vol. I, Catania.

(1998) *Sophocles' Ajax*, Warminster.

Gellie, G. H. (1972) *Sophocles: a Reading*, Melbourne.

Gellrich, M. (1995) 'Interpreting Greek Tragedy', pp. 38–58 in Goff ed.

Gentili, B. (1964) 'Studi su Simonide, II. Simonide e Platone', *Maia* 16: 278–306.

(1988) *Poetry and its Public in Ancient Greece*, trans. Cole, T., Baltimore and London.

Gera, D. L. (1993) *Xenophon's Cyropaedia: Style, Genre and Literary Technique*, Oxford.

Gernet, L. (1981, orig. 1936) 'Dolon the Wolf', pp. 125–39 in *Anthropology of Ancient Greece*, trans. Hamilton, S. J. and Nagy, B., Baltimore and London.

Ghiron-Bistagne, P. (1976) *Recherches sur les acteurs dans la Grèce antique*, Paris.

Gigon, O. (1956) *Kommentar zum zweiten Buch von Xenophons Memorabilien*, Basle.

Gill, C. (1979) 'Plato's Atlantis Story and the Birth of Fiction', *Philosophy and Literature* 3: 64–78.

(1980) 'Bow, Oracle and Epiphany in Sophocles' *Philoctetes*', *G&R* 27: 137–46.

(1990) 'The Articulation of the Self in Euripides' *Hippolytus*', pp. 76–107 in *Euripides, Women and Sexuality*, Powell, A., ed., London.

(1993) 'Plato on Falsehood – Not Fiction', pp. 38–87 in Gill and Wiseman eds.

Gill, C., and Wiseman, T. P., eds. (1993) *Lies and Fiction in the Ancient World*, Exeter.

Gilsenan, M. (1976) 'Lying, Honor and Contradiction', pp. 191–219 in *Transactions and Meaning: Directions in the Anthropology of Exchange and Symbolic Behaviour*, Kapferer, B., ed., Philadelphia.

Gleason, M. W. (1990) 'The Semiotics of Gender: Physiognomy and Self-Fashioning in the Second Century C. E.', pp. 389–415 in Halperin, Winkler and Zeitlin eds.

(1995) *Making Men: Sophists and Self-Presentation in Ancient Rome*, Princeton.

Goff, B. (1990) *The Noose of Words: Readings of Desire, Violence and Language in Euripides' Hippolytos*, Cambridge.

ed. (1995) *History, Tragedy, Theory: Dialogues on Athenian Drama*, Austin.

Goffman, E. (1969) *The Presentation of Self in Everyday Life*, Harmondsworth.

(1974) *Frame Analysis: an Essay on the Organization of Experience*, London.

Goldhill, S. D. (1984) *Language, Sexuality, Narrative: the Oresteia*, Cambridge.

(1986) 'Rhetoric and Relevance: Interpolation at Euripides *Electra* 367–400', *GRBS* 27: 157–71.

(1988a) *Reading Greek Tragedy*, Cambridge.

(1988b) 'Battle Narrative and Politics in Aeschylus' *Persae*', *JHS* 108: 189–93.

(1990) 'The Great Dionysia and Civic Ideology', pp. 97–129 in Winkler and Zeitlin eds.

(1991) *The Poet's Voice: Essays on Poetics and Greek Literature*, Cambridge.

(1995) 'Representing Democracy: Women at the Great Dionysia', pp. 267–305 in *Ritual, Finance, Politics. Athenian Democratic Accounts Presented to David Lewis*, Osborne, R. and Hornblower, S., eds., Oxford.

(1997) 'The Language of Tragedy: Rhetoric and Communication', pp. 127–50 in Easterling ed.

(1999) 'Programme Notes', pp. 1–29 in Goldhill and Osborne eds.

Goldhill, S. D., and Osborne, R., eds. (1999) *Performance Culture and Athenian Democracy*, Cambridge.

Gomme, A. (1933) *The Population of Athens in the Fifth and Fourth Centuries B.C.*, Oxford.

(1938) 'Aristophanes and Politics', *CR* 52: 97–109.

(1956) *An Historical Commentary on Thucydides*, vol. II, Oxford.

Goodrich, P. (1987) *Legal Discourse: Studies in Linguistics, Rhetoric, and Legal Analysis*, New York.

Gordon, R. L., ed. (1981) *Myth, Religion and Society*, Cambridge.

Graff, G. (1989) 'Co-optation', pp. 168–81 in *The New Historicism*, Veeser, H., ed., London and New York.

Gramsci, A. (1971) *Selections from the Prison Notebooks*, Hoare, Q. and Nowell-Smith, G., eds. and trans., London.

Greenblatt, S. (1980) *Renaissance Self-Fashioning from More to Shakespeare*, Chicago and London.

Gregory, J. (1991) *Euripides and the Instruction of the Athenians*, Ann Arbor.

Griffith, M. (1995) 'Brilliant Dynasts: Power and Politics in the *Oresteia*', *CA* 14: 62–129.

Grimaldi, W. H. (1980) *Aristotle Rhetoric I, a Commentary*, New York.

Guthrie, W. K. C. (1971) *A History of Greek Philosophy*, vol. III, Cambridge.

(1975) *A History of Greek Philosophy*, vol. IV, Cambridge.

Haft, A. (1984) 'Odysseus, Idomeneus, and Meriones: the Cretan Lies of *Odyssey* 13–19', *CJ* 79: 289–306.

Hall, E. (1989) *Inventing the Barbarian: Greek Self-Definition Through Tragedy*, Oxford.

(1995) 'Lawcourt Dramas: the Power of Performance in Greek Forensic Oratory', *BICS* 40: 39–58.

(1996) *Aeschylus' Persians*, Warminster.

(1997) 'The Sociology of Athenian Tragedy', pp. 93–126 in Easterling ed.

Halleran, M. (1995) *Euripides' Hippolytus*, Warminster.

Halliwell, S. (1980) 'Aristophanes' Apprenticeship', *CQ* 30: 33–45.

(1984) 'Aristophanic Satire', *Yearbook of English Studies* 14: 6–20.

(1993) 'Comedy and Publicity in the Society of the Polis', pp. 321–40 in Sommerstein et al. eds.

(1994) 'Philosophy and Rhetoric', pp. 222–43 in Worthington ed.

(1997) 'Between Public and Private: Tragedy and the Athenian Experience of Rhetoric', pp. 121–42 in Pelling ed.

Halperin, D. M. (1989) 'The Democratic Body: Prostitution and Citizenship in Classical Athens', pp. 88–112 in *One Hundred Years of Homosexuality and Other Essays on Greek Love*, New York.

(1992) 'Plato and the Erotics of Narrativity', pp. 95–131 in Hexter and Selden eds.

Halperin, D. M., Winkler, J. J. and Zeitlin, F., eds. (1990) *Before Sexuality: the Construction of Erotic Experience in the Ancient Greek World*, Princeton.

Handley, E., and Rea, J. (1957) *The Telephus of Euripides*, *BICS* Supplement 5, London.

Hansen, M. H. (1975) *Eisangelia: the Sovereignty of the People's Court in Athens in the Fourth Century B.C. and the Impeachment of Generals and Politicians*, Göttingen.

(1980) 'Eisangelia in Athens: a Reply', *JHS* 100: 89–95.

(1984) 'Two Notes on Demosthenes' Symbouleutic Speeches', *C&M* 35: 57–70.

(1985) *Demography and Democracy: The Number of Athenian Citizens in the Fourth Century B.C.*, Herning.

Hanson, V., ed. (1991) *Hoplites: the Classical Greek Battle Experience*, London.

Harding, P. (1988) 'Athenian Defensive Strategy in the Fourth Century', *Phoenix* 42: 61–71.

Harris, E. M. (1995) *Aeschines and Athenian Politics*, Oxford.

Harris, W. V. (1989) *Ancient Literacy*, Cambridge, Mass.

Harrison, A. R. W. (1968–71) *The Law of Athens*, 2 vols., Oxford.

Harrison, J. E., and Verrall, M. de G. (1890) *Mythology and Monuments of Ancient Athens*, London.

Harrison, T. (2000) *The Emptiness of Asia. Aeschylus' Persians and the History of the Fifth Century*, London.

Harvey, F. D. (1985) '*Dona Ferentes*: some Aspects of Bribery in Greek Politics', pp. 76–117 in Cartledge and Harvey eds.

(1990) 'The Sykophant and Sykophancy: Vexatious Redefinition', pp. 103–21 in Cartledge, Millett and Todd eds.

Heath, M. (1987a) *The Poetics of Greek Tragedy*, London.

(1987b) *Political Comedy in Aristophanes*, Göttingen.

(1989) *Unity in Greek Poetics*, Oxford.

(1990) 'Some Deceptions in Aristophanes', *Papers of the Leeds International Latin Seminar* 6: 229–40.

(1997) 'Aristophanes and the Discourse of Politics', pp. 230–49 in Dobrov ed.

Henderson, J. (1990) 'The Demos and Comic Competition', pp. 271–313 in Winkler and Zeitlin eds.

(1993) 'Comic Hero versus Political Elite', pp. 307–19 in Sommerstein et al. eds.

Henrichs, A. (1975) 'Two Doxographical Notes: Democritus and Prodicus on Religion', *HSCP* 79: 93–123.

Herman, E. S., and Chomsky, N. (1988) *Manufacturing Consent: the Political Economy of the Mass Media*, New York.

Herzfeld, M. (1985) *The Poetics of Manhood: Contest and Identity in a Cretan Mountain Village*, Princeton.

Hesk, J. P. (1999a) 'The Rhetoric of Anti-Rhetoric in Athenian Oratory', pp. 201–30 in Goldhill and Osborne eds.

(1999b) Review of Yunis (1996), *JHS* 119: 183.

(2000) 'Intratext and Irony in Aristophanic Comedy' in *Intratextuality and Classical Literature*, Sharrock, A. and Morales, H., eds., Oxford.

Hexter, R., and Selden, D., eds. (1992) *Innovations of Antiquity*, London and New York.

Heza, E. (1974) 'Ruse de guerre: trait caractéristique d'une tactique nouvelle dans l' oeuvre de Thucydide', *Eos* 62: 227–44.

Hinds, A. E. (1967) 'The Prophecy of Helenus in Sophocles' *Philoctetes*', *CQ* 17: 169–80.

Hirsch, S. (1985) *The Friendship of the Barbarians: Xenophon and the Persian Empire*, Hanover and London.

Hooker, J. (1980) *The Ancient Spartans*, London.

Hornblower, S. (1991) *A Commentary on Thucydides*, vol. I, Oxford.

Hubbard, T. K. (1991) *The Mask of Comedy: Aristophanes and the Intertextual Parabasis*, Ithaca.

Humphreys, S. (1985) 'Social Relations on Stage: Witnesses in Classical Athens', *History & Anthropology* I: 313–69.

Hunter, V. J. (1986) 'Thucydides, Gorgias and Mass Psychology', *Hermes* 114: 412–29.

(1994) *Policing Athens: Social Control in the Attic Lawsuits, 420–320 B.C.*, Princeton.

Hurwit, J. (1985) *The Art and Culture of Early Greece 1100–480 B.C.*, Ithaca and London.

Hussey, E. (1985) 'Thucydidean History and Democritean Theory', pp. 118–38 in Cartledge and Harvey eds.

Jaeger, W. (1966) 'Tyrtaeus on the True Virtue', pp. 101–42 in *Five Essays*, trans. Fiske A., Montreal.

Jameson, M. H. (1956) 'Politics and the *Philoctetes*', *CP* I:217–27.

Janaway, C. (1995) *Images of Excellence. Plato's Critique of the Arts*, Oxford.

Jarratt, S. (1991) *Rereading the Sophists: Classical Rhetoric Refigured*, Carbondale.

Jeanmaire, H. (1913) 'La Cryptie Lacédémonienne', *REG* 26: 121–50.

(1939) *Couroi et courètes: Essai sur l' éducation spartiate et sur les rites d' adolescence dans l' antiquité Hellénique*, Lille.

Jebb, R. (1898) *Sophocles: The Plays and Fragments. Part IV: the Philoctetes*, Cambridge.

(1962) *Sophocles: The Plays and Fragments. Part VII: the Ajax*, Amsterdam.

Jenkins, I. (1985) 'The Ambiguity of Greek Textiles', *Arethusa* 18: 109–32.

Johnson, L. M. (1991) 'Rethinking the Diodotean Argument', *Interpretation* 18: 53–62.

Jones, A. H. M. (1957) *The Athenian Democracy*, Oxford.

Jones, J. (1962) *On Aristotle and Greek Tragedy*, London.

Jones, N. (1995) *Soundbites and Spin Doctors. How Politicians Manipulate the Media and Vice Versa*, London.

Jones, R. V. (1978) *Most Secret War: British Scientific Intelligence 1939–1945*, London.

Jones, W. H. (1923) *Hippocrates, Volume II*, Cambridge, Mass.

Kagan, D. (1961) 'The Origin and Purposes of Ostracism', *Hesperia* 30: 393–401.

Kahn, L. (1978) *Hermès passe; ou les ambiguités de la communication*, Paris.

Kahn, C. H. (1981) 'The Origins of Social Contract Theory in the Fifth Century B.C.', pp. 92–108 in Kerferd ed.

Kamerbeek, J. C. (1980) *The Plays of Sophocles. Commentaries Part VI: Philoctetes*, Leiden.

Kassel, R., ed. (1971) *Aristotelis Ars Rhetorica*, Berlin.

Katz, M. (1991) *Penelope's Reknown: Meaning and Indeterminacy in the Odyssey*, Princeton.

Kearns, E. (1989) *The Heroes of Attica*, London.

Kellner, H. (1989) *Language and Historical Representation: Getting the Story Crooked*, Madison.

Kells, J. H. (1963) 'Sophocles *Philoctetes* 1142–5', *CR* 13: 7–9.

(1973) *Sophocles Electra*, Cambridge.

Kennedy, G. (1963) *The Art of Persuasion in Greece*, London.

Kennell, N. M. (1995) *The Gymnasium of Virtue: Education and Culture in Ancient Sparta*, Chapel Hill and London.

Kerferd, G. B. (1981a) *The Sophistic Movement*, Cambridge.

ed. (1981b) *The Sophists and their Legacy*, Wiesbaden.

Kerr, P., ed. (1990) *The Penguin Book of Lies*, London.

Kindstrand, J. F. (1982) *The Stylistic Evaluation of Aeschines in Antiquity*, Uppsala.

Kirk, G. S., Raven, J. E. and Schofield, M. (1983) *The Presocratic Philosophers*, Cambridge.

Kitto, H. D. F. (1954) *Greek Tragedy*, London.

Knox, B. (1952) 'The *Hippolytus* of Euripides', *YCS* 13: 3–31.

(1961) 'The *Ajax* of Sophocles', *HSCP* 65: 1–37.

(1964) *The Heroic Temper: Studies in Sophoclean Tragedy*, Berkeley.

Konstan, D. (1993) 'Rhetoric and the Crisis of Legitimacy in Cicero's *Catilinarian Orations*', pp. 14–25 in Poulakos ed.

Kovacs, P. D. (1980) *The Andromache of Euripides: an Interpretation*, Michigan.

Kristeva, J. (1980) *Desire in Language: a Semiotic Approach to Literature and Art*, trans. and ed. Roudiez, L., Oxford.

Kritzman, L., ed. (1988) *Michel Foucault: Politics, Philosophy, Culture*, London and New York.

Krön, U. (1976) *Die zehn attischen Phylenheroen: Geschichte, Mythos, Kult und Darstellungen*, Berlin.

Kurke, L. (1991) *The Traffic in Praise: Pindar and the Poetics of Social Economy*, Ithaca, New York and London.

Lada, I. (1993) '"Empathetic Understanding": Emotion and Cognition in Classical Dramatic Audience-Response', *PCPS* 39: 94–140.

Laín Entralgo, P. (1970) *The Therapy of the Word in Classical Antiquity*, trans. Rather, L. J. and Sharp, J. M., New Haven.

Landfester, M. (1967) *Die Ritter des Aristophanes*, Amsterdam.

Lavency, M. (1964) *Aspects de la logographie judiciaire attique*, Louvain.

Lee, K. (1975) 'Euripides' *Andromache*: Observations on Form and Meaning', *Antichthon* 9: 4–16.

Lefkovitz, M. (1986) *Women in Greek Myth*, London.

Lesky, A. (1965) *Greek Tragedy*, London.

Levi, M., and Nelken, D., eds. (1996) *The Corruption of Politics and the Politics of Corruption*, Oxford.

Levine, D. (1985) 'Symposium and the *Polis*', in Figuera and Nagy eds.

Levinson, R. B. (1953) *In Defence of Plato*, Cambridge, Mass.

Lévy, E. (1988) 'La Kryptie et ses contradictions', *Ktema* 13: 245–52.

Linforth, I. M (1956) '*Philoctetes*: the Play and the Man', *University of California Publications in Classical Philology* 15 (3): 95–156.

Lipsius, J. H. (1905) *Das Attische Recht und Rechtsverfahren 1: Gerichtsverfassung*, Leipzig.

Lissarrague, F. (1989) 'The World of the Warrior', pp. 39–51 in *A City of Images: Iconography and Society in Ancient Greece*, trans. Lyons, D., Bérard, C. et al., eds., Princeton.

Lloyd, G. E. R. (1970) *Early Greek Science: Thales to Aristotle*, London.

(1979) *Magic, Reason and Experience: Studies in the Origin and Development of Greek Science*, Cambridge.

(1983) *Science, Folklore and Ideology: Studies in the Life Sciences in Ancient Greece*, Cambridge.

Lloyd. M. (1992) *The Agōn in Euripides*, Oxford.

(1994) *Euripides' Andromache*, Warminster.

Lloyd-Jones, H., and Wilson, N. G. (1990) *Sophoclea: Studies in the Text of Sophocles*, Oxford.

Loraux, N. (1982) 'Mourir devant Troie, tomber pour Athènes: de la gloire du héros à l' idée de la cité', pp. 27–43 in *La Mort, les morts dans les sociétés anciennes*, Gnoli, G., and Vernant, J.-P., eds., Cambridge and Paris.

(1986) *The Invention of Athens: the Funeral Oration in the Classical City*, trans. Sheridan, A., Cambridge, Mass.

(1993) *The Children of Athena*, trans. Levine, C., Princeton.

Lord, C. (1981) 'The Intention of Aristotle's *Rhetoric*', *Hermes* 109: 326–39.

Lowry, E. (1991) *Thersites: a Study in Comic Shame*, London and New York.

Lucas, D. W. (1950) *The Greek Tragic Poets*, London.

Lushnig, C. A. E. (1988) *Time holds the Mirror: a Study of Knowledge in Euripides' Hippolytus*, Leiden.

Lynn-George, M. (1987) *Epos: Word, Narrative and the Iliad*, Basingstoke.

Ma, J. (1994) 'Black Hunter Variations', *PCPS* 40: 49–82.

MacC. Armstrong, A. (1958) 'The Methods of the Greek Physiognomists', *G&R* 5: 52–6.

MacDowell, D. M. (1978) *Law in Classical Athens*, London.

(1982) *Gorgias: Encomium of Helen*, Bristol.

(1983) 'The Nature of Aristophanes' *Akharnians*', *G&R* 30: 143–62.

(1990) *Demosthenes: Against Meidias*, Oxford.

(1995) *Aristophanes and Athens: an Introduction to his Plays*, Oxford.

Macleod, C. (1978) 'Reason and Necessity: Thucydides III 9–14, 37–48', *JHS* 98: 64–78.

Maloney, G. and Frohn, W. (1984) *Concordance des oeuvres hippocratiques*, Hildesheim.

Manuwald, B. (1979) 'Der Trug des Diodotos (zu Thukydides 3. 42–48)', *Hermes* 107: 407–22.

Martin, V., and de Budé, G. (1927–8) *Eschine: Discours*, Paris.

Martindale, C. (1993) *Redeeming the Text*, Cambridge.

Mastronarde, D. (1994) *Euripides: Phoenissae. Edited with Introduction and Commentary*, Cambridge.

Maugham, 1st Viscount Frederic M. (1941) *Lies as Allies: or Hitler at War*, London.

Maxwell-Stuart, P. G. (1970) 'Remarks on the Black Cloaks of the Ephebes', *PCPS* 16: 113–16.

Michelini, A. (1987) *Euripides and the Tragic Tradition*, Madison.

Michels, R. (1962, orig. 1915) *Political Parties: a Sociological Study of the Oligarchical Tendencies of Modern Democracies*, trans. Paul, E., and Paul, C., New York.

Miller, G. R., and Stiff, J. B. (1993) *Deceptive Communication*, London.

Millett, P. (1989a) Review of Ober (1989) *TLS* 1449.

(1989b) 'Patronage and its Avoidance in Classical Athens', pp. 15–48 in *Patronage in Ancient Society*, Wallace-Hadrill, A., ed., London and New York.

(1991) *Lending and Borrowing in Ancient Athens*, Cambridge.

(1993) 'Warfare, Economy and Democracy in Classical Athens', pp. 177–97 in *War and Society in the Greek World*, Rich, J., and Shipley, G., eds., London and New York.

Mills, S. (1997) *Theseus, Tragedy and the Athenian Empire*, Oxford.

Missiou, A. (1992) *The Subversive Oratory of Andokides: Politics, Ideology and Decision-Making in Democratic Athens*, Cambridge.

Montgomery, H. (1983) *The Way to Chaeronea: Foreign Policy, Decision-Making and Political Influence in Demosthenes' Speeches*, Bergen.

Mossman, J. (1995) *Wild Justice: a Study of Euripides' Hecuba*, Oxford.

Most, G. (1985) *The Measures of Praise: Structure and Function in Pindar's Second Pythian and Seventh Nemean Odes*, Göttingen.

Mourelatos, A. P. D. (1970) *The Route of Parmenides*, New Haven and London.

Muecke, F. (1977) 'Playing with the Play: Theatrical Self-Consciousness in Aristophanes', *Antichthon* 1: 52–67.

Munn, M. H. (1993) *The Defence of Attica. The Dema Wall and the Boiotian War of 378–375 B.C.*, Berkeley.

Murnaghan, S. (1987) *Disguise and Recognition in the Odyssey*, Princeton.

Murphy, C. T. (1938) 'Aristophanes and the Art of Rhetoric', *HSCP* 49: 69–114.

Murray, J. S. (1988) 'Disputation, Deception and Dialectic: Plato on the True Rhetoric (*Phaedrus* 261–266)', *Philosophy and Rhetoric* 21: 279–89.

Murray, P. (1996) *Plato on Poetry*, Cambridge.

Murray, R. J. (1987) 'Aristophanic Protest', *Hermes* 115: 146–54.

Mussurillo, R. (1974) 'The Problem of Lying and Deceit and the Two Voices of Euripides' *Hippolytus* 925–931', *TAPA* 104: 231–8.

Nagy, G. (1985) 'Theognis and Megara: a Poet's Vision of his City', pp. 8–44 in Figuera and Nagy eds.

(1990) *Pindar's Homer: the Lyric Possession of an Epic Poet*, Baltimore and London.

Napolitano Valditara, L. M. (1994) *Lo sguardo nel buio: Metafore visive e forme grecoantique della razionalità*, Rome.

Nehamas, A. (1998) *The Art of Living: Socratic Reflections from Plato to Foucault*, Berkeley.

Neils, J. (1987) *The Youthful Deeds of Theseus*, Rome.

Nestle, W. (1910) 'Sophokles und die Sophistik', *CP* 5: 129–57.

(1940) 'Xenophon und die Sophistik', *Philologus* 94: 31–50.

Newiger, H.-J. (1980) 'War and Peace in the Comedy of Aristophanes', *YCS* 29: 219–317.

Newman, W. L. (1902) *The Politics of Aristotle*, vol. IV, Oxford.

Nightingale, A. W. (1995) *Genres in Dialogue: Plato and the Construct of Philosophy*, Cambridge.

Nill, M. (1985) *Morality and Self-Interest in Protagoras, Antiphon and Democritus*, Leiden.

Nisetich, F. (1989) *Pindar and Homer*, Baltimore and London.

Norris, C. (1987) *Derrida*, London.

(1992) *Uncritical Theory. Postmodernism, Intellectuals and the Gulf War*, London.

North, H. (1952) 'The Use of Poetry in the Training of the Ancient Orator', *Traditio* 8: 1–33.

(1966) *Sophrosyne: Self-Knowledge and Self-Restraint in Greek Literature*, Ithaca.

Nouhaud, M. (1982) *L' Utilisation de l' histoire par les orateurs attiques*, Paris.

(1990) *Dinarque: Discours*, Paris.

Nussbaum, M. (1976) 'Consequences and Character in Sophocles' *Philoctetes*', *Philosophy and Literature* 1.1: 25–53.

Ober, J. (1985a) *Fortress Attica: Defense of the Athenian Land Frontier 404–322 B.C.*, Leiden.

(1985b) 'Thucydides, Pericles and the Strategy of Defense', pp. 171–88 in *The Craft of the Ancient Historian: Essays in Honour of Starr*, Eadie, J. and Ober, J. eds., Lanham.

(1989) *Mass and Elite in Democratic Athens: Rhetoric, Ideology and the Power of the People*, Princeton.

(1991) 'Hoplites and Obstacles', pp. 173–96 in Hanson ed.

(1994) 'Power and Oratory in Democratic Athens: Demosthenes 21, *Against Meidias*, pp. 85–108 in Worthington ed.

(1998) *Political Dissent in Democratic Athens: Intellectual Critics of Popular Rule*, Princeton.

Ober, J., and Hedrick, C., eds. (1996) *Démokratia: a Conversation on Democracies Ancient and Modern*, Princeton.

Ober, J., and Strauss, B. (1990) 'Drama, Political Rhetoric and the Discourse of Athenian Democracy', pp. 237–70 in Winkler and Zeitlin eds.

O' Regan, D. (1992) *Rhetoric, Comedy and the Violence of Language in Aristophanes' Clouds*, Oxford.

Osborne, R. (1985a) *Demos: the Discovery of Classical Attika*, Cambridge.

(1985b) 'The Erection and Mutilation of the Hermai' *PCPS* 31: 47–74.

(1990) 'Vexatious Litigation in Classical Athens: Sykophancy and the Sykophant', pp. 83–102 in Cartledge, Millett and Todd eds.

Ostwald, M. (1986) *From Popular Sovereignty to the Sovereignty of Law: Law, Society and Politics in Fifth-Century Athens*, Berkeley.

(1988) Ἀνάγκη *in Thucydides*, Atlanta.

Page, C. (1991) 'The Truth about Lies in Plato's *Republic*', *Anc. Phil.* 11: 1–33.

Page, D. (1938) *Greek Poetry and Life*, Oxford.

Parke, H. (1977) *Festivals of the Athenians*, London.

Parker, L. P. (1991) 'Eupolis or Dicaeopolis?', *JHS* 111: 203–8.

Parker, R. (1983) *Miasma: Pollution and Purification in Early Greek Religion*, Oxford.

(1996) *Athenian Religion: A History*, Oxford.

Pearson , L. (1941) 'Historical Allusions in the Attic Orators', *CPh* 36: 209–29.

(1962) *Popular Ethics in Ancient Greece*, Stanford.

(1976) *The Art of Demosthenes*, Meisenheim.

Pélékidis, C. (1962) *Histoire de l' éphébie attique, des origines à 31 av. J. C.*, Paris.

Pelling, C. B. R., ed. (1997a) *Greek Tragedy and the Historian*, Oxford.

(1997b) 'Aeschylus' *Persae* and History', pp. 1–20 in Pelling ed.

Perlman, S. (1961) 'The Historical Example, Its Use and Importance as Political Propaganda in the Attic Orators', *SH* 7: 150–66.

(1963) 'The Politicians in the Athenian Democracy of the Fourth Century B.C.', *Athenaeum* 41: 327–55.

(1964) 'Quotations from Poetry in Attic Orators of the Fourth Century B.C.', *AJP* 85: 155–72.

ed. (1973) *Philip and Athens*, New York.

Phillippo, S. (1995) 'Family Ties: Significant Patronymics in Euripides' *Andromache*', *CQ* 45: 355–71.

Pilger, J. (1994) *Distant Voices*, London.

Podlecki, A. (1966) 'The Power of the Word in Sophocles' *Philoctetes*', *GRBS* 7: 233–50.

Poole, W. (1994) 'Euripides and Sparta', pp. 1–33 in Powell and Hodkinson eds.

Popper, K. (1966) *The Open Society and its Enemies, vol. 1, The Spell of Plato*, 5th edn, London.

Porta, D. della, and Mény, Y., eds. (1997) *Corruption and Democracy in Europe*, London.

Poulakos, T., ed. (1993) *Rethinking the History of Rhetoric: Multidisciplinary Essays on the Rhetorical Tradition*, Boulder.

Powell, A. (1989) 'Mendacity and Sparta's Use of the Visual', pp. 173–92 in *Classical Sparta: Techniques Behind her Success*, Powell, A., ed., London.

(1994) 'Plato and Sparta: Modes of Rule and of Non-Rational Persuasion in the *Laws*', pp. 273–321 in Powell and Hodkinson eds.

Powell, A., and Hodkinson, S., eds. (1994) *The Shadow of Sparta*, London.

Prato, C., ed. (1968) *Tyrtaeus*, Rome.

Pratt, L. (1993) *Lying and Poetry from Homer to Pindar: Falsehood and Deception in Archaic Greek Poetics*, Ann Arbor.

Pritchett, W. K. (1971) *The Greek State at War Part I*, Berkeley.

(1974) *The Greek State at War Part II*, Berkeley.

(1979) *The Greek State at War Part III: Religion*, Berkeley.

Pucci, P. (1977) *Hesiod and the Language of Poetry*, Baltimore.

(1987) *Odysseus Polytropos: Intertextual Readings in the Odyssey and the Iliad*, Ithaca.

Rabel, R. (1992) 'The Theme of Need in *Iliad* 9–11', *Phoenix* 45: 285–95.

Rabinowitz, N. S. (1993) *Anxiety Veiled: Euripides and the Traffic in Women*, Cornell.

Radermacher, L. (1951) *Artium Scriptores*, Vienna.

Rankin, H. D. (1986) *Antisthenes Sokratikos*, Amsterdam.

Rawson, E. (1969), *The Spartan Tradition in European Thought*, Oxford.

Reckford, K. (1987) *Aristophanes' Old and New Comedy*, Chapel Hill.

Reeve, C. D. (1988) *Philosopher-Kings: the Argument of Plato's Republic*, Princeton.

Reeve, M. (1973) 'Interpolation in Greek Tragedy, III', *GRBS* 14: 145–71.

Reinmuth, O. W. (1971) *The Ephebic Inscriptions of the Fourth Century B.C.*, Leiden (= *Mnemosyne* Supp. 14.).

Rhodes, P. J. (1972) *The Athenian Boule*, Oxford.

(1979) 'ΕΙΣΑΓΓΕΛΙΑ in Athens', *JHS* 99: 103–14.

(1981) *A Commentary on the Aristotelian Athenaion Politeia*, Oxford.

Ridley, F. F., and Doig, A., eds. (1995) *Sleaze: Politicians, Private Interests and Public Reaction*, Oxford.

Ridley, F. F., and Thompson, B., eds. (1997) *Under the Scott-Light: British Government Seen Through the Scott Report*, Oxford.

Ridley, R. (1979) 'The Hoplite as Citizen: Athenian Military Institutions in their Social Context', *AC* 48: 508–48.

Roberts, J. T. (1982) *Accountability in Athenian Government*, Wisconsin.

(1994) *Athens on Trial: the Anti-Democratic Tradition in Western Thought*, Princeton.

Roberts, J. W. (1984) *City of Sokrates: an Introduction to Classical Athens*, London.

Robinson, D. B. (1969) 'Topics in Sophocles' *Philoctetes*', *CQ* 19: 34–56.

Robinson, T. M. (1979) *Contrasting Arguments: an Edition of the Dissoi Logoi*, New York.

Romilly, J. de (1956) *Histoire et raison chez Thucydide*, Paris.

(1975) *Magic and Rhetoric in Ancient Greece*, Cambridge, Mass. and London.

(1992) *The Great Sophists in Periclean Athens*, trans. Lloyd, J., Oxford.

Rorty, R. (1989) *Contingency, Irony and Solidarity*, Cambridge.

Rose, P. W. (1992) *Sons of the Gods, Children of the Earth: Ideology and Literary Form in Ancient Greece*, Ithaca and New York.

(1995) 'Historicizing Sophocles' *Ajax*', pp. 59–90 in Goff ed.

Rosenbloom, D. S. (1995) 'Myth, History and Hegemony in Aeschylus', pp. 91–130 in Goff ed.

Rosenmeyer, T. G. (1955) 'Gorgias, Aeschylus and *Apatê*', *AJP* 76: 225–60.

Rosivach, V. (1987) 'Some Fifth- and Fourth-Century Views on the Purpose of Ostracism', *Tyche* 2: 161–70.

Rösler, W. (1980) 'Die Entdeckung der Fiktionalität in der Antike', *Poetica* 12: 283–319.

Rothwell, K. S. (1990) *Politics and Persuasion in Aristophanes' Ecclesiazusae*, Leiden.

Rowe, G. (1966) 'The Portrait of Aeschines in the *Oration on the Crown*', *TAPA* 97: 397–406.

Ruschenbusch, E. (1968) *Untersuchungen zur Geschichte des athenischen Strafrechts*, Cologne and Graz.

Saïd, S. (1978) *La Faute tragique*, Paris.

Saïd, S., and Trédé, M. (1985) 'Art de la Guerre et expérience chez Thucydide', *C&M* 36: 65–85.

Ste Croix, G. E. M. de (1972) *The Origins of the Peloponnesian War*, London.

Sandys, J. E. (1979, orig. 1890) *Demosthenes' Speech Against the Law of Leptines*, Cambridge.

Schäfer, A. (1856–8) *Demosthenes und seine Zeit*, vols. I–III, Leipzig.

Scheibe, K. E. (1979) *Mirrors, Masks, Lies and Secrets: the Limits of Human Predictability*, New York.

Schmid, W., and Stählin, O. (1940) *Geschichte der griechischen Literatur*, vol. III, Munich.

Schmitt-Pantel, P. (1977) 'Athéna Apatouria et la Ceinture. Les Aspects féminins des Apatouries à Athènes.' *Annales E.S.C.* 32: 1059–73.

Scodel, R. (1980) *The Trojan Trilogy of Euripides*, Göttingen.

Seaford, R. (1984) *Euripides: Cyclops*, Oxford.

(1994a) *Reciprocity and Ritual: Homer and Tragedy in the Developing City-State*, Oxford.

(1994b) Review of Rabinowitz (1994) 'Woman as Fetish', *TLS* 4787.

(1995) 'Historicizing Tragic Ambivalence', pp. 202–21 in Goff ed.

Sealey, R. (1956) 'Callistratos of Aphidna and his Contemporaries', *Historia* 5: 178–203.

(1967) 'Athens and the Archidamian War', pp. 75–110 in *Essays in Greek Politics*, New York.

Segal, C. (1962) 'Gorgias and the Psychology of the Logos', *HSCP* 66: 99–155.

(1978) ' "The Myth was Saved": Reflections on Homer and the Mythology of Plato's *Republic*', *Hermes* 106: 315–36.

(1981) *Tragedy and Civilization: An Interpretation of Sophocles*, Cambridge, Mass.

(1982) *Dionysiac Poetics and Euripides' Bacchae*, Princeton.

(1986) *Interpreting Greek Tragedy: Myth, Poetry, Text*, Cornell.

(1988) 'Confusion and Concealment in Euripides' *Hippolytus*: Vision, Hope and Tragic Knowledge', *Metis* 3: 263–83.

(1995) *Sophocles' Tragic World*, Cambridge, Mass.

Shapiro, A. (1986) 'The Attic Deity Basile', *ZPE* 63: 134–6.

Shaw, M. (1982) 'The ἦθος of Theseus in the *Suppliant Women*', *Hermes* 110: 3–19.

Shey, H. (1976) 'Tyrtaeus and the Art of Propaganda', *Arethusa* 9: 5–28.

Siewart, P. (1977) 'The Ephebic Oath in Fifth-Century Athens', *JHS* 97: 102–11.

Silk, M. S., ed. (1996) *Tragedy and the Tragic: Greek Theatre and Beyond*, Oxford.

Simmel, G. (1950) *The Sociology of Georg Simmel*, Glencoe.

Sinclair, R. K. (1988) *Democracy and Participation in Athens*, Cambridge.

Slater, N. (1993) 'Space, Character and ἀπάτη: Transformation and Transvaluation in *Acharnians*', pp. 397–417 in Sommerstein et al. eds.

Smith, J. S. (1986) 'Plato's Use of Myth in the Education of the Philosophic Man', *Phoenix* 40: 20–34.

Smith, W. D. (1967) 'Expressive Form in Euripides' *Suppliants*', *HSCP* 71: 151–70.

Snyder, T. (1981) 'The Web of Song: Weaving Imagery in Homer and the Lyric Poets', *CJ* 76: 193–6.

Sommerstein, A. H. (1980) *Aristophanes: Acharnians*, Warminster.

(1981) *Aristophanes: Knights*, Warminster.

(1996) *Aeschylus*, Bari.

Sommerstein, A. H., Halliwell, S., Henderson, J. and Zimmermann, B., eds. (1993) *Tragedy, Comedy and the Polis*, Bari.

Sourvinou-Inwood, C. (1989) 'Assumptions and the Creation of Meaning: Reading Sophocles' *Antigone*', *JHS* 109: 134–48.

Spence, I. G. (1993) *The Cavalry of Classical Greece: a Social and Military History with Particular Reference to Athens*, Oxford.

Stanford, W. B. (1954) *The Ulysses Theme*, Oxford.

Stevens, P. (1971) *Euripides' Andromache*, Oxford.

Stinton, T. (1976) 'Si credere dignum est. Some Expressions of Disbelief in Euripides and Others', *PCPS* 22: 80–99.

Stockton, D. (1990) *The Classical Athenian Democracy*, Oxford.

Storey, I. (1989) 'Domestic Disharmony in Euripides' *Andromache*', *G&R* 36: 16–27.

(1993) 'Notus est omnibus Eupolis?' pp. 373–96 in Sommerstein et al. eds.

Strauss, B. (1996) 'The Athenian Trireme, School of Democracy', pp. 313–26 in Ober and Hedrick eds.

Sutton, D. F. (1980) *The Greek Satyr Play*, Meisenheim.

(1981) 'Critias and Atheism', *CQ* 31: 33–8.

Svenbro, J. (1976) *La Parole et le Marbre: aux Origines de la Poétique Grecque*, Lund.

Swearingen, C. J. (1991) *Rhetoric and Irony: Western Literacy and Western Lies*, New York and Oxford.

Taplin, O. (1977) *The Stagecraft of Aeschylus*, Oxford.
   (1983) 'Tragedy and Trugedy', *CQ* 33: 331–3.
   (1985) 'Fifth-Century Tragedy and Comedy: a Synkrisis', *JHS* 106: 163–74.
   (1990) 'Agamemnon's Role in the *Iliad*', pp. 60–82 in *Characterization and Individuality in Greek Literature*, Pelling, C., ed., Oxford.
   (1996) 'Comedy and the Tragic', pp. 188–202 in Silk ed.
   (1999) 'Spreading the Word through Performance', pp. 33–57 in Goldhill and Osborne eds.
Tarkow, T. (1983) 'Tyrtaeus 9D: The Role of Poetry in the New Sparta', *AC* 52.
Tatum, J. (1989) *Xenophon's Imperial Fiction: on the Education of Cyrus*, Princeton.
Thalheim, T. (1901) *Lysiae Orationes*, Leipzig.
Thalmann, W. G. (1984) *Conventions of Form and Thought in Early Greek Epic Poetry*, Baltimore.
Thomas, R. (1989) *Oral Tradition and Written Record in Classical Athens*, Cambridge.
Tigerstedt, E. N. (1965) *The Legend of Sparta in Classical Antiquity*, Uppsala.
Todd, S. (1990) 'The Purpose of Evidence in Athenian Courts', pp. 19–39 in Cartledge, Millett and Todd eds.
   (1993) *The Shape of Athenian Law*, Oxford.
Todd, S., and Millett, P. (1990) 'Law, Society and Athens', pp. 1–18 in Cartledge, Millett and Todd eds.
Todorov, T. (1977) *The Poetics of Prose*, trans. Howard, R., Oxford.
Too, Y. L. (1995) *The Rhetoric of Identity in Isocrates: Text, Power, Pedagogy*, Cambridge.
   (1998) 'Xenophon's *Cyropaedia*: Disfiguring the Pedagogical State,' pp. 282–302 in *Pedagogy and Power: Rhetorics of Classical Learning*, Too, Y. L., and Livingstone, N., eds., Cambridge.
Trendall, A. D., and Webster, T. B. L. (1971) *Illustrations of Greek Drama*, London.
Trevett, J. (1992) *Apollodoros the Son of Pasion*, Oxford.
Turner, F. M. (1981) *The Greek Heritage in Victorian Britain*, London.
Turner, V. (1967) *The Forest of Symbols*, Ithaca.
   (1969) *The Ritual Process: Structure and Anti-Structure*, Chicago.
Unger, R. M. (1986) *The Critical Legal Studies Movement*, Cambridge, Mass. and London.
Untersteiner, M. (1954) *The Sophists*, trans. Freeman, K., Oxford.
Usher, S. (1965) 'Individual Characterization in Lysias', *Eranos* 63: 99–119.
   (1976) 'Lysias and his Clients', *GRBS* 17: 31–40.
Usher, S., and Edwards, M. (1985) *Greek Orators I: Antiphon and Lysias*, Warminster.
Ussher, R. (1990) *Sophocles Philoctetes*, Warminster.
Valesio, P. (1980) *Novantiqua: Rhetorics as a Contemporary Theory*, Bloomington.
Van Gennep, A. (1960, orig. 1909) *The Rites of Passage*, London.

Verdenius, W. J. (1981) 'Gorgias' Doctrine of Deception', pp. 116–28 in Kerferd ed.

Vernant, J.-P. (1968) *Problèmes de le guerre en Grèce ancienne*, Paris.

(1992) *Mortals and Immortals*, Princeton.

Vernant, J.-P., and Vidal-Naquet, P. (1988) *Myth and Tragedy in Ancient Greece*, trans. Lloyd, J., Brighton.

Vickers, B. (1988) *In Defence of Rhetoric*, Oxford.

Vickers, M. (1987) 'Alcibiades on Stage: *Philoctetes* and *Cyclops*', *Historia* 36: 171–97.

Vidal-Naquet, P. (1968) 'The Black Hunter and the Origin of the Athenian Ephebeia', *PCPS* 14: 49–64.

(1986a) *The Black Hunter: Forms of Thought and Forms of Society in the Greek world*, Baltimore and London.

(1986b) 'The Black Hunter Revisited', *PCPS* 32: 126–44.

(1988, orig. 1981) 'Sophocles' *Philoctetes* and the Ephebeia', pp. 161–79 in Vernant and Vidal-Naquet.

Vince, C., and Vince, J. (1926) *Demosthenes' De Corona and De Falsa Legatione*, Cambridge, Mass.

Von Arnim, H. (1923) *Xenophons Memorabilien und Apologie des Sokrates*, Copenhagen.

Von Reden, S. (1995) *Exchange in Ancient Greece*, London.

Von Reden, S., and Goldhill, S. (1999) 'Plato and the Performance of Dialogue', pp. 257–92 in Goldhill and Osborne eds.

Walcot, P. (1970) *Greek Peasants, Ancient and Modern: a Comparison of Social and Moral Values*, Manchester.

(1977) 'Odysseus and the Art of Lying', *Anc. Soc.* 8: 1–19.

(1996) 'Greek Attitudes Towards Women', pp. 91–102 in *Women in Antiquity*, McAuslan, I. and Walcot, P., eds., Oxford.

Walker, H. J. (1995) *Theseus and Athens*, New York and Oxford.

Walsh, G. (1984) *The Varieties of Enchantment: Early Greek Views of the Nature and Function of Poetry*, Chapel Hill.

Wänkel, H. (1976) *Demosthenes: Rede für Ktesiphon über den Kranz*, Heidelberg.

Wardy, R. (1996a) 'Mighty is the Truth and it Shall Prevail?', pp. 56–87 in *Essays on Aristotle's Rhetoric*, Rorty, A. O., ed., Berkeley.

(1996b) *The Birth of Rhetoric: Gorgias, Plato and Their Successors*, London.

Waterfield, R. (1998) *The Histories: Herodotus*, Oxford.

Waugh, P. (1984) *Metafiction. The Theory and Practice of Self-Conscious Fiction*, London.

Webster, T. B. L. (1970) *Sophocles' Philoctetes*, Cambridge.

Weil, W. H. (1883–6) *Les Plaidoyers politiques Démosthène*, Paris.

Wheeler, E. L. (1988) *Stratagem and the Vocabulary of Military Trickery*, Leiden.

(1991) 'The General as Hoplite', pp. 134–50 in Hanson ed.

Wheeler, J. R. (1887) 'An Attic Decree: The Sanctuary of Kodros', *AJA* 3: 38–9.

White, H. (1978) *Tropics of Discourse*, Baltimore.

(1987) *The Content of the Form: Narrative Discourse and Historical Representation*, Baltimore.

White, J. B. (1985) *Heracles' Bow: Essays on the Rhetoric and Poetics of the Law*, Wisconsin.

Whitehead, D. (1988) 'Κλοπὴ πολέμου: Theft in Ancient Greek Warfare', *C&M* 39: 40–55.

(1990) *Aineias the Tactician*, Oxford.

Wilamowitz-Möellendorff, T. von (1917) *Die dramatische Technik des Sophokles*, Berlin.

Wilamowitz-Möellendorff, U. von (1893) *Aristoteles und Athen*, Berlin.

Wild, J. (1963) 'Plato as an Enemy of Democracy', pp. 105–28 in *Plato: Totalitarian or Democrat?* Thorison, T. L., ed., Englewood Cliffs.

Wilson, P. J. (1991) 'Demosthenes 21 (*Against Meidias*): Democratic Abuse', *PCPS* 37: 164–95.

(1996) 'Tragic Rhetoric: The Use of Tragedy and the Tragic in the Fourth Century', pp. 310–31 in Silk ed.

(1999) 'The *Aulos* in Athens', pp. 58–95 in Goldhill and Osborne eds.

Winiarczyk, M. (1987) 'Nochmals das Satyrspiel "Sisyphos"', *WSt* 100: 35–45.

Winkler, J. (1990a) 'The Ephebes' Song: Tragoidia and Polis', pp. 20–62 in Winkler and Zeitlin eds.

(1990b) 'Laying Down the Law: the Oversight of Men's Sexual Behaviour in Classical Athens', pp. 171–209 in Halperin, Winkler and Zeitlin eds.

Winkler, J., and Zeitlin, F., eds. (1990) *Nothing to do with Dionysos?*, Princeton.

Winnington-Ingram, R. P. (1965) 'Τὰ Δέοντα Εἰπεῖν: Cleon and Diodotus', *BICS* 12: 70–82.

(1969) 'Euripides: Poietes Sophos', *Arethusa* 2: 127–42.

(1979) 'Sophoclea', *BICS* 26: 1–12.

(1980) *Sophocles: an Interpretation*, Cambridge.

(1983) *Studies in Aeschylus*, Cambridge.

Woodhead, A. G. (1967) 'ΙΣΗΓΟΡΙΑ and the Council of 500', *Historia* 16: 129–40.

(1970) *Thucydides on the Nature of Power*, Cambridge, Mass.

Wooten, C. W. (1989), 'Dionysius of Halicarnassus and Hermogenes on the Style of Demosthenes', *AJP* 110: 576–88.

Worthington, I. (1992) *A Historical Commentary on Dinarchus: Rhetoric and Conspiracy in Later Fourth-Century Athens*, Ann Arbor.

ed. (1994) *Persuasion: Greek Rhetoric in Action*, London and New York.

Wycherley, R. E. (1960) 'Neleion', *BSA* 55: 60–6.

Yunis, H. (1988a) 'The Debate on Undetected Crime and an Undetected Fragment from Euripides' *Sisyphus*', *ZPE* 75: 39–46.

(1988b) *A New Creed: Fundamental Religious Beliefs in the Athenian Polis and Euripidean Drama*, Göttingen.

(1996) *Taming Democracy: Models of Political Rhetoric in Classical Athens*, Ithaca and London.

Zeitlin, F. (1978) 'Dynamics of Mysogyny in the *Oresteia*', *Arethusa* 11: 149–84.

(1980) 'The Closet of Masks: Role-playing and Myth-making in the *Orestes* of Euripides', *Ramus* 9: 51–77.

(1981) 'Travesties of Gender and Genre in Aristophanes' *Thesmophoriazousae*', pp. 169–217 in Foley ed.

(1985) 'The Power of Aphrodite: Eros and the Boundaries of the Self in Euripides' *Hippolytus*', pp. 53–111 in Burian ed.

(1986) 'Thebes: Theater of Self and Society in Athenian Drama', pp. 101–41 in *Greek Tragedy and Political Theory*, Euben, P., ed., Berkeley, Los Angeles and London.

(1990) 'Playing the Other: Theatre, Theatricality and the Feminine in Greek Drama', pp. 63–96 in Winkler and Zeitlin eds.

(1999) 'Aristophanes: the Performance of Utopia in *Thesmophoriazousae*', pp. 167–200 in Goldhill and Osborne eds.

Zuntz, G. (1963) *The Political Plays of Euripides*, Manchester.

Index locorum

Index

accountability, 81
Achilles,
  in Homer, 195
  in Plato, 121–2
  in Sophocles, 195
advantage-taking, *see pleonexia*
Aeschines, 207–17, 231–40, 294
  admits ability, 211
  defines good *rhētōr*, 216–7
  on Ctesiphon's non-normative lies,
    234–6
  on Demosthenes' mimetic lying, 231–2
  on Demosthenes' mimicry, 226
  on Demosthenes' sophistry, 208, 211,
    214, 216
  on Demosthenes' *technai*, 207–8
  on Demosthenes' tongue, 211
Aeschines: works,
  Against Ctesiphon, 211, 216–17, 232–6
  Against Timarchus, 214
  On the Embassy, 207, 231–2
Aeschylus, 119, 143, 107–8
Ajax,
  in Antisthenes, 119–21
  in Pindar, 118
  in Sophocles, 118
alazōneia (charlatanry, being an
  impostor), 232–3, 261
Alcibiades, 31–2, 189
alētheia ('truth'),
  and *lēthē*, 145–9
  and Parmenides, 149–50
  and Plato, 145–51, 162
  archaic conceptions of, 145–7, 149–50
  Detienne's interpretation of, 145–51
  in Aeschines, 216, 232–6
  in Demosthenes, 229
  in oratory, 239
  laicization of, 146
Anaximenes of Lampsacus, 210–12
Andocides
  and persuasion, 170–1

and Sparta, 171–2
and topoi, 230
on 'noble lie', 152, 169–72, 194, 252
on deceiving the demos, 169–72
on generals, 152, 194
Andrewes, A., 253
anthropological approaches, 7–9, 21–2
Antiphon, 182, 285
anti-rhetoric, 4–5, 202–241, 248–89,
  293–6
  see also 'rhetoric'
Antisthenes, 35, 118–21
Apatē, 107–8
apatē, 7–11
  and *alētheia*, 146–51
  and *doxa*, 145–50, 239
  as 'fiction', 146–7
  see also 'deception'
Apatouria, festival of, 29
Apollodorus, 58–61, 221–9
Archilochus, 80
Arendt, H., 296
Aristophanes, 215, 218, 255–74
  Acharnian chorus in, 265–6
  Agoracritus in, 255–8, 289–91
  and anti-rhetoric, 247, 255–8, 260–74,
    294
  and emerging demagogues, 255–8
  and logography, 267–9
  and parabasis, 269–74
  and sophistry, 267–9
  and Thucydides, 255–8
  and topoi of orators, 270–4
  and tragedy, 266–9
  Cleon in, 255–8, 259, 263–4, 289–90
  Demos in, 255–8, 289–91
  Dicaeopolis in, 259–74
  ending of *Knights*, 289–91
  Euripides in, 266–9
  identification with Dicaeopolis, 263–4,
    272–4
  metatheatre in, 259–63, 266–9

STUART

GOODWIN

THE

LEGEND

OF DINOSAUR

GEORGE MULDOON

GOODROW
PRODUCTIONS

goodrowproductions.co.uk

Book Cover by Goodrow Productions
Illustrations by Goodrow Productions with
Midjourney
1st edition 2023
Edited by Alan Rowe.
Written by Stuart Goodwin.

ISBN: 9798869760173